Remember the Former Things

SOCIETY
OF BIBLICAL
LITERATURE

DISSERTATION SERIES

Number 161

REMEMBER THE FORMER THINGS

by
Patricia Tull Willey

Patricia Tull Willey

REMEMBER THE FORMER THINGS

The Recollection of Previous Texts in Second Isaiah

Society of Biblical Literature
Dissertation Series

Scholars Press
Atlanta, Georgia

Remember the Former Things
The Recollection of Previous Texts in Second Isaiah

by
Patricia Tull Willey

Library of Congress Cataloging in Publication Data
Willey, Patricia Tull, 1955–
Remember the former things : the recollection of previous texts in Second Isaiah / Patricia Tull Willey.
p. cm. — (Society of Biblical Literature dissertation series ; no. 161)
Thesis (Ph. D.)—Emory University, 1996.
Includes bibliographical references.
ISBN 0-7885-0364-2 (cloth : alk. paper)
1. Bible. O.T. Isaiah XL–LV—Criticism, interpretation, etc.
2. Intertextuality in the Bible. I. Title. II. Series:
Dissertation series (Society of Biblical Literature) ; no. 161.
BS1520.W54 1997
224'.106—DC21 97-21732
CIP

Printed in the United States of America
on acid-free paper

Acknowledgements

It is difficult to study intertextuality without being reminded continually of one's own precursors and conversation partners. Without other voices first echoing within me, I would have no thoughts or words to call my own.

I want to thank Shifra Epstein, now at Emory University, who taught me to love the Hebrew language as a freshman at the University of Texas, and Harold Liebowitz of the University of Texas, who opened the world of Jewish biblical interpretation to me. I also want to thank Prescott Williams, professor emeritus at Austin Presbyterian Theological Seminary, who first challenged me to consider graduate education in Hebrew Bible. I am grateful that his love for the Bible and for exegesis was so contagious.

My mentors and friends in the Graduate Division of Religion at Emory have been invaluable sources of ideas, questions, and insights. Gail O'Day introduced me to the discussion of intertextuality in the wider field of literature and offered many helpful suggestions both substantive and stylistic during the writing of this dissertation. John Hayes introduced me to Michael Fishbane's work and the concept of inner-biblical exegesis, fed my curiosity through many conversations on the composition of Isaiah, and helped greatly with bibliographical references, both early in the process and late. Fred Craddock enriched the conversation throughout my years at Emory through study of homiletical theory and practice. His insights not only into preaching itself but into the related issues of memory, liturgy, rhetoric, and community formation helped me to conceptualize this study, and his careful reading and responses at several junctures helped focus my questions. I have benefitted in countless ways from his insight, faith, grace, and encouragement.

It is impossible to reduce to words what I have learned from my dissertation director, Carol Newsom. Not only did the initial observation that inspired this dissertation come from her, but it was she who introduced me to Bakhtin as well as a host of other thinkers who revolutionized my understanding of scripture and of the religious enterprise itself. Her patient and critical reading of draft after endless draft of these chapters continually challenged me to sharpen my own thinking. Her collegial bearing helped me to develop an inner sense of authority, and her delight in my successes and those of her other students made those successes all the more significant. I have learned from Carol's example a great deal not only about doing scholarship myself but also about nurturing the thinking of others.

In the course of this study, there have been opportunities to present integral parts of the work in a variety of settings at SBL and elsewhere. I am grateful for the feedback and encouragement of many colleagues, especially Walter Reed of Emory's English Department, and Mark Biddle, Roy Melugin, Marvin Sweeney, Claire Mathews, and other members of the Formation of the Book of Isaiah Seminar.

My colleagues at Louisville Presbyterian Theological Seminary have not only allowed me time and intellectual space to finish this project, but have responded with encouragement and critical engagement to parts of it along the way. Special thanks go to David Hester for allowing me to think out loud to him, Gene March for extensive reading of this manuscript in various stages, and Melissa Nebelsick and Robyn Garrison McMullen for proofreading and helping sort out the endless rules of bibliography and footnoting.

Most of all I need to thank my family. My parents, Catherine and Bob Tull, instilled in me long ago an intellectual inquisitiveness that has always made the quest for learning its own adventure. My mother-in-law Frances Willey has many times been a third parent to our children, and has been a frequent source of encouragement. My husband Frank not only patiently survived two cross-country moves, five years of graduate studies, and toxic levels of fast food, but has listened, read, responded, encouraged, consoled, and listened yet again without ever complaining that Daughter Zion had moved in with us. Our children, Claire and Ian, though for some obscure reason not particularly eager actually to read my dissertation, sat with me at the dining room table most every afternoon, each of us doing our homework, throughout their elementary school years. To these two I dedicate this, the world's longest book report.

Table of Contents

Abbreviations

AB	Anchor Bible
ASTI	*Annual of the Swedish Theological Institute*
BET	Beiträge zur evangelischischen Theologie
BZAW	Beihefte zur *ZAW*
CBQ	*Catholic Biblical Quarterly*
CQR	*Church Quarterly Review*
EncJud	*Encyclopedia Judaica*
GSAT	Geistliche Schriftlesung
HAT	Handbuch zum Alten Testament
IB	*The Interpreter's Bible*
IDB	*The Interpreter's Dictionary of the Bible*
ICC	International Critical Commentary
Int	*Interpretation*
JBL	*Journal of Biblical Literature*
JR	*Journal of Religion*
JSOT	*Journal for the Study of the Old Testament*
JSOTSup	*JSOT* Supplement Series
NCB	New Century Bible
OTL	Old Testament Library
OTWSA	*Die Ou Testamentiese Werkgemeenskap in Suid-Afrika*
SBLDS	Society of Biblical Literature Dissertation Series
VT	*Vetus Testamentum*
VTSup	*Vetus Testamentum* Supplements
ZAW	*Zeitschrift für die alttestamentliche Wissenschaft*

Introduction
"Remember the Former Things of Old"

It has long been recognized that Isaiah 40–55 partakes of the themes and forms of a variety of other biblical texts: not only other prophetic books, but also pentateuchal stories and several psalms and laments. I will argue that this correspondence is quite intentional, that a driving force of Second Isaiah's rhetoric is the recollection, or re-collection, of other, already familiar texts into its own poetry. By reusing words known to the exilic community, Second Isaiah reapplied the "former things of old," shaping them into a "new thing" for a society in a radically altered situation, a people reevaluating their national self-understanding in the wake of the destruction of their capital city, monarchy, and temple.

The time is ripe for such a study. Scholarly interest in the similarities between Second Isaiah and other texts has increased steadily in recent years. A generation ago the discussion focused on Second Isaiah's thematic resemblance to pentateuchal traditions and formal similarity to various psalms and prophetic texts. But lately, stimulated by interest in the related phenomena of "intertextuality" and "inner-biblical exegesis," various scholars have suggested that some of the poet's echoes are in fact deliberate textual allusions.

While the puzzles of inner-biblical exegesis fascinate some scholars, such inquiries may appear to others to be esoteric exercises in source-hunting, curious but insignificant for interpreting Second Isaiah's meaning. A major premise of this dissertation, however, is that traditional historical criticism is partly correct—recovering a text's context is indeed crucial for understanding its message. In fact, many students of intertextuality would contend that it is impossible for texts to have meaning apart from their contexts. This claim will be discussed at length in chapter 2, but a few introductory words will be helpful here.

As historical critics have long understood, the poetry of Second Isaiah arose in reference to a particular sequence of historical events, that is, the destruction of Jerusalem, the exile of portions of the Judahite population to Babylon, and the eminent change in world affairs represented by the activities of Cyrus of Persia. But whereas historical criticism has focused on setting texts within historical or archaeological contexts, an equally crucial context is rhetorical. That is, what shapes thought (and therefore texts) is not so much an event itself but the discourse by which the event comes to be interpreted.

The Russian literary theorist Mikhail Bakhtin recognized the inseparability of a particular text from surrounding discourse when he noted that no artistic work is ever "a self-sufficient and closed authorial monologue, presuming only passive listeners," but rather is, "a rejoinder in a given dialogue, whose style is determined by its interrelationship with other rejoinders in the same dialogue."[1] This is true even in works of fiction: the concatenation of various voices within a novel, for instance, is not merely a creation of the author's imagination, but rather reflects the various voices and viewpoints competing in the world in which the author lives. By creating characters whose speech echoes these various voices, and by orchestrating their interactions within a novel, an author organizes and comments upon the various discourses in the author's own environment. This weighing and distributing of voices is the means for negotiating the reality that:

> Between the word and its object . . . there exists an elastic environment of other, alien words about the same object, the same theme. . . . The word, directed toward its object, enters a dialogically agitated and tension-filled environment of alien words, value judgments and accents, weaves in and out of complex interrelationships, merges with some, recoils from others, intersects with yet a third group: and all this may crucially shape discourse, may leave a trace in all its semantic layers, may complicate its expression and influence its entire stylistic profile.[2]

---

[1] M. M. Bakhtin, *The Dialogic Imagination*, ed. Michael Holquist (Austin, TX: University of Texas Press, 1981, originally published in Russian in 1975) 274.

[2] Ibid., 276.

If Bakhtin was correct in stating that rhetorical context crucially shapes discursive decisions, then a key to understanding Second Isaiah is recognizing what other voices in its milieu it reflects, and in what ways the text exhibits merging with some, recoiling from others, and intersecting with still others—that is, how Second Isaiah, by recollecting the voices of others, organizes and manages the variety of viewpoints present at the end of the exile.

But, it may be argued, even granting the importance of rhetorical context, how can it be recovered? How can we know what voices were sounding around this author, when the echoes of those voices died out some 2600 years ago? We certainly do not have access to the oral conversations in the thick culture surrounding the poet. We cannot even imagine that we possess all that was written in response to the catastrophic events of the sixth century. If the discovery of numerous ancient texts has taught us anything, it is that the Hebrew Bible has preserved only a sliver of all that was written by ancient Judahites. The texts that the nation did preserve, however, were evidently viewed as many of Judah's most significant religious writings. Therefore, if it is discovered that some of these texts were known by thinkers who themselves created significant texts, it should not come as a great surprise. Rather, it would be more surprising if these literate writers never displayed awareness of any text that was already in the process of being preserved, and that continued to survive subsequently.

Second Isaiah indeed displays such a significant density of linguistic correspondence to certain other biblical texts—and only certain texts—that the similarities between them could not easily have happened by coincidence, similar traditioning, or the work of secondary redactors. Even if we cannot recover all the conversations Second Isaiah was entering, we may still, through careful examination, recover some of them. Recognition of what Second Isaiah was choosing to engage and not to engage, and of how this text was situated in relation to other texts, will help us understand more closely the prophet's rhetorical choices.

It should immediately be apparent that one of the greatest obstacles to this discussion is the dating of texts. Late in the nineteenth century, when dating was heatedly debated as a point of religious as well as scholarly concern, one method used to garner support for a particular viewpoint was to search for references in one text to another. Scholars wishing to demonstrate, for instance, that the book of Isaiah was composed in its entirety in the eighth century would point to the similarities of Isaiah 40–66 to sixth-century prophets such as Jeremiah, Zephaniah, and Nahum, contending that those later prophets borrowed their ideas from Isaiah. This argument cuts two ways, however, and other scholars were using the same evidence to reach the opposite conclusion. Around the time that some were beginning to argue the uselessness of dating texts by means of such comparisons, source criticism took over the field with such force that the subject became largely irrelevant. The texts became viewed as so riddled with interpolation that the dating of one verse meant nothing for the dating of the next verse. Source critics, however, continued to date texts, verse by verse, on far less evidence than had already been discredited by their predecessors.

Asserting intertextual relations in order to date texts proved a risky and inconclusive venture. As I will show in chapter 1, the source-critical atomization of texts and the resultant radical uncertainty concerning their dating, combined with other, related, assumptions about the nature of prophecy, rendered further discussion of relationships between texts virtually unthinkable for several decades. But as the historical integrity and literary coherence of certain texts began to be asserted once again, a new possibility for understanding the literary relationships of Second Isaiah emerged. This possibility was articulated by Norman Gottwald in 1954. In his widely read volume entitled *Studies in the Book of Lamentations*, Gottwald observed that:

> OT scholarship has the good fortune in the case of Lamentations and Isaiah 40–66 to possess two documents that have been dated by means of criteria other than a subjective idea about who borrowed from whom. With fixed dating possible, the literary relations of the two works become of immense interest.[3]

---

[3] Norman Gottwald, *Studies in the Book of Lamentations*, Studies in Biblical Theology, no. 14 (London: SCM Press, 1954) 44.

Gottwald's suggestion concerning the recoverability of literary connections between Lamentations and Second Isaiah, though quite original in twentieth-century study, does have considerable precedent in earlier interpretation. Its precursors include not only the work of Max Löhr, on which Gottwald depended, and stray suggestions that date back at least to the time of Bishop Robert Lowth (1778),[4] but also at least two witnesses from long-standing Jewish traditions. First, Jewish liturgy has associated the two texts for centuries: Lamentations is read each year on the Ninth of Ab, the traditional commemoration of the destruction of both the first and second temples, and Isaiah 40 is read on the following Sabbath, the Sabbath of Comfort.[5] Second, the midrashic commentary Lamentations Rabbah, compiled in fifth-century C.E. Palestine, likewise associates the two texts. According to this text, "Because they sinned from *alef* to *tav*, they were comforted from *alef* to *tav*. So you will find that as to all the harsh prophecies that Jeremiah issued against the Israelites, Isaiah first of all anticipated each and pronounced healing for it."[6] Supposed Isaian responses (before the fact) to every verse of Lamentations 1 follow.

Gottwald himself pointed out parallel phrases, themes, and rhetorical strategies, which he understood to demonstrate Second Isaiah's familiarity with and use of Lamentations. Not only did he include a lengthy list of particular words and phrases from Lamentations that were echoed in Second Isaiah, but he noted a whole list of form-critical categories shared by the two works, such as oracular comfort announcements, rhetorical questions inviting comparison, ironic mocking songs against the enemy "daughter," and "songs

---

[4] Max Löhr, "Der Sprachgebrauch des Buches der Klagelieder," *ZAW* 14 (1894) 31–50; Robert Lowth, *Isaiah: A New Translation with a Preliminary Dissertation and Notes* (London: Nichols, 1778).

[5] See Max Lansberg, "Ab, Ninth Day of," in *The Jewish Encyclopedia*, vol. 1 (New York: Funk and Wagnalls Co., 1901) 23–25, and Meir Ydit, "Av, the Ninth of," in *EncJud*, vol. 3 (Jerusalem: Keter Publishing House, 1971) cols. 936–40.

[6] Jacob Neusner, ed., *Lamentations Rabbah: An Analytical Translation* (Atlanta: Scholars Press, 1989) 127.

bewailing national suffering under the figure of a person enduring great pain and ostracism."[7]

In her response to a 1992 paper by Gottwald on ideologically motivated omissions in Second Isaiah, Carol Newsom cited Gottwald's own previous findings to supplement his more recent work.[8] In her view, Second Isaiah did not merely repeat the Judahite language of Lamentations, but also responded to it directly and selectively. Newsom explored the contribution of Second Isaiah's responses to Lamentations to the prophet's overall rhetorical strategy of reinterpreting the exile to prepare the way for the problematic return from Babylon. Second Isaiah answered and reversed the complaints of Lamentations, speaking of comfort for comfortless Zion, festive garments to replace Zion's unclean ones, sacredness instead of defilement, returning instead of scattering. Yet, Newsom observed, not all the language of Lamentations was recollected in Second Isaiah. Whereas Lamentations described in detail the suffering of Jerusalem's people, these people disappeared in Second Isaiah, having been incorporated into the symbolic mother Zion, waiting to welcome her children home from exile. And whereas Lamentations described the exiled population ambivalently, not only as children, but also as princes, kings, priests, prophets, and elders, the ones who had led them astray, Second Isaiah chose only to call them Zion's children. Thus an examination of Second Isaiah's strategic engagement of Lamentations helped Newsom clarify the social and rhetorical interests of the community Second Isaiah represented.

The observations of both Gottwald and Newsom were brief and more programmatic than exhaustive. However, they do suggest a relatively secure path into the subject. If, like Second Isaiah, Lamentations and a few other texts from the same time period can be reasonably firmly dated, and if Second Isaiah shows substantial

---

[7] Gottwald, *Studies*, 45.

[8] N. Gottwald, "Social Class and Ideology in Isaiah 40–55: An Eagletonian Reading," *Semeia* 59 (1992) 43–57; Carol Newsom, "Response to Norman Gottwald, 'Social Class and Ideology in Isaiah 40–55: An Eagletonian Reading,'" *Semeia* 59 (1992) 73–78.

awareness of these other texts, then its habits of textual recollection in these relationships can be explored to form a basis for understanding what conversations this poetry was entering, what the state of the conversation was at the time, and what kinds of discourse Second Isaiah was choosing to remember, what to forget, and what to reconfigure—with what Second Isaiah saw fit to "merge," from what to "recoil"—and how Second Isaiah's particular message is thereby shaped.

It is important to clarify what this study includes and excludes. It is limited to Second Isaiah's use of texts that are either generally understood, or can convincingly be argued, to predate Second Isaiah. Texts that arguably postdate and recollect Second Isaiah, such as Third Isaiah, Job, and Baruch, are bracketed out. This study is further limited to texts that can be demonstrated to show specific verbal similarities to Second Isaiah. Vaguer thematic or formal resemblances, and fainter, less demonstrable verbal echoes, while intriguing, lend themselves to more speculation than enlightenment.

In a context in which oppositional thinking concerning literary and historical methods sometimes occurs, it is perhaps necessary to point out that this study draws from literary theory in order to ask unapologetically historical questions. Through reexamining the past, I will in the end suggest implications of Second Isaiah's situation and rhetorical methods both for current interpretation of the text and for contemporary biblical hermeneutics. Thereby I hope to demonstrate one of many ways in which historical, sociological, and literary methodologies can join forces.

Chapter 1 will trace developments in Second Isaiah's history of interpretation, pointing out relevant paradigm shifts in the study of prophetic books in the past two centuries. The growth of recent understandings of Second Isaiah as an integrated composition deeply related to previous texts will be traced. I will outline several discussions of the text's literary relations with the Pentateuch, Psalms, pre-exilic prophecy (particularly First Isaiah), and Lamentations, and will draw particular attention to two long-standing assumptions which this study calls into question: first, that Second

Isaiah's primary prophetic precursor and theological inspiration was First Isaiah; and second, that certain clearly related texts, particularly Psalm 98 and Jeremiah 30–31, are post-exilic compositions indebted to Second Isaiah. I will also note methodological problems in recent discussions of Second Isaiah's literary relations.

Chapter 2 will explore contemporary theoretical frameworks of intertextual study, particularly as they relate to biblical interpretation, and will offer a methodology for inquiry, making use of Bakhtin's notions of discursive environment. Particular attention will be paid to the role of memory in the negotiation of change in textually oriented religious communities, and to the language within Second Isaiah that announces the text's self-positioning in relation to its rhetorical environment. I will also attend to the indispensable question of dating and availability of relevant biblical texts as they are understood in contemporary scholarship, and on the basis of these preliminary considerations preview the path my individual intertextual discussions will take.

Chapters 3 through 6, the heart of this study, will examine in depth the primary intertextual recollections found in Isaiah 49–54, traditionally called the Zion/Jerusalem section. Although there will be occasion to refer to other parts of Second Isaiah, the clearest intertextual allusions occur here, and further study must necessarily build outward from what is most evident. Because these chapters are primarily concerned with the two figures Daughter Zion and YHWH's Servant, discussions of intertextual relations will be interspersed with discussions of the connections between and functions of these two important characters. Throughout the study there will be occasions to note the impact of intertextual study not only on larger interpretive decisions but also on details of translation.

Chapter 3 begins with brief discussions of the alternating appearances of Daughter Zion and the Servant in chapters 49–54 and of Zion's origins as a figure, before proceeding to a detailed study of the second Zion section, Isa 51:9–52:12, the single portion of Second Isaiah that most directly quotes known biblical texts. Here Second Isaiah's interpretive range can be discerned in the wide variety of texts involved (including Lamentations, Nahum,

Jeremiah, several Psalms, and exodus and wilderness traditions in the Pentateuch), and in its flexible repertoire of allusive tropes, which extends beyond quotation to such practices as misquotation, recontextualization, rearrangement, and fusion.

Chapter 4 surveys the relationships between the Zion and the servant by exploring Second Isaiah's negotiation of speakers and addressees, drawing attention particularly to the frequent identification of Israel with "YHWH's servant" and the positioning of the historical audience in relation to both the servant and Daughter Zion. This prepares the way for an intertextual discussion of Isa 49:1–50:3, in which the two figures are presented back to back in terms especially of key texts in Jeremiah, with some echoes of Lamentations, Psalm 98, and Deuteronomy as well.

Chapter 5 focuses on the two remaining servant passages, Isa 50:4–11 and Isa 52:13–53:12. After a discussion of the servant's textual precursors, I will examine these passages in relation to precedents found especially in Lamentation 3. This will allow discussion of the trajectories on which both the servant and Zion travel in their development from previous texts through Second Isaiah and into subsequent understanding, and the interests displayed in the prophet's use of each figure.

Chapter 6 examines Isaiah 54, the final Zion passage, and its strategy of repairing damaged connections, especially with psalmic and pentateuchal traditions. Here particular attention is drawn to Second Isaiah's redistribution of roles already present in previous tradition but problematized by the fall of the monarchy.

Chapter 7 concludes with a summary of Second Isaiah's various methods for responding to diverse precursor texts and a final discussion of hermeneutical implications suggested by Second Isaiah's strategy of reaching toward the past in order to rebuild language for Judah's future.

Chapter 1
"Look to the Rock from Which You Were Hewn": A History of the Discussion of Isaiah 40–55's Recollection of Biblical Text and Tradition

Second Isaiah's history of interpretation is, like any history, a study in itself of intertextuality—of the transumption of previous thoughts and words into continually new forms. This history is not one of evolutionary development or organic growth, but of rhetorical viewpoints reacting to one another, often merging with previous ideas, and just as often diverging from what was said before when it no longer suits new questions and tastes.

Early Views

Before the eighteenth century, commentators on Isaiah tended to view its textual parallels synchronically, as aids to interpretation, but to engage in little or no discussion of temporal linkages between similar texts. Abraham Ibn Ezra, for instance, writing in the twelfth century, referred to other texts in order to help explicate the meaning of unusual or ambiguous words.[1] John Calvin, whose lengthy 1551 commentary on Isaiah took the form of a phrase-by-phrase meditation for contemporary believers, portrayed the prophet as addressing the Church.[2] Although he pointed out the prophet's mentions of the exodus from Egypt, which he evidently viewed more as references to history than to text, he otherwise seldom referred to other texts, and then more because they supported a theological or pastoral point than because they clarified Isaiah. He was as likely to cite a New Testament text as any

---

[1] Abraham Ibn Ezra, *The Commentary of Ibn Ezra on Isaiah* (New York: P. Feldheim, 1948, reprinted from edition edited by M. Griedlander, London, 1873).

[2] John Calvin, *Commentary on the Book of the Prophet Isaiah,* 5 vols. (Grand Rapids, MI: Eerdmans, 1948, originally published in Latin in 1551).

other. By contrast, the Westminster Assembly's *Annotations Upon All the Books of the Old and New Testament,* written in 1645 and expanded in 1651 by "Learned Divines," included a very detailed system of cross-referencing of parallels not only of themes and phrases but even of syntax.[3]

Robert Lowth (1778) concentrated on explicating the prophet's poetry, and on evaluating the manuscript evidence for textual emendations. He also, from time to time, noted parallel passages with an eye to both historical sequence and rhetorical effect. Although his assumption of Isaianic authorship for the whole book renders his conclusions problematic today, and although his statements evoke a quaint mental picture of the prophets as learned scholars, he is to be credited for having contributed to a more historically and rhetorically sensitive discussion of biblical literature. For instance, on Isaiah 52:11 ("Depart, depart ye; go ye out from thence . . ."), noting a strong parallel with Lam 4:15 that is very seldom recognized ("Depart; ye are polluted, depart; depart ye, forbear to touch . . ."), he commented:

> The Prophet Jeremiah seems to have had his eye on this passage of Isaiah, and to have applied it to a subject directly opposite. It is here addressed by the Prophet in the way of encouragement and exhortation to the Jews coming out of Babylon: Jeremiah has given it a different turn, and has thrown it out as a reproach of the heathen upon the Jews, when they were driven from Jerusalem into captivity.[4]

Late in the eighteenth century, non-Isaianic authorship for chapters 40–66 was suggested by several scholars.[5] Gesenius's book

---

[3] For instance, for 51:9 it was noted: "*Awake awake*—so verse 17, chap. 52:1. So also Jer 6:22, and 25:32. . . . The redoubling of the word intimates the vehemency of their affection, and earnest desire of speedy relief and release. See the like, Judg 5:12, chap. 52:1. So Psalm 13:1 and 94:3." *Annotations upon All the Books of the Old and New Testament* (1651, additional annotations London: printed by J. Legatt and J. Raworth, 1658), vol. 2 on Isa 52:9, no page numbers used.

[4] Lowth, 361.

[5] There is some disagreement over who was the first to suggest this idea. Most historians credit J. G. Eichhorn (*Einleitung ins AT*, vol. 3, Leipzig: Weidmann, 1783) and J. C. Döderlein (*Esaias. Ex resensione textus Hebraei . . .*, Altdorf, 1789) with this insight. See for instance O. Eissfeldt, *The Old Testament:*

on Isaiah (1821) was the first major commentary to presuppose exilic dating for these chapters.[6] Otherwise his understanding of the prophetic writing process remained similar to Lowth's. Whereas Lowth asserted, for instance, that Nahum (2:1) had copied Isaiah (52:7), Gesenius made the same assertion the other way around: "Fast wörtlich so Nah 2:1, welchen unser Dichter vielleicht vor Augen hatte."[7] Similarly, J. A. Alexander (1847), who held to the eighth-century authorship of the book, offered a detailed reading of Isa 52:12 and its multiple and dense allusions to the exodus story, noting the language that may have been familiar to original "readers."[8]

Heinrich Ewald (1840–41) noted that Isa 51:11 repeats Isa 35:10 nearly verbatim.[9] Because of this, he judged the verse not to be original ("ursprünglich") to Second Isaiah. He judged that either this verse was a later interpolation from Isa 35:10, or else both prophets had borrowed it from an even earlier work, in which case

---

An Introduction (New York: Harper and Row, 1965, originally published in German in 1934) 304. John Rogerson, in *Old Testament Criticism in the Nineteenth Century* (Philadelphia: Fortress Press, 1985) 23, contends that it was J. B. Koppe, in *D. Robert Lowth's Jesaias übersetzt mit einer Einleitung und kritischen philologischen und erläuternden Anmerkungen*, vol. 3 (Leipzig, 1780) 206, who first argued that Isaiah 40–66 had been written during the Babylonian exile. However, both E. J. Young, in *Who Wrote Isaiah?* (Grand Rapids, MI: Eerdmans, 1958) and Theodore Friedman, in "Isaiah," in *EncJud*, vol. 9, col. 45, state that Koppe suggested merely that chapter 50 may not have come from the prophet, and that it was Döderlein who extended this contention to the last 27 chapters of the book. For discussions of these issues see R. Smend, "Lowth im Deutschland," in *Epochen der Bibelkritik*, BET 109 (Munich: Chr. Kaiser, 1991) 43–62, and M. Mulzer, "Döderlein und Deuterojesaja," *Biblische Notizen* 66 (1993) 15–22. The difficulty of locating the origin of the suggestion in a single source only underscores the corporate nature of ideas and the complexity of intertextual relations.

[6] W. Gesenius, *Philologisch-kritischer und historischer Kommentar über den Jesaia*, 3 vols. (Leipzig: F. C. W. Vogel, 1821).

[7] Ibid., 157.

[8] J. A. Alexander, *Commentary on the Prophecies of Isaiah* (Grand Rapids, MI: Zondervan, 1953, originally published as *The Later Prophecies of Isaiah* in 1847) 2/282.

[9] H. Ewald, *Die Propheten des Alten Bundes* (Göttingen: Vandenhoeck & Ruprecht, 1968, originally published in 1840–41) 3/87.

he believed it fit more clearly after Isa 52:6, where he consequently placed it in his own translation. In doing this he foreshadowed two confusions that would reign among early twentieth-century critics. The first was the confusion of two understandings of the term "ursprünglich." At some points this word was used to mean that a phrase was used first by this prophet and not borrowed from any other text. At other points it meant that a phrase was actually used by the prophet and was not inserted by a later redactor. Often these two different kinds of originality were not distinguished—if the prophet did not say it before anyone else, the prophet did not say it at all. The second confusion Ewald foreshadowed concerned the role of modern commentators, who began to see themselves less as interpreters of the canonical text and more as editors of the text into a form that was thought to have predated the final form—that is, to have been more "original."

Throughout the rest of the century, commentators continued to use evidence of intertextual relationship to support contentions on the dating and authorship of Isaiah 40–66. C. W. E. Nägelsbach (1877) used comparative word lists to show that the eighth-century prophet authored the entire book.[10] Prominent among his arguments was a list of passages in Isaiah 40–66 that parallel portions of other prophets, including Jeremiah, Zephaniah, Ezekiel, and Nahum. He recognized that other scholars might view these as the exilic Isaiah's quotations of other prophets. Nevertheless he attempted to demonstrate that the eighth-century prophet was the original author, basing his arguments on the notion that Isaiah sounded bolder or more poetic, without explicating the relationship between boldness and originality.

T. K. Cheyne (1881) devoted two full essays to the phenomenon of parallel passages and the question of intertextual dependence.[11] He suggested that Second Isaiah's connections with First Isaiah

---

[10] C. W. E. Nägelsbach, *The Prophet Isaiah Theologically and Homiletically Expounded* (New York: Charles Scribner's Sons, 1884, originally published in German in 1877).

[11] T. K. Cheyne, *The Prophecies of Isaiah*, vol. 2 (London: C. Kegan Paul & Co., 1881).

might be explained by understanding the sixth-century prophet operating as a *sofer*, who creatively combined old material with new in the manner of mosaic-work, who "not only put old ideas and phrases into a new setting, but also incorporated the substance of connected discourses of . . . Isaiah."[12] While cautioning that there are several possible ways to account for parallels with other texts, and that the study of parallels can become an overrated enterprise when used to argue unity of authorship or chronological priority, he nevertheless maintained that "the exaggerated value sometimes attached to the argument from parallel passages must not drive us to the other extreme of treating them as non-existent or unimportant."[13] He provided extensive lists of passages from various other parts of the Bible that he saw as paralleling First Isaiah and the "disputed portions" of Isaiah. He perceived particularly strong relationships between Isaiah 40–66 and the Pentateuch, Job, Jeremiah, and several minor prophets. Psalms, he maintained, quoted Isaiah 40–66, and Lamentations was not part of his discussion. Consonant with his findings was his depiction of the prophets as "free from morbid craving for originality":[14]

> Self-abnegation is the mark of prophetic writers quite as much as that of their editors. They experienced no *Sturm und Drang,* no 'storm and stress' of an unchastened individuality. They never attempted to set themselves on high, on the pedestal of original genius. Isaiah . . . is as dependent on his less famous predecessors as a Marlowe or a Shakespeare.[15]

In contrast to Cheyne's notion of the prophet as *sofer*, a very different conception of prophets was emerging from nineteenth-century European romanticism, one perhaps best characterized by Julius Wellhausen's description (1878).[16] Distinguishing prophets

---

[12] Ibid., 206.

[13] Ibid., 217.

[14] Ibid., 229.

[15] Ibid., 217.

[16] J. Wellhausen, *Prolegomena to the History of Ancient Israel* (Cleveland, OH: World Publishing Co., 1957, originally published in German in 1878 as *Geschichte Israels,* vol. 1).

from priests, who "take their stand . . . entirely on tradition,"[17] Wellhausen said:

> The prophets have notoriously no father, their importance rests on the individuals . . . resting on nothing outside themselves. . . .
>
> The element in which the prophets live is the storm of the world's history, which sweeps away human institutions, in which the rubbish of past generations with the houses built on it begins to shake, and that foundation alone remains firm, which needs no support but itself. . . . They do not preach on set texts; they speak out of the spirit which judges all things and itself is judged of no man. Where do they ever lean on any other authority than the truth of what they say; where do they rest on any other foundation than their own certainty?[18]

Wellhausen went on to assert the death of God's relationship with Israel, and the incompatibility of the servant in Isaiah 40–66 with the priestly "Torah of Moses." Rather, the Torah which will go out to the whole world "might most fitly be compared with the Logos of the prologue of John."[19] Modern readers have little difficulty discerning the speculative and anti-Jewish nature of many of Wellhausen's assumptions, but his conception of the prophets carried itself into Christian European and American criticism for over half a century.[20] Notions of the prophets as respectful interpreters of their traditions all but disappeared for several decades.

Duhm and Beyond

If the prophets spoke only God's words and not human tradition, then the words that are not so new are not the prophet's own—and these were many. Bernhard Duhm (1892) understood

---

[17] Ibid., 397.

[18] Ibid., 398–99.

[19] Ibid., 401.

[20] For discussions of these issues see Rolf Rendtorff, "Toward a Common Jewish-Christian Reading of the Hebrew Bible," in his *Canon and Theology: Overtures to an Old Testament Theology*, ed. M. Kohl (Minneapolis: Fortress Press, 1993, originally published in German in 1991) 33, M. H. Goshen-Gottstein, "Christianity, Judaism and Modern Bible Study," *VT Supp* 28 (Leiden: E. J. Brill, 1975) 78, and Lou Silberman, "Wellhausen and Judaism," *Semeia* 25 (1982) 75–82.

the book to have undergone an extremely long and gradual history of development that did not end until about a century before the common era.[21] Even chapters 40–55, the core of which Duhm dated to around 540 B.C.E., continued to be subject to major additions and glosses throughout the history of the book's development.

Duhm's concern in explicating the text was to find a pure version of the original poetry. In his translation he freely deleted phrases and even whole verses that he perceived as insertions. He also rearranged lines and added words when he thought the meter required them. A description of some of his strategies with Isa 51:9–20 will illustrate his method. In this section, one verse is eliminated completely from his translation (verse 11), another verse is moved (verse 18), the authenticity of six more verses (verses 9, 12–16) is for various reasons and to varying degrees questioned, and textual emendations are prescribed, or at least suggested, for most of the remaining verses. Most of Duhm's reasons for alterations have to do with problems of repetition. For instance, verse 11 is deleted because it repeats Isa 35:10. The authenticity of verse 9 is questioned on the basis of its similarity with Isa 52:1, "denn Dtjes. wird nicht so geschmacklos gewesen sein, in ein und demselben Zusammenhang das Gleiche von Jahves Arm und von Zion auszusagen."[22] Duhm's revisions of the text attempted to sever or at least to attenuate the major relationships between the poet's words and other biblical texts (even other writings of the same poet), in order that the remnant that remained might approach the state of originality that Wellhausen had declared to be the hallmark of God's prophets.

Soon after Duhm's time, form-critical analysis of Hebrew poetry began to be employed. Hugo Gressmann (1914) divided Second Isaiah into 49 independent, originally oral prophetic speeches.[23] Many of these speeches owed their form, he said, to the prophetic

---

[21] B. Duhm, *Das Buch Jesaia* (Göttingen: Vandenhoeck & Ruprecht, 1892).

[22] Ibid., 361.

[23] H. Gressmann, "Die literarische Analyse Deuterojesajas," *ZAW* 34 (1914) 254–97.

genres, but the forms of many were borrowed from "foreign" genres, particularly that of sacred hymns. In fact, according to Gressmann, Second Isaiah used the hymn form more than any previous prophet. Gressmann saw the hymns being used not for their own sake but in order to support the prophet's message. Whereas hymnic language in the psalms was used to praise and thank God, Second Isaiah used the language as a means to persuade, exhort, and instruct. According to Gressmann, only three verses of the sixteen chapters (52:4–6) derived from the hand of a later glossator. He did not argue directly with Duhm's notion of massive interpolation in the book, but his understanding of the prophet's orality and flexible use of genres suggested an alternative explanation for the book's less than obvious structure.

Sigmund Mowinckel (1921) had also noted the use of mixed forms in Second Isaiah's poetry. Second Isaiah's hymnic sections were dependent, he said, upon preexilic "enthronement festival" psalms such as Psalms 93–100, which reflected festal celebrations of preexilic Israel.[24] "The ideas associated with the enthronement festival have come to life again as a message about the future for his own time, and as a promise of restoration. They became the natural vehicle of the message of consolation and joy which he had to proclaim."[25]

But Mowinckel's understanding of Second Isaiah as a borrower of forms and ideas did not take him so far as to perceive Second Isaiah as a *sofer* echoing specific texts. He furthermore proposed that the various short oral units perceived by Gressmann and others as the building blocks of Second Isaiah were assembled on the basis of "Stichwörter," catchwords loosely connecting one unit with the

---

24 S. Mowinckel, *Psalmenstudien*, 6 vols. (Amsterdam: Verlag P. Schippers, 1961, originally published in 1921–24) 2/49–50, 195–201. His stance is quite distinct from that of his contemporary Hermann Gunkel (*The Psalms: A Form-Critical Introduction*, Philadelphia: Fortress, 1967, originally published in German in 1930, 36–37), who argued that these psalms were postexilic heirs to Second Isaiah's original formulations.

25 S. Mowinckel, *He that Cometh* (New York: Abingdon Press, 1954, originally published in Norwegian in 1951) 143.

next.[26] Though far less radical than Duhm, Mowinckel was much quicker than Gressmann to see the repetition of material as later interpolation.

Joachim Begrich's study (1938) furthered the form-critical investigation of Second Isaiah.[27] He perceived the poetry not as a series of prophetic utterances but as a written work imitating speech. Unlike many of his predecessors, Begrich included a discussion of the relationship of Second Isaiah to previous religious tradition. Not only did he note Second Isaiah's use of pentateuchal stories, prophetic warnings, and psalmic motifs, but he also drew attention to the way in which Second Isaiah's rhetoric presumed the audience's knowledge of these traditions. He pointed out the prophet's use of the breadth of the tradition in order to support his new message, and he distinguished Second Isaiah from earlier prophets as one who recognized "neben seiner prophetischen Autorität eine in der bisherigen Überlieferung gegebene Autorität also massgebend und gültig an."[28] Begrich's attention to the rhetorical use of transformed genre, as well as his pointing out of the broad range of Second Isaiah's use of tradition, made his a significant work long after his own time.

Despite Mowinckel's and Begrich's interest in Second Isaiah's reuse of preexilic forms and traditions, most German scholars early in this century followed the analytical programs of Duhm, in reconstructing the original author's text, and of Gressmann, in discovering small oral units comprising the text. Ludwig Köhler (1923) wrote a translation and critical analysis of Second Isaiah which deleted forty-three verses or half-verses as "undeuterojesajanisch," and combined Duhm's textual emendations with many of his own to create a text whose seventy small units were metrically

---

[26] S. Mowinckel, "Die Komposition des deuterojesanischen Buches," *ZAW* 49 (1931) 87–112.

[27] J. Begrich, *Studien zu Deuterojesaja* (Munich: Chr. Kaiser Verlag, 1963, originally published in 1938).

[28] Ibid., 94.

orderly.[29] J. Fischer (1925) and P. Volz (1932), and even scholars as late as G. Fohrer (1964), while more restrained than Duhm and Köhler in their assumption of interpolations into Second Isaiah's text, nevertheless cited numerous glosses and suggested many emendations.[30]

English-speaking scholars were less convinced by this methodology. C. C. Torrey (1928), who believed that Isaiah 40–66 was written in postexilic Judah by a single author, objected to "the spectacle of dissection, rearrangement, and excision . . . the constant alteration of the text to suit the present theory of the book, and the condemnation of numerous passages as unintelligible—that is, under the present theory."[31] He lamented:

> We have here a good example of that which has happened not a few times in the history of literary criticism, where scholars have felt obliged to pare down a writing to make it fit a mistaken theory. The paring process, begun with a penknife, is continued with a hatchet, until the book has been chopped into hopeless chunks.[32]

E. J. Kissane (1943) also viewed Isaiah 40–66, with the exception of two prose sections, to have had a single, albeit exilic, author, suggesting, "even though there be abrupt breaks in the sense, it may be that the various fragments are related to each other as integral parts of a single theme."[33] Moreover, Kissane, finding it necessary to account for this section's points of continuity with Isaiah 1–39, saw this author as having been saturated with the thought and language of Isaiah, alluding to and even quoting the eighth-century prophet. He suggested that the prophecies in chapter 1–35 are genuine to Isaiah, and that the exilic prophet who

---

[29] L. Köhler, *Deuterojesaja stilkritisch untersucht*, BZAW 37 (Giessen: Töpelmann, 1923) 1.

[30] J. Fischer, *Das Buch Isaias übersetzt und erklärt*, II Teil: Kap. 40–66 (Bonn: P. Hanstein, 1939); P. Volz, *Jesaja II* (Leipzig: Verner Scholl, 1932); G. Fohrer, *Das Buch Jesaja*, vol. 3 (Stuttgart: Zwingli Verlag, 1964).

[31] C. C. Torrey, *The Second Isaiah: A New Interpretation* (Edinburgh: T. & T. Clark, 1928) 15.

[32] Ibid., 13.

[33] E. J. Kissane, *The Book of Isaiah: Translated from a Critically Revised Hebrew Text with Commentary*, vol. 2 (Dublin: Browne and Nolan, 1943) xxii.

wrote Isaiah 40–66 also collected and edited the prophecies of Isaiah and added chs 36–39 from Kings. Since the heavy dependence of the exilic prophet on the earlier prophet was evident to Kissane, the further possibility that other verses may be quoted from other writings such as Jeremiah was "no reason for doubting their genuineness."[34]

Despite the hegemony of source and form criticism, a few scholars during the early part of the century, particularly Jewish scholars who rejected Wellhausen's views about prophecy, had continued to note with interest Second Isaiah's citing of other texts. Umberto Cassuto was one of many Jewish scholars of the early twentieth century who utilized the principles and findings of higher biblical criticism, but rejected the Graf-Wellhausen hypothesis.[35] In a series of articles on Second Isaiah published in Italian from 1911 to 1913 (not published in English until 1973), Cassuto drew conclusions that were quite distinct from those being drawn in German scholarship:

> Without doubt, the style of Isaiah the Second bears in general the undeniable stamp of originality, but in certain particulars we can discern, not infrequently, the influence of other biblical writers. In phrases, in expressions, in hemistichs—and at times even in entire verses of our prophet—we often find echoes, and on occasion even the *ipsissima verba*, of other books of Scripture.[36]

He described extensive parallels between Second Isaiah and Jeremiah, especially the idol section in Jer 10:1–16, the prophecies of consolation in chapters 30–31, the oracle against Babylon in chapters 50–51 (which he considered dependent upon Second

---

[34] Ibid., 165.

[35] I. Abrahams and C. Roth, "Cassuto, Umberto," in *EncJud*, vol. 5, cols. 234–36, and H. D. Hummel, "Bible," in *EncJud*, vol. 4, col. 907. In 1940, Cassuto presented a series of eight lectures disputing the claims and arguments of the documentary hypothesis. These lectures were translated into English by I. Abrahams as *The Documentary Hypothesis and the Composition of the Pentateuch* (Jerusalem: Magnes Press, 1961).

[36] U. Cassuto, "On the Formal and Stylistic Relationship between Deutero-Isaiah and other Biblical Writers," in *Biblical and Oriental Studies* (Jerusalem: Magnes, 1973) 1/141.

Isaiah), and several other miscellaneous sections. He argued for heavy dependence of Second Isaiah upon Nahum and Zephaniah, but concluded that Second Isaiah's parallels with Ezekiel could for the most part be explained on the basis of their shared dependence upon Jeremiah. Recognizing the many alternative explanations for the presence of parallel passages, Cassuto attempted to work critically and cautiously, and to draw his conclusions in concert with contemporary historical investigation.[37]

In 1935 Moshe Seidel published an article in Hebrew which was filled with examples of phrases and even passages several verses long echoing parts of the Psalms.[38] He updated his findings in a 1956 article in which he added many additional phrases and verses that he had found or that had been suggested to him.[39]

H. L. Ginsberg (1958) drew on Seidel's work to discuss the repetition of the phrase "arm of YHWH," which recurs frequently in Isaiah 51–63, and otherwise with great frequency only in the Psalms, especially Psalm 89.[40] In this article he pointed out several similarities in phrasing and thought between passages of Second Isaiah and Psalms 89 and 98. On the basis of this and other evidence he suggested a translation of Isa 53:10–11 in which זֶרַע ("seed") is emended to זְרוֹעַ ("arm") and several phrases of the poetry are rearranged. Although his conclusion is improbable, the findings on which he built this conclusion are worth noting.

---

[37] Israel Abrahams, in his translator's foreword to the English edition in which this essay appears, shed light on the changing labels attached to opponents of Wellhausen's theories when he remarked about Cassuto: "Occasionally his intrepid scholarship attracted, from the less perceptive, the reproach of 'fundamentalism.' What these critics meant, though they did not realize it, was 'iconoclasm.' Cassuto was an idol-breaker; he shattered some of the venerated thought-stereotypes on which the faithful devotees of the Documentary Hypothesis based their vivisection of the Biblical text," ibid., v-vi.

[38] M. Seidel, "Parallels between the Book of Isaiah and the Book of Psalms," in *Minhah leDavid* (Jerusalem: Reuben Mas, 1935) 23–47 [Hebrew].

[39] Seidel, "Parallels between the Book of Isaiah and the Book of Psalms," *Sinai* 38 (1956) 149–72 [Hebrew].

[40] H. L. Ginsberg, "The Arm of YHWH in Isaiah 51–63 and the Text of Isa 53:10–11," *JBL* 77 (1958) 152–56.

The Present Generation

Beginning in the 1950s, dramatic shifts took place away from several assumptions reigning among earlier scholars. First, although the rest of Isaiah was still understood as having a long and complex redactional history, Second Isaiah began to be conceived as having originated nearly whole in Babylon in the late exilic period. Second, the complexity of Second Isaiah's forms and inter-poetic relationships were explained by some as having resulted from the poetry's origin as a written, rather than oral, document. Third, and most importantly, the romantic understanding of Israelite prophets as individuals standing over against tradition was all but abandoned, and Second Isaiah was seen as an inheritor and radical reinterpreter of traditional formulations. These developments were heralded by earlier interpreters, but were combined with new force in James Muilenburg's 1956 commentary, and have been refined in various ways since.[41]

Before Muilenburg's time, a few commentators, notably Budde, Torrey, Begrich, and Kissane, suggested that Second Isaiah began its life as a written composition rather than as a series of oral prophecies. Similarly, Muilenburg argued against the common form-critical practice of segmenting the poetry according to genre and equating the shifts in form to the beginning and ending of short oral speeches. Rather, he said:

> The poems of SI exhibit numerous signs of literary craftsmanship; they are so elaborate in their composition and in the detail of technical devices that they must have been written. . . . Nor may we suppose that his work was designed primarily to be read, although this possibility must not be excluded. He may have delivered his poems to his fellow exiles, or he may have sent them to various groups among the exiles.[42]

Since written composition both fixes the form of the poetry more than oral tradition and allows for more complex relationships between disparate parts, Muilenburg was disinclined to attribute variety in form or content to multiple authorship. For instance,

---

[41] J. Muilenburg, "Isaiah 40–66," in *IB* 5, ed. G. A. Buttrick et al. (New York: Abingdon Press, 1956) 381–773.

[42] Ibid., 386.

against Duhm and most others at the time, Muilenburg argued that the servant passages belonged originally to Second Isaiah. He listed many linguistic parallels between them and surrounding passages.

Furthermore, Muilenburg asserted that Second Isaiah's roots lay deep within the Israelite tradition. "He is steeped in it, knows where its central points lie, and how it bears relevantly upon the broken era in which he has been called to prophesy."[43] Yet "despite his familiarity with the words and ways of his predecessors, and despite their influence upon him, he goes his own way with an almost sovereign independence."[44]

Since Muilenburg's time, these issues have been much discussed. Some, such as H. C. Spykerboer (1976), have agreed that Second Isaiah originated as a written document.[45] Others, such as John McKenzie (1968), while viewing Second Isaiah as a "speaker first and writer second," have nevertheless understood the prophet to have edited his own speeches.[46] Even form critics reluctant to admit written composition have qualified their arguments that the poetry originated orally. For instance, Claus Westermann (1966), who understood the book as the product of a long process beginning with oral tradition, admitted that "the longer poems like 49:14–26 and 51:9–52:3 may have been literary productions from the beginning."[47] Yehoshua Gitay (1981) saw this discussion of Second Isaiah's compositional origin as being overly concerned with differentiating between oral and written composition. This distinction was "not so clear in the period before the invention of printing. . . . Even if DI wrote his prophecies, they were not read in

---

[43] Ibid., 398.

[44] Ibid., 397.

[45] H. C. Spykerboer, *The Structure and Composition of Deutero-Isaiah with Special Reference to the Polemics against Idolatry* (Meppel: Krips Repro, 1976).

[46] J. McKenzie, *Second Isaiah*, AB 20 (Garden City, New York: Doubleday & Co., 1968) xxxv.

[47] C. Westermann, *Isaiah 40–66*, OTL (Philadelphia: Westminster Press, 1969, originally published in German in 1966) 28.

silence but aloud. Hence, the prophet, in order to appeal to his audience, chose his words carefully for their aural effect."[48]

In terms of the text's unity, many scholars since Muilenburg's time have become increasingly reluctant to claim interpolations. While once nearly every phrase that duplicated a line from elsewhere in the Bible was viewed as a harmonizing gloss, more recent scholars have based their evaluations primarily on perceived discontinuity in the argument of the text. Westermann and McKenzie, for instance, differed over which texts they considered secondary, but each in his own way made a bid for the primacy of texts once assumed to be postexilic. More recently, Richard Clifford (1984) marked the trend toward assertions of the book's unity by identifying only six verses (44:20, 48:22, and 52:3–6) as glosses.[49]

Intricate hypotheses concerning Second Isaiah's growth over the course of several generations are still being suggested, especially among German redaction scholars. For instance, O. H. Steck (1992), concentrating on Isaiah 47–55, traced nine stages of redactional composition in detail, ranging from the sixth to the early third centuries.[50] Steck's student Reinhold Kratz (1991), concentrating especially on Isaiah 40–48, identified five stages of composition beginning in 539 and ending around 450.[51] In the U.S. and Great Britain, their work has been received with admiration for attention to detail mixed with skepticism over their hypercritical methodology, their precise matching of posited historical settings and hypothetical redactional layers, and their confident conclusions. Despite the questionable assumptions on which their claims are founded, it is important to note that the aims of these redaction scholars differ significantly from those of their predecessors. Rather

48 Y. Gitay, *Prophecy and Persuasion: A Study of Isaiah 40–48* (Bonn: Lingusitica Biblica, 1981) 45.

49 R. Clifford, *Fair Spoken and Persuading: An Interpretation of Second Isaiah* (New York: Paulist Press, 1984).

50 O. H. Steck, *Gottesknecht und Zion: Gesammelte Aufsätze zu Deuterojesaja* (Tübingen: Mohr [Paul Siebeck], 1992), see especially chart on p. 125.

51 R. G. Kratz, *Kyros im Deuterojesaia-Buch: Redaktionsgeschichtliche Untersuchungen zu Entstehung*, FAT 1 (Tübingen: Mohr [Paul Siebeck], 1991), see especially chart on p. 217.

than devalue the work of biblical redactors as effacers of an originally pure prophetic word, they perceived theological and compositional coherence in the strata of rewritings they posited.

Muilenburg's claim that Second Isaiah knew and used the traditions of Judah is far less developed in his commentary than his contention of written composition, but is much more widely accepted. Within a decade the ground shifted dramatically on this issue in relation not only to Second Isaiah but to all the prophets. The consensus has been summarized by Gene Tucker (1985), who stated: "The dependence of the prophets on older traditions—including traditions of law—has now become obvious."[52] He cited Gerhard von Rad's *Old Testament Theology* (1960) as the most influential work on this question.[53] In von Rad's view, the prophets neither created new theology nor merely repeated what had come before, but rather reinterpreted the tradition for their contemporary days of crisis:

> It is now, of course, apparent that when the prophets spoke of coming events, they did not do so directly, out of the blue, as it were; instead, they showed themselves bound to certain definite inherited traditions, and therefore even in their words about the future they use a dialectic method which keeps remarkably close to the pattern used by earlier exponents of Jahwism. It is this use of tradition which gives the prophets their legitimation. At the same time, they go beyond tradition—they fill it even to bursting-point with new content or at least broaden its basis for their own purposes.[54]

Von Rad went on to discuss Second Isaiah's reinterpretation of three election traditions (related to the exodus, David, and Zion) and of the tradition of creation. The prophet's relationship to these traditions was both positive and negative, involving new formulations that von Rad thought were probably shocking to

---

[52] G. Tucker, "Prophecy and Prophetic Literature," in *The Hebrew Bible and its Modern Interpreters*, ed. D. Knight and G. Tucker (Chico, CA: Scholars Press, 1985) 331.

[53] Ibid., 328.

[54] G. von Rad, *Old Testament Theology*, vol. 2: *The Theology of Israel's Prophetic Traditions* (New York: Harper & Row, 1965, originally published in German in 1960) 239.

contemporaries.[55] Though appealing to the election of David, the prophet "democratises" it as applying to the nation as a whole, removing its messianic content.[56] The world's creation is seen as the first of God's saving acts, and Israel's creation is synonymous with its redemption in the exodus.[57] The prophet recalls the original exodus only to assert that "the new exodus will far surpass the old in wonders":

> One must be clear about what is implied here. In referring as he does to the new exodus, Deutero-Isaiah puts a question mark against 'Israel's original confession'; indeed, he uses every possible means to persuade his contemporaries to look away from that event which so far had been the basis of their faith, and to put their faith in the new and greater one.[58]

According to von Rad, the "former things," the "saving history that began with the call of Abraham and the exodus from Egypt and ended with the destruction of Jerusalem," have in Second Isaiah's understanding come to an end; the prophet announces a new beginning.[59]

Commentators since von Rad's time have come to take virtually for granted the importance of Israelite traditions in the formulation of Second Isaiah's poetry. Westermann devoted a section of the introductory chapter of his commentary to this subject. The exodus from Egypt was so critical to Second Isaiah that, in Westermann's words: "An arch which spans the nation's entire history has as its one pillar the release from Egypt and as its other the new, imminent release from Babylon."[60] He also highlighted Second Isaiah's continuity with preexilic prophecy. The poetry's affinity with the Psalms received the greatest share of Westermann's attention. His suggestions will be described below.

Others have followed suit. P.-E. Bonnard (1972), like Westermann, included a discussion of the text's relationships to the

---

[55] Ibid., 238–50; see especially 247.

[56] Ibid., 240.

[57] Ibid., 240–41.

[58] Ibid., 246.

[59] Ibid., 246–48.

[60] Westermann, *Isaiah 40–66*, 22.

Pentateuch, psalms, and prophets, as well as the dependence of later biblical literature on Second Isaiah.[61] R. N. Whybray (1975) also pointed out Second Isaiah's frequent use of forms and expressions from earlier poetry.[62] Though Whybray viewed this trait as a weakness, Richard Clifford claimed it as a strength: to persuade fellow exiles to fulfill God's will by returning to Jerusalem, the poet "arranged the venerable national tradition to speak to the new situation, doing so with wonderful rhetorical skill and sensitivity to the popular temper."[63]

As a result of the increased interest in the unity and textuality of Second Isaiah and the increased recognition of its relationship with antecedents, studies of the use in Second Isaiah of previous biblical texts have begun to proliferate. The depth, breadth, and implications of many of these will be described below.

Second Isaiah and the Pentateuch

By far the most attention has been paid to Second Isaiah's use of pentateuchal themes: the exodus from Egypt especially, but also wilderness, patriarchal, pre-patriarchal, and creation stories. In his 1956 work B. J. van der Merwe studied all of these traditions in relation to Second Isaiah. He concluded that even though much of the Pentateuch was probably available during the exile, and even though Second Isaiah referred to many traditions of the Pentateuch, the poet rarely if ever quoted explicitly from those narratives.[64] Second Isaiah even refrained from using well-known phrases regarding the exodus common among preexilic prophets. Rather, Second Isaiah's language more closely resembles that of Israel's hymns.

---

61 P.-E. Bonnard, *Le Second Isaïe: Son disciple et leurs éditeurs, Isaïe 40–66* (Paris: J. Gabalda, 1972) 71–81.

62 R. Norman Whybray, *Isaiah 40–66*, NCB. (Grand Rapids, MI: Eerdmans, 1975) 28.

63 Clifford, 4.

64 B. J. van der Merwe, *Pentateuchtradisies in die Prediking van Deuterjesaja* (Groningen: J. B. Wolters, 1956). The one possible quotation he recognized is the use of the word בְחִפָּזוֹן in Isa 52:12 (see Ex 12:11; Deut 16:3). However, he preferred to recognize this as a reference to a Passover liturgy (158–60; 264).

Other studies have tended to focus on one portion of the tradition, particularly the exodus from Egypt. Walther Zimmerli (1963) contrasted Second Isaiah's use of the exodus tradition with Ezekiel's (particularly in Ezek 20:32–44), pointing out Second Isaiah's depiction of the new exodus from Babylon as an anti-type of the original exodus.[65] The poet bids the returnees to go without haste (לֹא בְחִפָּזוֹן) and to take none of the Babylonian spoils, leaving Babylon very differently from the way their ancestors had left Egypt (Isa 52:11, 12; see Exod 12:11; Deut 16:3; Exod 3:21–22; etc.). The hearers, Zimmerli observed, are even invited to forget the former things (Isa 43:16–21), because YHWH's new action—to make a way in the wilderness rather than in the sea—stands so much in contrast with former events.

Bernhard Anderson (1962) saw Second Isaiah's recollections as typological interpretations of the original exodus from Egypt.[66] He provided a comprehensive list of passages in Second Isaiah alluding to the patriarchal, exodus, and wilderness traditions. His 1976 article pointed out Second Isaiah's peculiar silence concerning the Sinai tradition. This omission was striking because Second Isaiah referred to all the other traditions and "must have known the pentateuchal tradition in approximately the form given to it by the Priestly Writer."[67] In omitting this portion of the pentateuchal story, Anderson believed, Second Isaiah was, unlike Hosea, Jeremiah, and Ezekiel, taking exception to the conditional Mosaic covenant, and showing preference instead for the unconditional Noachic and Davidic covenants.

---

[65] W. Zimmerli, "Der 'neue Exodus' in der Verkündigung der beiden grossen Exilspropheten," in his *Gottes Offenbarung: Gesammelte Aufsätze zum Alten Testament*, Theologische Bücherei 19 (München: Chr. Kaiser Verlag, 1963) 192–204. Original publication date of essay, 1960.

[66] B. Anderson, "Exodus Typology in Second Isaiah," in *Israel's Prophetic Heritage: Essays in honor of James Muilenburg*, ed. B. W. Anderson and W. Harrelson (New York: Harper and Brothers, 1962) 177–95.

[67] Anderson, "Exodus and Covenant in Second Isaiah and Prophetic Tradition," in *Magnalia Dei: The Mighty Acts of God*, ed. F. M. Cross et al. (New York: Doubleday, 1976) 342.

Dale Patrick (1984) called the language used to describe Second Isaiah's new exodus "epiphanic imagery," that is, imagery in which God "comes to intervene for (or against) His people in a time of crisis."[68] Patrick showed that such epiphanies involved God's coming from a distant place on earth, on a journey that is accompanied and announced by disturbances in nature. In Patrick's view, Second Isaiah's descriptions of YHWH's intervention on behalf of exiled Jerusalem drew upon epiphanic descriptions of the crossing of the Red Sea such as in Psalms 77 and 114 and Exodus 15. Patrick also reflected upon the disjunction between the language of the Pentateuch and that of Second Isaiah, and suggested that Second Isaiah's language may be more influenced by hymnic poetry than by narrative prose.

In the same year that Gene Tucker declared prophetic dependence upon tradition a consensus, Michael Fishbane published his comprehensive work on inner-biblical exegesis, *Biblical Interpretation in Ancient Israel.* Fishbane explored the variety of ways in which exegetical reinterpretation of biblical texts occurs within the Bible itself. Some texts obtained their present form, Fishbane argued, by a process of growth in which scribes or interpreters supplemented earlier texts which they viewed as having become obscure, limited, or unacceptable. Other texts, especially many prophetic texts, were created as aggadic reinterpretations of already authoritative texts, necessitated by new social contexts and disseminated in new prophetic genres. Although the most pervasive prophetic reformulations of tradition emphasized fundamental continuity between past and present, prophets also engaged in re-presentation of historical memories and, at times, in asserting the newness of their word over against an obsolete tradition. This was not done for the sake of the past but for the present:

> Characteristically, aggadic transformations are not articulated "for the sake of" the *traditum* from which they are derived. . . . Any given aggadic *traditio* may reinforce the authority of the *traditum* whose language and ideas it reuses, even as some instances of aggadic exegesis can be understood to be

[68] D. Patrick, "Epiphanic Imagery in Second Isaiah's Portrayal of a New Exodus," *Hebrew Annual Review* 8 (1984) 126.

> "for the sake of" the covenantal tradition as a whole. . . . Aggadic exegeses do not explicitly clarify, resolve, harmonize, or even reauthorize earlier traditions. What they rather do is to serve the *traditio*—and its particular concern—"by means of" the *traditum*.[69]

Like von Rad, Fishbane viewed these prophetic reformulations as being inextricably tied to the past, and yet freely fashioned into dynamic new applications. But whereas von Rad discussed traditions which the prophets reused, Fishbane discussed texts. Occasionally he identified relationships between texts on the basis of direct citation, but since, in his view, "the vast majority of cases of aggadic exegesis involve implicit or virtual citations," they were identified more frequently on the basis of "multiple and sustained lexical linkages between two texts . . . where the second text (the putative *traditio*) uses a segment of the first (the putative *traditum*) in a lexically reorganized and topically rethematized way."[70]

Fishbane's work on Second Isaiah mostly involved its revision or typological reuse of pentateuchal traditions, including the creation story of Gen 1:1–2:4a, the figures Eden, Noah, and Abraham, and especially the exodus from Egypt. His work on Genesis texts will be discussed presently; at this point his suggestions concerning the exodus will be summarized.

The exodus and conquest stories, Fishbane said, "dominate the prophetic consciousness of Deutero-Isaiah."[71] This is especially seen in the typological relationship to the exodus, both positive and negative, expressed in Isa 43:16–21, where the audience is first reminded of YHWH who made a way in the sea, and then exhorted to forget the former things, because now YHWH is making a way in the wilderness. "Quite clearly, the original exodus event is not only a prototype for what will soon transpire but a warrant for it as well. . . . Here, YHWH himself reinforces the validity of his present promise by reference to earlier, constitutive acts of his own

[69] M. Fishbane, *Biblical Interpretation in Ancient Israel* (Oxford: Clarendon Press, 1985), 415–16.

[70] Ibid., 285.

[71] Ibid., 363.

doing."[72] Fishbane noted many individual parallels of theme and even of term between the pentateuchal exodus and wilderness stories and the language of Second Isaiah. Among these are a direct allusion to a grammatical construction otherwise used only in Exod 15:13 and 16 (עַם־זוּ), the ironic reversal in Isa 52:12 of the Exod 12:11 instructions to eat the Passover in haste (בְּחִפָּזוֹן), and the multivalent creation-exodus-new exodus language in Isa 51:9–11. In an essay on this theme in *Text and Texture*, he noted the ambiguities of myth/history and of past/present/future, observing that in this ambiguity "the modern reader can experience an ironic correlative to the hesitations and confusions of the original audience."[73]

Examining more particular themes of the exodus tradition, Claude Chavasse (1964), Graham Ogden (1978), and J. G. Janzen (1989) compared elements of Second Isaiah with the stories of Moses and Abraham.[74] All three of these authors, like Fishbane, saw Second Isaiah using the Pentateuch as a written source. Their claims can only be evaluated by means of some reasonable criteria for discerning intertextual dependence; here it should simply be noted that they exemplify the trend to explore Second Isaiah's relationship to the Pentateuch as an intertextual, rather than tradition-historical, study.

Several scholars in the past generation have investigated ties between Second Isaiah's poetry and Genesis accounts. A. S. Kapelrud (1964) and Moshe Weinfeld (1968), followed by Fishbane, have seen Second Isaiah as exegetically reappropriating the creation account in Gen 1:1–2:4a.[75] However, according to Weinfeld, Second Isaiah rejects and spiritualizes many of the details

---

72 Ibid., 364.

73 M. Fishbane, *Text and Texture: Close Readings of Selected Biblical Texts* (New York: Schocken Books, 1979) 138.

74 C. Chavasse, "The Suffering Servant and Moses," *CQR* 165 (1964) 152–63; G. Ogden, "Moses and Cyrus," *VT* 28 (1978) 195–203; J. G. Janzen, "An Echo of the Shema in Isaiah 51:1–3," *JSOT* 43 (1989) 69–82.

75 A. Kapelrud, "The Date of the Priestly Code (P)," *ASTI* 3 (1964) 58–64; M. Weinfeld, "God the Creator in Genesis 1 and in the Prophecy of Second Isaiah," *Tarbiz* 37/2 (1968) 105–32 [Hebrew]; Fishbane, *Biblical Interpretation*, 326.

of the creation account. In particular, against Gen 1:2, Isa 45:7 claims YHWH as the creator of darkness and Isa 45:18 denies its primordial chaotic state. Against Gen 1:26, Isa 40:18, 25 and 46:5 assert that no likeness of YHWH is to be found anywhere, and Isa 44:24 and 40:13–14 assert respectively that YHWH was alone, and did not consult with anyone else at the time of creation. Against Gen 2:2–3, Isa 40:28 states that YHWH has no need to rest. As Fishbane saw it, even in the act of appropriating creation tradition in order to maintain it in a newly understood way, Second Isaiah rejected elements of the Genesis text.[76]

Many individual suggestions have been made concerning thematic linkages, and more lately verbal links, between Second Isaiah and various portions of the Pentateuch. But aside from Fishbane's work, these suggestions have frequently been limited by narrowness of scope and lack of methodological rigor. Even Fishbane, because of his nearly exclusive concentration on the reuse of pentateuchal texts, has offered many suggestions without comparing the pentateuchal influence on Second Isaiah with the influence of other sources. Additionally, Second Isaiah's unmistakable knowledge of pentateuchal traditions is at times confused with reliance on particular Exodus texts. As my study will show, the prophet uses pentateuchal traditions freely, but the dearth of direct, continuous citation of pentateuchal passages renders it difficult to discern what form or version of the text Second Isaiah knew. Moreover, the continuing flux of opinions concerning pentateuchal dating and redaction adds uncertainty to any claims that can be made in this regard.

---

[76] Other brief studies relating Second Isaiah to patriarchal texts include D. Gunn, "Deutero-Isaiah and the Flood," *JBL* 94 (1975) 493–508; E. Conrad, *Patriarchal Traditions in Second Isaiah* (Ph.D. diss., Princeton, 1974); G. Jones, "Abraham and Cyrus: Type and Anti-Type?" *VT* 22 (1972) 304–19; and K. Baltzer, "Schriftauslegung bei Deuterojesaja? Jes 43,22–28 als Beispiel," in *Die Väter Israels: Beiträge zur Theologie der Patriarchenüberlieferungen im AT*, ed. Manfred Görg (Stuttgart: Katholisches Bibelwerk, 1989) 11–16.

Second Isaiah and the Prophets

Several studies have appeared concerning Second Isaiah's relationship to preexilic prophets, especially Jeremiah. Werner Tannert (1956) detailed several literary and theological relationships between Jeremiah and Second Isaiah, noting the contours of Second Isaiah's relationship to the previous prophet.[77] Shalom Paul (1969), like Cassuto and Tannert, viewed Isaiah 40–66 as heavily influenced by Jeremiah as well as by several other literary sources.[78] Paul offered a wealth of short verbal echoes culled from a wide range of chapters in both books. Many of his suggestions offer solutions to textual difficulties in Second Isaiah. Victor Eldridge's 1978 dissertation examined the suggestions of both Cassuto and Paul, and concluded that Second Isaiah borrowed from Jeremiah's phrases, images, and theology, not adopting the earlier prophet's message wholesale but only selectively, mostly from the parts of Jeremiah that Mowinckel had classified as "Source A" and "Source D."[79]

Both Joel Eakins (1970) and Dieter Baltzer (1971) studied Ezekiel in relation to Second Isaiah.[80] Eakins concluded that "Ezekiel had no significant influence on Exilic Isaiah in matters of style, phraseology, and vocabulary," but that the similarity of their theological themes indicated that Second Isaiah was influenced by Ezekiel on the level of ideas.[81] Unfortunately, though he laid out a methodology for critical exploration of verbal ties, he offered no

---

[77] W. Tannert, *Jeremia und Deuterojesaja: Eine Untersuchung zur Frage ihren literarischen und theologischen Zusammenhanges* (Ph.D. diss., Karl Marx University in Leipzig, 1956).

[78] S. Paul, "Literary and Ideological Echoes of Jeremiah in Deutero-Isaiah," in *Proceedings of the Fifth World Congress of Jewish Studies,* ed. Pinchas Peli (Jerusalem: R. H. Hacohen Press, 1969).

[79] V. Eldridge, *The Influence of Jeremiah on Isaiah 40–55* (Ph.D. diss., Southern Baptist Theological Seminary, 1978).

[80] J. K. Eakins, *Ezekiel's Influence on the Exilic Isaiah* (Ph.D. diss., Southern Baptist Theological Seminary, 1970); D. Baltzer, *Ezechiel und Deuterojesaja: Berührungen in der Heiserwartung der beiden grossen Exilspropheten,* BZAW 121 (Berlin: Walter de Gruyter, 1971).

[81] Eakins, 144.

similar controls for exploring theological connections. Baltzer observed that while Ezekiel's language was rooted in priestly tradition, Second Isaiah's language was psalmic. Though he noted that the substance of their messages was similar, Baltzer was more cautious than Eakins about concluding that Second Isaiah was directly dependent upon Ezekiel.

Very little work has been done on Second Isaiah's connections with minor prophets, with the exception of some brief notes in an article by Richard Coggins (1982) referring to similarities between Nahum and Second Isaiah, and an article by B. J. van der Merwe (1964/65) suggesting echoes of Hosea in Second Isaiah.[82]

Quite a bit more has been written on the links between Second Isaiah and Isaiah 1–39. While few would deny the existence of thematic and verbal links among the parts of the book, how these links are understood is closely tied to perceptions of Isaiah's development. It is clear to many that major sections of "First Isaiah" are quite late.[83] But it has been difficult to reach agreement on the extent or significance of postexilic redactions of Isaiah's words. Suggestions in recent times have ranged widely. On the one hand, John Hayes and Stuart Irvine (1987) have understood chapters 1–33 as having been composed by the son of Amoz and delivered in nearly the order in which they now appear.[84] Otto Kaiser (1983), on the other hand, viewed Isaiah's earliest collection to date from the fifth century and even then to consist only of sayings in

---

[82] R. Coggins, "An Alternative Prophetic Tradition?" in *Israel's Prophetic Tradition: Essays in Honour of Peter Ackroyd*, ed. R. Coggins et al. (Cambridge: Cambridge University Press, 1982) 77–94; B. J. van der Merwe, "Echoes from Teaching of Hosea in Isaiah 40–55," *OTWSA* (1964/65) 90–99.

[83] According to a survey of recent scholarship by Rolf Rendtorff, "The scholarly discussion shows that there is broad agreement on the 'secondary' character of elements like chs. 13–23, 24–27, and also of smaller units like 2:1–5, 4:2–6, 12:1–6 and others." R. Rendtorff, "The Book of Isaiah: A Complex Unity. Synchronic and Diachronic Reading," *Society of Biblical Literature Seminar Papers* (Atlanta: Scholars Press, 1991) 16–17.

[84] John H. Hayes and Stuart A. Irvine, *Isaiah: The Eighth-Century Prophet* (Nashville: Abingdon Press, 1987).

chapters 1 and 28–31.[85] Rolf Rendtorff and Peter Ackroyd have questioned whether First Isaiah ever existed as a separate book before its postexilic compilation with chapters 40–66.[86]

Neither an understanding of First Isaiah as a unified written work nor as a growing set of traditions necessarily dictates the effect of First Isaiah (or its core) on Second Isaiah. The once popular understanding of the three Isaiahs as separate books brought together after their writing neither necessitates nor precludes First Isaiah's having influenced the thought and writing of Second Isaiah, because First Isaiah would simply have taken its place alongside Jeremiah, Hosea, and the other prophetic books available for Second Isaiah's use or rejection.[87] Those like Ackroyd and Rendtorff who understand First Isaiah as a composition based on some amount of eighth-century prophecy and a great deal of postexilic growth have attended to textual relationships among the parts of the book, but not necessarily in terms of First Isaiah's influence on Second Isaiah. An understanding of First Isaiah as a largely postexilic composition might be counterindicated if it could be shown that Second Isaiah responded to a great deal of literature and thought ranging throughout the first thirty-nine chapters. But if significant intertextual relationships between 40–55 and 1–39 cannot be discovered, or if these relationships can be just as easily

---

[85] O. Kaiser, *Isaiah 1–12: A Commentary*, 2nd ed., OTL (Philadelphia: Westminster Press, 1983, originally published in German in 1981) 1.

[86] Rolf Rendtorff, "The Book of Isaiah," as well as *The Old Testament: An Introduction* (Philadelphia: Fortress Press, 1986, originally published in German in 1983), in which he states, "The numerous passages in I [First Isaiah] which echo II [Second Isaiah] clearly indicate that the composition of the first part in its present form cannot be understood apart from the composition of the book of Isaiah as a whole," 200. See also his "The Composition of the Book of Isaiah," in *Canon and Theology*, 146–69; P. Ackroyd, "Isaiah 1–12: Presentation of a Prophet," in his *Studies in the Religious Tradition of the Old Testament* (London: SCM Press, 1987, originally published in 1978) 79–104.

[87] O. H. Steck has proposed a contemporary modification of this theory by viewing Isaiah 1–39* and 40–62* as having been completed before their having been linked together by chapter 35, in *Bereitete Heimkehr: Jesaja 35 als redaktionelle Brücke zwischen dem Ersten und dem Zweiten Jesaja* (Stuttgart: Verlag Katholisches Bibelwerk, 1985) 101.

understood as the editorial insertion of Second Isaiah's ideas and words into the first part of the book, then an understanding of the relationships as resulting from First Isaiah's growth would remain unchallenged.

One recently revived notion about Isaiah's development, however, depends positively upon finding a strong intertextual influence of First Isaiah upon Second Isaiah: the idea that Second Isaiah was originally created as an addition to and interpretation of an already extant First Isaiah. An early form of this theory was the notion of a continuous school of Isaiah's disciples who not only helped edit and preserve the prophet's oracles, but who finally composed and added chapters 40–66. The idea seems to have first been proposed by Mowinckel (1946), and was taken up by D. R. Jones (1955), John Eaton (1959), and others, but has few adherents today.[88]

A recent modification of this idea does not posit a continuous succession of Isaiah disciples, but rather perceives Second Isaiah's self-understanding to be that of heir and interpreter of Isaiah of Jerusalem. Brevard Childs took a step in this direction by suggesting that, although the original setting of Second Isaiah might have been more particular, "the canonical editors of this tradition employed the material in such a way as to eliminate almost entirely those concrete features and to subordinate the original message to a new role within the canon"—as a continuation of Isaiah of Jerusalem's message.[89] He interpreted Second Isaiah's "former things" as now only meaning the prophecies of First Isaiah, and viewed Second Isaiah without First Isaiah as "only a

---

[88] S. Mowinckel, *Prophecy and Tradition* (Oslo: J. Dybwad, 1946) 68–69; D. R. Jones, "The Traditio of the Oracles of Isaiah of Jerusalem," *ZAW* 67 (1955) 226–46; John Eaton, "The Origin of the Book of Isaiah," *VT* 9 (1959) 138–57. Rainer Albertz, "Das Deuterojesaja-Buch als Fortschreibung der Jesaja-Prophetie," in *Die Hebraische Bibel und ihre zweifache Nachgeschichte: FS Rolf Rendtorff*, ed. E. Blum et al. (Neukirchen: Neukirchener Verlag, 1990), is perhaps the most recent advocate of an unbroken tradition of thought descending from the eighth-century prophet.

[89] Brevard Childs, *Introduction to the Old Testament as Scripture* (Philadelphia: Fortress Press, 1979) 325.

confused fragment."[90] He concluded, "In the light of the present shape of the book of Isaiah the question must be seriously raised if the material of Second Isaiah in fact ever circulated in Israel apart from its being connected to an earlier form of First Isaiah."[91] But he also viewed Isaiah 1–39 as having been considerably redacted to "assure that its message was interpreted in the light of Second Isaiah."[92] Although Childs was vague on the identity of that redactor, he did credit "Second Isaiah" (presumably not the prophet but the editors who must have deleted the prophet's historical particularity and circulated the prophet's words) with bringing the first chapter of Isaiah together.[93]

Ronald Clements (1982 and 1985) and, more recently, Christopher Seitz (1990 and 1991) and H. G. M. Williamson (1994) have taken up Childs's interpretation of Second Isaiah's "former things," agreeing with Childs that Second Isaiah developed primarily in response to some form of First Isaiah.[94] Clements discussed at length the relationships among the parts of Isaiah, and contended that "from the time of their origin, the prophetic sayings of Isaiah 40–55 were intended as a supplement and sequel to a collection of the earlier sayings of the eighth-century Isaiah of Jerusalem."[95]

> The issue here appears to me to be a deeper one than simply whether the so-called Deutero-Isaiah was familiar with, and alluded to, sayings of Isaiah of Jerusalem. Rather it raises the question whether the existence of the

---

[90] Ibid., 329.

[91] Ibid., 329.

[92] Ibid., 333.

[93] Ibid., 331.

[94] R. Clements, "The Unity of the Book of Isaiah," *Int* 36 (1982) 117–29, and "Beyond Tradition-History: Deutero-Isaianic Development of First Isaiah's Themes," *JSOT* 31 (1985) 95–113); C. Seitz, "The Divine Council: Temporal Transition and New Prophecy in the Book of Isaiah," *JBL* 109 (1990) 229–47, and *Zion's Final Destiny: The Development of the Book of Isaiah. A Reassessment of Isaiah 36–39* (Minneapolis: Fortress Press, 1991); H. G. M. Williamson, *The Book Called Isaiah: Deutero-Isaiah's Role in Composition and Redaction* (Oxford: Clarendon Press, 1994).

[95] Clements, "Beyond Tradition-History," 101.

> earlier Isaianic prophecies has not provided the primary stimulus in the shaping of much of the contents of chs. 40–55."[96]

To demonstrate his point, Clements traced the theme of blindness and deafness from a starting point in Isaiah 6, which he perceived as predating Second Isaiah. The theme, he argued, reappeared in Isaiah 42 and 43, and then emerged in the later Isa 35:5 and 29:18. He also saw Second Isaiah's theme of Israel's election as presupposing Isaiah 1–39's claim that God had rejected Israel.

In his 1990 article, Seitz explored Isa 40:1–11 especially as it related to Isaiah 6. He showed linguistic and structural similarities linking the two chapters and, on the basis of these and other data, proposed a variety of new ideas concerning the character of Isaiah 40–55. Although he was a little more cautious than Clements about presuming the nature and historical sequence of intertextual relationships, citing "the existence of complex reciprocal relationships among the various subsections of Isaiah," Seitz still accepted the prevailing view that Isa 40:1–11 was "exegetically composed on the basis of, and literarily coordinated with, Isa 6:1–13."[97]

Seitz's 1991 book was less cautious. In this monograph he presupposed Clements's understanding of Second Isaiah's growth out of a pre-existent core of "former things" in Isaiah 1–39.[98] In

---

[96] Ibid., 113.

[97] Seitz, "The Divine Council," 240.

[98] It is interesting to note the trajectory of this discussion. Childs merely suggested that the language "former things" in its *present* context points back to First Isaiah. This observation prompted Rendtorff to raise the question of what that expression might have meant before 40–66 was combined with 1–39, according to Childs's understanding (Rendtorff, "The Book of Isaiah," 17). Clements moved beyond Childs, claiming: "When 'Second Isaiah' speaks of 'former things' therefore, the reader will naturally recognize that things prophesied in chs. 1–39 are being referred to" (Clements, "Beyond Tradition History," 97). Interpreting the "former things" as the prophecies of First Isaiah became a key feature in Seitz's determination that Second Isaiah was from the beginning consciously exegeting First Isaiah (Seitz, *Zion's Final Destiny*, 199–202). By way of contrast, Fishbane, noting the variety of usages of the motifs of "former things" and "new things" in Second Isaiah, suggested a more nuanced range to the meaning of the terms. In his view, the "former things" alluded not only to the preexilic oracles of doom, but also (especially in Isa 43:18) to the exodus event (Fishbane, *Text and Texture*, 132–33).

view of First Isaiah's composite character, however, Seitz said, "it is necessary to determine in more precise terms what is meant by 'First Isaiah,'" out of which Second Isaiah grew.[99] Seitz sought to claim, contrary to Clements, that chapters 36–39 were not only a part of the preexilic corpus of First Isaiah, but were "the pivot on which the entire tradition process turns, explaining the puzzle of Isaiah's growth, on the one hand, and much of the shape and character of Second Isaiah, on the other."[100]

The early inclusion of the Hezekiah narratives in the Isaianic corpus does not in itself either require or prove that First Isaiah was the ground out of which Second Isaiah grew. Seitz, however, argued that chapters 40–55 "give evidence of a conscious relationship to chapters 36–38 one might term exegetical."[101] He cited as evidence: 1) the phrase in Isa 40:6, "all flesh is grass," as a reference to Isa 37:27; 2) the references to "former things" (Isa 21:22, 43:18, 46:9, and 48:3) and similar phrases, which he viewed as deriving from 37:26; and 3) an analogy between Isa 52:13–53:12 and Hezekiah's sickness in Isaiah 38 based on the admittedly controversial idea that Zion is the servant of YHWH.

Recent, more cautious, articles by Graham Davies (1989) and Rolf Rendtorff (1989) have drawn attention to the overstatements in this debate.[102] Davies's article highlighted passages in First Isaiah that may be deliberately echoed in Second Isaiah, such as the "sign to the nations" (Isa 5:26, 11:10–12; see 49:22), the "arousing" of foreigners (13:17; see 41:25), the downfall of imperial power (10:6–7; see 47:6–7), and the motif of world government (9:1–6, 11:1–9; see 55:3–5). Yet, he cautioned, two conditions must be met to prove that the later section was composed to supplement the earlier one:

---

[99] Seitz, *Zion's Final Destiny*, 34.

[100] Ibid., 208.

[101] Ibid., 207–8.

[102] Graham Davies, "The Destiny of the Nations in the Book of Isaiah," in *The Book of Isaiah—Le Livre d'Isaïe*, ed. J. Vermeylen (Leuven: University Press, 1989) 93–120, and Rolf Rendtorff, "Isaiah 6 in the Framework of the Composition of the Book," in *Canon and Theology*, 170–80. Essay originally published in German in 1989.

> First, the alleged sources of Deutero-Isaiah's ideas and expressions must either be the only passages from which he could have derived them or at least they must in some way be more likely to have been his inspiration than other possible passages. Secondly, it must be plausible, when the whole of Deutero-Isaiah's thought and language is considered, to envisage Isaiah 1–39 as being to a special degree presupposed by the later prophet, more than any other known prophetic collection or collections.[103]

He noted the close parallels presented by the book of Jeremiah, showing that the "blind and deaf" passages in Second Isaiah to which Clements had appealed are as closely matched in Jer 5:21 as in Isa 6:9–10. He opted to remain open to the possibility that "Deutero-Isaiah was dependent, not exclusively on the Isaiah tradition, but on a more extensive prophetic corpus which was already being brought together, perhaps in Deuteronomistic circles."[104]

While Rolf Rendtorff's work on Isaiah in the early 1980s leaned toward making assertions concerning the dependence of much of both First and Third Isaiah on a rather unified and independent Second Isaiah, his more recent articles have become more cautious: "It seems to me more important first to keep one's gaze free for observations on the synchronic level of the present text, without simultaneously making the attempt in each case to answer to questions that arise on the diachronic level."[105] Like Childs, Clements, and Seitz, Rendtorff explored the intertextual relationships among elements of the Isaiah 6 "throneroom" narrative, some of the language of Isaiah 1, and some similar themes in Isaiah 40 and the chapters following. He pointed out verbal links between these passages as well as structural similarities between the sequences of Isaiah 6 and 40. While he noted that the classical answers to these puzzles would either be the dependence of one text on the other, or the dependence of both of them on a common source, he pointed out that both texts relate mutually to each other:

> It is obvious that without the preceding judgment the announcement of salvation has no function. But conversely, we saw in connection with the

[103] Davies, 116.

[104] Ibid., 116.

[105] Rendtorff, "Isaiah 6," 179.

> statement about the hardening of the hearts in Isa 6:8ff that its annulment is found for the first time only in Isa 40ff. So in the same sense the first part of chapter 6 could also be formulated with an eye to chapter 40 and in mutual relationship to that chapter.[106]

Rendtorff's article on Isa 56:1 also balanced on the edge of making diachronic assertions.[107] On the one hand he viewed this verse, which brings together First Isaian and Second Isaian usages of the word צְדָקָה, as a redactional key to the book, pulling the historically and theologically diverse sections together for a postexilic audience. On the other hand, he recognized that such a pronouncement presupposed a substantial body of prophecy from Isaiah of Jerusalem, enough to define the word צְדָקָה in a way that had to be squared after the fact with Second Isaiah's usage. Once again, rather than articulate a necessarily vague or complex diachronic theory, he laid out the evidence as he saw it and cautioned that "we are still at the beginning, in reading the book of Isaiah as a whole."[108]

Such cautions notwithstanding, H. G. M. Williamson recently built a comprehensive theory of Second Isaiah's dependence upon First Isaiah around perceived similarities between the Isaiahs, similarities such as linguistic and thematic echoes between Isaiah 6 and 40, the name "Holy One of Israel," and several themes found not only in the two Isaiahs but also in Jeremiah or the Psalms: the blindness motif, the theme of devastated cities, and a variety of other correspondences such as the potter and the clay, fading flowers, the references to Rahab. His work, which aimed to demonstrate the primacy of First Isaiah for Second Isaiah, advanced the most compelling possibilities of dependence and argued them exhaustively.

Exploration of all suggested exegetical connections is important for insight into the book's origin, whether the conclusions are positive or negative. For that reason Williamson's contribution is

---

[106] Ibid., 179.

[107] Rendtorff, "Isaiah 56:1 as a Key to the Formation of the Book of Isaiah," in *Canon and Theology*, 181–189.

[108] Ibid., 189.

valuable. His aim, however, was to demonstrate that First Isaiah was Second Isaiah's primary precursor. He acknowledged, citing Davies, that to do so he would also have to demonstrate the overall lack of comparable influence of other texts.[109] But this was not an issue he was prepared to address.[110] Despite this rather large omission, Williamson asserted that Second Isaiah:

> . . . was familiar with an early form of the book of Isaiah and that both consciously and sometimes also, no doubt, unconsciously he took up various of its themes, images, and modes of expression in the course of his own ministry, and that he did so in a way that is not true to anything like the same extent of his use of any other single body of earlier OT literature.[111]

Arguments for relationships within the book of Isaiah were thoroughly explored in the course of my research. In fact, I assumed initially that First Isaiah would play a major role in this study, and was disappointed to discover that substantial connections with First Isaiah did not turn up in the chapters I will discuss, and were rather scattered even in chapters 40–48 where claims are usually made. I found little evidence that First Isaiah's themes and language were uppermost in Second Isaiah's memory, and very much to suggest otherwise. While reconstructing the book of Isaiah's redactional history lies well outside the parameters of the present work, readers interested in that issue may find it useful to compare the quality and intensity of recollections that I will observe in this study with those that have been claimed for First Isaiah.[112]

---

[109] Williamson., especially pp. 14–15, 18.

[110] Ibid., 241.

[111] Ibid., 94.

[112] A dissertation exploring similar questions with somewhat different methodologies came to my attention too late to be discussed at length here: Benjamin Sommer, *Leshon Limmudim:* The Poetics of Allusion in Isaiah 40–66 (Ph.D. diss., University of Chicago, 1994). See his article, "Allusions and Illusions: The Unity of the Book of Isaiah in Light of Deutero-Isaiah's Use of Prophetic Tradition," in *New Visions of Isaiah,* ed. Roy Melugin and Marvin Sweeney, JSOTSup 214 (Sheffield: Sheffield Academic Press, 1996) 156–86, which also cautions against overdrawing the relationship between First and Second Isaiah.

Second Isaiah and the Psalms

Although the recognition of Second Isaiah's use of hymnic forms dates back at least to Gressmann, the notoriously difficult problem of dating most psalms has rendered exploration of Second Isaiah's relationship to particular ones very problematic. As a result, although mention of Second Isaiah's use of psalmic material and forms is now standard fare in studies and commentaries, the question of literary borrowing has not been widely studied. Not only has the possibility of Second Isaiah's use of specific psalms not been explored, but there do not seem to be many significant studies since Seidel's time that map out the verbal similarities even without hypothesizing a particular historical relationship between them.

Otto Eissfeldt, in his 1962 essay, noted that Psalm 89 originated during the time of the monarchy, and suggested that it inspired much of the prophet's language.[113] Eissfeldt listed many words and phrases he found common to the two works that were not common elsewhere, such as "chosen" and "servant" used in connection with each other, "Rahab," "fullness," and several others. In the end, however, because Second Isaiah used this language not in connection with the hope of the return of monarchy, but with an understanding of Israel's taking over the king's role as God's servant, Eissfeldt viewed the relationship between these two texts as "formal and superficial" only. "In terms of content, the latter passage is entirely different from the former."[114] Although he noted the difference of opinion concerning monarchy between Second Isaiah on the one hand and Jeremiah, Ezekiel, Haggai, and Zechariah on the other, Eissfeldt did not apparently view Second Isaiah's transumption of the language and symbols of the monarchic psalm as a rhetorical coup, but rather as an indication of lack of relationship.

---

[113] O. Eissfeldt, "The Promises of Grace to David in Isa 55:1–5," in *Israel's Prophetic Heritage: Essays in Honor of James Muilenburg*, ed. B. W. Anderson and W. Harrelson (New York: Harper and Brothers, 1962) 196–97.

[114] Ibid., 206.

In his 1961 volume on the Psalms, Claus Westermann entered the debate carried on a generation before between Gunkel, Mowinckel, and others concerning the relationship of the enthronement psalms to Second Isaiah.[115] "It is of decisive importance for the total understanding of these psalms whether that cry ["YHWH has become king"] has its origin in the Psalms or in Second Isaiah."[116] He presented six reasons for understanding Second Isaiah as the originator, and the psalms as postexilic imitators, of this form. Unfortunately, he presented these reasons only in thesis form, without supporting evidence.

It is hard to tell from Westermann's treatment of the subject in his 1966 commentary on Isaiah 40–66 whether his views on this issue had changed. In an introductory section entitled "Traditions in the Prophecy of Deutero-Isaiah," he commented quite extensively on the prophet's debt to the Psalter:

> Almost every page in Deutero-Isaiah reveals affinities between his proclamation and the language of the Psalter. . . . Because of the circumstances in which the exiles found themselves, the psalms which the prophet most frequently echoes are inevitably the psalms of lamentation; however, since the Psalter shows that lament and praise are essentially co-related, we may logically expect to find Deutero-Isaiah's diction influenced by the psalms of praise as well. The influence is, in actual fact, much stronger than has hitherto been realized.[117]

Although Westermann confined his comments for the most part to Second Isaiah's reuse of forms and motifs of the Psalter and not of particular words of particular psalms, his commentary was an important introduction to the wide range of Second Isaiah's influences. He commented, if only briefly, on Second Isaiah's relationship not only to psalmic motifs but also to prophecy and Pentateuch. His failure to comment on Second Isaiah's admitted close relationship to the enthronement psalms stands out as a

---

[115] C. Westermann, *The Praise of God in the Psalms* (Richmond: John Knox Press, 1961, originally published in German in 1961). This discussion is also addressed in his book, *Sprache und Struktur der Prophetie Deuterojesajas* (Stuttgart: Calwer Verlag, 1981).

[116] Westermann, *Praise*, 146.

[117] Westermann, *Isaiah 40–66*, 23.

rather glaring omission of a topic he had once viewed as being of decisive importance.[118] A further peculiarity of Westermann's discussion was his understanding of Second Isaiah's responses to lament psalms. Recognizing a response to a community lament in Isa 40:27 ("Why do you say, O Jacob, and speak, O Israel, 'My way is hid from YHWH, and my right is disregarded by my God'?"), Westermann said:

> Here Deutero-Isaiah obviously quotes words of a community lament, using them to express Israel's complaint and protest against the way in which God acted; and his quotation is, in fact, the central part in a lament, the "charge brought against the deity." The "why" with which he begins combats the "why" that introduced the charge which the nation made against God, which would have run: "O Lord, why is our way hid from thee? our right disregarded by thee?"[119]

Commenting that similar laments are known from Lamentations and the Psalms, Westermann concluded, "We may therefore take it for granted that here in verse 27 Deutero-Isaiah cites words from a lament in actual use by the exiles at the time."[120] Likewise, in dealing with the acknowledgments of Zion's distress in Isa 51:17b–20, Westermann again posited a lament which Second Isaiah took on word for word:

> Verses 17b–20 continue the community lament, here practically without alteration: it is simply put in the form of God's addressing Israel. The original is perfectly easy to reconstruct: "Thou didst give us, Lord YHWH, the cup of thy wrath to drink, made us drink to the dregs the bowl of staggering." . . . We can therefore be quite certain in saying that here Deutero-Isaiah takes up the words of a community lament such as was made both in the exiles' worship and in that of the people who were not deported. These sentiments, expressed word for word, were perfectly familiar to everyone who heard them.[121]

The assumption Westermann made in both these cases was that Second Isaiah necessarily quoted laments word for word, only

---

[118] Ibid., 102 and 250.

[119] Ibid., 59.

[120] Ibid., 60.

[121] Ibid., 245. In deference to Jewish reverence for the divine name, I have wherever possible altered quotations from other authors by substituting "YHWH" for "Yahweh." Bibliographical titles remain unaltered.

exchanging the subjects and objects to create a divine response. Even though in both cases he pointed out the similarities of Second Isaiah's language to the words of Lamentations and lament psalms, his assumption that intertextual relationships had to be exact led him to posit texts without any evidence and prevented him from exploring possible relationships with texts that did exist. The problem here is similar to that noted above in connection with Eissfeldt's work: a narrow understanding of the interactions of texts, which does not take into account the freedom with which a new text might reformulate another's terms, has forestalled significant recognitions.

Linda Deming's 1978 dissertation also involved form-critical analysis of Second Isaiah's hymnic sections.[122] She concluded that Second Isaiah's hymnic language could more aptly be termed "calls to praise" than actual hymns. These functioned always in connection with YHWH's own speech describing the exiles' return from Babylon. Deming recognized the form, if not the contents, of these calls to praise as having been borrowed from the enthronement psalms and used to support the prophet's proclamation of salvation.

Like Deming, Tryggve Mettinger (1986) discovered a close relationship between some of Second Isaiah's hymnic material—especially Isa 42:10–13; 52:9–10, and 55:12–13—and enthronement psalms such as 96 and 98.[123] He noted expressions closely echoed that were otherwise rare or unknown in the Bible. He declined, however, to discuss the issue of intertextuality, saying, "May it suffice to say that the similarities pointed out above seem to have as their minimum prerequisite that the Prophet of the Consolation drew from the same tradition as the YHWH malak psalms."[124]

---

122 L. Deming, *Hymnic Language in Deutero-Isaiah: The Calls to Praise and their Function in the Book* (Ph.D. diss., Emory University, 1978).

123 T. Mettinger, "In Search of the Hidden Structure: YHWH as King in Isaiah 40–55," in *Svensk Exegetisk Årsbok 51–52* (Lund, Sweden: CWK Gleerup, 1986).

124 Ibid., 156–57.

Second Isaiah and Lamentations

As I have already noted, the book of Lamentations and its place in the development of scripture has not been widely studied. I have already mentioned the contributions of Gottwald and Newsom. Mention should also be made of the comments of Norman Porteous, Alan Mintz, Mary Donovan Turner and Tod Linafelt.

In a 1961 article entitled "Jerusalem-Zion: The Growth of a Symbol," Norman Porteous briefly traced the theme of the symbolic significance of Jerusalem from preexilic writings through postexilic reformulations and into intertestamental and New Testament literature. Echoing Gottwald, Porteous remarked that "the Book of Lamentations is a very definite link between Jerusalem's past and the remarkable development which followed. In particular, as soon as it is grasped that the greater part, if not the whole, of the book precedes the prophecies of the Second Isaiah, it gains very considerably in value as a probable influence upon the Second Isaiah in his recreation of Israel's religion."[125] Porteous noted especially the development in Lamentations of Daughter Zion, who had already begun to take shape as a female personification of the city in preexilic and exilic prophecy, and the glimmerings of hope in Lamentations 3, which are extended much further in Second Isaiah. But like Gottwald, Porteous moved quickly away from these observations, laying out suggestions for study of an issue which he did not carry into detail.

Alan Mintz (1984) offered a sensitive and detailed literary analysis of Lamentations 1–3.[126] Although his discussion of the response of Second Isaiah to the laments of Jerusalem was brief, he did point out the prophetic literature's "strategic sensitivity to the suffering and despondency in the aftermath of the Destruction":

> The text of Second Isaiah displays a consciousness of its role as an antidote to the discourse of lamentation. Through echoes and quotations from the

---

[125] N. Porteous, "Jerusalem-Zion: The Growth of a Symbol," in *Verbannung und Heimkehr*, ed. Arnulf Kuschke (Tübingen: J. C. B. Mohr, 1961) 238.

[126] A. Mintz, *Hurban: Responses to Catastrophe in Hebrew Literature* (New York: Columbia University Press, 1984).

> poetry of communal complaint, the prophet emphasized that it is precisely this discourse that has been superseded by the discourse of consolation.[127]

Mintz pointed out the interplay between Lamentations' question, "Who can console you?" and Second Isaiah's insistence that God is the consoler of Israel. Mintz also observed that the prophet's reuse of the female Zion figure in Lamentations "constitutes one of the most powerful correspondences to the discourse of lamentation."[128]

Mary Turner's 1992 dissertation explored the personification of Jerusalem as "Daughter Zion" in the prophetic books and Lamentations.[129] An entire chapter was devoted to detailing the responses of Isaiah 40, 49–52, and 54 to the poetry of Lamentations. According to her, Second Isaiah "uses images and motifs from Lamentations and transforms them from elements of lamentation into elements of restoration."[130] She noted particularly the responses of YHWH that guaranteed a future to the childless widow Zion. Since her dissertation aimed at tracing the metaphor through several books, Turner's work was more descriptive than analytical, and methodological issues of inner-biblical exegesis, while obviously in the background, were not highlighted.

Tod Linafelt's 1995 article explored Lamentations as a lament unanswered by God within the book, and suggested the survival of this difficult book through its interpretation not only by Second Isaiah but by its Targumic translation.[131] He was particularly attentive to the interplay of dramatic voices. Although Lamentations presented several voices, including those of Zion, the poet, and the community, and although these voices pleaded for divine response to their descriptions of destruction, the divine voice was conspicuously absent from the book. Isaiah 49:14–26, Linafelt

---

127 Ibid., 44.

128 Ibid., 45.

129 M. Turner, *Daughter Zion: Lament and Restoration* (Ph.D. diss., Emory University, 1992).

130 Ibid., 184.

131 T. Linafelt, "Surviving Lamentations," *Horizons in Biblical Theology* 17 (1995) 45–61.

suggested, was "a direct answer to Lamentations . . . able to hold together the divine response and the survival of the children."[132] This was accomplished by identifying Zion's children not as the dead, but as the returning exilic community. In response to Lamentations's bitterest language, Linafelt concluded, Second Isaiah articulated the survival not only of children but of the community as a whole.

Conclusion

Understanding Second Isaiah's use of previous biblical material has become increasingly important in recent decades. While some exegetes throughout time have recognized literary connections between Second Isaiah and other parts of the Bible, it took two major movements in biblical scholarship to refine this insight. The first task was a historicizing of concerns: recognition of Second Isaiah's historical independence from the eighth-century prophet Isaiah, and recontextualization of Isaiah 40–55 in the late sixth century. While authorial independence was first suggested around 1800, a century of discussion and refinement was necessary to establish consensus on this issue.

Arguing this stance necessitated isolating Second Isaiah's literature only from that of First Isaiah. Nevertheless, in the midst of the debate, suggestions of continuity between Second Isaiah and other literature were ignored. Observations by Cassuto and Cheyne concerning Second Isaiah's interpretive relationship with First Isaiah and other prophets were overlooked along with anti-critical claims of Alexander, Nägelsbach, and others. Meanwhile, source-critical studies offered scholars a new tool for creating Second Isaiah's isolation from its textual environment. Armed with the presupposition, as expressed by Wellhausen, that prophets spoke not out of their tradition but out of "the spirit which judges all things and itself is judged of no man," many critics isolated all speech that repeated phrases found in other parts of the Bible, and relegated these repetitions to the harmonizing efforts of later

132 Ibid., 56.

scribes. Duhm, Köhler, Fischer, Volz, Fohrer, and others carried forward this program, dividing the text into increasingly small and disjointed units. Thus the first task carried out in refining understanding of Second Isaiah was that of isolation: historically, textually, and even intratextually.

The second major task that followed, and still continues, may broadly be described as one of putting the pieces back together. Once the authorial independence of the exilic prophecy had been accepted, accounting had to be made of its continuity—both internal continuity as a poetic work with flow and purpose, and external continuity with literary contexts: the book of Isaiah, the prophets, and the Bible as a whole. Early pioneers in this work were Mowinckel, who placed Second Isaiah in a cultic context reutilizing psalmic tradition and in a prophetic context continuing the tradition of First Isaiah, and Begrich, who recognized Second Isaiah's use of Pentateuch, prophets, and psalms, noting the interaction of the prophet's audience with such familiar material.

By the 1950s this work of integration had begun in earnest. The climate of scholarship had changed sufficiently to allow exploration of Second Isaiah as a planned, coherent literary work. Scholars such as Muilenburg, followed by Westermann and McKenzie, and even more by Spykerboer, Gitay, and Clifford, have departed from the practice of dividing the book into small oral and redactional sources, and have explored the original exilic prophet's responsibility for the book's final form. Consequently these critics have sought, and found, poetic purpose in the order of Second Isaiah as it stands today.

At the same time that Second Isaiah's own textuality has been explored, scholars have also noted the ties that bind the poetry to its surroundings in Judahite literature. Commentators such as Muilenburg, followed by Westermann, Bonnard, and Clifford, have recognized Second Isaiah's references to previous tradition, especially pentateuchal themes, psalmic language, and preexilic prophecy. In addition, many more detailed suggestions of Second Isaiah's relationships to individual genres and books have been published. While early ventures into this discussion usually developed the more guarded suggestion that Second Isaiah depended upon traditions and forms that may also be seen in other biblical literature, the past ten or fifteen years have witnessed a growing interest in identifying written texts as precursors, thus enabling a more precise exploration of Second Isaiah's strategies.

Even though Lamentations is without doubt one of the books most closely related to Second Isaiah both temporally and thematically, and even though recognition of its relevance to Second Isaiah predates modern scholarship by over a millennium, this most promising of relationships has been very little explored. Brief suggestions have been made concerning textual citations of Lamentations in Second Isaiah by Gottwald, Porteous, and more recently by Mintz, Newsom, Turner, and Linafelt, but there is still a great deal to be gained in following up these brief and mostly programmatic observations.

More research has been carried out concerning Second Isaiah's relationship to preexilic prophets, especially First Isaiah. Scholars attempting to account for the exilic prophet's connection with First Isaiah have pointed out thematic, and occasionally verbal, relationships among the parts of the book, which some, such as Clements, Seitz, and Williamson, have regarded as resulting from Second Isaiah's conscious exegetical relationship with First Isaiah's tradition. However, Rendtorff and Davies have suggested alternative reasons for these connections. According to Rendtorff, similarities that exist between First and Second Isaiah may be evidence of a postexilic effort to bring the two prophets together along with the later prophecies that comprise Third Isaiah. According to Davies, Second Isaiah may be exegetically dependent not upon First Isaiah alone, but on a more extensive corpus of prophetic writings, including particularly the book of Jeremiah. The discussion of the intertextual relationships within the book of Isaiah is a very complex and problematic one because there is no consensus on just how much of Isaiah 1–39 predated the exile.

A few scholars have also drawn connections between Second Isaiah and other prophets, especially Jeremiah. The first major work on this was that of Cassuto in 1911, who perceived Second

Isaiah's strong textual connections with Jeremiah, Nahum, and Zephaniah, but not with Ezekiel. His work on Jeremiah was corroborated more than a half century later by Tannert, Paul and Eldridge, and his work on Ezekiel has been corroborated negatively by Eakins and Baltzer. Just what this evidence might mean for the formation of Second Isaiah—especially such questions as why it might show more intimate ties to Jeremiah than to the prophet whose name is now associated with it, and why it follows the Jerusalemite Jeremiah rather than the Babylonian Ezekiel (who was also, though in very different ways, closely related to Jeremiah)—these questions have not been explored.

Many have indicated interest in Second Isaiah's relationship with the Psalms, but few have explored the issue in depth. Claims by Mowinckel that Second Isaiah reutilized preexilic enthronement psalms and contrary claims by Gunkel that these psalms were actually postexilic eschatological hymns based on Second Isaiah both find adherents today. At times, scholarly expectation that any exegetical use by Second Isaiah of a psalm follow a precise, perhaps even wooden, pattern and cohere completely with the psalm's message has made it difficult to recognize the relationships that do exist.

Finally, the relationship of Second Isaiah to pentateuchal traditions, and to the Pentateuch itself, has been explored more than all of the others put together. Because exodus and creation motifs stand out, and because names such as Eden, Noah, and Abraham are easy to identify, recognizing thematic relationships between Second Isaiah and the Pentateuch is far simpler than recognizing the more diffuse psalmic, lament, or prophetic language. However, the issue that was raised by van der Merwe in 1956 has yet to be addressed adequately—even if the Pentateuch and its stories were available during the exile and had already been used frequently by Hosea, Jeremiah, and Ezekiel, nevertheless the language of Second Isaiah often does not reflect pentateuchal vocabulary so closely as it does psalms that recount the same themes. Studies such as those by von Rad, Zimmerli and Anderson, thematic rather than intertextual in nature, have pointed out in what ways Second Isaiah coheres with pentateuchal tradition, but are not equipped methodologically to be more precise. More recent studies that have attempted to take language itself into account, such as Fishbane's, have yielded interesting positive results, but since the evidence that has been examined has been somewhat scanty, and has not been compared with the strength of evidence for Second Isaiah's relationships with other texts, it remains inconclusive.

Clearly, the many scholars who have noted Second Isaiah's deep roots in Judah's themes, traditions, and semantic forms have discovered an aspect of the book that warrants fuller exploration. But while this possibility has been mentioned in passing by commentators, and has been explored in depth in terms of relatively isolated intertextual relationships, it is not a subject that has been engaged in any prolonged or systematic way. In fact, the relationships that have been explored the most—those with the Pentateuch and with First Isaiah—have turned out to be less promising than some others that have not been so studied, and the one book of the Bible that may be closest to Second Isaiah in time, theme, and theology has been virtually overlooked.

Even more importantly, the questions asked about these relationships have primarily concerned tradition history, dating, and redaction. Contributions of intertextual study to the interpretation of Second Isaiah as a literary and theological text have been minimal. The vocabulary of the discussions suggests that this is largely due to a prevailing understanding of textual relationships as "influence" by precursor texts on "dependent" receptor texts, rather than as active appropriation on the part of new texts.[133] Romantic views prevailing in the nineteenth century literary world, echoed among biblical scholars, encouraged this understanding by valuing literary works only insofar as they displayed unique and independent imagination.

---

[133] For thorough discussions of the links and disjunctures between models of influence and models of intertextuality, see J. Clayton and E. Rothstein, eds., *Influence and Intertextuality in Literary History* (Madison: University of Wisconsin Press, 1991).

More recent literary critics such as Mikhail Bakhtin, however, have turned the discussion around, viewing intertextual recollection positively rather than negatively. Calling these echoes not "dependence upon predecessors," but "rejoinders in a given dialogue," Bakhtin viewed the reuse of language as a means of taking over previous thought in order to shape it to new purposes. Many literary critics now see intertextuality as basic to all communication. It is no longer enough to ask, therefore, whether or not Second Isaiah reuses previous texts. Rather, it becomes more fruitful to inquire whether any of the texts it uses are still available to us, what kinds of texts it uses, how it uses them, and how the use of familiar words, phrases, images, and thought patterns contributes to its message. In the next chapter I will outline theoretical perspectives for approaching these questions, and propose a methodology for exploring Second Isaiah's relationships to previous texts.

Chapter 2
"The Former Things I Declared Long Ago": An Intertextual Approach to Second Isaiah

It is clear from the preceding discussion that the role of other biblical texts in Second Isaiah's crafting is gaining interest among contemporary biblical scholars. Although scholars in the eighteenth and nineteenth centuries began investigating this question, it was neglected for several decades while source, form, and redaction inquiries were made. During this time, most scholars ignored the book's close verbal congruences to other books, and attributed similarities too obvious to ignore to the work of later scribes. However, as understanding of biblical prophecy has shifted away from a model of intensely personal and individualistic revelation and toward a model of continuity with tradition, the interaction of prophets with their spiritual and intellectual predecessors has become more obvious.

In the past generation, the positive relationships of Second Isaiah to preexilic prophets and to Judah's pentateuchal and liturgical traditions have been generally recognized, and individual studies have explored some of these relationships. Yet the question is still new, and much methodological uncertainty prevails. While some have expected precise repetitions, others have allowed too much imprecision. Some have let uncertainty about dating keep them from making intertextual claims, while others have ignored the problematic nature of dating, or even allowed perceived intertextual relationships to determine it. Many have kept the scope of their investigation too narrow to compare the strength of a relationship with one text to that with another.

But the most important of all these problems is a question of purpose. What does it matter if Second Isaiah responds to other texts? Many have noted, for instance, that a verse of Nahum appears in Isaiah 52. A more interesting question is, what is it doing there? Is the later prophet simply not up to creating an eloquent expression at that moment, and so lets Nahum do the thinking? Or are both prophets using a stock sentence? Or is there rhetorical strategy involved in invoking these presumably familiar words, and if so, what is it? Is the citing of other texts an enactment of a relationship with past writings only, or is it also, or perhaps primarily, a signal to a contemporary audience and a communication about the future? If, as students of biblical poetics rightly claim, rhetorical strategy involves the choice of sounds, metaphors, wordplays, parallelisms, and genre transgressions, creating certain meanings and effects, what are the meanings and effects of using familiar speech? Identification of Second Isaiah's precursors is only a preliminary step toward exploring how these precursors are employed for the sake of the poet's own moment and message.

What is needed is a method of inquiry sensitive to historical uncertainties, attentive to literary possibilities, and flexible enough to recognize the wide variety of ways that one text might respond to another and incorporate, revise, repudiate or ignore its claims. This inquiry should be comprehensive enough to provide a map of the relative importance of various texts and traditions in Second Isaiah's formation. And it should be prepared to use this increased awareness of the text's discursive context to shed light on its messages.

Before proposing a methodology I will comment on the subject of intertextuality, first as a theory governing all texts, and second, as it relates to communities and their scriptures. Then I will examine some preliminary features of Second Isaiah that indicate its overt orientation toward other texts.

"No Text Is an Island"

The title of this section is lifted from a recent article by Timothy Beal. Beal quoted the sentence directly from Peter Miscall, who renovated the insight from John Donne's famous line, "no man is an island."[1] The phrase illustrates the variety of paths an idea may take as it travels from one text to another: it may leap from one genre to another (Beal's quotation became my title); it may reappear verbatim with citation (Miscall's quip became Beal's quotation); it may allude to an unnamed but widely recognized precursor (John Donne's meditation about human community became Miscall's quip about texts). It may even debate an informal, prevailing assumption: Donne's words presuppose, if not an actual statement, oral or written, then at least a tacit assumption that an individual person resembles an island, "intire of it selfe."

By using the overt metaphor of geography and the more subtly embedded metaphor of human community, the sentence asserts that all texts, all systems of communicative symbols, are unavoidably intertextual: they are semiotic patterns created by the reutilization of previously understood words, signs, or codes. As Julia Kristeva, who coined the term "intertextuality," has often been quoted as saying, "Any text is constructed as a mosaic of quotations; any text is the absorption and transformation of another."[2]

On the most general level, no verbal text can be composed without words, words arising from other texts. Likewise, a new text can only be read by reference to previous encounters with the words and syntactical forms that comprise the text. "Intertextuality is the defining condition for literary readability. Without intertextuality, a literary work would simply be unintelligible, like speech in a

---

[1] Peter D. Miscall, "Isaiah: New Heavens, New Earth, New Book," in *Reading Between Texts*, ed. Danna Nolan Fewell (Louisville: Westminster/John Knox Press, 1992) 45; Timothy Beal, "Glossary," same volume, 23; John Donne, *Selected Prose*, ed. Helen Gardner and Timothy Healy (Oxford: Clarendon Press, 1967, originally published in 1624 as *Devotions*) 101.

[2] Julia Kristeva, *Desire in Language: A Semiotic Approach to Literature and Art* (New York: Columbia University Press, 1980, originally published in French in 1969) 66. It is interesting to note that even Kristeva understood this influential description not as her own new idea but as a description of "an insight first introduced into literary theory by [Mikhail] Bakhtin," 66.

language one has not yet learned."[3] Whether and in what way a word or phrase in a newly read work is understood depends upon previous encounters. This holds true whether those encounters are consciously remembered or not.

Intertextual connections of this sort abound in multitude—they are so thickly woven around each person that the individual strands are for the most part impossible to discern, nor is such an exercise necessarily useful. Intertextualists inquiring on this level into the "quotations of which a text is made [which] are anonymous, untraceable, and nevertheless *already read*"[4] are not interested in discerning individual traces and temporal sources, but rather in describing semiotic spaces and patterns: the fabric or matrix of sign systems that make linguistic or cultural understanding possible or render it problematic. Some intertextualists attempt to limit the discussion to that level.[5]

Not all intertextual connections are so invisible, however. Sometimes a writer or speaker knows precisely to whom is owed a word, phrase, or whole paragraph, and is willing to disclose the

---

[3] Laurent Jenny, "The Strategy of Form," in *French Literary Theory Today: A Reader*, ed. T. Todorov (Cambridge University Press, 1982, originally published in French in 1976) 34.

[4] Roland Barthes, "De l'oeuvre au texte," in *Revue d'esthetique* 3 (1971) 229, translated and quoted in Jonathan Culler, *The Pursuit of Signs: Semiotics, Literature, Deconstruction* (Ithaca, NY: Cornell University Press) 103.

[5] For instance, Leon S. Roudiez, in his introduction to Kristeva's *Desire in Language*, includes a glossary in which he defines intertextuality negatively as having "nothing to do with matters of influence by one writer upon another, or with the sources of a literary work" (15), even though Kristeva's various works, as well as the works of Bakhtin to whom she is indebted, both introduce a variety of understandings of intertextuality, including the instancing of individual allusions to specific literary sources. Laurent Jenny rightly protests against limitations such as Roudiez's, but himself limits the definition in the opposite direction: "Intertextuality in the strict sense is not unrelated to source criticism: it designates not a confused, mysterious accumulation of influences, but the work of transformation and assimilation of various texts that is accomplished by a focal text which keeps control over the meaning" (39–40). Jenny's assertion notwithstanding, this discussion in itself demonstrates that neither author, in fact, can manage to maintain control of the meaning of the word "intertextuality."

source. In that case the phenomenon of intertextuality takes the form of a quotation or citation which is anything but anonymous and untraceable, and often arises from the fact that it may *not* in fact be "already read." Quotations and citations enlarge the audience's understanding by putting the immediately present text's conversational partners on display, making them accessible so that the audience can place, by a strategy of mental triangulation, the thoughts of the present writer. Writers who use quotations are not doing so in lieu of other forms of intertextuality; rather, direct quotations are surrounded by a myriad of fragments of other, often anonymous texts.

In between the manifestations of intertextuality described as quotation on the one hand and as anonymous and untraceable codes on the other is a wide middle ground of arguably specific, but often unspecified, intertextual relationship. This is the realm of allusion, response, appropriation, recollection, and echo. In this realm the author's sources, while perhaps difficult to trace or even no longer traceable, are hardly anonymous. In fact, for the audience fully to appreciate the richness and resonance of the new text, the precursor must be known. Operating on this level, the instance cited above, "No text is an island," invokes Donne's poem about community. Numerous book titles also partake of this intertextual trope: *Who's Afraid of Virginia Woolf?* by Edward Albee, *Fair Spoken and Persuading*, by Richard Clifford, *All Creatures Great and Small*, by James Herriot, *The Catcher in the Rye*, by J. D. Salinger, and *The Grapes of Wrath*, by John Steinbeck refer respectively to a fairy tale and children's song (and a writer), a Shakespearean history, a Protestant hymn, a folk song, and a civil war song which is itself a recollection of Isaiah 63, which in turn partakes of a metaphor already in use (see Jer 25:30, Lam 1:15).

If the purpose of reusing the speech of another were only to adopt a phrase more desirable than the author's own, then it would not matter whether the audience recognized it or not. In fact, the writer's perceived ability might be enhanced by a plagiaristic fiction of greater verbal power.[6] However, allusion has a richer potential: when the words of a familiar other are reused, these words subtly awaken in the audience a recollection of their previous context. As Richard Hays put it, "Allusive echo functions to suggest to the reader that text B should be understood in the light of a broad interplay with text A, encompassing aspects of A beyond those explicitly echoed."[7] For instance, William Faulkner's title *The Sound and the Fury* recalls not only the phrase "sound and fury" from Macbeth but also its immediate context, "It [life] is a tale told by an idiot, full of sound and fury, signifying nothing."[8] This fuller context becomes indirect commentary on Faulkner's story, a tale told not simply by an "idiot," but by several different characters possessing various levels of mental and spiritual perceptiveness, each signifying their story differently. Though a new text is usually intelligible even if the allusion goes unnoted, recognized allusions enrich the author-reader communication. Allusions recall for audiences what they already know, making connections between the "already read" and the "now being read," so that the new word partakes of qualities already inherent in the previous text.

---

[6] Peter Rabinowitz, in "'What's Hecuba To Us?': The Audience's Experience of Literary Borrowing," in *The Reader in the Text: Essays on Audience and Interpretation*, ed. S. Suleiman and I. Crossman (Princeton, NJ: Princeton University Press, 1980), classified categories of literary "recycling" according to what the author expects the audience to know about a previous work. On one end of his list is plagiarism, in which the authorial audience is not aware of the previous work, and their finding out will diminish the effect of the present work. The system works its way through various levels of audience awareness, through categories of adaptation, retelling, parody, and criticism, to "revision," in which the narrative audience treats the original work as non-fiction but untrue, and "expansion," in which the narrative audience knows the original and believes it to be true non-fiction.

[7] Richard Hays, *Echoes of Scripture in the Letters of Paul* (New Haven: Yale University Press, 1989), 20. Or, in the language of Jenny, intertextual allusion creates a text that is "studded with bifurcations that gradually expand its semantic space," conferring exceptional richness and density on the text (45).

[8] W. Shakespeare, *Macbeth*, act v, scene 5, in *William Shakespeare: The Complete Works*, ed. Alfred Harbage (Baltimore: Penguin Books, 1969). John Hollander also discussed this allusion, in *The Figure of Echo: A Mode of Allusion in Milton and After* (Berkeley: University of California Press, 1981) 106.

A further dimension of the practice of reusing familiar texts is one well known by form critics. That is the practice of recalling not an individual text but a genre of texts, by reutilizing elements of the genre's forms or common phrases. Satirical movies depend heavily on genre recognition. For instance, in the famous "Holy Hand Grenade" scene in Monty Python's "In Search of the Holy Grail," a monk reading holy writ imitates *ad nauseum* the repetitiveness of Levitical commandments. Similarly, Second Isaiah's use of כֹּה אָמַר יְהוָה, "Thus has YHWH said," recalls not a specific phrase of a certain precursor but the genre of divine speech in earlier prophetic books. By utilizing this pattern, Second Isaiah signals that this text is to be read as prophecy, in continuity with previous prophetic literature that employs the same formula.

Up to this point, what has been claimed is that a specific text may exhibit varying degrees of relationship to precursor texts, ranging from the most general and unrecognizable to the most specific and direct, with a vast middle range of echoes offered for recognition without specific citation. Most discussions of Second Isaiah's intertextual relationships deal with this dimension: whether or not Second Isaiah is citing other texts, which other texts it may be citing, and sometimes, how extensively the precursor texts are used. But the degree of presence of precursor texts in new texts is only one dimension of intertextual relationship. Another dimension is the degree to which the recollection of a previous text is a friendly merger.

On the one hand, a text may reuse another text with full approval. Because of the dynamics of power between old and new texts, an approving citation has more than one dimension. If the audience already grants authority to the previous text, citing it augments the credibility of the new text. But if the previous text has been forgotten or neglected, the new text's citation may assist the audience's recollection of it.[9] The risk involved for the new work is that it may be viewed as having nothing new to add.

---

[9] According to T. S. Eliot in "Tradition and the Individual Talent," in *American Literature: The Makers and the Making*, vol 2, ed. Cleanth Brooks et

On the other hand, previous writers are not always cited approvingly. While a negative citation is clearly intended to undercut the authority of a previous work, it can also pose risks for the new work, because it locates the present writer over against an authority, and because in the process of citing the previous work the writer points out the road not taken, leaving open the possibility that the audience may take that road instead of the writer's own. Writers who diverge from other texts generally proceed by a variety of rhetorical methods to weaken the credibility of their precursors, by claiming that the new way is truer to a more broadly conceived past, for instance, or is more relevant to the present. Both of these strategies will become apparent in Second Isaiah's speech.

Just as the degree of presence of a previous text in a new one can be viewed on a continuum from the most general and anonymous to the most specifically quoted, so also the positioning of the present text in relation to a previous text may be seen on a continuum. Complete harmony and complete disharmony are two ends of a spectrum; in between, a text may claim all kinds of partial or provisional agreement: "An intertextual citation is never innocent or direct, but always transformed, distorted, displaced, condensed, or edited in some way in order to suit the speaking subject's value system."[10] This dimension is overlooked by studies such as Eissfeldt's on Second Isaiah and Psalm 89, mentioned in chapter 1. Though he observed that Second Isaiah echoes many terms and phrases from the psalm, he considered the relationship superficial, because the psalm concerned the fortunes of YHWH's "servant" and "chosen," the Davidic king, and Second Isaiah

---

al. (New York: St. Martin's Press, 1973) 2830, the arrival of a new piece of work rearranges the existing order of past works: the past is altered by the present as much as the present is directed by the past.

[10] Thaïs Morgan, "The Space of Intertextuality," in *Intertextuality and Contemporary American Fiction*, ed. P. O'Donnell and R. C. Davis (Baltimore: Johns Hopkins University Press, 1989) 260. She credits Kristeva for this idea. Morgan's essay is an extremely helpful guide to the thinking of a wide variety of critics and theorists on the subject of intertextuality.

conferred these titles not on a king but on the nation of Israel itself. Recognition of a new text's freedom to reinterpret the terms of a precursor text might have led to a different conclusion.

Some theorists have attempted taxonomies describing these complex relationships. Laurent Jenny (1982) classified intertextual allusions in terms of "figures," that is, the "types of alterations undergone by texts in the course of intertextual processing," so that the new text may "subdue the borrowed text to its own requirements."[11] These are: 1) paronomasia: "an alteration of the original text which consists in retaining the sounds while modifying the spelling, so as to give the text a new meaning"; 2) ellipsis: "the truncated repetition of a text or architext"; 3) amplification: "the transformation of the original text by development of its semantic possibilities"; 4) hyperbole: "the transformation of a text by superlativization of its descriptive terms"; 5) inversion: changes that can be quite varied, and may involve a change in the speaker or the addressee; a change in the modifiers so as to be characterized antithetically; a reversal of the dramatic situation by negative or passive transformation; or a reversal of symbolic values; 6) change in the level of meaning.[12] These strategies involve deviations from or even reversals of meaning. While some of his categories may be awkward and less systematic than they may at first appear, what is helpful about his approach is that his descriptions focus on textual alterations that can be materially observed.

Harold Bloom (1973) differed from Jenny by focusing not on the texts but on their authors.[13] He reconstructed out of various poets' works the personalities of sons driven by oedipal anxiety to kill off their poet "fathers." His "revisionary ratios" involved various forms of discontinuity, mostly expressed in the language of struggle resulting in the diminishment, or even the literary "death," of the precursor. While sometimes a new poet may simply offer a

---

[11] Jenny, 54–55, 58.

[12] Ibid., 57–58.

[13] Harold Bloom, *The Anxiety of Influence: A Theory of Poetry* (London: Oxford University Press, 1973).

correction or completion of a previous work, the poet in other instances may attempt to repress its memory, or even try to make it appear anachronistically indebted to the new poet's own writing. Thus the "reading" of a previous work is an act of willful misreading in competition with that work.

Bloom's study forcefully points out the power dynamics between texts. There are serious limitations to its applicability, however. Anxiety and competition are, by Bloom's own admission, not always central to poetic consciousness.[14] "Anxiety of influence" is only one of many possible reasons for trying to control interpretation. Moreover, Bloom's work took on a certain one-dimensionality in that he viewed each new poet in terms of a single precursor. Even his genetic analogy breaks down readily—no one is ever born of a single father, but of two parents. (The mother in Bloom's schema is the Muse, so apparently is a womb without genetic consequences for the son.) And each parent is also born of two parents, and those of two, and so on, so that within a few generations even the most detailed genealogies become increasingly anonymous. Similarly, no text has a single precursor, but rather a variety of known and unknown predecessors. In fact, when a text places itself in relation to one precursor, it often simultaneously places itself in relation to several others.

Mikhail Bakhtin's anti-formalist understanding did not lend itself to a systematization of relationships between texts, even one as awkward as Jenny's or Bloom's. Rather, Bakhtin described the complex relationships among utterances—not merely written texts, but all discourse—not taxonomically but imagistically. Bakhtin's version of Bloom's precursor poet and Jenny's original text is not one utterance, but a complex web of utterances already produced, which already fills both all objects that may be discussed and all audiences that may be addressed. New discourse must find its way through this web of alien speech:

> No living word relates to its object in a *singular* way: between the word and its object, between the word and the speaking subject, there exists an elastic

---

[14] Ibid., 11.

> environment of other, alien words about the same object, the same theme. . . .
>
> Indeed, any concrete discourse (utterance) finds the object at which it was directed already as it were overlain with qualifications, open to dispute, charged with value, already enveloped in an obscuring mist—or, on the contrary, by the "light" of alien words that have already been spoken about it. . . . The word, directed toward its object, enters a dialogically agitated and tension-filled environment of alien words, value judgments and accents, weaves in and out of complex interrelationships, merges with some, recoils from others, intersects with yet a third group: and all this may crucially shape discourse, may leave a trace in all its semantic layers, may complicate its expression and influence its entire stylistic profile.[15]

The complexity of Bakhtin's description, though difficult at times to pin down, does more justice than most descriptions to the multitudinous possibilities involved in intertextual relationships. Bakhtin addressed the connections not simply between certain poets (Bloom) or written texts (Jenny) but among all communications on a subject, written or spoken. Moreover, he pointed out the relationships not simply between texts and precursors but between texts and their own subjects, rivals, and audiences:

> The word is born in a dialogue as a living rejoinder within it; the word is shaped in dialogic interaction with an alien word that is already in the object. A word forms a concept of its own object in a dialogic way.
>
> But this does not exhaust the internal dialogism of the word. It encounters an alien word not only in the object itself: every word is directed toward an *answer* and cannot escape the profound influence of the answering word that it anticipates.
>
> The word in living conversation is directly, blatantly, oriented toward a future answer-word: it provokes an answer, anticipates and structures itself in the answer's direction.[16]

This broadening of the conversation is important for envisioning Second Isaiah not as a learned scholar writing in response to other learned scholars, but as a prophet negotiating through the maze of other words that may claim authority, in order to assert a new understanding of the divine will in the exilic situation. Second Isaiah was created not in a vacuum of voices, but in full awareness

---

[15] Bakhtin, 276.

[16] Ibid., 279–80.

of the multiplicity of other possibilities, and it was designed to answer, anticipate, and overcome those alien words.

In summary, the subject of intertextuality covers a wide range of relationships among texts. In a broad sense, no text can be anything but derivative. But there are times when texts refer so concretely to other texts that they seem to demand that the audience recognize a connection. This sort of recollection may be as specific as a footnote with bibliography, or as general as the echo of a refrain common to a certain kind of speech. Since the recollection directs the audience toward text lying beyond what is explicitly stated, recognition of the recollection contributes to fuller appreciation of the new text.

But the identification of a textual recollection is only the first step to describing the shape of an intertextual relationship. The position that a new text takes in relation to previous texts also warrants exploration. A conflictual relationship is just as important as, and may in fact be more interesting than, a harmonious one. Furthermore, relationships between a text and its precursors are not negotiated one at a time, but simultaneously and variously. While analysis necessitates the isolation of one echo or complex of echoes at a time, the artificial nature of this isolation should always be borne in mind.

Finally, creators of texts work not only in reference to other texts, but also in relation to an audience whose thoughts, understandings, and even actions they hope to influence. In doing so they must take into account other texts already presumed to be dwelling in the audience's minds, with which they must negotiate in order to be heard.

The Word of God and Second Isaiah

Michael Fishbane borrowed an apt phrase from Thomas Mann to describe the textuality of western religious-cultural heritage: "zitathaftes Leben," which translates literally as "citationous life" or periphrastically as "citation-filled life." By this term Fishbane meant "the dependence of the great religious-cultural formation on authoritative views which are studied, reinterpreted, and adapted to ongoing life."[17] He drew from the domain of intertextuality the recognition that readers are constituted not simply by the memories passed down to them but also by the texts they read.[18] People oriented to scriptures think, speak, and act within the possibilities presented by their texts as they are interpreted by religious tradition.

As long as texts remain relevant and coherent, there is continuity in the way they are interpreted. But when a conflict arises between what adherents to a text understood and what they see, new efforts of interpretation are needed to find in the authoritative texts resources for changed situations. Some religious traditions, such as Judaism and Roman Catholicism, affirm the importance of interpretation as the need arises. But even when the understanding of scripture in a religious community leaves insufficient room for its adherents to update textual interpretation consciously, such as has often been the case in Protestant communities with a heavy emphasis on "*sola scriptura*" and the perceived goal of "getting back to the original meaning," believers will still reinterpret as needed, masking their new meanings as, "just reading what is there," that is, drawing out ideas which they think existed in the text all along without having been recognized previously.[19]

Thus, among "People of the Book"—religious communities who ascribe authority to a received text—two needs exist in tension with each other. First, there is the need to find resources for living from a text that is understood to possess a transcendent authority, "the Word of God." It is not enough for a religious comunity's leadership to have voted on the course of action that seems most wise or even most traditional. The authorization for important actions or understandings must have come from above, must be understood

---

[17] Fishbane, *Biblical Interpretation*, 1.

[18] Fishbane, *The Garments of Torah: Essays in Biblical Hermeneutics* (Bloomington: Indiana University Press, 1989) 127.

[19] Fishbane, *Biblical Interpretation*, 2.

to be in some sense a communication of the divine will, mediated through sacred text. Second, as new situations inspire new questions, texts are called upon to address problems they did not address before. When new interpretations are called forth from this need, they too must find some means of acquiring authority. The authority for a new interpretation is closely tied to its ability to demonstrate rhetorically that it stands in continuity with the past, that it was in fact present in the text all along, waiting to be revealed—in short, that it is authorized by the living deity.

So in a situation like the Babylonian exile, which is so traumatic that radical departure from the established order is critical and a variety of responses seems possible, it is in the best interest of a new interpretation to anchor itself as deeply as it can in authorized understanding and familiar text. Not just anything can be said: new interpretations tend to be circumscribed by what the tradition, interpreted according to the community's exegetical norms, will yield. The indwelling of authoritative text in the audience necessitates the indwelling of authoritative text in new interpretation. The self-recognition of interpreters as heirs to a distinct tradition means that their creative freedom is limited to living "within the ideologies of the theological *traditum* and its literary fund."[20]

---

[20] Fishbane, *Biblical Interpretation*, 435. Studying the issue of social memory, Paul Connerton, in *How Societies Remember* (Cambridge: Cambridge University Press, 1989) 6, echoed from a sociological perspective the recognition of intertextualists that recollection is essential to intelligibility. Even in moments of major social upheaval and change, the new is defined by what is understood from the past: "The absolutely new is inconceivable. It is not just that it is very difficult to begin with a wholly new start, that too many old loyalties and habits inhibit the substitution of a novel enterprise for an old and established one. More fundamentally, it is that in all modes of experience we always base our particular experiences on a prior context in order to ensure that they are intelligible at all; that prior to any single experience, our mind is already predisposed with a framework of outlines, of typical shapes of experienced objects."

This recognition of the crucial role of the remembered past in shaping understanding of the social present is underscored by contemporary research into what is sometimes called "the invention of tradition": the conscious

In fact, it is not enough to resemble the tradition and its ideas. Because audiences live by words and not merely concepts, the more concretely recognizable the new words are, the more acceptable they will be. So exegetes, like their audiences, live with "'texts-in-the-mind'—that is, with texts . . . which [provide] the imaginative matrix for evaluating the present, for conceiving the future, for organizing reality . . . and even for providing the shared symbols and language of communication."[21]

Because twentieth-century observers live at such a great distance from the inception of biblical texts, and stand in fact on the receiving end of interpretations long established and assumed, it is difficult for us to recognize the tensions that were involved in speaking new words in times long past. The biblical prophets themselves were far more acutely aware than we can be of the claims with which they competed and the problems their own interpretations occasioned.[22] These tensions are inscribed in the texts, however, and illustrate well Bakhtin's description of the entrance of new speech into disputed contexts: "The word, directed toward its object, enters a dialogically agitated and tension-filled

---

searching of storehouses of cultural memory for stories and practices that can be used to help redefine the present. Fascinating anecdotal accounts of this phenomenon in nations whose cultural identities are in flux can be found in *The Invention of Tradition*, ed. Eric Hobsbawm and Terence Ranger (Cambridge: Cambridge University Press, 1983), especially Prys Morgan, "From a Death to a View: The Hunt for the Welsh Past in the Romantic Period," 43–100; and in *Commemorations: The Politics of National Identity*, ed. John R. Gillis (Princeton, NJ: Princeton University Press, 1994), especially Yael Zerubavel, "The Historic, the Legendary and the Incredible: Invented Tradition and Collective Memory in Israel," 105–23.

21 Fishbane, *Biblical Interpretation*, 435.

22 John Barton ("History and Rhetoric in the Prophets," in *The Bible as Rhetoric: Studies in Biblical Persuasion and Credibility*, ed. Martin Warner, London: Routledge, 1990, 51–64) has argued that the prophets' interpretations of Israel's history, "form a considerable rhetorical *tour de force*" (52). The prophets ingeniously transformed the ambiguous events of history into divine necessities. According to Barton, the fact that even modern readers are inclined to take prophetic messages as accurate portrayals of God's judgment is a tribute to the prophets' rhetorical skill.

environment of alien words, value judgments and accents . . . and all this may crucially shape discourse, may leave a trace in all its semantic layers, may complicate its expression and influence its entire stylistic profile."[23]

Tensions concerning the difficulty of claiming authority over against competing words indeed influence Second Isaiah's rhetoric, which self-consciously articulates the intent to assert a word that subdues other possible interpretations. This can be seen on Second Isaiah's surface in two specific ways: first, the relativization of past words, and second, the relativization of present, competing speech.

The Relativization of Past Words: "(Do not) remember the former things"

"Old and new make the warp and woof of every moment."[24] But the dynamic relationship between past text and present need is not easily negotiated. Tensions erupt between the conserving impulse of old speech and the radical demands of unexpected situations. Yet when new demands threaten to overcome the articulative ability of words that were not written to address them, uncertainty arises, and the last thing desired is yet another new word, unconnected with themes of the past. Therefore, when new words come they often come already insisting that they are in fact old words, "in the beginning with God."[25]

The negotiation of this tension between past and present words becomes visible on the semantic level in Second Isaiah in its interplay between "former things" and "new things." On the one hand, the poetry stresses over and over continuity with Israel's past, with YHWH who made promises long ago:

---

[23] Bakhtin, 276.

[24] R. W. Emerson, "Quotation and Originality," in *The Complete Works of Ralph Waldo Emerson*, vol. 8 (Boston: Houghton Mifflin Co., 1875) 178.

[25] For a discussion of this archaizing feature of intertextuality, see M. Fishbane, "Revelation and Tradition: Aspects of Inner-Biblical Exegesis," *JBL* 99 (1980) 346.

Remember the former things of old,
for I am God, and there is no other,
God, and there is none like me,
telling from the beginning the end,
and from ancient times things not yet done,
saying, "My purpose will stand,
and I will do all that I wish." (Isa 46:9–10)[26]

On the other hand, the poetry also introduces discontinuity with the past, thus relativizing and revising it. After a clearcut reminder that YHWH is "the creator of Israel, your king . . . who makes a way in the sea, a path in the mighty waters," destroying chariot and warrior (43:15–17), an abrupt and ironic twist occurs:

Do not remember the former things,
and the things of old do not consider.
I am doing a new thing;
now it springs up, do you not perceive it?
I will make a way in the desert
and in the wilderness, rivers. (43:18–19)

Clearly, in view of the preceding reminder that "your king" is the creative one, the same one who saved Israel from Egypt in the past, "do not remember" cannot quite be taken at face value. In fact, YHWH's "new thing" bears strong analogies to the "former things": not only is it a creative act along the lines of the fashioning of Eden, but it also stands in antithetic parallel to the exodus act: in the past, God made a way in the sea; now God will make a way in the wilderness. In the past, God created dry land in the midst of water; now, says Second Isaiah, God will create water in the midst of dry land. The similarity-but-difference becomes a means of articulating the idea that what is new is not really new at all, but was implicit all along, for those who, in the text's terms, can perceive it. It is only the new situation, with its need to cross a desert rather than a sea, that has brought forth the old word in this new way. "Do not remember" becomes a call for the community to loosen its hold

---

26 All translations of biblical texts are my own.

on the way things were and to expect something new, yet recognizable by means of analogy.

The freedom with which Second Isaiah both uses and relativizes the past echoes the words of Emerson: "We cannot overstate our debt to the Past, but the moment has the supreme claim. The Past is for us; the sole terms on which it can become ours are its subordination to the Present."[27] Throughout this study there will be many occasions to note how Second Isaiah remembers the past, but remembers in a particular, sometimes revisionary way, and beckons the audience to do the same. This is by no means a hidden agenda in Second Isaiah. Rather, the paradoxical instructions both to remember and to forget the past openly declare Second Isaiah's revisionary relationship to tradition and text.

The Relativization of Competing Words: "The word of our God will stand"

Second Isaiah competes not only with the past, but with other real and potential rival voices in the present. James Muilenburg noted Second Isaiah's fondness for the rhetorical device of "quoting" speech attributed to others such as Zion, Israel, the servant of YHWH, Babylon, anonymous voices, and, above all, YHWH.[28] Speakers and speech abound in the text, from the initial bluntly cited claim of Israel ("My way is hidden from YHWH, and by my God is my right disregarded," 40:27) to the corresponding complaint of Zion ("YHWH abandoned me, and the Lord forgot me," 49:14); from the grandiose crows of Babylon ("I am, and there is none beside me," 47:8, 10) to the counterclaim of Zion's herald ("Your God reigns," 52:7) and the admission of the surrounding nations ("God is among you alone, and there are no others, no other gods," 45:14). Even the mountains and the hills, the sea and the coastland, the heavens and the earth are drawn into this concatenation of voices.

---

[27] Emerson, 204.

[28] Muilenburg, 389.

This chorus of differing voices employed in Second Isaiah, which is by no means limited to the material between quotation marks, resembles to a certain extent what Bakhtin described as the "internally dialogic quality of discourse."[29] To Bakhtin, the plurality of voices depicted in novelistic prose enact a drama not contained by the text "in its own single hermetic context," but reflected from without, in the "elastic environment of other, alien words."[30]

Bakhtin contended that the voices in a work of fiction cannot fail to reflect the competing words of the novel's environment. This is true in Second Isaiah's discourse as well, where the speaking characters not only are analogous to the people in the author's world, but even bear the same names. When Israel is questioned directly ("Why do you say, Jacob, and declare, Israel, 'My way is hidden from the Lord . . .'" Isa 40:27), no other character stands between the speaker and the addressees. Thus, the world created by the poet within the text, with all its competing voices, cannot be securely sealed off from the world in which the text and its addressees reside. YHWH's rebuke of characters within the text becomes the poet's commentary on other, competing discourses.

The novels that Bakhtin portrayed as dialogical novels *par excellence*, those of Dostoevsky, reflected competing voices without resolving whose voice should be taken as authoritative. In that sense they are very different from Second Isaiah which, though shot through with dialogue, allows one voice to dominate over all others from beginning ("Grass withers, flowers fade; but the word of our God will stand forever," 40:8) to end ("So is my word which proceeds from my mouth; it shall not return to me empty, but it shall carry out my intent . . ." 55:11). No counselor taught or advised YHWH (40:13); no competing gods have any words to speak even when challenged (41:21–24). Only YHWH and YHWH's

[29] Bakhtin, 269. Norman Gottwald ("Social Class," 46) listed the incorporation of "audience objections" into Second Isaiah's discourse as one of several indications of its "dialogical, even conflictual matrix." Accordingly, "We are hearing one voice in a community debate in which contrary voices reverberate."

[30] Bakhtin, 274–76.

herald, who speaks so much in concert with YHWH that they are at times difficult to distinguish, are authorized to interpret the coming events. In this way Second Isaiah, like every other text, enters a discursive environment already filled with competing words; yet it portrays, and if successful, enacts, the silencing of any voice but its own.

To summarize, intertextuality is a property not only of texts, but of the people who read those texts. Religious communities oriented toward texts must negotiate the reality that words of the past must be updated to address new and unexpected concerns. New interpretations that are suggested must negotiate the problem of authority: if they are too much like the old word, they risk irrelevance, but if they are too dissimilar, they risk rejection.

Throughout this study, traces of rhetorical tension will be seen in the ways Second Isaiah negotiates relationships with other texts. However, even on the surface level, before any other texts are explored, traces can already be seen in Second Isaiah's rhetorical relativization both of voices from the past and of competing voices in the present. Second Isaiah deals with the past by instructing the audience both to remember and to forget—that is, to remember the story in a new way. It deals with the present by representing competing words within the text, passing judgment upon those words, and presenting its own message, that is, its "word of YHWH" as the one word that supersedes all other claims.

Methodology: Reconstruction of Intertextual Surfaces

If Second Isaiah's meaning is necessarily created in relation to other texts, and if many of those other texts are indeed available to us, the next question is how to go about examining and discussing the evidence. Finding intertextual relations is not simply a matter of reading with an attentive ear or an open concordance, although both are necessary. Problems of historical distance, of difference between the present audience and the intended audience, our knowledge and theirs, our needs and theirs, must be taken into account as well. The problem of an adequate methodology for this task may best be addressed by showing the differences between what I am doing and what Michael Fishbane did.

Fishbane's *Biblical Interpretation in Ancient Israel*, which was discussed in chapter 1 for its contributions to the study of Second Isaiah, is a massive work reviewing not only aggadic exegesis in the prophets, but also scribal and legal revisions of pentateuchal law, the rewriting of Samuel-Kings in Chronicles, and what Fishbane calls mantological exegesis in late, apocalyptic literature. Fishbane's aim was to show that exegetical practices known in post-biblical Judaism were rooted in the development of the Bible itself. He did this by separating out the strata within the Bible between text and subsequent interpretation leading to new text, to show the inner workings of the ongoing interpretive process.

Fishbane's purpose was not to set out a history of the writing of the Bible or a catalog of the relationships between particular books, but rather to describe an interpretive impulse in a great variety of manifestations ranging over most of the biblical corpus, and to identify in general a trajectory of interpretation. Therefore, he was more inclined to presume than to demonstrate details such as the provability, or even plausibility, of individual examples. In fact, while the vast majority of his examples are compelling, some display a confidence about sequence, date, and purpose that other scholars do not necessarily share.

For instance, in his discussion of Isa 48:21 ("They did not thirst when he led them through the deserts; water from a rock he made flow for them; he split open a rock and water gushed out," (***וַיִּבְקַע־צוּר וַיָּזֻבוּ מָיִם***),[31] Fishbane claimed to find a "literal pentateuchal allusion."[32] Clearly, the verse refers to the tradition of the "water from the rock," which is known primarily from Exodus and Numbers. Inspection of the wording of the Isaiah passage reveals,

---

[31] Here and elsewhere, bold italics in Hebrew phrases point out the use of the same words in two or more different passages. Since interested readers will examine the examples, and since I do not wish to add confusion, I have not created hierarchies of markers to distinguish the use of exact or nearly exact forms of the same words (as here).

[32] Fishbane, *Biblical Interpretation*, 364.

however, that its linguistic linkages with parallel passages in Exod 17:6 and Num 20:8 are rather slight. Deuteronomy 8:15 is a closer parallel, but even there several opportunities for verbal links are missed. Rather, the closest parallel to Isa 48:21 is not in the Pentateuch at all, but in Psalm 78. There the splitting of the rock is described first in verse 15: "he split open rocks in the desert," יְבַקַּע צֻרִים בַּמִּדְבָּר, and again in verse 20: הִכָּה־צוּר וַיָּזוּבוּ מַיִם, "he struck a rock and water gushed out." If Second Isaiah's description derived from any previous text which we still have, it is much more likely to be a fusion of these two psalmic phrases than a rewording of any of the pentateuchal texts. This suggestion is substantiated further by the probable preexilic dating of the psalm and the fact that it shares other language and phrasing with Second Isaiah. Therefore the memory being evoked here is not that of the Pentateuch itself, with its particular slant on the tradition, but more likely the episode as it is described in the hymn.

This example shows the importance of a careful and cautious methodology for examining parallel passages. There do exist very real problems of slippage between the allusions a writer may intend and the allusions a reader may recognize.[33] Obviously, any reader's recognition of the "already read" in the text is a product of that reader's own repertoire of texts and memories. Furthermore, the reader's interpretation of an echo is based on several factors including her or his (intuitive or painstaking) assessment of the echo's intended meaning and its relative importance for the text. No two readers' repertoires are identical. In order to communicate with readers, authors must make countless judgments of the readers' repertoires and interpretive skills. If author and intended readers share a similar community of interpretation—that is, if they possess similar repertoires and similar interpretive assumptions—

[33] Hollander (64) distinguished between intended recollections and unconscious ones by calling the first "allusion" and the second "echo." These are helpful theoretical distinctions, but in practice they describe the recognition of readers more than the plans of authors. Yet as he showed, what may begin as an echo in a reader's ear may be explored until a case can be made for a direct allusion.

this task is far easier than if their backgrounds differ substantially. And if—as when modern readers interpret scripture—the actual readers are far removed from the original community temporally and culturally, the possibility of slippage between the echoes readers hear and the texts authors recollected multiplies.

On the one hand, modern readers will hear echoes which, because of anachronism, cultural difference, or simple authorial choice, may have nothing to do with the original text. For Christians, Isaiah is filled not only with echoes recalling the Apostle Paul, the synoptic gospels, and the Book of Revelation, but also librettos to Handel's *Messiah,* while Jews may hear in Isaiah echoes of shabbat prayers and summer haftaroth—all subsequent layers of meaning ringing in modern ears, influencing interpretation. In fact, one of the greatest difficulties for interpreting Isaiah is that, especially for Christians, many parts of the book have been thoroughly overlaid with later texts that seem to claim theological, if not historical, precedence—as struggles over the identity of "YHWH's servant" readily testify.

The reverse of hearing unintended echoes is failing to hear intended ones, particularly when an author recollects a specific precursor text that no longer exists for the reader. When Second Isaiah asks, "Why do you say, Jacob, and declare, Israel, 'My way is hidden from YHWH, and by my God is my right disregarded'?" (Isa 40:27), modern readers will search in vain for that quotation. They will not be able to determine whether the text is echoing a particular lament well known to the first audience but subsequently lost, mimicking a question heard on the street, paraphrasing the gist of many lament questions, including some still known in Psalms and Lamentations, or even imputing to the audience words the author only assumes they are thinking.[34] Unless a precursor text is

[34] As was discussed above, Westermann, *Isaiah 40–66*, reconstructs from these words a literal community lament: "O Lord, why is our way hid from thee? our right disregarded by thee?" He asserts, "We may therefore take it for granted that here in verse 27 Deutero-Isaiah cites words from a lament in actual use by the exiles at the time" (59–60). He may be right. But since

actually known by the reader, even direct quotations cannot be heard.

It can also happen that what a reader knows from a single text the author may have known from many texts, or even from a popular phrase. This can happen in two ways. First, the phrase may have a literary source, but may have bounced from user to user so many times that the original source no longer determines its meaning. In that case, a reader who correctly identifies the source but does not recognize the indirect route the phrase has taken may overinterpret it. Or if the phrase, having become a pervasive cliché with its original coinage forgotten, is written down widely, but only one or two instances happen to be preserved, these instances may seem to a distant reader more directly linked than they originally were. Many genre categories of form criticism are based on the assumption—which can be neither proved nor disproved—that one or two known instances of a form represent dozens or hundreds of similar texts. Here, again, it is difficult to know without supporting evidence whether a single instance was always unique or is simply the remnant that remains, and caution is in order.

These pitfalls in the interpretive process do not mean that the search for an ancient text's discursive context should be abandoned, and that the texts should be interpreted as if they were closed literary systems. Nor does it mean some sort of "objectifying" of the text to minimize or disregard the reader's role in interpretation, which, as reader-response critics point out, is futile. Nor, on the other hand, should the entire reconstructive project be abandoned and interpretation limited to twentieth-century "readings" devoid of historical assumption, as if assumption could be avoided. What they do mean is that suspected recollections of other texts ought to be traced cautiously, with the recognition that much will be missed and interpretations will necessarily be partial and provisional. The success of such interpretations depends not only on the interpreter's own claims to recognize a specific textual

---

misquoting is as powerful a rhetorical move as quoting, this reconstruction cannot be taken for granted.

recollection, but also on the readers' agreement that the recollection is supported by textual evidence, and is likely to have been intended by the author and recognized by the author's community.[35]

Although my project resembles Fishbane's in theoretical presupposition, in methodology it resembles more the work of Richard Hays (1989). Like Fishbane, Hays recognized intertextuality as a link between authoritative text and subsequent interpretation. His interest was not exegetical reworking within the Hebrew canon, but the reappropriation of the Septuagint by one New Testament writer, Paul. By comparing Paul's interpretation of Deut 30:11–14 with a radically different interpretation offered by a talmudic story, Hays pointed out the open-ended and creative nature of both interpretations. Modern responses to Paul's interpretive idiosyncrasies have ranged, Hays said, "along a spectrum from outraged dismissal to fervent apology."[36] But they must be understood, Hays argued, against the backdrop of inner-biblical exegesis as Fishbane delineated it. Paul "saw himself as a prophetic figure, carrying forward the proclamation of God's word as Israel's prophets and sages had always done, in a way that reactivated past revelation under new conditions."[37]

While Paul often cited scripture directly, his writing was also saturated with unidentified allusions, some unmistakable, others faint and nearly indiscernible. According to Hays, Paul's recollections of scripture functioned to enrich his letters metaleptically: the replaying of a phrase of scripture was meant to call the reader's attention to correspondences between the two texts moving beyond those explicitly stated. Hays's aim was to make explicit for modern readers elusive meanings that Paul's echoes generated in the "'cave

[35] Hays (25–29) laid out in detail arguments for recognizing the validity and necessity of all these various factors in the recognition of allusions.

[36] Ibid., 6.

[37] Ibid., 14.

of resonant signification' that enveloped him: Scripture."[38] Since Hays's purpose was to work out individual examples, bringing to light a fuller range of possible meanings embedded in Paul's allusions, it was more important to him than to Fishbane to seek an exacting methodology. And indeed, one of the most valuable traits of Hay's study is the methodological clarity with which he approached this new and mostly uncharted subject.

Hays outlined seven "tests" for allusions in Paul's letters.[39] These are:

1) *Availability:* Was the proposed source available to the author? Judging this requires assessment of the time and place of a previous text's composition, as well as recognition of the ways it was disseminated in the culture.

2) *Volume:* As Hays conceived it, volume "is determined primarily by the degree of explicit repetition of words or syntactical patterns."[40] But it can also involve the rhetorical stress the precursor text receives within the present text.

3) *Recurrence:* Similar to volume, this category involves recognition of the frequency with which that same scriptural passage is elsewhere cited within the present text.

4) *Thematic Coherence:* It is not enough that words and phrases be echoed. Their meanings in prior settings must fit the line of argument being developed in the present text. If their original meaning is irrelevant to the present text's themes, an allusion is less likely. Assessment of thematic coherence can be complicated by the fact that the present text's aim in using the precursor text may be to negate or to realign its meaning.

---

[38] Ibid., 21. Gail O'Day, working on similar lines, illustrated well the potential of intertextual study not only to enhance interpretation in more general ways, but even to add precision to the reading of grammatically ambiguous texts, correcting what may actually be long-standing misreadings. See her "Jeremiah 9:22–23 and 1 Corinthians 1:26–31: A Study in Intertextuality," *JBL* 109 (1990) 259–67.

[39] Ibid., 29–32.

[40] Ibid., 30.

5) *Historical Plausibility:* This involves a more general assessment of whether the new text, as its historical and sociological context and message are understood, could have intended the echo as it is being interpreted. Does it make sense in context and add to the meaning of the new message, or merely confuse it?

6) *History of Interpretation:* This is the least reliable category because exegetes have not historically attended to reading books intertextually. However, suggestions that have been made do serve as cues to the perceptions of others, and may help one recognize allusions that might otherwise be missed.

7) *Satisfaction:* This is Hays's most intuitive category, asking most generally, "Does the proposed reading make sense? Does it illuminate the surrounding discourse? Does it produce for the reader a satisfying account of the effect of the intertextual relation?"[41] Even if this category had not been explicitly stated, a satisfying reading is an implicit hope for curious readers. Reviewers of Fishbane's and Hays's books have emphasized not assessments of the theoretical validity of their work but rather appreciation for the particular examples that made for thought-provoking interpretations. No matter how theoretically objective scholarship strives to be, the bottom line is often whether an interpretation satisfies the thirst for perspectives that seem both less than obvious (and therefore interesting) and evident upon closer inspection (and therefore convincing).

A major difference between Hays's study and mine is the temporal relationship between the texts we are interpreting and the texts we perceive them echoing. Because Hays was studying Pauline epistles in relation to Septuagint texts, his work was both easier and more difficult. It was easier in that the Septuagint clearly preceded Paul, so the question of the relative dating of texts was not a problem. At the same time, because several centuries had elapsed since the writing and translating of these texts, it is not easy to assess the effect of more contemporary Jewish and even Christian readings, and at times it may be questioned whether Paul's readings

[41] Ibid., 31.

came directly from scripture or from prevailing words in the surrounding culture. Added to this is the complication that Paul's interpretations often depart radically from the received tradition, not only restating theology but also positioning a new word for a different, mostly gentile, community.

Second Isaiah, by contrast, is closer to the parent texts in time, space, community, and basic theological assumption, and in that sense my work is somewhat easier. On the other hand, work on intertextuality within the Hebrew scriptures necessitates caution concerning the dating of texts. Before turning to the exploration of actual texts, therefore, I will outline contemporary understandings of the dating of Second Isaiah and the precursor texts prominent in this study, indicating where a consensus exists and what problems are involved with certain texts. I will discuss availability of precursor texts not only in terms of simple dating, but also in terms of geographical and cultural location and use.

Dating and Availability of Key Texts

Second Isaiah

Second Isaiah's dating has inspired unusually wide agreement, thanks in large part to the particularity and distinctiveness of its message, which not only instructs exiles to "go out from Babylon, flee from Chaldea" (Isa 48:20) but also specifies Cyrus as their deliverer (Isa 44:28, etc.). These details indicate that the text can most naturally be understood in relation to the Persian conquest of Babylon and Cyrus's edicts mandating the return of conquered peoples to their homelands and the restoration of their sanctuaries. To find contentions that Second Isaiah must be dated earlier, it is necessary to go back to works maintaining, against critical consensus, the authorial unity of the entire book of Isaiah.[42] Among

[42] See, for instance, E. J. Young, *Studies in Isaiah* (London: Tyndale Press, 1954); *Who Wrote Isaiah?* (cited above in chapter 1, note 5); and *The Book of Isaiah*, 3 vols. (Grand Rapids, MI: Eerdmans, 1965–72); and R. Margalioth, *The Indivisible Isaiah: Evidence for the Single Authorship of the Prophetic Book* (New York:

scholars agreeing on the authorial unity of Second Isaiah, the range of suggestions extends from about 550 to 538 B.C.E, with most agreeing that the book addresses an audience in Babylon.[43] Scholars who see redactional growth in Second Isaiah date the earliest strata to the end of the Babylonian period and understand the book's growth in terms of the continuing issues of diaspora and reconstruction.[44]

Sura Institute for Research, Jerusalem Yeshiva University, 1964). Of great interest is the computer-assisted research of Yehuda T. Radday, *The Unity of Isaiah in the Light of Statistical Linguistics* (Hildesheim: H. A. Gerstenberg, 1973). Radday began his project attempting to defend the authorial unity of Isaiah by demonstrating a close linguistic similarity among the parts of the book, but became convinced that this was not to be found. He concluded, in fact, that Isaiah 1–12 and 40–48 are so dissimilar that they could not have been written by the same person. The significance of his finding may not lie so much in the linguistic evidence itself as in the recognition that this scholar's own research caused such a radical change in his position.

43 Interpreters before this century posited many locations for the author of Isaiah 40–66, including Egypt and Palestine as well as Babylon. Bernhard Duhm suggested Lebanon, although as Seitz pointed out, it was Duhm's separation of the final eleven chapters from Second Isaiah that helped enable subsequent interpreters to note the particularly exilic concerns of Isaiah 40–55. Although the consensus concerning Babylonian authorship is (I think correctly) quite predominant now, see Seitz, *Zion's Final Destiny*, 1–35, for a dissenting voice. In my chapter 4, I will discuss the placement of the prophet's audience both geographically and in relation to the various addressees posited in the book.

44 For a more detailed discussion of the state of present understanding of Second Isaiah, see chapter 1. While I myself tend to presuppose a relatively high degree of authorial and temporal unity for Second Isaiah, and perceive methodological problems in intricate redactional reconstruction, I recognize that some disjunctures within Second Isaiah lend themselves to the suggestion of redactional and compositional, rather than authorial, unity. Perceiving rhetorical intentionality, poetic skill, and fairly consistent message throughout the work, however, I prefer to bow out of the discussion of Second Isaiah's internal redactional development. The main point here is, whether completed in the sixth century or later, Second Isaiah did not precede Lamentations and the other texts to be discussed.

Lamentations

Lamentations is viewed by nearly all recent scholars as datable to the early or mid-sixth century. Such is the view of Kraus (1960), Albrektson (1963), Ackroyd (1968), Hillers (1972), and Gordis (1974).[45] Disagreements with this consensus have been voiced by Otto Kaiser (1981), Iain Provan (1991), and, concerning chapter 3 only, Claus Westermann (1994).[46] Except for these, there is scant argument and even less evidence for disputing the availability of the five poems of Lamentations within a few decades of Jerusalem's destruction in 587.

While each of the five poems is seen by most as a unity on the basis of the regular acrostic form, there is disagreement on whether the whole book was composed by the same author. Differences in style, voice, and subject matter, as well as inconsistencies in the acrostic's use, suggest that the book could be a collection of separate laments. Within each lament, except for two anomalous fourth lines (1:7b and 2:19d), the acrostic form is so regular as to render extensive later additions unlikely. So it is safe to assume that

---

[45] H.-J. Kraus, *Klagelieder* (Neukirchen: Neukirchener Verlag, 1960); B. Albrektson, *Studies in the Text and Theology of the Book of Lamentations* (Lund, Sweden: CWK Gleerup, 1963); P. Ackroyd, *Exile and Restoration: A Study of Hebrew Thought of the Sixth Century B.C.* (Philadelphia: Westminster Press, 1968); D. R. Hillers, *Lamentations*, AB 7A (Garden City, New York: Doubleday and Co., 1972); R. Gordis, *The Song of Songs and Lamentations: A Study, Modern Translation and Commentary* (New York: Ktav Publishing House, 1974).

[46] O. Kaiser, "Klagelieder," in *Sprüche, Prediger, Das Hohe Lied, Klagelieder, Das Buch Esther*, ed. H. Ringgren et al., ATD 16 (Göttingen: Vandenhoeck & Ruprecht, 1981) 300–302; Iain Provan, *Lamentations*, NCB (Grand Rapids, MI: Eerdmans, 1991) 11; C. Westermann, *Lamentations: Issues and Interpretation* (Minneapolis: Augsburg Fortress, 1994, originally published in German in 1990) 104. Kaiser placed chapter 3 in the fourth century and the other chapters in the fifth century. Though this late dating is characteristic for Kaiser, Westermann (55) noted that he has more recently abandoned this hypothesis. Iain Provan expressed doubt that the book's date can be determined with certainty. Claus Westermann agreed with the vast majority that Lamentations 1, 2, 4 and 5 arose during the exile. He maintained, however, that the third chapter originated much later, and was composite in origin. However, he did not offer evidence standing against the lament's earlier origin, nor did he venture even an approximate date.

if one part of that chapter was known to Second Isaiah, the rest of it was known as well. This cannot necessarily be assumed between chapters. But as I will show, sufficient use of each of the chapters of Lamentations can be found to justify the supposition that that they were all known to Second Isaiah.

Lamentations displays little interest in the plight of those who have left Jerusalem. Its people are seen enduring life in the destroyed city. Observation of this interest in Jerusalem has led to the conclusion that the laments were written in Judah and reflect the interests of those left in the city after the Babylonian conquest.[47] Nothing is certain concerning the early use of this poetry, although its formal and thematic resemblance to psalms of lament, its connections with Deuteronomy and preexilic psalms,[48] and the use of plural speakers in the fifth chapter all point to its having mostly likely served public purposes. External evidence, that is, Lamentations' later (and continuing) annual liturgical use on the ninth of Ab, the traditional anniversary of the destruction of both the first and second temples, also suggests that the poetry may have served a liturgical purpose even before the temple was rebuilt.[49] Although almost nothing is known about worship in Jerusalem during the exile, Jer 41:5 records an instance of men from Shechem, Shiloh, and Samaria "with their beards shaved and

---

[47] See especially Newsom's discussion of the Judahite speech of Lamentations (75).

[48] See Albrektson, 214–39.

[49] W. C. Gwaltney, Jr., in "The Biblical Book of Lamentations in the Context of Near Eastern Lament Literature," in *Scripture in Context II: More Essays on the Comparative Method*, ed. W. W. Hallo et al. (Winona Lake, IN: Eisenbrauns, 1983) 209–10, suggested on the basis of Sumerian usage that Lamentations may have found its origin on the occasion of the temple's restoration. F. W. Dobbs-Allsopp, in *Weep, O Daughter of Zion: A Study of the City-Lament Genre in the Hebrew Bible* (Rome: Pontifical Biblical Institute Press, 1993) 92–94, disagreed. He understood Lamentations' final two verses to introduce the hope of restoration only to dash them in the final line, which, being quite pessimistic, is unlikely to have been composed for the rebuilding of the temple. "Rather, it seems more likely that the poems of Lamentations were composed to give voice to the community's profound grief and to protest the injustice of the city's destruction and the people's suffering."

their clothes torn, and their bodies gashed," bringing offerings to the temple site. Zechariah 7:1–5 as well indicates an understanding late in the sixth century that fasting and lamenting in the fifth month (Ab) had been practiced in Jerusalem since the time of the temple's destruction.[50]

If Second Isaiah indeed originated in the Babylonian community and reflects its interests, an important consideration is whether the laments would have been known there. Other than literary evidence, there is no positive proof on this question one way or the other. However, Babylon was clearly a literary center for Judaism both during and after the exile. Both Jeremiah and Ezekiel bear witness to the continuation of communication between the two communities. Therefore, it seems quite likely that these laments would have made their way to Babylon where, as Newsom has pointed out, they would have been perceived to be "someone else's speech"—that is, the speech of the community remaining in the land of Judah.[51]

What attitude the exiled community would have taken to such Judahite language can only be surmised. The ambivalence Lamentations displays toward the nation's leaders suggests that the exilic community's relationship to the laments could not have been entirely comfortable. The one lament available that was clearly written in Babylon, Psalm 137, contains no element of self-blame. Moreover, Ezekiel represents the exilic community, rather than the Jerusalem community, as those favored by God.[52] Some amount of

---

[50] Westermann, *Lamentations*, 62, commented that it is widely recognized that the rites mentioned in Zechariah 7 and 8 refer to ceremonies commemorating the day on which Jerusalem was destroyed, and went so far as to claim that the passages "indicate that the laments of the Book of Lamentations early on formed a part of the liturgy for the Ninth of *Ab* within Jewish cultic tradition." Evidence in Zechariah for this last claim is not at all clear to me, however.

[51] Newsom, 75.

[52] See Ezek 11:14–25, for example.

friction between the two communities, their interests and outlooks, seems clear.[53]

Both Lamentations and Second Isaiah deal with the same time period and the same concerns, that is, Jerusalem, its destruction, and its need for restoration. Both books share very similar motifs—the suffering of Daughter Zion and her children, her abandonment by YHWH and her need for a comforter, the problem of faith in distress, and the problem of foes and oppressors. Attention to the language and motifs of Lamentations reveals a deeply contrapuntal relationship between the two books.

As I will show, the most prominent intertextual recollections of Lamentations occur in Isaiah 51–52, in which Daughter Zion is depicted as an abandoned, suffering woman being called to awaken and arise to her restoration. Less thoroughgoing but still quite discernible echoes are found throughout chapters 49–54, especially wherever Daughter Zion appears, but also in relation to the servant. Whereas YHWH's voice was conspicuously absent throughout Lamentations, it is heard in Second Isaiah as an answer to Daughter Zion's complaints, reversing her sufferings and transferring them to her enemies.

Jeremiah

The dating of Jeremiah is far more complex than that of Second Isaiah and Lamentations. Two characteristics have prompted much of the critical debate on Jeremiah's redactional history: its clear relationship in some sections to Second Isaiah, and the diverse forms of composition that comprise the book. At the heart of the early debate was the similarity of Jeremiah 30–31 to Second Isaiah. F. C. Movers (1837) set out a full argument against the authenticity

---

[53] Ideological friction between the two communities, and its impact on Second Isaiah, are explored in Gottwald's "Social Class" and Newsom's response, as well as in another response by John Millbank ("'I Will Gasp and Pant': Deutero-Isaiah and the Birth of the Suffering Subject," *Semeia* 59, 1992: 59–71) and an article by Robert Carroll appearing in the same volume ("The Myth of the Empty Land," *Semeia* 59, 1992: 79–93).

of certain passages of Jeremiah on this basis.[54] The point was debated throughout the nineteenth century. K. H. Graf (1862) and Heinrich Ewald (1868) argued against Movers's claims, pointing out, for instance, the similarity of Jeremiah 30–31 to sections of Jeremiah 3 that were (and still are) considered authentic to the prophet.

Toward the turn of this century, commentators such as C. H. Cornill (1891; 1905), Bernhard Duhm (1901), and F. Giesebrecht (1907) began breaking up the passages in question into smaller units, assigning some parts to Jeremiah and other parts to exilic and postexilic redactors. Although these three commentators disagreed quite markedly on their conclusions, they all denied Jeremiah's authorship of portions of the Book of Consolation that resembled Second Isaiah, particularly parts of 31:7–14. Umberto Cassuto's article claiming Second Isaiah's dependence on Jeremiah, published in 1911–13, demonstrated that the textual relationships of the two books extend far beyond what was commonly recognized, deep into the poetry considered original to both books. However, his arguments did not receive any noticeable attention.

Mowinckel's work (1914) became foundational to all debates on Jeremiah's redaction in this century.[55] He considered chapters 46–52 later additions, and divided the remainder of the book into four literary sources: Source A, primarily poetic oracles found in chapters 1–25 and originating from the prophet himself, perhaps collected by a redactor between 580 and 480; Source B, the prose narrative found in chapters 26–45, written somewhat later; an even

---

[54] Information on nineteenth-century critical debate was obtained from S. Herrmann, *Jeremia: Der Prophet und das Buch* (Darmstadt: Wissenschaftliche Buchgesellschaft, 1990) 148–49; N. Lohfink, "Der junge Jeremia als Propagandist und Poet: Zum Grundstock von Jer 30–31," in *Le Livre de Jérémie: Le Prophète et son Milieu, Les Oracles et Leur Transmission,* ed. P. M. Bogaert (Leuven: Leuven University Press, 1980) 352, and Cassuto, "Formal and Stylistic Relationship," 149–52. Further information on these early commentaries is listed in my bibliography.

[55] S. Mowinckel, *Zur Komposition des Buches Jeremia* (Oslo: J. Dybwad, 1914).

later Source C, comprised of prose speeches reflecting a Deuteronomistic style and theology; and Source D, oracles about the future in chapters 30–31. This source, according to Mowinckel, began as an anonymous collection of older prophecies over Ephraim, which were inserted by a redactor to form the core, Jer 30:1–31:28, to which 31:29–40 were later appended.

Most subsequent scholars of Jeremiah have accepted, with modifications, the formal divisions proposed by Mowinckel, but have generally dated the redactions much earlier. One area of widespread agreement throughout modern critical discussion has been the understanding that many poetic oracles in the early part of the book are the most "authentic" to the prophet. Even Robert Carroll, who is currently the critic most prone to seek postexilic contexts for the book's origin, suggested placing the oracles in Jeremiah 2–6 between 605 and 587.[56] Although most scholars have viewed Jeremiah's call in Jer 1:4–10 as an authentic report of the prophet, there are some, such as McKane and Carroll, who view this section as an editorial introduction summarizing the vocation of Jeremiah.[57]

A major point of disagreement in Jeremiah scholarship has been over the origin of the poetry of Mowinckel's undateable "D," often called the Book of Consolation. The problem, in a nutshell, has been that on the one hand these chapters are characterized by frequent references not only to Jacob and Israel but to Ephraim, Samaria, and Rachel—terms associated with the Northern Kingdom no longer relevant to Second Isaiah's time—and that on the other hand they contain material that sounds very much like Second Isaiah.

Early proposals by Cornill, Duhm, and others that parts of these oracles addressing Ephraim were delivered by Jeremiah during the reign of Josiah have held much more sway than has Mowinckel's suggestion. Volz (1922) argued that most of the oracles were

---

[56] R. Carroll, *Jeremiah*, OTL (Philadelphia: Westminster Press, 1986) 116.

[57] W. McKane, *A Critical and Exegetical Commentary on Jeremiah*, vol. 1, ICC (Edinburgh: T. & T. Clark, 1986) 6–14; Carroll, *Jeremiah*, 94–101.

directed by Jeremiah toward the former Northern Kingdom between 594 and 588 B.C.E.[58] Rudolph (1947) dated the oracles even earlier, before the death of Josiah.[59] Hyatt (1956) proposed to date them during the time of Gedaliah's governorship.[60] Modifications on these theories of early origin for the bulk of these chapters have continued, and today Carroll is nearly alone in doubting the preexilic or exilic origin of many parts of these chapters.[61]

But just how much of these chapters to attribute to Jeremiah is still debated. Bright's assessment—that most concede Jer 31:2–6 and 15–22 to the prophet—still holds true,[62] and some argue that much larger blocks are preexilic in origin.[63] Curiously, some commentators whom one might expect to attempt to bring as much of chapters 30–31 as possible into a Jeremian or exilic time frame, such as Bright and Holladay, have been influenced by the presence of similarities to Second Isaiah to view portions of the section as postexilic interpolations, without asking whether enough evidence exists to determine which way influence has traveled. Bright's comments especially illustrate the limited way in which connections between the two works have been seen. In his view, writing similar to Second Isaiah's is found "only at a few places (especially in 30:10; 31:7–14), not generally throughout these chapters or elsewhere in the book, and specifically not in the unquestionably genuine sayings addressed to northern Israel in 31:2–6, 15–22."[64]

---

[58] P. Volz, *Der Prophet Jeremia* (Leipzig: A. Deichert, 1922).

[59] W. Rudolph, *Jeremia* (Tübingen: Mohr [Paul Siebeck], 1947) 159–60.

[60] J. P. Hyatt, "Jeremiah," in *IB*, vol. 5, ed. G. A. Buttrick et al. (New York: Abingdon Press) 1022.

[61] W. McKane, *A Critical and Exegetical Commentary on Jeremiah*, vol. 2, ICC (Edinburgh: T. & T. Clark, 1996) clvii.

[62] J. Bright, *Jeremiah*, AB 21 (Garden City, NY: Doubleday and Co., 1965) 284.

[63] For instance, Marvin Sweeney ("Jeremiah 30–31 and King Josiah's Program of National Restoration and Religious Reform," *ZAW* 108, 1996: 569–583) argued on redaction-critical grounds that Jer 30:5–31:26 and 31:35–37 are preexilic.

[64] Bright, 285; see also W. Holladay, *Jeremiah 2*, Hermeneia (Minneapolis: Fortress Press, 1989) 155–67.

Images found in Jeremiah 30 and 31 do indeed appear in Second Isaiah, especially in the characterizations of YHWH and the returning exiles in Isa 51:11–16, and in the frequent repetitions in the early part of the book of the phrases "do not fear," "I am with you," and "my servant Jacob." These themes so prominently and frequently characterize Second Isaiah's message that the temptation to take them as the later prophet's own creation is understandable. But the intertextual relationships between Second Isaiah and Jeremiah run far deeper than a few isolated phrases in Jeremiah 30–31. In fact, much of my discussion of Second Isaiah's recollections of this book will concern chapters 1–3. In coming chapters I will demonstrate that the relationships for which to be accounted between these two prophets amount to far more than Bright has reckoned. Two other observations about the nature of Jeremiah 30–31 are relevant as well: its close relationships with early parts of Jeremiah, and its relationships with Hosea, both of which account for this section far more adequately than supposed dependence on Second Isaiah would. Notes concerning these relationships are contained in an appendix for readers interested in pursuing the matter further.

Though the vast majority have viewed the early poetry in the book as authentic to the prophet, it is helpful to remember that my argument does not rest on attribution to the prophet Jeremiah, but rather on the presence of these passages in Jeremiah's corpus by the time of Second Isaiah's composition much later in the century. My question is not what Second Isaiah owes to another prophet, but how the poet makes use of tradition, and of traditional words, associated with Judah's earlier prophets—what constraints these words exercised on the poet's new words, with what freedom these prophecies were interpreted in a new setting.

Modern stereotypical and imprecise descriptions of Jeremiah as the prophet of doom and Second Isaiah as the prophet of consolation may suggest initially that the two books' intents and messages may be inimical to each other.[65] However, just as the first prophet is portrayed as a prophet of doom before the destruction and consolation after, the second prophet's consolation is time-sensitive as well: it comes only when Jerusalem's "time of service is past, her penalty paid" (Isa 40:2), and asserts several times that destruction was well deserved (see Isa 42:24–25; 43:28). Second Isaiah's reversals of Jeremiah's themes rarely call the former literature's judgments into question, but rather update and expand the language incipient in Jeremiah 30–31, using terms already available from Jeremiah's early poetry. Jeremiah's time and message are the logical antecedents of Second Isaiah's time and message—there can be no return without an exile, no divine forgiveness without divine anger, no comfort without a sorrow over which to be comforted, no redemption without a predicament from which to be redeemed. The most fully developed reutilizations of Jeremiah occur in the three Daughter Zion sections, in Isaiah 49, 51, and 54.

Nahum

Second Isaiah's uses of Nahum are quite brief, as the book of Nahum itself is. As poetry celebrating—or voicing expectation of—the defeat of Assyria's capital city Nineveh in 612, Nahum is particularly well suited for adaptation into the celebration—or expectation—of the defeat of the subsequent empire's capital city of Babylon. Nahum is widely understood to coincide with the decline of the Assyrian empire—so Roberts (1991), Christensen

[65] In Carroll's view, it would be out of character for Jeremiah to prophesy salvation, because Jeremiah is portrayed in the book as "sour and alienated from all communal activities and incapable of speaking kindly without adding even more words of judgment" (*Jeremiah,* 588). Of course, to construct a personality for Jeremiah by attending to certain portions of the book and excluding other portions, and then to base the exclusion of those passages on this constructed personality, is to reason in a circle. See T. Raitt, *A Theology of Exile: Judgment/Deliverance in Jeremiah and Ezekiel* (Philadelphia: Fortress Press, 1977) 109, who said that because Second Isaiah is taken as *the* prophet of salvation, "all earlier prophetic words of deliverance either shrink under comparison with his words or have their authenticity doubted."

(1985), Westermann (1962), Maier (1959), Pfeiffer (1941), Eissfeldt (1934), and many others.[66] Argument over Nahum's dating has generally to do with pinpointing it more precisely within the seventh century.

One of Second Isaiah's quotations of Nahum is quite lengthy, and simply reapplies to the Babylonians what was already said before about Nineveh. Other uses of imagery and wording found in Nahum show coherence with, though not in-depth interest in, the previous book. It is difficult to tell whether Nahum directly inspired these sayings or whether they were more general clichés of lament and divine description.

Psalms

Dating some of the psalms used in this study is problematic not only because they lack specific referents, but also because of the flexibility of their use throughout time. Indications that many psalms were edited or combined in various formulations in new settings also complicate any discussion of specific psalms before the canon was fixed. Therefore, it is safest to talk about the poet's use of certain types of psalms and psalmic language, with the complex of theology and proclamation implied by that language, and to attend to the ways particular language was applied to the specific setting Second Isaiah addressed.

As Seidel and others have shown, bits and pieces from a wide variety of psalmic settings can be discerned in Second Isaiah. Rather than chase down small phrases, however, I will concentrate

---

[66] J. J. M. Roberts, *Nahum, Habakkuk, and Zephaniah: A Commentary*, OTL (Louisville, KY: Westminster/John Knox Press, 1991) 38; D. Christenson, "Nahum," in *Harper's Bible Commentary*, ed. J. L. Mays et al. (San Francisco: Harper and Row, 1988) 736; C. Westermann, *Handbook to the Old Testament* (Minneapolis: Augsburg, 1967, originally published in German in 1962) 194; W. Maier, *The Book of Nahum: A Commentary* (St. Louis: Concordia Publishing House, 1959) 27–40; R. Pfeiffer, *Introduction to the Old Testament* (New York: Harper and Brothers, 1941) 596; O. Eissfeldt, *The Old Testament*, 415. For an extended description of the discussion throughout the first half of this century, see Maier.

on larger, more clearly discernible patterns. Four related kinds of psalmic material make major appearances in Second Isaiah:

1) royal psalms interpreting the Davidic king's just reign, especially Psalms 72 and 89;
2) a psalm associated with Zion's divine protection, Psalm 46;
3) laments mourning national disaster, such as Psalms 44, 74, 77, and 89; and
4) enthronement psalms, especially 93 and 98.

All these types converge on the issue of Jerusalem's security. Clearly, when YHWH is understood to have appointed the monarch, and the king's reign is understood to promote divine justice, human and divine reign are closely associated. As Psalm 89 demonstrates, a hymn celebrating YHWH's choice of the Davidic king can also become a lament for that monarchy's downfall. At the end of the exile, when the reconstitution of Judah without a king became a possibility, the issue of distinguishing between human and divine kingship became crucial for understanding the basis of Jerusalem's renewed existence and security. As we will see, themes from all of these psalm types find striking new configurations, especially in chapters 51–52.

There is not much debate about the preexilic existence of royal and Zion psalms very similar to those appearing in the canonical Psalter. Psalms 46, 72, and at least the hymnic portion of Psalm 89, are generally considered monarchical.[67] Various theories have been advanced on the original setting of the lament portion of Psalm 89. Most often these converge on the late seventh and early sixth centuries, although occasionally an early postexilic setting is

---

[67] See for instance Peter Craigie, *Psalms 1–50*, Word Biblical Commentary 19 (Waco: Word Books 1983) 343; James L. Mays, *Psalms*, Interpretation (Louisville: John Knox Press, 1994) 236, 288; H.-J. Kraus, *Psalms 60–150: A Commentary* (Minneapolis: Augsburg, 1989) 77, 203; A. A. Anderson, *The Book of Psalms*, NCB (Grand Rapids, MI: Eerdmans, 1989, originally published in 1972) 1/518; 2/631; and Mitchell Dahood, *Psalms II: 51–100*, AB 17 (Garden City, NY: Doubleday & Co., 1968) 179, 311.

suggested.[68] It is safe to say that language Second Isaiah uses that resembles these psalms is language borrowed from Judah's liturgical tradition. As we shall see, several verses of each psalm are recalled close together in Second Isaiah, indicating that these particular psalms, in a form close to if not the same as that in which we have them, are the source texts.

There is also not much debate on Psalm 74, which is nearly always associated with Jerusalem's destruction in 587.[69] Psalm 77, which is regarded by many as a communal lament in content even though the speaker is singular, and Psalm 44, a communal lament, are both difficult to date, and when suggestions are made they range from the early monarchic period to the time of the Maccabees.[70] The use of laments to occasion divine answers in Second Isaiah suggests strongly that what is new in this text is not the question but the response. Still, the indefinite dating and possibly composite nature of Psalms 44 and 77 necessitate caution concerning the exact form of the laments appropriated.

The group of psalms (47, 93, 96–99) clustering around the theme "YHWH reigns," usually called "enthronement hymns," have occasioned the largest problems in relation to Second Isaiah. Psalms 93 and 98 are the most important to be considered here. Formal features and vocabulary resembling ancient Canaanite hymns have led most to view Psalm 93 as quite early.[71] But the dating of Psalm 98—like that of Jeremiah 30–31—has been much

---

[68] See for instance M. Tate, *Psalms 51–100,* Word Biblical Commentary 20 (Dallas: Word Books, 1990) 417.

[69] See for instance Mays, 244; Kraus (who thinks it closer to the end of the exile than the beginning), *Psalms,* 97; A. A. Anderson, 2/58; and Dahood, *Psalms II,* 199.

[70] See Mays, 178–79; Kraus, *Psalms,* 114; A. A. Anderson, 1/337, 2/224; Dahood, *Psalms I: 1–50,* AB 16 (Garden City, NY: Doubleday & Co., 1965) 265; *Psalms II,* 224.

[71] See Kraus, *Psalms,* 233; Dahood, *Psalms II,* 339. See also J. D. Shenkel, "An Interpretation of Ps. 93:5" (*Biblica* 46, 1965) 401–2; John Gray, *The Biblical Doctrine of the Reign of God* (Edinburgh: T. & T. Clark, 1979) 46; and Helen Jefferson, who studied the hymn's vocabulary in depth in "Psalm 93," *JBL* 71 (1952) 155–60.

debated on account of the psalm's linguistic resemblance to parts of Second Isaiah. Some interpreters have gone so far as to view Second Isaiah as author of the enthronement psalms; others have argued that the poet authored hymnic language later recollected in these psalms.[72] An increasing number of scholars, however, view the psalms as Second Isaiah's preexilic precursors.[73] John Day (1988) argued for this view on the basis of three points.[74] First, Second Isaiah is explicitly monotheistic, whereas the enthronement psalms assume the existence of other gods. Second, the theme of YHWH as redeemer, a major emphasis in Second Isaiah, is absent from the psalms. Third, Ps 99:1 refers to the cherubim and Ps 47:6 appears to presuppose the ark, neither of which existed in the postexilic temple. As I will show, very strong resemblances to Psalm 98 not only occur several times in Second Isaiah, but occur in sections saturated with recollections of other literature, strongly suggesting that this psalm predated and inspired the prophetic hymns.

Second Isaiah's psalmic references generally function like "good old hymns" in modern worship. The psalms are mined for remembrances and cadcnces. Their familiar language is often used

---

[72] The debate between Mowinckel and Gunkel on this point, as well as more recent contributions to the question, have already been noted in chapter 1. For the idea that Second Isaiah was the author, see M. Buttenwieser, *The Psalms* (Chicago: University of Chicago Press, 1938) 317–43. He attributed not only Psalm 98 to Second Isaiah, but Psalms 93, 96, and 97 as well. For the second viewpoint see Kraus, *Psalms*, 263–64, who based his understanding of Psalm 98 as a postexilic hymn on its similarity to Second Isaiah.

[73] See for instance Dahood, *Psalms II*, 365, on Psalm 96; David M. Howard, *The Structure of Psalms 93–100* (Ph.D. diss. University of Michigan, 1986) 112; John Day, "Prophecy," in *It Is Written: Scripture Citing Scripture*, ed. D. A. Carson and H. G. M. Williamson (Cambridge: Cambridge University Press, 1988) 47–48.

[74] Day, 47. See also his *Psalms*, Old Testament Guides (Sheffield: Sheffield Academic Press, 1990) 71–73, where he added the following arguments: 1) The words "sing to YHWH a new song" (Pss 96:1; 98:1; Isa 42:10) are characteristic of psalmody rather than prophecy (see Pss 33:3; 40:3; 144:9); and 2) there is abundant evidence elsewhere of Second Isaiah's dependence on psalmic forms and themes.

to sanctify new and uncertain situations, to connect the perceived new acts of God with language celebrating YHWH's past power and ascendancy. Even the lament psalms remember deeds of YHWH from the past.

The Pentateuch

Though Second Isaiah refers often to traditions found in the Pentateuch, sustained literal resemblances to the Pentateuch's terms are rather rare. Perhaps this has to do with the nature of the source itself: unlike the material Second Isaiah reutilizes from other texts, most of the Pentateuch is prose, and therefore may not come to a writer's mind as literally as poetry does, which not only relies on exact words and cadences for its meanings, but may have been repeated orally in worship settings. In addition, the stories may not be recalled from the Pentateuch itself, but rather from hymns or liturgies, some of which we may no longer possess.

A thorough exploration of the complex issues surrounding the Pentateuch's redaction history would be unsatisfying in light of current upheavals surrounding the subject, as well as disproportionate in view of the Pentateuch's relatively few appearances in this study. A few general observations are in order, however, and attention will be paid to the issue of dating on a case-by-case basis as specific intertextual recollections are noted.

Classic source theory as set out in Julius Wellhausen's *Prolegomena to the History of Ancient Israel* supported the existence and availability during the exile of all parts of the Pentateuch except for the texts considered "Priestly," which were thought to have been added to the Pentateuch in the fifth century.[75] As is widely acknowledged, however, source theory is in a state of disarray today.[76] Scholars holding a spectrum of opinions agree with the

---

[75] Wellhausen, 405.

[76] For comments to this effect, see for instance R. N. Whybray, *Introduction to the Pentateuch* (Grand Rapids, MI: William B. Eerdmans, 1995) 12–13; D. Knight, "The Pentateuch," in *The Hebrew Bible and its Modern Interpreters,* ed. D. Knight and G. Tucker (Chico, CA: Scholars Press, 1985) 264; D. Clines, "Introduction to the Biblical Story: Genesis-Esther," in *Harper's Bible*

fundamental point *that* some variety of written sources were redacted together to create the Pentateuch. But the dating, content, nature, and interrelationships of these sources are now in dispute, and it is not clear how any new consensus will be achieved.

Some scholars have placed the Priestly Source earlier: Jacob Milgrom (1991), Menahem Haran (1981), and Avi Hurvitz (1982) have argued that P derives from the time of the first temple, preceding the Deuteronomistic writings.[77] Others, such as Frederick Winnett (1965) and John Van Seters (1975), have posited a "Late Yahwist" in the exilic or postexilic period.[78] Rolf Rendtorff (1977) and Hans Heinrich Schmid (1976), working independently, both dispensed with the existence of the Yahwist altogether and

---

Commentary, ed. J. L. Mays et al. (San Francisco: Harper and Row, 1988) 82–83; and J. Blenkinsopp, *The Pentateuch: An Introduction to the First Five Books of the Bible* (New York: Doubleday, 1992) 25. For a comprehensive discussion of developments up to the mid–1980s, see R. N. Whybray, *The Making of the Pentateuch: A Methodological Study*, JSOTSupp 53 (Sheffield: Sheffield Academic Press, 1987). R. Rendtorff, in *The Problem of the Process of Transmission in the Pentateuch*, JSOTSupp 89 (Sheffield: Sheffield Academic Press, 1990, originally published in German in 1977) 175, announced the breakdown of the documentary hypothesis most directly when he said, "I cannot at present discern what contribution the documentary hypothesis makes to the question of the formation of the Pentateuch from the smallest units (and their prehistory), across the larger units or the complexes of tradition, to the present synthetic whole. On the contrary, I see numerous important reasons which . . . speak against the currently reigning view of pentateuchal sources within the meaning of the documentary hypothesis."

[77] J. Milgrom, *Leviticus 1–16*. AB 3 (Garden City, NY: Doubleday and Co., 1991); M. Haran, "Behind the Scenes of History: Determining the Date of the Priestly Source," *JBL* 100 (1981) 321–33; A. Hurvitz, *A Linguistic Study of the Relationship Between the Priestly Source and the Book of Ezekiel* (Paris: Gabalda, 1982); see also R. Friedman, "Torah (Pentateuch)," in *The Anchor Bible Dictionary*, vol. 6, ed. D. N. Freedman et al. (New York: Doubleday, 1992) 605–622.

[78] F. Winnett, "Re-examining the Foundations," *JBL* 84 (1965): 1–19; J. Van Seters, *Abraham in History and Tradition* (New Haven: Yale University Press, 1975); see also *In Search of History: Historiography in the Ancient World and the Origins of Biblical History* (New Haven: Yale University Press, 1983); *Prologue to History: The Yahwist as Historian in Genesis* (Louisville, KY: Westminster/John Knox Press, 1992).

suggested that the assimilation of traditions into a continuous whole pentateuchal narrative could only be associated with deuteronomistic efforts.[79] A common element among all these various innovations is the collapsing of the time period of the Pentateuch's development from a span of five centuries or more to one of less than three centuries. Rather than viewing the diversity among the sources as resulting from centuries of development, there is more inclination to view distinctions as resulting from diverse and even polemical theological agendas.

Given the current lack of consensus, it is important to distinguish which elements of this discussion have real implications for study of Second Isaiah. The following should be noted:

1) No matter what the finer points are, very few people have suggested a date later than the end of the exile for any pentateuchal material besides P.

2) An increasing number of scholars are entertaining the possibility, or even making the claim, that P material was also available before the exile.

3) Most pentateuchal traditions that I will discuss are referred to so explicitly in Second Isaiah that they have been unmistakable to scholars for several centuries, both before and after the rise of the documentary hypothesis. The question these references leave open is not which story are they citing, but rather which manifestation of a particular story. For instance, when a motif from the wilderness wandering is mentioned, the remembered context could be a psalm that recounts the story, a prior form of the pentateuchal text itself, or the present canonical form of the passage in either Exodus/Numbers or Deuteronomy. Where continuous linguistic similarity is lacking, some caution against over-interpretation is in order. As prophetic references to Jacob (Hos 12:2–4) and to Miriam (Mic 6:4) demonstrate, the stories were not universally remembered with the same details and nuances.

---

[79] Rendtorff, *The Problem of the Process of Transmission in the Pentateuch*; H. H. Schmid, *Der Sogenannte Jahwist: Beobachtungen und Fragen zur Pentateuchforschung* (Zurich: Theologischer Verlag, 1976).

References to pentateuchal stories regularly appeal to tradition in order to draw parallels: "Like the waters of Noah this is to me" (Isa 54:9); "Look to Abraham your father, and to Sarah who bore you" (Isa 51:2); "Are you not the one drying the sea, the waters of the great deep?" (Isa 51:10). The most important interpretive issue for such easily recognizable traditions is their significance in the new context. Some echoes are not as obvious initially, but other echoes within their immediate context can be very helpful as cues not only to the presence of allusions but also to their import.

Conclusion

As we have seen, readers have long recognized close relationships between Second Isaiah and other biblical books. Recent scholarship has begun investigating the possibility that at least some of the verbal similarities result from Second Isaiah's direct use of other written texts that are still available to us.

In recent years, semiotics theory and studies of inner-biblical exegesis have reshaped the questions: If all texts necessarily derive from other texts, the question is no longer *whether* Second Isaiah recollects the words of others, but rather *whose* words it recollects, and to what extent this interaction can be reconstructed. If texts are free to reshape their precursors for a new time, the issue is not one of influence by previous texts upon a debtor text so much as appropriation by a new text of previous words, and the entrance of a text into dialogue with other conceptions. Not all cultural or even textual precursors of Second Isaiah are recoverable. But the poet's apparent inclination to write in terms recognizable from other parts of the Bible, as well as the increasing importance of textuality in the exilic community, enable us to trace more of Second Isaiah's recollections than may be possible with earlier literature.

This kind of reconstruction, far from being an exercise in source hunting, can lead to an understanding of the rhetorical context of the prophet—what else was being said on the subjects this prophet addressed—and thus aid in interpreting the prophet whose language was shaped by these conversations. Even though these earlier texts provided Second Isaiah's imaginative matrix, making available images, phrases, and theological constructions to be appropriated by prophet and audience, they did not say everything that needed to be said in the changing times. Much of the new message involved reframing the audience's understanding in relation to older words, by reiterating, revising, re-collecting, and often reversing what had been said before.

The vast majority of texts to be examined in this study are widely recognized to predate Second Isaiah, can reasonably be understood as having been available to the poet, and share concerns and themes important to Second Isaiah's rhetoric. Though the similarity of language in Jeremiah 30–31 and Psalm 98 to that in Second Isaiah has led some to view them as postexilic pieces, more and more scholars are coming to the opinion that these too are preexilic texts. Evidence will be presented in chapter 3 in support of this understanding.

Not all sections of Second Isaiah recollect previous texts with equal clarity. Chapters 49–54, which allude most explicitly and directly to other extant biblical texts, form the core of my discussion. In chapter three, following some initial observations on the structure of Second Isaiah, I will examine the section displaying the most intense interest in previous texts, Isa 51:9–52:12. The exegetical methods employed in this section vary widely. Close inspection will illuminate the range of ways in which previous speech appears in Second Isaiah, and will allow identification of the most obvious still available precursors. On the basis of this study, in chapters four, five, and six, I will examine echoes of these same precursors in Isa 49:1–50:3; 50:4–11 (with reference also to 52:13–53:12); and 54:1–17.

As the study unfolds, larger issues of intertextual reutilization of characters and speaking voices will emerge, especially in reference to Daughter Zion and the Servant of YHWH. Within each section of the intertextual inquiry, I will provide first my own translation, which will be as literal as it can intelligibly be, and introduce basic features of the passage's structure and argument. Then I will compare parts of the section with previous texts that display the most evident parallels, in order to argue *that* the other texts in question formed part of Second Isaiah's fund of textual sources. Then I will look for texts that may be densely clustered around those parallels, which in themselves may not provide strong evidence, but taken as a whole can be found convincing. Because the material is so abundant, fainter echoes that others have claimed will not always figure prominently in my work. As I proceed I will analyze the significance and import of clear allusions individually and as a system. Although I will make explicit reference back to the categories and criteria for recognizing intertextual recollections from time to time, especially at first, I deem it unnecessarily tedious to walk intelligent readers through that process in every instance, and will often simply make strategic remarks to remind readers of the framework of interpretation implicit throughout this study. Sometimes I will argue for direct relationships between particular texts; at other times I will be content to argue that a particular known text or complex of texts is the nearest available record of the kind of language Second Isaiah seems to be echoing. In all cases the aim is to clarify what happens to known words when Second Isaiah reuses them, what new meanings result, and how these contribute to Second Isaiah's overall message and its strength.

Chapter 3
"Awake, Awake, Put on Your Strength": Isaiah 51:9–52:12

In this chapter and in the three following, I will examine specimen sections of Second Isaiah that can be shown to recollect previous biblical texts. A study like this, once begun, could become an endless pursuit of talmudic proportions, of fainter and fainter echoes, but that is not my intent. Rather, I will begin with the obvious, and from there explore possibilities which become clearer once the obvious is noted.

Although intertextual allusions may be found throughout Second Isaiah, the most prominent and continuous ones are found in the book's second half, which has traditionally been called the Zion/Jerusalem section. This designation serves to highlight Zion's appearance as an addressee in large portions of these chapters, and her virtual absence from the first half of Second Isaiah, which primarily addresses Israel/Jacob. But it is a misleading designation—major chapters of this section do not concern Zion at all. Attention in chapters 49–54 actually alternates between Zion and the other metaphorical figure, the so-called "servant of YHWH," who sometimes speaks and sometimes is spoken for. Three sections are devoted to each figure. These sections alternate with one another:

Isa 49:1–13	Servant section
Isa 49:14–50:3	Zion section
Isa 50:4–11	Servant section
[Isa 51:1–8	Section addressed to masculine plural "you"]
Isa 51:9–52:12	Zion section
Isa 52:13–53:12	Servant section
Isa 54:1–17	Zion section

These two characters, embedded as they are in the texts I will examine, will figure prominently in this study. Because of the interpretive weight traditionally given to the servant, relationships between the two entities have only recently begun to be examined. This chapter, which concerns only Daughter Zion, will introduce her significance both in previous literature and in Second Isaiah. In chapter 4, before examining Isa 49:1–50:3, in which the two figures appear back to back, I will survey the relationships between these two figures and a third entity addressed throughout the text, a masculine plural "you." In chapter 5 I will discuss the role of the servant in relation both to previous literature and to Daughter Zion, and in chapter 6, show how these characters reach resolution.

Daughter Zion's Literary Past

In Second Isaiah the city of Zion is personified as a woman bitterly lamenting her own destruction. This image of the city as weeping "Daughter Zion" shares important characteristics not only with previous Judahite literature, especially Lamentations, but also with Mesopotamian city laments. Many, including W. C. Gwaltney and Delbert Hillers, have claimed direct relationships between the ancient near eastern figures.[1] F. W. Dobbs-Allsopp nuanced this idea, suggesting that a literary relationship between similar genres in different cultures need not be direct, but may be linked by intermediaries.[2] Exploring in depth the similarities between the two bodies of literature, he concluded that while the development of the city-lament genre in Israel was influenced by similar genres in neighboring cultures, Israelite usage developed native characteristics reflecting its own theology and imagery.

Dobbs-Allsopp examined a long list of characteristics common to Lamentations and Mesopotamian laments, including the interplay of various voices, the use of contrast and reversal, the theme of divine abandonment, the descriptions of destruction, the divine

---

[1] Gwaltney, 191–211; Hillers, 32–39. For a discussion that is critical of Gwaltney's arguments and conclusions see P. W. Ferris, Jr., *The Genre of Communal Lament in the Bible and the Ancient Near East*, SBLDS 127 (Atlanta: Scholars Press, 1992).

[2] Dobbs-Allsopp, 6.

agency, and the disaster's social ramifications. Most importantly, Mesopotamian lament literature highlighted the motif of the "weeping goddess," the protector of her people, mourning her destroyed city and interceding in the divine assembly. Israelite literature adapted the weeping goddess motif to its monotheistic world by creating a female personification of the city itself. Dobbs-Allsopp noted five important similarities between the Mesopotamian goddess and Daughter Zion as she appears in Lamentations: the descriptions of her mourning; the authorial viewpoints with which the poet addresses her; the understanding of the temple and its contents as belonging personally to her; the imagery of her as "mother" of the city's citizens; and the use of exile and enslavement language to describe her reduced condition. Dobbs-Allsopp also noted the epithets paralleling epithets of ancient near eastern goddesses, such as "virgin," "daughter," and "enthroned one."

Mark Biddle further elucidated the variations on the weeping goddess figure by bringing west semitic texts into the discussion.[3] In Mesopotamian literature, where the word "city" is masculine or neuter, the goddess functioned as a patron, mother of the unpersonified city. In west semitic languages "city" was feminine. The city itself was understood as a goddess, married to the patron god of the city. Monotheistic Israelite literature similarly personified the female city itself, but could not make her divine.

Thus Zion is depicted in Judahite literature as both a city and a woman, related to the city's population as mother. Though she occasionally appears in literature related to monarchical times,[4] Daughter Zion emerges most prominently in Lamentations. Throughout the book she is the only figure given a name. In chapters 1 and 2, she speaks at length. Her voice alternates with

---

[3] M. Biddle, "The Figure of Lady Jerusalem: Identification, Deification and Personification of Cities in the Ancient Near East," in *The Biblical Canon in Comparative Perspective*, ed. K. L. Younger et al., (Lewiston, NY: Edwin Mellen, 1991) 173–94. See also A. Fitzgerald, "The Mythological Background for the Presentation of Jerusalem as a Queen and False Worship as Adultery in the OT," *CBQ* 34 (1972) 403–16.

[4] See 2 Kings 19:21; Isa 1:8; 10:32; 16:1; 37:22; Mic 1:13; 4:8, 10, 13; Zeph 3:14.

that of a sympathetic observer of her grief—an observer whose own gender is never revealed. This observer describes Zion as a lonely widow, weeping bitterly in the night with no comforter. Her princes have fled, her roads are empty, and her inhabitants grieve. Zion herself draws YHWH's attention to the deaths of her inhabitants, the taunts of her enemies, and the depths of her distress. She even expresses outrage at the crimes God has allowed.

Zion, her observer, and her citizens fill four of the book's five laments, chapters 1, 2, 4, and 5, with both Zion and her observer finally giving way toward the end of chapter 4 to the plural voice of Jerusalem's people, which continues throughout chapter 5 to the end. Another sufferer comes to life as well, in the third, middle chapter. This is a male figure who describes himself as the man, the *geber*, who "saw affliction under the rod of his wrath." As I will show in chapter 5, this figure in many ways parallels Daughter Zion.[5]

Female personifications of Zion as well as of other cities both within and without Judah appear in preexilic prophetic literature as well. An unnamed female figure emerges as "wife" of YHWH in Hosea 2. Similar female figures appear in Jeremiah, sometimes called Zion or Jerusalem, other times called virgin Israel, "daughter of my people," and even Rachel, or left unidentified. In much of

---

[5] The counting of these various voices differs from interpreter to interpreter. W. F. Lanahan, "The Speaking Voice in the Book of Lamentations," *JBL* 93 (1974) 41–49, counts five, counting the speaker in chapter 4 as different from the narrator in chapters 1–2. Provan (7) counts only three, combining the speaker of chapters 1, 2, and 4 with the one in chapter 3. Because of the difference in characteristics between chapter 3's *geber* and the other speaker (being obviously male rather than ungendered, describing himself in terms that are analogous to the descriptions of Zion) I differentiate that figure from the observer in the other chapters. But I see no cause to call the ungendered speaker in chapter 4 a "bourgeois" as Lanahan did and differentiate that voice from the similarly unidentified, and similarly functioning, speaking voice in the first two chapters.

Of course, it is more important to note the interplay of voices within laments than between them. For a discussion of the movement in the first two laments from speech *about* Jerusalem to speech *of* Jerusalem, see B. Kaiser, "Poet as 'Female Impersonator': The Image of Daughter Zion as Speaker in Biblical Poems of Suffering," *JR* 67 (1987) 164–82.

Jeremiah the female's role as faithless or suffering woman, and thus as representative of the people's faithlessness or suffering, seems more important than her identification with the city of Jerusalem. In chapters 2, 3, and 13, where the majority of the judgments against the female figure occur, her identity is unstable. For instance, in the prose introduction in Jer 2:2 she is called Jerusalem, but in the subsequent poetry the addressee immediately becomes the masculine plural "house of Jacob" and "families of the house of Israel." Along with the variations in names and pronouns, imagery shifts frequently and dramatically in these sections. However, in some sections of Jeremiah, particularly chapters 4–6, her role becomes more similar to that in Lamentations. There she is called Daughter Zion (Jer 4:31; 6:2, 23), distinguished from the people as their mother, and heard voicing lament over her suffering.

Isaiah 51:9–52:12

Although in Second Isaiah Zion appears first in the prologue (Isa 40:1–11), she disappears immediately and only resurfaces again as a character eight chapters later. In Isa 49:14 she breaks in as lamenting Zion. From this point to chapter 54 she is addressed three times by the prophet. Zion's three sections display the most prevalent and pointed allusions in Second Isaiah to previous texts. The middle one, Isa 51:9–52:12, in which a change in her fortune is outlined, is by far the most referential of all of Second Isaiah's poetry. Discussing it first will clarify not only the full scope of the poet's intertextual usage, but the special role designated for Zion within the book.

51:9	Awake, awake, put on strength,	עוּרִי עוּרִי לִבְשִׁי־עֹז
	arm of YHWH.	זְרוֹעַ יְהוָה
	Awake as in days of old,	עוּרִי כִּימֵי קֶדֶם
	generations long ago.	דֹּרוֹת עוֹלָמִים
	Are you not she, the crusher of Rahab,[6]	הֲלוֹא אַתְּ־הִיא הַמַּחְצֶבֶת רַהַב
	the piercer of the dragon?	מְחוֹלֶלֶת תַּנִּין
51:10	Are you not she, the one drying the sea,	הֲלוֹא אַתְּ־הִיא הַמַּחֲרֶבֶת יָם
	the waters of the great deep,	מֵי תְּהוֹם רַבָּה
	the one making the depths of the sea a road	הַשָּׂמָה מַעֲמַקֵּי־יָם דֶּרֶךְ
	for the redeemed to pass?	לַעֲבֹר גְּאוּלִים
51:11	Then let the ransomed of YHWH return	וּפְדוּיֵי יְהוָה יְשׁוּבוּן
	and come to Zion with singing,	וּבָאוּ צִיּוֹן בְּרִנָּה
	and everlasting gladness on their head.	וְשִׂמְחַת עוֹלָם עַל־רֹאשָׁם
	Let joy and gladness overtake them;	שָׂשׂוֹן וְשִׂמְחָה יַשִּׂיגוּן
	let suffering and groaning flee.[7]	נָסוּ יָגוֹן וַאֲנָחָה
51:12	I, I am he, your comforter.	אָנֹכִי אָנֹכִי הוּא מְנַחֶמְכֶם
	Who are you that you fear the human who will die,	מִי־אַתְּ וַתִּירְאִי מֵאֱנוֹשׁ יָמוּת
	the mortal who will fade like grass,	וּמִבֶּן־אָדָם חָצִיר יִנָּתֵן
51:13	and that you forget YHWH your maker—	וַתִּשְׁכַּח יְהוָה עֹשֶׂךָ
	the one stretching out the heavens	נוֹטֶה שָׁמַיִם
	and founding the earth—	וְיֹסֵד אָרֶץ
	and that you fear continually all the day	וַתְּפַחֵד תָּמִיד כָּל־הַיּוֹם
	before the wrath of the oppressor,	מִפְּנֵי חֲמַת הַמֵּצִיק
	when he intends to destroy?	כַּאֲשֶׁר כּוֹנֵן לְהַשְׁחִית
	And where is the wrath of the oppressor?	וְאַיֵּה חֲמַת הַמֵּצִיק

---

[6] The use of participles to describe YHWH's actions, as here and elsewhere in this passage, is quite prevalent in Second Isaiah. Although most translators convert these to finite verbs, Erich Zenger, in "The God of Exodus in the Message of the Prophets as Seen in Isaiah," in *Exodus: A Lasting Paradigm*, ed. Bas Van Iersel and Anton Weiler (Edinburgh: T. & T. Clark, 1987) 26, noted that the use of participles emphasizes that "Exodus is not quoted as an event concluded in the past: rather YHWH's action at the Exodus is seen as profoundly characteristic and continuously constitutive of his nature."

[7] Here I follow Clifford, 165, and the JPS translation in employing the jussive, which in many plural forms is indistinguishable from the imperfect. Jon Levenson likewise translated this verse in the jussive, in his *Creation and the Persistence of Evil: The Jewish Drama of Divine Omnipotence* (Princeton, NJ: Princeton University Press, 1988) 11.

51:14	The fettered one shall quickly be released,	מִהַר צֹעֶה לְהִפָּתֵחַ
	and he will not die in the pit,	וְלֹא־יָמוּת לַשַּׁחַת
	and he will not lack bread.	וְלֹא יֶחְסַר לַחְמוֹ
51:15	I am YHWH your God:	וְאָנֹכִי יְהוָה אֱלֹהֶיךָ
	"who stills the sea, though its waves roar—[8]	רֹגַע הַיָּם וַיֶּהֱמוּ גַּלָּיו
	YHWH Sabaoth is his name."	יְהוָה צְבָאוֹת שְׁמוֹ
51:16	And I put my words in your mouth,	וָאָשִׂים דְּבָרַי בְּפִיךָ
	and in the shadow of my hand I hid you,	וּבְצֵל יָדִי כִּסִּיתִיךָ
	stretching out[9] the heavens and founding the earth,	לִנְטֹעַ שָׁמַיִם וְלִיסֹד אָרֶץ
	and saying to Zion, my people you are.	וְלֵאמֹר לְצִיּוֹן עַמִּי־אָתָּה
51:17	Wake yourself, wake yourself,	הִתְעוֹרְרִי הִתְעוֹרְרִי
	rise up, Jerusalem,	קוּמִי יְרוּשָׁלִַם
	who has drunk from YHWH's hand	אֲשֶׁר שָׁתִית מִיַּד יְהוָה
	the cup of his wrath.	אֶת־כּוֹס חֲמָתוֹ
	The goblet of reeling	אֶת־קֻבַּעַת כּוֹס הַתַּרְעֵלָה
	you have drunk, you have drained.	שָׁתִית מָצִית
51: 18	There is no one to guide her	אֵין־מְנַהֵל לָהּ
	among all the children she bore,	מִכָּל־בָּנִים יָלָדָה
	and there is no one to grasp her hand	וְאֵין מַחֲזִיק בְּיָדָהּ
	among all the children she raised.	מִכָּל־בָּנִים גִּדֵּלָה
51:19	These two things have happened to you	שְׁתַּיִם הֵנָּה קֹרְאֹתַיִךְ
	—who will grieve over you?	מִי יָנוּד לָךְ
	—devastation and destruction and famine and sword	הַשֹּׁד וְהַשֶּׁבֶר וְהָרָעָב וְהַחֶרֶב
	—how will I comfort you?[10]	מִי אֲנַחֲמֵךְ

---

[8] For discussion of this translation of רֹגַע, see below, note 25.

[9] With the Syriac and most modern translations, and in agreement with verse 13, I am emending נטע, "plant," to נטה, "stretch out."

[10] At first glance, emendation of this phrase seems necessary for sense, and it is generally emended with 1QIsa[a] to 3ms to correspond to the parallel question just previous, "Who will grieve over you?" However, its odd syntax, combined with the phrase מִי יָנוּד לָךְ and the word שֹׁד, "devastation," unite to point toward Nah 3:7 as a parallel and possible source:

Nineveh is devastated;	
who will grieve over her?	*שָׁדְּדָה נִינְוֵה מִי יָנוּד לָהּ*
Where will I seek comforters for you?	*מֵאַיִן אֲבַקֵּשׁ מְנַחֲמִים לָךְ*

On the basis of the similarity of the Nahum passage and the usage of מִי as "how" in Amos 7:2 and 5 and in post-biblical usage, I have, with Cassuto

51:20	Your children fainted;	בָּנַיִךְ עֻלְּפוּ
	they lay at the head of every street	שָׁכְבוּ בְּרֹאשׁ כָּל־חוּצוֹת
	like an antelope in a net,	כְּתוֹא מִכְמָר
	filled with the wrath of YHWH,	הַמְלֵאִים חֲמַת־יְהוָה
	the rebuke of your God.	גַּעֲרַת אֱלֹהָיִךְ
51:21	Therefore hear this, afflicted one,	לָכֵן שִׁמְעִי־נָא זֹאת עֲנִיָּה
	drunk, but not from wine:	וּשְׁכֻרַת וְלֹא מִיָּיִן
51:22	Thus says your Lord YHWH,	כֹּה־אָמַר אֲדֹנַיִךְ יְהוָה
	your God, who will contend for his people,	וֵאלֹהַיִךְ יָרִיב עַמּוֹ
	See, I have taken from your hand	הִנֵּה לָקַחְתִּי מִיָּדֵךְ
	the cup of reeling.	אֶת־כּוֹס הַתַּרְעֵלָה
	The goblet of my wrath	אֶת־קֻבַּעַת כּוֹס חֲמָתִי
	you will no longer drink.	לֹא־תוֹסִיפִי לִשְׁתּוֹתָהּ עוֹד
51:23	But I will put it	וְשַׂמְתִּיהָ
	into the hand of your tormentors,	בְּיַד־מוֹגַיִךְ
	who said to you,	אֲשֶׁר־אָמְרוּ לְנַפְשֵׁךְ
	"Bow down, and let us pass.	שְׁחִי וְנַעֲבֹרָה
	Make your back like the ground,	וַתָּשִׂימִי כָאָרֶץ גֵּוֵךְ
	and like the street for those passing through."	וְכַחוּץ לַעֹבְרִים
52:1	Awake, awake,	עוּרִי עוּרִי
	put on your strength, Zion!	לִבְשִׁי עֻזֵּךְ צִיּוֹן
	Put on your splendid garments,	לִבְשִׁי בִּגְדֵי תִפְאַרְתֵּךְ
	Jerusalem, the holy city;	יְרוּשָׁלַםִ עִיר הַקֹּדֶשׁ
	for he shall no longer come into you,	כִּי לֹא יוֹסִיף יָבֹא־בָךְ עוֹד
	uncircumcised and unclean.	עָרֵל וְטָמֵא
52:2	Shake yourself from the dust, rise up,	הִתְנַעֲרִי מֵעָפָר קוּמִי
	sit down, Jerusalem.	שְׁבִי יְרוּשָׁלָםִ
	Loose the bonds on your neck,	הִתְפַּתְּחִי מוֹסְרֵי צַוָּארֵךְ
	captive daughter Zion!	שְׁבִיָּה בַּת־צִיּוֹן
52:3	For thus YHWH said:	כִּי־כֹה אָמַר יְהוָה
	You (mpl) were sold for nothing,	חִנָּם נִמְכַּרְתֶּם
	and without money you (mpl) will be redeemed.	וְלֹא בְכֶסֶף תִּגָּאֵלוּ
52:4	For thus has the Lord YHWH said:	כִּי כֹה אָמַר אֲדֹנָי יְהוִה
	To Egypt my people went down	מִצְרַיִם יָרַד־עַמִּי
	long ago to reside there.	בָרִאשֹׁנָה לָגוּר שָׁם
	And Assyria without cause has oppressed them.	וְאַשּׁוּר בְּאֶפֶס עֲשָׁקוֹ

("Formal and Stylistic Relationship," 169), Gottwald (*Studies*, 44), and the JPS translation, resisted emending this line.

52:5	And now what have I here—word of YHWH—	וְעַתָּה מַה־לִּי־פֹה נְאֻם־יְהוָה
	for my people are taken away without payment;	כִּי־לֻקַּח עַמִּי חִנָּם
	their rulers howl—word of YHWH—	מֹשְׁלָיו יְהֵילִילוּ נְאֻם־יְהוָה
	and continually all the day	וְתָמִיד כָּל־הַיּוֹם
	my name is despised.	שְׁמִי מִנֹּאָץ
52:6	Therefore my people will know my name;	לָכֵן יֵדַע עַמִּי שְׁמִי
	therefore, in that day,	לָכֵן בַּיּוֹם הַהוּא
	that I am he who speaks. Here I am.	כִּי־אֲנִי־הוּא הַמְדַבֵּר הִנֵּנִי
52:7	How beautiful upon the mountains	מַה־נָּאווּ עַל־הֶהָרִים
	are the feet of a messenger,	רַגְלֵי מְבַשֵּׂר
	a proclaimer of peace, a messenger of good,	מַשְׁמִיעַ שָׁלוֹם מְבַשֵּׂר טוֹב
	a proclaimer of salvation,	מַשְׁמִיעַ יְשׁוּעָה
	one who says to Zion, your God reigns!	אֹמֵר לְצִיּוֹן מָלַךְ אֱלֹהָיִךְ
52:8	The voice of your watchmen!	קוֹל צֹפַיִךְ
	They lift up their voice; together they cry out!	נָשְׂאוּ קוֹל יַחְדָּו יְרַנֵּנוּ
	For eye-to-eye they see	כִּי עַיִן בְּעַיִן יִרְאוּ
	the return of YHWH to Zion.	בְּשׁוּב יְהוָה צִיּוֹן
52:9	Break forth, cry out together,	פִּצְחוּ רַנְּנוּ יַחְדָּו
	ruins of Jerusalem!	חָרְבוֹת יְרוּשָׁלָםִ
	For YHWH has comforted his people;	כִּי־נִחַם יְהוָה עַמּוֹ
	he has redeemed Jerusalem.	גָּאַל יְרוּשָׁלָםִ
52:10	YHWH has bared his holy arm	חָשַׂף יְהוָה אֶת־זְרוֹעַ קָדְשׁוֹ
	for the eyes of all the nations,	לְעֵינֵי כָּל־הַגּוֹיִם
	and all the ends of the earth have seen	וְרָאוּ כָּל־אַפְסֵי־אָרֶץ
	the salvation of our God.	אֵת יְשׁוּעַת אֱלֹהֵינוּ
52:11	Depart! Depart! Go out from there!	סוּרוּ סוּרוּ צְאוּ מִשָּׁם
	Unclean! Do not touch!	טָמֵא אַל־תִּגָּעוּ
	Go out from its midst, purify yourselves,	צְאוּ מִתּוֹכָהּ הִבָּרוּ
	carriers of the vessels of YHWH!	נֹשְׂאֵי כְּלֵי יְהוָה
52:12	For not in haste will you go out,	כִּי לֹא בְחִפָּזוֹן תֵּצֵאוּ
	and not in flight will you go.	וּבִמְנוּסָה לֹא תֵלֵכוּן
	For the one going before you is YHWH,	כִּי־הֹלֵךְ לִפְנֵיכֶם יְהוָה
	and your rearguard is the God of Israel.	וּמְאַסִּפְכֶם אֱלֹהֵי יִשְׂרָאֵל

This section of Second Isaiah follows a very clear structure in its largest patterning. It forms a triptych, all of its three parts sharing a nearly identical beginning. The first part, 51:9–16, begins with a doubled qal feminine singular imperative addressed to the "arm of YHWH":

Isa	Awake, awake, put on strength,	עוּרִי עוּרִי לִבְשִׁי־עֹז
51:9	arm of YHWH.	זְרוֹעַ יְהוָה
	Awake as in days of old,	עוּרִי כִּימֵי קֶדֶם
	generations long ago.	דֹּרוֹת עוֹלָמִים
	Are you not she, the crusher of Rahab,	הֲלוֹא אַתְּ־הִיא הַמַּחְצֶבֶת רַהַב
	the piercer of the dragon?	מְחוֹלֶלֶת תַּנִּין

The second section, 51:17–23, begins with a similar call to arise, expressed once again as a twice-repeated feminine singular imperative form of the same verb עור. Here, however, the verb appears not in the qal, but in the reflexive form, and it is addressed not to YHWH's arm but to Jerusalem. Like the previous opening, it is followed immediately by recollection of the past. Here the recollection is of more recent times:

Isa	Wake yourself, wake yourself,	הִתְעוֹרְרִי הִתְעוֹרְרִי
51:17	rise up, Jerusalem,	קוּמִי יְרוּשָׁלַםִ
	who has drunk from YHWH's hand	אֲשֶׁר שָׁתִית מִיַּד יְהוָה
	the cup of his wrath.	אֶת־כּוֹס חֲמָתוֹ
	The goblet of reeling	אֶת־קֻבַּעַת כּוֹס הַתַּרְעֵלָה
	you have drunk, you have drained.	שָׁתִית מָצִית

The third section likewise addresses Jerusalem. Only now, she is placed fully in parallel with YHWH, addressed with the same twice-repeated qal verb with which YHWH's arm was addressed in 51:9. She is likewise bid to "put on strength," so that the first four words of the section are nearly identical. Only at the end of the line is it discovered that it is Zion, not YHWH's arm, who is being addressed. Here the emphasis is not on the past but on the future:

Isa	Awake, awake,	עוּרִי עוּרִי
52:1	put on your strength, Zion!	לִבְשִׁי עֻזֵּךְ צִיּוֹן
	Put on your beautiful garments,	לִבְשִׁי בִּגְדֵי תִפְאַרְתֵּךְ
	Jerusalem, the holy city;	יְרוּשָׁלַםִ עִיר הַקֹּדֶשׁ
	for he shall no longer come into you,	כִּי לֹא יוֹסִיף יָבֹא־בָךְ עוֹד
	uncircumcised and unclean.	עָרֵל וְטָמֵא

These three opening verses form the basic structure of the section, and set out the major themes of the verses that follow. The concern governing the first panel of this triptych, Isa 51:9–16, is the role of

YHWH in relation to the world in general and God's people in particular. In a deft combination of motifs of YHWH's work at both creation and exodus, divine power over the world's elements is recalled, and YHWH is asked to exercise that power on behalf of the people. In response, assuming the role of the people's comforter, YHWH announces divine ascendancy over oppressors. The language of Jeremiah 31 figures prominently in this section.

The second panel, Isa 51:17–23, is a retrospective look at Zion's immediate past. She is bidden to awaken herself from the stupor caused by drinking the cup of divine wrath. In terms quite reminiscent of Lamentations, especially of chapter 4, the tragic fate of her children is reviewed. She is then promised an end to her sufferings: YHWH will take the cup from her hands and give it to her tormentors.

In the third panel, Isa 52:3–6 interrupts the flow of the poetry with prose of a very different nature, with a quite different vocabulary.[11] These verses are almost universally considered a very late gloss, and for our purposes they will not be considered. Although the remainder of this section (Isa 52:1–2, 7–12) continues to address Zion, its tone is quite different from that of the previous two. Here the focus is fully on the future. Utilizing the imagery from Lamentations of Zion and her mourners sitting on the ground in disheveled or filthy garments, the speaker now bids Zion to arise from the dust and put on splendid garments. God's return to Zion is announced, and the ruins of Jerusalem are invited to celebrate YHWH's comfort and redemption. In terms reminiscent of a wide variety of texts, the exiles are instructed to depart from the unclean foreign city and accompany YHWH home.

This section richly illustrates the range of texts contributing to Second Isaiah's thought, the range of attitudes Second Isaiah took toward previous discourse, and the range of ways in which Second Isaiah's language was able to recall, use, misuse, and appropriate

[11] Notice, for instance, the change in gender and number of the addressees, the sudden reference to Assyria, the apparent prose, and the sudden shift in tone and subject matter.

those texts. Some of the recollections to be observed in this section of Isaiah are very distinct quotations, unmistakably direct, and these will be considered first. These recollections, once observed, will guide the discussion of less obvious allusions in this and other sections of Second Isaiah, as I note, section by section, recollections which are less distinct linguistically, yet which respond to, or correspond to, complaints, prayers, images, and motifs present in other texts associated with the destruction of Jerusalem. After discussing these modes of recollection and their illustrations in Isa 51:9–52:12, I will show how the passage intertwines these varieties of recollection to create a new whole.

Discernible Quotations from Israel's Texts

Unlike some later literature, but like its precursors and contemporaries, Second Isaiah never names the sources from which it draws. Rarely does it even quote other texts word for word. It is much more common for Second Isaiah to refer to other texts, if directly at all, only by short phrases and brief images, which necessitate a modern reader's sustained attention to hear the echoes behind Second Isaiah's words.

In Isa 51:9–52:12, however, four distinct texts are quoted directly and at unusual length, and several others are referred to with a clarity that renders them virtually unmistakable. These texts are so deeply woven into the fabric of Second Isaiah that they may not be removed as glosses without serious damage to the whole. In most cases, they are also so deeply woven into the precursor texts that they must be considered original there as well. First I will examine three quotations in Isa 52:7–12, and then one quotation in Isa 51:15.

Quotations in Isaiah 52:7–12

Quotations of whole lines of Nah 2:1, Ps 98:3, and Lam 4:15 appear in Isa 52:7, 10, and 11 respectively. These three quotations are not only set side by side, but are also interlaced with one another and with several distinct references to the exodus story.

Second Isaiah uses this old and familiar language to validate the new calling that the poet urges upon Judah's exiles. The traditional language does not simply embellish Second Isaiah's new words. Rather, Second Isaiah's bold suggestion that the exiles' future lies in returning to Jerusalem is expressed nearly exclusively in terms of previous text, suggesting to hearers that this radically new word is only the uncovering of meanings hidden in the tradition all along, now open to plain sight by all.

Nahum 2:1

First, Isa 52:7 quotes from Nahum, a late seventh-century text which celebrated the defeat of Nineveh by Babylon in 612.[12] Nahum's similarity to Second Isaiah in circumstance and theme render it quite amenable for adaptation. Its first chapter had announced God's powerful rage, culminating in verses 12–14: by divine decree, Nineveh was to be cut off, its name and its gods forgotten, and its bonds snapped from Judah's neck. Immediately the prophet responded:

Nah	Look! On the mountains	הִנֵּה ***עַל־הֶהָרִים***[13]
2:1	the feet of a messenger,	***רַגְלֵי מְבַשֵּׂר***
	a proclaimer of peace.	***מַשְׁמִיעַ שָׁלוֹם***
	Celebrate, Judah, your festivals,	חָגִּי יְהוּדָה חַגַּיִךְ
	fulfill your vows!	שַׁלְּמִי נְדָרָיִךְ
	For he will no longer	***כִּי לֹא יוֹסִיף עוֹד***
	pass into you, the wicked one—	***לַעֲבָר־בָּךְ*** בְּלִיַּעַל
	he is utterly cut off.	כֻּלֹּה נִכְרָת

Isaiah 52:7 expands on the first line of this announcement:

---

[12] Cassuto ("Formal and Stylistic Relationship," 168–69) noted this similarity, along with several others. Porteous (247) noted it as well.

[13] The bold italics in the Hebrew text denote words with linguistic parallels in Second Isaiah.

Isa 52:7
How beautiful upon the mountains
are the feet of a messenger,
a proclaimer of peace, a messenger of good,
a proclaimer of salvation,
one who says to Zion, your God reigns!

מַה־נָּאווּ עַל־הֶהָרִים
רַגְלֵי מְבַשֵּׂר
מַשְׁמִיעַ שָׁלוֹם מְבַשֵּׂר טוֹב
מַשְׁמִיעַ יְשׁוּעָה
אֹמֵר לְצִיּוֹן מָלַךְ אֱלֹהָיִךְ

The six-word phrase of Nahum that is repeated in Second Isaiah appears nowhere else in the Bible. No part of this phrase occurs anywhere else. In fact, the term מְבַשֵּׂר itself occurs only three times outside of Second Isaiah and Nahum, and only in narratives (1 Sam 4:17; 2 Sam 4:10 and 18:26). In terms of the tests of intertextual allusions outlined by Hays (see chapter 2): 1) Availability: it would be difficult to imagine the Nahum passage, referring to the defeat of Assyria less than a century before, being unavailable to a Judahite community at the end of the exilic period; 2) Volume: its six-word phrase is echoed precisely in Second Isaiah, displaying a remarkable level of explicit repetition; 3) Recurrence: as seen below, another portion of this verse recurs in Isa 52:1; 4) Thematic coherence: the themes cohere precisely: both the Nahumic passage and the Isaianic passage celebrate the announcement of the defeat of conquering cities; 5) Historical plausibility: application to Babylon of words once applied to the previous oppressor is highly plausible historically, given the many analogies drawn between the two empires and their activities against Israel and Judah; and 6) History of interpretation: as was shown in chapter 1, this allusion has been frequently recognized even by some who viewed Second Isaiah as historically prior to Nahum.

Reutilizing the line from Nahum precisely except to expand the beginning slightly, Second Isaiah then enlarges on Nahum by repeating each of the two participles, מְבַשֵּׂר ("messenger") and מַשְׁמִיעַ ("proclaimer"), supplying each with additional objects, טוֹב ("good") and יְשׁוּעָה ("salvation") that ascend step by step from the first object, שָׁלוֹם ("peace"), in a crescendo of good news that finally culminates in the contents of the message itself: מָלַךְ אֱלֹהָיִךְ ("your God reigns").

In Nahum, as in Second Isaiah, the messenger's arrival is announced as if he were already visible ("Look!"). Yet in both texts this deliverance is still beyond the horizon, seen only with prophetic expectation. Like the passage in Second Isaiah, Nahum 2:1 is preceded by a confession that the enemies are still at full strength, along with a promise that even so, they will be cut off, and Judah's bonds (וּמוֹסְרֹתַיִךְ, see Isa 52:2: "loose the bonds, מוֹסְרֵי, on your neck") will be snapped.

In a briefer citation that would be hardly noticeable without 52:7, the last line of the Nahum passage is recollected in the opening verse of this section:

Isa	Awake, awake,	עוּרִי עוּרִי
52:1	put on your strength, Zion!	לִבְשִׁי עֻזֵּךְ צִיּוֹן
	Put on your beautiful garments,	לִבְשִׁי בִּגְדֵי תִפְאַרְתֵּךְ
	Jerusalem, the holy city;	יְרוּשָׁלַםִ עִיר הַקֹּדֶשׁ
	for he shall no longer come into you,	**כִּי לֹא יוֹסִיף יָבֹא־בָךְ עוֹד**
	uncircumcised and unclean.	עָרֵל וְטָמֵא

The contexts of the two passages are quite similar. As in the Nahum passage, the announcement of the enemy's departure is preceded by a call to festivity. Likewise, as in the Nahum passage, the city is addressed in the feminine singular, and the enemy is discussed in the masculine singular. Nahum's use of the verb עבר—to pass—to describe the enemy's activity in the city is reflected in Second Isaiah in the verse just preceding this one, in which the enemy is portrayed as saying, "Bow down, and let us pass (נַעֲבֹרָה). Make your back like the ground, and like the street for those passing through (עֹבְרִים)." Several echoes of other texts are also embedded in Isa 52:1, and these will be unfolded in the course of this chapter.

What is Nahum's significance here? Modern readers can only guess what attitude was taken toward Babylon's defeat of Assyria, and toward literature celebrating that defeat, once Babylon became a threat to Judah itself. On the one hand, Assyria's replacement by yet another foreign oppressor surely quelled the unqualified glee displayed in Nahum. On the other hand, Nahum's reminder of the vulnerability of even the most powerful enemy, the one that had destroyed Israel, Syria, and the majority of Judah, may well have supplied hope for the exiles' future. If Nineveh was no greater than

Thebes, the strong city that fell (Nah 3:8–10), surely Babylon was no greater than Nineveh. Such a hope from Judah's past is being invoked in Second Isaiah's use of language once associated with Nineveh to exult over the humiliation of Babylon. By invoking a familiar articulation of Nineveh's defeat, Second Isaiah confers historic significance on new events. In addition, by drawing this explicit analogy, the poet renders Nahum's surrounding rhetoric available as a key for interpreting Babylon's fate: Babylon, like Nineveh, will soon cease to be a world-crushing power.

Duane Christensen has suggested that Nahum's structural symmetry may indicate musical influence, that the book "bears the mark of original musical composition and performance within an ancient Israelite liturgical setting."[14] If he is correct, then even before Second Isaiah's writing, the use among exiles of Nahum's imprecations against Assyria as coded imprecations against Babylon is not inconceivable. In that case Second Isaiah would not be recollecting and adapting past ideas so much as directly appealing to formulations—and reinterpretations of them—already available.

Psalm 98:3

The second major quotation is to be found in Isa 52:8–10, which directly cites Psalm 98. Psalmic refrains resembling the enthronement psalms in general and Psalm 98 in particular have long been observed recurring at strategic moments throughout Second Isaiah.

Isaiah 42:10–12, the first occurrence of this doxological language, echoes extended strings of phrases found in Psalm 98 so precisely that its immediate relationship with some form of the psalm is unmistakable. Isaiah 42:10 opens with the first words of Psalm 98: שִׁירוּ לַיהוָה שִׁיר חָדָשׁ ("Sing to YHWH a new song"). It continues in its first line with a near echo of the reference in Ps 98:3 to the "ends of the earth," followed by a very close parallel to verse 7 (four words long if the necessary textual emendation of one word is made) and also repeats scattered vocabulary of Psalm 98 and other enthronement psalms such as "mountains" (Ps 98:8,

---

[14] Christensen, 736.

etc.), "coastlands" (Ps 97:1), "lift voices" (Ps 93:3), and "ascribe to YHWH honor" (Ps 96:7 and 8). The words of Isa 42:10–12 that reflect enthronement vocabulary are highlighted below:

Isa 42:10	Sing to YHWH a new song,	***שִׁירוּ לַיהוָה שִׁיר חָדָשׁ***
	his praise from the ends of the earth.	תְּהִלָּתוֹ מִקְצֵה ***הָאָרֶץ***
	Let thunder the sea and its fullness,	יוֹרְדֵי ***הַיָּם וּמְלֹאוֹ***
	the coastlands and their inhabitants.	***אִיִּים וְיֹשְׁבֵיהֶם***
42:11	Let the desert and its towns lift up [their voice],	***יִשְׂאוּ מִדְבָּר*** וְעָרָיו
	the villages that Kedar inhabits.	***חֲצֵרִים תֵּשֵׁב*** קֵדָר
	Let the inhabitants of Sela cry out;	***יָרֹנּוּ יֹשְׁבֵי*** סֶלַע
	from the top of the mountains let them shout aloud.	מֵרֹאשׁ ***הָרִים*** יִצְוָחוּ
42:12	Let them give YHWH honor,	יָשִׂימוּ ***לַיהוָה כָּבוֹד***
	and his praise in the coastlands let them declare.	וּתְהִלָּתוֹ ***בָּאִיִּים יַגִּידוּ***

Phrases from the psalm appear likewise in Isa 44:23, 49:13, 51:3, and 55:12, often in combination with the declaration that "YHWH has comforted." In Isa 52:10 an extensive quotation of Ps 98:3 appears, with references preceding it to verses 1, 2, 4, and 8. The psalm had said:

Ps	A Psalm.	מִזְמוֹר
98:1	Sing to YHWH a new song,	שִׁירוּ *לַיהוָה* שִׁיר חָדָשׁ
	for he has done wonders!	כִּי־נִפְלָאוֹת עָשָׂה
	It has brought salvation for him, his right hand	***הוֹשִׁיעָה***־לּוֹ יְמִינוֹ
	and his holy arm.	***וּזְרוֹעַ קָדְשׁוֹ***
98:2	YHWH has made known his salvation	הוֹדִיעַ ***יְהוָה יְשׁוּעָתוֹ***
	before the eyes of the nations,	***לְעֵינֵי הַגּוֹיִם***
	he has revealed his righteousness.	גִּלָּה צִדְקָתוֹ
98:3	He remembered his steadfast love and his faithfulness	זָכַר חַסְדּוֹ וֶאֱמוּנָתוֹ
	to the house of Israel.	לְבֵית יִשְׂרָאֵל
	All the ends of the earth have seen	***רָאוּ כָל־אַפְסֵי־אָרֶץ***
	the salvation of our God.	***אֵת יְשׁוּעַת אֱלֹהֵינוּ***
98:4	Shout to YHWH, all the earth!	הָרִיעוּ *לַיהוָה* כָּל־הָאָרֶץ
	Break forth and cry out and sing . . .	***פִּצְחוּ וְרַנְּנוּ*** וְזַמֵּרוּ
98:8	Let the rivers clap their hands;	נְהָרוֹת יִמְחֲאוּ־כָף
	let the hills cry out together!	***יַחַד*** הָרִים ***יְרַנֵּנוּ***

Isaiah 52:8–10 draws from this psalm extensively, beginning with two-word phrases that build up to a final seven-word quotation of Ps 98:3:

Isa	The voice of your watchmen!	קוֹל צֹפַיִךְ
52:8	They lift up their voice;	
	together they cry out!	נָשְׂאוּ קוֹל יַחְדָּו יְרַנֵּנוּ
	For eye-to-eye they see	כִּי עַיִן בְּעַיִן יִרְאוּ
	the return of YHWH to Zion.	בְּשׁוּב יְהוָה צִיּוֹן
52:9	Break forth, cry out together,	פִּצְחוּ רַנְּנוּ יַחְדָּו
	ruins of Jerusalem!	חָרְבוֹת יְרוּשָׁלָםִ
	For YHWH has comforted his people;	כִּי־נִחַם יְהוָה עַמּוֹ
	he has redeemed Jerusalem.	גָּאַל יְרוּשָׁלָםִ
52:10	YHWH has bared his holy arm	חָשַׂף יְהוָה אֶת־זְרוֹעַ קָדְשׁוֹ
	before the eyes of all the nations,	לְעֵינֵי כָּל־הַגּוֹיִם
	and all the ends of the earth have seen	וְרָאוּ כָּל־אַפְסֵי־אָרֶץ
	the salvation of our God.	אֵת יְשׁוּעַת אֱלֹהֵינוּ

Here a phrase from Ps 98:8, יַחַד . . . יְרַנֵּנוּ, "cry out together," is adapted into both verse 8, where it applies to the watchmen, and verse 9, where it applies to the ruins of Jerusalem. In its second repetition it is overlapped with a similar phrase from Ps 98:4, פִּצְחוּ וְרַנְּנוּ, "break forth and cry out," to produce the composite "break forth, cry out together." The first of these phrases only occurs otherwise in the later Job 38:7, where the verb is infinitive. The second never occurs anywhere else. The reason for all the noise is announced in the second line of Isa 52:9: "YHWH has comforted his people." This crucial announcement will be discussed at greater length below.

The first line of verse 10 condenses and joins phrases from Ps 98:1–2, זְרוֹעַ קָדְשׁוֹ ("his holy arm") and לְעֵינֵי הַגּוֹיִם ("before the eyes of the nations"). The second line repeats nearly precisely—with the addition of a single vav—the seven-word second line of Ps 98:3: רָאוּ כָל־אַפְסֵי־אָרֶץ אֵת יְשׁוּעַת אֱלֹהֵינוּ ("All the ends of the earth have seen the salvation of our God."). The phrase לְעֵינֵי הַגּוֹיִם ("before the eyes of the nations") does occur elsewhere in the Bible: it is used in Lev 26:45 to refer to YHWH's bringing the ancestors out of Egypt "before the eyes of the nations," and is repeated in Ezekiel to refer both to the exodus from Egypt and to the return of the exiles from Babylon (see especially Ezek 20:9, 14, 22, and 41). These usages add further resonance to the phrase from Psalm 98, indicating that Second Isaiah was not alone in understanding the psalmic language, and the international scope of its claims, in terms of these major acts of deliverance. The other two phrases in verse 10 are, like the phrases used in verse 9, unique to these two places in the Bible.

Once again, the relationships between the two passages are quite clear. The volume of explicit repetition is quite high. Recurrence of this psalm throughout Second Isaiah has already been highlighted. The themes cohere: both the psalm and the passages in Second Isaiah celebrate YHWH's reign as manifested in divine deliverance. Scholars have differed over whether the psalm inspired the hymnic passages in Second Isaiah, or was inspired by them. As was noted in chapters 1 and 2, more and more arguments have been mounted in recent years for the psalm's priority. Its occurrence here in the midst of other clearly quoted texts suggests very strongly that Second Isaiah is the borrower. In fact, as shall be shown, if that were not the case, verse 10 would be the only portion of these verses that was composed freely by the prophet.

This psalmic allusion, along with the other allusions to Psalm 98, serves to underscore in a new way liturgically expressed understandings of the relationship of Judah and its God to the rest of the world. The "YHWH-malak" psalms themselves had affirmed the ongoing reign of YHWH over all the known world, asserting that YHWH was on the verge of judging and setting straight all that refused to conform to the divine reign. This understanding had been shaken, perhaps overturned in the minds of many, by the events of the previous two generations, in which another nation and its gods gained domination over YHWH's worshippers.

Second Isaiah asserts unyieldingly YHWH's control over the events of history, even the disastrous ones, and YHWH's ascendancy over other deities. In such an argument, frequent and strategic insertions of old psalmic affirmations both buttress the prophet's claims with language that rings familiar, and redefine the enthronement language itself: in the place of judgment (which could signify either redemption or condemnation), Second Isaiah narrows the possibilities of YHWH's present activity solely to that which favors the people: YHWH is coming to redeem, save, and comfort.

Second Isaiah links Nahum's messenger announcement to psalmic tradition by placing the cry in the messenger's mouth: the message of peace, of good, and of salvation is the proclamation to Zion that "your God reigns" (מָלַךְ אֱלֹהָיִךְ). As I will show below, this regnal proclamation has been anticipated by the recollection of several national lament psalms, and of another enthronement hymn, Psalm 93, at the beginning of this section. Immediately after the messenger's dramatic announcement of the enthronement theme, YHWH is envisioned returning in victory to the regnal city, and echoes of Psalm 98's celebration of YHWH's reign begin to sound, faintly at first, like the strains of approaching musicians, and then gaining both strength and frequency till they take over completely in verse 10.

Linkage of the themes of YHWH as victorious returning warrior and as king of Israel is also seen in the lament psalms echoed in the beginning of this section, which will be discussed below.[15] Echoes

---

[15] Frank Cross, in *Canaanite Myth and Hebrew Epic: Essays in the History of the Religion of Israel* (Cambridge: Harvard University Press, 1973) 91–111, demonstrated the relationships of this complex of themes to neighboring stories of Baal's battle with Yam, and Marduk's with Tiamat, in which the victorious warrior is rewarded with kingship. T. Mettinger, who had also studied the references in Canaanite and Mesopotamian myth, noted a strong linkage between the themes of YHWH as divine warrior and as king, and of Zion as God's royal abode, especially in Isaiah 51–52 but also throughout Second Isaiah ("In Search of the Hidden Structure"). Patrick Miller, in *The Divine Warrior in Early Israel* (Cambridge: Harvard University Press, 1973) 83, noted some distinctions between the usage in Canaanite and Mesopotamian literature and that in Hebrew literature. In particular he noted that the stories of YHWH are historicized, so that the decisive battle occurs not with other gods but with the earthly enemies of Israel. Bernhard Anderson ("Exodus and Covenant," 345–49) understood the stories of the exodus and the motifs of mythological battles to have been fused and blended in the Jerusalem cult: "the meaning of the Exodus is enhanced by mythical motifs, derived primarily

of those laments anticipate the final vision emerging at the end of this section, in which YHWH's return to reign is announced in terms of Psalm 98. These recollections celebrate the divine reign in a changed setting, a setting in which the future of the human, Davidic reign is highly uncertain or even altogether out of the question. Reuse of this language suggests that a new era in YHWH's reign has begun. YHWH has indeed returned.

Use of the Nahum text involved no swerve in interpretation, but simply a reapplication of old language to an analogous new setting. In using the psalmic text, Second Isaiah points to, or perhaps creates, an analogy that is less obvious, given the clear alterations in political setting. No mention is made here of the other elements once concomitant with the divine reign: no human king, no independence from foreign control. Nevertheless, Second Isaiah asserts the analogy, suggesting strongly that God's supremacy is not dependent upon these human verities. Rather, according to verse 9, divine reign is recognizable in YHWH's restoration, against all odds, of the destroyed nation. Use of the psalm suggests that God's re-establishment of Jerusalem will make visible to all nations a power to save that could not originate from any structures of the weakened community itself, a power belonging to the divine ruler alone. This theme of witness, of the nations' witnessing YHWH's "arm," is continued in the section that follows, in which the nations are startled to see God's restoration of the weakened and despised servant.

Lamentations 4:15

Immediately following the hymn, Isa 52:11 cites, and reverses, Lam 4:15. That chapter had concerned itself with the fates of various people of Jerusalem, from the children, who had been devalued, denied food, and even eaten by their mothers, to the king, who was pursued and captured in the enemy's pits. As shall be

---

from Canaan, with the result that YHWH's historical deeds are seen in the spacious perspective of his cosmic rule" (346). He understood both Isa 51:9–11 and 52:7–8 to reflect this fusion of motifs.

shown further on, a high linguistic correspondence exists between that chapter and the section concerning Zion's children in Isa 51:17–23. According to the lament, the sins of the prophets and iniquities of the priests precipitated the city's unbelievable destruction. Their end was vividly portrayed: defiled by the innocent blood they had shed, wandering blindly, garments untouchable, they were treated by the nations as lepers:[16]

Lam 4:15	"Depart! Unclean!" they shouted at them;	**סוּרוּ טָמֵא** קָרְאוּ לָמוֹ
	"Depart! Depart! Do not touch!"	**סוּרוּ סוּרוּ אַל־תִּגָּעוּ**
	For they became fugitives and wanderers;	כִּי נָצוּ גַּם־נָעוּ
	it was said among the nations,	אָמְרוּ בַּגּוֹיִם
	"They will no longer stay."	**לֹא יוֹסִיפוּ** לָגוּר

In a remarkable cooptation of Lam 4:15 recorded in Isa 52:11, those who once became wanderers and fugitives on account of their own iniquity reverse roles with the nations among whom they dwell:[17]

Isa 52:11	Depart! Depart! Go out from there!	**סוּרוּ סוּרוּ** צְאוּ מִשָּׁם
	Unclean! Do not touch!	**טָמֵא אַל־תִּגָּעוּ**
	Go out from its midst, purify yourselves,	צְאוּ מִתּוֹכָהּ הִבָּרוּ
	carriers of the vessels of YHWH!	נֹשְׂאֵי כְּלֵי יְהוָה

The shout **טָמֵא**, "Unclean," was used, according to pentateuchal law, to warn the healthy against those with leprosy (Lev 13:45). The protocol prescribed torn clothing, disheveled hair, and social isolation. Outside of Leviticus, the expression **טָמֵא** is relatively rare. The words סוּרוּ and **אַל־תִּגָּעוּ** are even more rare. The combination of these words into one phrase with the repeated סוּרוּ סוּרוּ is not only unique to these two passages, but also quite unlikely to occur by coincidence. The high degree of thematic continuity

---

16 Provan, 118, suggested that the "they" in this verse referred not just to the priests and prophets of verse 13 but to the scattered community as a whole. Perhaps so.

17 Gottwald (*Studies*, 44) noted this correspondence in his list of phrases shared by Second Isaiah and Lamentations; he did not, however, discuss it in depth. As was mentioned in the first chapter, the correspondence was noted at least as long ago as 1778, by Robert Lowth (361).

between the two texts, the probability of Lamentations' availability to Second Isaiah's community, the volume of this echo, and the recurrence of this lament's language in other verses nearby, all contribute to the recognition that here Second Isaiah refers explicitly to the formulation found in Lam 4:15.

If Second Isaiah's use of Psalm 98 adjusts previous themes to fit a new reality, its use of Lamentations constitutes nothing less than a full about-face. This pointed reversal in Second Isaiah of the rejection of Lam 4:15 recollects the fugitive state of Judah's leaders. However, their problematic condition is not directly acknowledged. Rather it is as if this statement, in all its similarity to the former rebuke, is meant to overwrite it. The new poetry exploits an ambiguity in the lament to reinterpret its import. "Depart! Unclean! Do not touch!" the exiles are again ordered. But the second line clarifies: it is not now the Babylonian exiles who are unclean and untouchable, but rather the gentile city in which they are dwelling. The devastating image of Jerusalem's religious leaders as wandering lepers, unfit for the company even of the uncircumcised nations, is sharply reversed as they are commissioned to separate themselves and the temple vessels from the now unclean city of Babylon, and to return with YHWH to Jerusalem.

This reversal of ignominious fate is first hinted in Isa 52:1, where elements of Lam 4:15 are blended with very similar wording already cited from Nah 2:1. Here it is not Israelites who are called unclean and forbidden entrance to other nations, but rather the uncircumcised gentiles who had invaded Jerusalem:

Isa	Awake, awake,	עוּרִי עוּרִי
52:1	put on your strength, Zion!	לִבְשִׁי עֻזֵּךְ צִיּוֹן
	Put on your beautiful garments,	לִבְשִׁי בִּגְדֵי תִפְאַרְתֵּךְ
	Jerusalem, the holy city;	יְרוּשָׁלַםִ עִיר הַקֹּדֶשׁ
	for he shall no longer come into you,	כִּי **לֹא** יוֹסִיף יָבֹא־בָךְ עוֹד
	uncircumcised and unclean.	עָרֵל ***וְטָמֵא***

As was shown above, the last line of this verse echoes Nah 2:1. The major alteration of Nahum in the Isaiah text was the deletion of Nahum's reference to בְּלִיַּעַל, and the substitution of עָרֵל וְטָמֵא

in its place. Now a reason for this alteration becomes visible: a blending of two texts, suggested perhaps by the shared phrase לֹא יוֹסִיף, "no longer," produces a more specific reference, not to "the wicked one," but to "uncircumcised and unclean." This identification of the invaders specifically as "unclean" prepares the audience to begin reinterpreting the exclamation "Unclean! Do not touch!" as a reference to Babylon rather than to the exiles even before they reach the phrase "go out from its midst" that clarifies it. The admonition to leave unclean Babylon and return carrying the temple vessels to the sanctified city of Jerusalem completes the separation between sacred and unclean that was begun with the promise in 52:1 that the unclean will no longer be able to enter the sacred city.

The allusion in verse 11 is very clear. But the subtle blending of terms from Nahum and Lamentations in verse 1 would not be so noticeable to us without the evidence of allusions to both verses further on. Such joining of sounds as this should probably not be seen as scribal precision, but as intuitive linking of felicitously similar phrases in a poet's ears. Verse 1 serves well to remind modern readers that Second Isaiah did not compose this symphony of voices for our rather deaf ears, but for an audience expected to recognize and enjoy its overtones and undertones. Even with careful analysis, much that is subtle will simply elude us.

The recollections of Lam 4:15 in Isa 52:1 and 11 are supplemented in Isa 52:8 by a reference to Lam 4:17. That text, following the description of the unclean, homeless leaders of Jerusalem, had described the sentinels of Jerusalem as they waited in vain for reinforcements against their enemies:

Lam 4:17	Still, our eyes wore themselves out—	עוֹדֵינוּ תִּכְלֶינָה **עֵינֵינוּ**
	for our help, in vain,	אֶל־עֶזְרָתֵנוּ הָבֶל
	from our watchpost we were watching	**בְּצִפִּיָּתֵנוּ צִפִּינוּ**
	for a nation that did not save.	אֶל־גּוֹי לֹא **יוֹשִׁעַ**

But in Second Isaiah the sentinels (literally, "watchers"; hence, "watchmen") are the first to see salvation approaching. In verse 7 a Nahumic messenger was glimpsed on the mountains, coming to herald peace, salvation (יְשׁוּעָה), and God's reign. Next the sentinels too rejoice at what becomes visible:

Isa	The voice of your watchmen!	קוֹל צֹפַיִךְ
52:8	they lift up their voice; together they cry out!	נָשְׂאוּ קוֹל יַחְדָּו יְרַנֵּנוּ
	For eye-to-eye they see	כִּי עַיִן בְּעַיִן יִרְאוּ
	the return of YHWH to Zion.	בְּשׁוּב יְהוָה צִיּוֹן

Like the hint of Lam 4:15 in Isa 52:1, this recollection would be far less apparent without the stronger allusion that follows three verses later. Once the plausibility of Second Isaiah's intent to reverse the devastating language of Lamentations 4 is confirmed, however, the sentinel imagery falls into place. The futile lookout during Jerusalem's siege that was described in Lamentations 4 is, like the wandering of the exiles, recalled in its reversal: when salvation finally approaches, it does so not in the form of a human ally, but in the return of the divine protector whose desertion had in the beginning occasioned the crisis. Whereas once the watchmen strained their eyes to see a salvation that never manifested itself, now their eyes behold in full view their divine leader, returning in triumph to the regnal city, inspiring no longer lament but psalmody ("together they cry out," see above).

A methodology which recognizes the power of receptor texts and the full range of stances they may take toward previous texts becomes critical here. An interpreter might say, as many have said in the past, that Nahum or Psalm 98 has influenced Second Isaiah. But "influence" cannot account for the choices Second Isaiah makes in their use. To speak of Lamentations as influencing Second Isaiah, or of Second Isaiah as being dependent upon the lament, is to obscure the fact that it is the later text that is exerting the intertextual pressure. Likewise, to consider Lamentations 4 and Isaiah 52 irrelevant to each other because they make contradictory claims is to miss the power of the new text, power to enter the fray of competing discourse and to utilize the language of others to stake its own claim. Continuity with psalmic and prophetic language becomes rhetorical ballast weighing in against such painful articulations of Judah's recent experience as are voiced in

Lamentations 4. When the lament's terms are not avoided, but are engaged in a radically different context which turns their meaning upside down, their stinging power is depleted.

Quotations of Nah 2:1, Ps 98:3, and Lam 4:15 have been highlighted in Isa 52:7, 10, and 11 respectively, and briefer phrases from these and surrounding verses have been discerned in verses 1, 8, and 9. These citations are interwoven to form a nearly solid fabric of citation-filled speech running continuously for five verses. I will now attend to two further points: the language of "comforter" in verse 9 and the pentateuchal language in the section's final verse.

Lamentations 1 and Zion's Comforter

The motif of Zion's comfort, though echoed only briefly in this section, is actually both Second Isaiah's most prominently positioned message and its most frequently recurring allusion to Lamentations. Strong echoes of Lamentations 4 in verses 1, 8, and especially 11 have already been noted. In the midst of echoes in verses 9 and 10 of Psalm 98, another recollection, this time of Lamentations 1, is deftly interwoven. According to verse 9, the reason for rejoicing is that נִחַם יְהוָה עַמּוֹ, "YHWH has comforted his people." This phrase repeats verbatim an announcement first heard in Isa 49:13, where it summarizes the preceding vision of returning exiles. Isaiah 51:3 repeats the phrase twice with different objects: "YHWH has comforted Zion, comforted all her ruins." The refrain echoes the opening words of the book, נַחֲמוּ נַחֲמוּ עַמִּי יֹאמַר אֱלֹהֵיכֶם, "Comfort, comfort my people, says your God" (Isa 40:1), and is further reinforced in Isa 51:19, where the prophet asks Zion, "How will I comfort you?" and in 54:11, where she is called "not comforted." Most prominently, in Isa 51:12 YHWH announces אָנֹכִי אָנֹכִי הוּא מְנַחֶמְכֶם, "I, I am he, your comforter."

As a freestanding theme, apart from anything said before, the claim of YHWH's comfort for suffering Jerusalem is quite compelling, and not at all obscure. But when heard against the background of Lamentations, its import is doubled. The most repeated phrase of Lamentations 1— indeed of the whole book—concerned the same subject, Zion's comforter, or rather her lack of one: she has "no comforter," אֵין מְנַחֵם.[18] Between the beginning and end of this lament the phrase recurs five times. It is repeated by both the sympathetic observer of Zion who opens the poem, and Zion herself, who closes it. In each instance the same piel masculine singular active participial form is used:

Lam 1:2b	There is no comforter for her among all who love her.	אֵין־לָהּ ***מְנַחֵם*** מִכָּל־אֹהֲבֶיהָ
1:9b-c	. . . And she fell extraordinarily— there was no comforter for her. "See, YHWH, my suffering, for the enemy is exalted!"	וַתֵּרֶד פְּלָאִים אֵין ***מְנַחֵם*** לָהּ רְאֵה יְהוָה אֶת־עָנְיִי כִּי הִגְדִּיל אוֹיֵב
1:16b	. . . For far from me is a comforter, a reviver of my strength.	כִּי־רָחַק מִמֶּנִּי ***מְנַחֵם*** מֵשִׁיב נַפְשִׁי
1:17a	Zion stretched out her hands— there was no comforter for her.	פֵּרְשָׂה צִיּוֹן בְּיָדֶיהָ אֵין ***מְנַחֵם*** לָהּ
1:21a	They heard how I was groaning; there was no comforter for me.	שָׁמְעוּ כִּי נֶאֱנָחָה אָנִי אֵין ***מְנַחֵם*** לִי

This masculine singular participial form appears otherwise in only two other verses of the Bible: the much later Eccl 4:1, and Isa 51:12, where YHWH announces, "I, I am he, your comforter" (מְנַחֶמְכֶם).[19]

---

[18] Unlike many others, this connection has not been easily seen by modern readers. It was not mentioned at all by either Gottwald or by Löhr. Porteous (246) hinted at a relationship between this phrase in the lament and the opening of Isaiah 40. Newsom (76) suggested a clear connection: "Second Isaiah dialogically engages Lamentations in terms of reversal. Where Lamentations says that Zion has no one to comfort her (Lam 1:2), Second Isaiah says that now YHWH will comfort Zion (Isa 51:3)."

[19] Mentions of YHWH's comfort, employing other forms of the verb, are relatively rare and fleeting, found in Isa 12:1 (generally considered late); Isa 66:13 and Zech 1:17 (late and probably dependent upon Second Isaiah); Jer 31:13 (which will be discussed below); and Pss 23:4; 71:21; 86:17; 119:76, 82.

The very least to be said about this particular correspondence between Lamentations 1 and Second Isaiah is that the prophetic text responds to concerns for comfort such as Lamentations 1 expresses. The directness of Second Isaiah's response to this particular lament is demonstrated, however, by the lament's probable availability to Second Isaiah, the two texts' common concern for war-racked Jerusalem, the characterization in both texts of the comfortless city as suffering Daughter Zion, the precise similarity, prominence, and recurrence of the wording in both texts, the reuse of other Lamentations texts in Second Isaiah, and the tight relationship, albeit revisionary, of Second Isaiah's theme of comfort to the lament's theme of comfortlessness. Most significantly, as I have shown here and will show again in the chapters that follow, whenever Zion's lament of comfortlessness is answered in Second Isaiah, the assurance is accompanied by other reversals of language and imagery of Lamentations, creating a density of reference that can hardly be considered coincidental.

Embedded in the doxological language of the psalm in verse 9 comes the announcement that Zion's comfortless condition, highlighted in the lament, has been addressed and rectified. This announcement of YHWH's comfort becomes the particular occasion for the psalm's rejoicing.

Pentateuchal Allusions

Although the exodus story and other pentateuchal traditions are often referred to in Second Isaiah, there is relatively little literal repetition of pentateuchal wording, none as extensive as that seen above in regard to Lamentations, Nahum, and Psalm 98. However, many interpreters throughout time have noted that Isa 52:12, the last verse of this citation-filled passage, refers quite distinctly to the exodus story.[20] They are certainly correct: in fact, Isa 52:11b–12 is filled with a montage of brief allusions:

---

[20] References to the exodus tradition here were already cited in chapter 1 in the work of Zimmerli and Fishbane. To get a sense of the range of people noting these connections see also for instance Ibn Ezra, 239; Calvin, 4/105;

Isa 52:11b	Go out from its midst, purify yourselves,	**צְאוּ מִתּוֹכָהּ** הִבָּרוּ
	carriers of the vessels of YHWH!	נֹשְׂאֵי כְּלֵי יְהוָה
52:12	For not in haste will you go out,	כִּי לֹא **בְחִפָּזוֹן תֵּצֵאוּ**
	and not in flight will you go.	וּבִמְנוּסָה לֹא תֵלֵכוּן
	For the one going before you is YHWH,	כִּי־הֹלֵךְ **לִפְנֵיכֶם יְהוָה**
	and your rearguard is the God of Israel.	**וּמְאַסִּפְכֶם** אֱלֹהֵי יִשְׂרָאֵל

The first two phrases are to be found in the story of the exodus itself, and the last two in descriptions of the tribes' marching orders during the journey through the desert to the promised land. Here they are adapted to describe both the new exodus from Babylon and the return across the wilderness to Jerusalem.

The first echo of an exodus motif is the phrase צְאוּ מִתּוֹכָהּ, "go out from its midst," which corresponds to Pharaoh's words when, after the Passover, he orders Moses to leave Egypt:

Exod 12:31	And he summoned Moses and Aaron	וַיִּקְרָא לְמֹשֶׁה וּלְאַהֲרֹן
	by night and said,	לַיְלָה וַיֹּאמֶר
	"Arise, go out from the midst of my people,	קוּמוּ **צְּאוּ מִתּוֹךְ** עַמִּי
	both you and the Israelites,	גַּם־אַתֶּם גַּם־בְּנֵי יִשְׂרָאֵל
	go and serve YHWH as you said."	וּלְכוּ עִבְדוּ אֶת־יְהוָה כְּדַבֶּרְכֶם

Even though the phrase in Exod 12:31 refers to a quite analogous situation (departure from the land of captivity), and is otherwise nearly unknown in the Bible, the echoing phrase צְאוּ מִתּוֹכָהּ is brief and would be insignificant were it not for what unfolds next.

The second phrase that awakens recollection is כִּי לֹא בְחִפָּזוֹן תֵּצֵאוּ, "for not in haste will you go out." The word חִפָּזוֹן is only found otherwise in Exod 12:11, where it refers to the manner in which the Passover should be eaten (בְּחִפָּזוֹן), and in Deut 16:3,

---

Alexander, 282; Franz Delitzsch, *The Prophecies of Isaiah*, vol 2, 4th ed., transl. S. R. Driver (Edinburgh: T & T Clark, 1889) 277; Torrey, 409; Volz, *Jesaja II*, 123; Kissane, 169; C. R. North, *The Second Isaiah* (Oxford: Clarendon, 1964) 225; von Rad, 2/246; Westermann, *Isaiah 40–66*, 253; Clifford, 172; and Frank Matheus, *Singt dem Herrn ein neues Lied: Die Hymnen Deuterojesajas* (Stuttgart: Katholisches Bibelwerk, 1990) 99. Although the connection with the phrase בְחִפָּזוֹן תֵּצֵאוּ is cited most frequently, all of the pentateuchal echoes I will discuss are also cited by various scholars.

where it describes the manner of the Israelites' departure from Egypt:

Deut	You must not eat with it anything leavened.	לֹא־תֹאכַל עָלָיו חָמֵץ
16:3	For seven days you shall eat with it	שִׁבְעַת יָמִים תֹּאכַל־עָלָיו
	unleavened bread, the bread of affliction,	מַצּוֹת לֶחֶם עֹנִי
	for in haste you went out	***כִּי בְחִפָּזוֹן יָצָאתָ***
	from the land of Egypt,	מֵאֶרֶץ מִצְרַיִם
	so that you would remember	לְמַעַן תִּזְכֹּר
	the day of your departure	אֶת־יוֹם צֵאתְךָ
	from the land of Egypt	מֵאֶרֶץ מִצְרַיִם
	all the days of your life.	כֹּל יְמֵי חַיֶּיךָ

Correspondence to this element of the exodus story is rendered as a contrast: this time there will be no need to hurry: כִּי לֹא בְחִפָּזוֹן תֵצֵאוּ, "for not in haste will you go out." Whether the exodus tradition was known and viewed as relevent to this departure is not a question: analogies between the two captivities are to be found not only elsewhere in Second Isaiah itself (see for instance Isa 51:10) but also in the wider textual arena (see especially Jer 16:14–15). The fact that this word recurs in both the Exodus and Deuteronomy recountings, even when used of two different activities, and nowhere else except Isaiah, underscores its importance as a key theme of the departure from Egypt. Its reuse here, in a passage describing another departure from another land of captivity, is highly noticeable even in its negation. Though the volume is slight, the recurrence of specific, unusual exodus language in two adjacent verses of Second Isaiah is striking. If the poet was willing to reverse what was ignominious in Lamentations, what was less than dignified in Exodus might certainly be revised.

The reason that this exodus may be a more stately procession is given next in phrases that correspond to, and enlarge upon, the descriptions of YHWH's guidance in the wilderness. In verse 12, YHWH's place in the procession is described in language that is otherwise used only to describe the journey of the Israelites in the wilderness. Here it is said, הֹלֵךְ לִפְנֵיכֶם יְהוָה, "the one going before you is YHWH"; likewise, in Num 14:14 (see also Exod 13:21, Deut 1:33), Moses describes to YHWH what is being said:

Num	They have heard that you, YHWH,	שָׁמְעוּ כִּי־אַתָּה יְהוָה
14:14	in the midst of this people,	בְּקֶרֶב הָעָם הַזֶּה
	are seen eye-to-eye; you, YHWH,	אֲשֶׁר־עַיִן בְּעַיִן נִרְאָה אַתָּה יְהוָה
	and your cloud is standing over them,	וַעֲנָנְךָ עֹמֵד עֲלֵהֶם
	and in a pillar of cloud	וּבְעַמֻּד עָנָן
	you go before them by day,	אַתָּה הֹלֵךְ לִפְנֵיהֶם יוֹמָם
	and in a pillar of fire by night.	וּבְעַמּוּד אֵשׁ לָיְלָה

It is not only the phrase הֹלֵךְ לִפְנֵיהֶם, striking as it is in itself, that corresponds to the description in Numbers. Moses' description of YHWH's visibility (עַיִן בְּעַיִן נִרְאָה, "seen eye-to-eye") otherwise appears in scripture only in Isa 52:8, where it forms, along with Lam 4:17 and Ps 98:8, yet a third allusion within the one verse:

Isa	The voice of your watchmen!	קוֹל צֹפַיִךְ
52:8	they lift up their voice; together they cry out!	נָשְׂאוּ קוֹל יַחְדָּו יְרַנֵּנוּ
	For eye-to-eye they see	כִּי עַיִן בְּעַיִן יִרְאוּ
	the return of YHWH to Zion.[21]	בְּשׁוּב יְהוָה צִיּוֹן

The descriptions of YHWH's travels before Israel in a cloud by day and in smoke by night in the Pentateuch do not mention YHWH's acting as rearguard, as Isa 52:12 asserts. However, the word מְאַסֵּף, "rearguard," is used otherwise only of the Israelite processions in the wilderness—see Num 10:25; Josh 6:9, 13. If this word, like the other phrases in this passage, is meant to call the former journey to mind, it emphasizes that the new journey will be even more divinely protected than the former one, since the rearguard is no longer a mere human force, but YHWH their king. In creating not only analogies to the exodus and wilderness story, but also contrasts that heighten the wonder, Second Isaiah displays a vector of increasing splendor and significance. Jeremiah 16:14–15 announced that the return from exile will outlast the exodus in

---

[21] The syntax may be even closer than it appears. Pointed as in the MT, the verb in Num 14:14 (נִרְאָה) is 3ms niphal. But if the BHS's suggested emendation of one vowel is followed, the word becomes the 1cp qal form נִרְאֶה, "we see you eye-to-eye," corresponding even more closely to the 3mp qal form in Isa 52:8.

Judah's religious imagination, but Second Isaiah provides verbal pictures to make it so.

The sudden density of clearly pentateuchal language in these two verses in Isaiah is quite unlikely to have resulted from a series of linguistic coincidences. Nor is it likely that Second Isaiah created this language, making it available for adoption later into a variety of pentateuchal passages. Rather it seems clear from the explicitness of referents, the recurrence of language, the coherence of themes, the allusive nature of this entire section in Second Isaiah, the revisionary nature of the recollections, and the history of interpretation itself, that Second Isaiah is here recollecting in brief synopsis major features of the exodus story as it is already known, in order to present the departure from Babylon as its typological heir.

As was discussed in the previous chapter, dating of pentateuchal passages is very much in dispute at this time, with some scholars arguing for an earlier dating of Priestly texts and others arguing for a later dating of J texts. In view of this debate, it is interesting to note that the recollections in Isa 52:11–12 cut straight across the boundaries as conceived by classic source critics: Exod 12:11 was generally considered P; Exod 12:31 belonged variously to a J or E narrative; Num 10:25 was generally considered a Priestly text; Num 14:14 was seen as an awkward and puzzling composite text variously thought to contain elements of J, E, or D; Deut 16:3 was attributed to D; and the Joshua passages were attributed by various scholars to J, E, or D.[22] The fact that these texts are melded into a sequence by

---

[22] For discussions of these see for example O. Eissfeldt, *The Old Testament* (201, 206); J. A. Soggin, *Introduction to the Old Testament*, OTL (Philadelphia: Westminster Press, 1976. Translated from the 2nd ed., published in Italian, 1974) 144; O. Kaiser, *Introduction to the Old Testament: A Presentation of its Results and Problems* (Minneapolis, MN: Augsburg, 1975. Translated from the 2nd edition, published in German,1970) 79; G. E. Wright, "Exodus, Book of," in *Interpreter's Dictionary of the Bible*, vol. 2 (Nashville: Abingdon, 1962) 193; R. C. Dentan, "Numbers, Book of," in *IDB*, vol. 3, 568; G. B. Gray, *A Critical and Exegetical Commentary on Numbers*. ICC (Edinburgh: T. & T. Clark, 1903) 90, 157; M. Noth, *Exodus: A Commentary*, OTL (Philadelphia: Westminster Press, 1962, originally published in German in 1959) 92–93; idem, *Numbers: A*

Second Isaiah does not necessarily mean that the poet found them already associated together, since this entire section consists of distinct texts juxtaposed in new combinations, but it certainly lends support to such a supposition.

Summary

From the above it is clear that Isa 52:7–12 is composed of quotation after quotation linked together, superimposed upon one another, intertwined with one another. Significantly, the psalm, the lament, and possibly the book of Nahum all found their original and usual setting in the worshipping congregation, as liturgical texts. It is not difficult to imagine that this could have been true as well for the some of pentateuchal pieces, that is, if they formed part of the Passover liturgy or if the Pentateuch were indeed already being read in public worship at that time. Most, possibly all, of this passage would then have rung familiar as oral, liturgical descriptions of the works of YHWH. Only here they are combined into a new synthesis, no longer primarily referring back to various events of the past (the exodus from Egypt, the defeat of Assyria, and the destruction of Jerusalem), but converging on a new event on the horizon, which all previous events are made to foreshadow.[23]

A Quotation in Isaiah 51:15: Jeremiah 31:35

While the section's final six verses contain the vast majority of direct quotations, one other quotation occurs in the first part: Isa 51:15 repeats precisely a seven-word description of YHWH found

---

Commentary, OTL (Philadelphia: Westminster Press, 1968, originally published in German in 1966) 109.

[23] On Isa 51:17–52:12, Muilenburg (602) said, "The poet . . . employs the materials of his literary predecessors (Nahum, Jeremiah, Ezekiel, Lamentations). The great historical traditions associated with the Exodus and the wandering are woven into a fresh eschatological context. Creative imagination and memory are focused upon a single event. Second Isaiah brings to a culmination the thought and aspiration of his people's past, and fashions the matrix of thought for succeeding centuries."

originally in Jer 31:35.[24] To understand the import of this quotation, it is necessary to backtrack briefly into the book of Jeremiah. In Jer 5:22, the disobedience of Israel is contrasted with the obedience of the sea in not transgressing boundaries set by YHWH:

Jer	Do you not fear me? says YHWH.	הַאוֹתִי לֹא־תִירָאוּ נְאֻם־יְהוָה
5:22	Do you not tremble before me,	אִם מִפָּנַי לֹא תָחִילוּ
	who placed the sand as a boundary for the sea,	אֲשֶׁר־שַׂמְתִּי חוֹל גְּבוּל לַיָּם
	an eternal rule, that it cannot transgress?	חָק־עוֹלָם וְלֹא יַעַבְרֶנְהוּ
	They toss but do not prevail,	וַיִּתְגָּעֲשׁוּ וְלֹא יוּכָלוּ
	its waves roar but they do not transgress it.	וְהָמוּ גַלָּיו וְלֹא יַעַבְרֻנְהוּ

Jeremiah 31:35–36 similarly invokes the rules of the natural order. Here, however, it is not to complain of Israel's unfaithfulness but to affirm YHWH's faithfulness:

Jer	Thus says YHWH,	כֹּה אָמַר יְהוָה
31:35	who gives the sun for light by day,	נֹתֵן שֶׁמֶשׁ לְאוֹר יוֹמָם
	the laws of the moon and stars	חֻקֹּת יָרֵחַ וְכוֹכָבִים
	for light by night,	לְאוֹר לָיְלָה
	who stills the sea, though its waves roar—[25]	רֹגַע הַיָּם וַיֶּהֱמוּ גַלָּיו
	YHWH Sabaoth is his name—	יְהוָה צְבָאוֹת שְׁמוֹ

[24] Cassuto, "Formal and Stylistic Relationship," 151; Paul, 115; Eldridge, 175–77.

[25] The qal verb רגע in this verse has usually been translated as "stirs up," even though other forms of the root have to do with "rest." The verb appears in relation to the sea in two other texts, Isa 51:15 which employs the exact same phrase, and Job 26:12, which also describes an act of YHWH to control the sea. Ibn Ezra (234) understood the word to mean "give rest" or "still." Both the KJV and Calvin (4/81) understood it as "divide" (see also REB, "cleft"). But the BDB translates the word in all three passages as "disturb," and Koehler-Baumgartner lists "stirs up" for all three, even while translating the niphal and hiphil respectively as "to keep quiet" and "to get some peace; to make peace."

Most recent translators, including the NRSV, have distinguished among the verses, translating the word in Job 26:12 "still," in accord with its context and the usual connotation of that root. The Jeremiah and Isaiah passages, however, have customarily been translated in this century with the opposite meaning: NRSV says, "who *stirs up* the sea so that its waves roar," and most other translations do the same. This may seem appropriate to the context if the vav

31:36 If these rules ever fail before me, says YHWH, then the seed of Israel also will cease from being a nation before me for all time.	אם־יָמֻשׁוּ הַחֻקִּים הָאֵלֶּה מִלְּפָנַי נְאֻם־יְהוָה גַּם זֶרַע יִשְׂרָאֵל יִשְׁבְּתוּ מִהְיוֹת גּוֹי לְפָנַי כָּל־הַיָּמִים

Here natural boundaries both temporal and spacial are invoked. The reference to the bounded sea has implications reaching beyond a simple pledge derived from the regularity of the natural world. A common description of enemy forces overrunning a city in Jeremiah is that of the sea which cannot be contained. Jeremiah 6:23, for instance, describes the nation that will invade from the north, saying קוֹלָם כַּיָּם יֶהֱמֶה, "their sound is like the roaring sea." In invoking the sea's boundaries and the rules of day and night in the midst of promises of restoration, the prophet portrays YHWH as pledging to keep the enemy "seas" from flooding Israel.[26]

---

prefix of וַיֶּהֱמוּ גַלָּיו, "its waves roar," is taken as a causative. But if it behaves like the vav prefix of וְהָמוּ גַלָּיו, "its waves roar" in Jer 5:22, that is, as an implied "though," there is no reason to create a new meaning for the same word, especially one that contradicts other meanings of the verb as well as other accounts of YHWH's action in the creation of the sea. The close thematic and linguistic relationship between Job 26:12 and Isa 51:9–10 (Yam, Rahab, pierce) also argues against translating the verb differently in three passages.

I have not found any recent commentator on Isaiah or Jeremiah who questioned the prevailing translation of רגע. However, Marvin Pope, in his notes on Job 26:12, in *Job,* AB 15 (Garden City, NY: Doubleday and Co., 1973) 185, observed that "perusal of the context [in both Jeremiah and Isaiah] makes it clear that the message of comfort to Israel is drawn from the appeal to YHWH's creative power and his defeat and control of the boisterous sea." M. K. Wakeman, in *God's Battle with the Monster: A Study in Biblical Imagery* (Leiden: E. J. Brill, 1973) 57–58, agreed with him, as do I.

[26] John Day, in *God's Conflict with the Dragon and the Sea: Echoes of a Canaanite Myth in the Old Testament* (Cambridge: Cambridge University Press, 1985) 120, suggested along similar lines that the notion of the inviolability of Jerusalem reflected in Psalms 46, 48, and 76 was a historicization of the myth of divine conflict with the waters.

Isaiah 51:15 echoes the seven-word description of YHWH in Jer 31:35 word for word, even to the point of reusing a third-person pronoun that is awkward in the new context:[27]

Isa 51:15	I am YHWH your God: "who stills the sea, though its waves roar— YHWH Sabaoth is his name."	וְאָנֹכִי יְהוָה אֱלֹהֶיךָ רֹגַע הַיָּם וַיֶּהֱמוּ גַּלָּיו יְהוָה צְבָאוֹת שְׁמוֹ

The volume of the echo here is obvious, as is its thematic coherence. As in Jeremiah, the phrase is used here in conjunction with other references to YHWH's power both to create the natural order and to sustain the nation of Israel, even in the face of enemy threats. Though this verse does not itself occur again in Second Isaiah, neighboring language in Jeremiah's book of consolation and other parts of Jeremiah will be seen frequently. The most controversial question about this echo, as was mentioned above in chapter 2, is one of priority: most scholars in the past century have assumed that language in Jeremiah 30–31 that resembles Second Isaiah is secondary, even when they think the rest of the section predated Second Isaiah. Yet the relationship of Jer 31:35 to Jeremiah 5 is clear. Moreover, while the echoed phrase fits smoothly into place in Jeremiah, it appears in Second Isaiah in a truncated form, violating grammatical rules, as if to call to mind as succinctly and literally as possible the previous formula.

The phrase, and with it Jeremiah's pledge, come to life richly in this new setting. Occurring just a few verses after the human plea that YHWH awake and defeat watery enemies as in times past, and in the midst of an extended discussion of the relationships among Zion, her enemies, and her God, this reminder of Jeremiah's formulation of YHWH as the one who "stills the sea" sets the direction the prophet's argument will take. The following verse, using another formulaic description of YHWH's work in creation (לִנְטֹעַ שָׁמַיִם וְלִיסֹד אָרֶץ, "stretching out the heavens, and founding the earth," see Jer 10:12), likewise connects YHWH's

---

[27] McKane, *Jeremiah*, vol. 2, notes this incongrence in person in Isa 51:15 which, he agrees, suggests that Jeremiah perserves the more original form.

power over the natural world with the nation's preservation (וְלֵאמֹר לְצִיּוֹן עַמִּי־אָתָּה, "and saying to Zion, my people you are"). As I will show, by referring to YHWH's power over natural forces at the beginning of this section, and to YHWH's return to reign as king at the end—together framing what will be a very difficult discussion of what Zion has suffered at her enemies' hands—Second Isaiah regathers the motifs that had once added up to the very understanding that Babylon had violated: the security of Zion. This complex of strong recollections of YHWH's power over natural and political worlds alike will enable the prophet to proclaim that the enemy can no longer enter the sacred city.

Conclusion

What has been outlined above is only the most obvious layer of intertextual citation manifest in Isa 51:9–52:12. These quotations demonstrate several characteristics of the compositional work of Second Isaiah:

First, the poet worked, in Fishbane's words, with "texts in the mind": the new ideas expressed in this poetry continually triggered, and were triggered by, remembrances not simply of events of Judah's tradition, but of particular verbal formulations of that tradition. These traditional words were not locked in the past but could be applied to present circumstances to yield new meanings.

Second, the prophet did not confine attention to one precursor at a time. Rather, texts from various and disparate sources that contained similar themes or key words were multiply superimposed upon one another to create new complexes of meaning.

Third, this passage echoes several texts that were prominent in Second Isaiah's world of meaning: not only Lamentations and Jeremiah, but also Nahum, Psalm 98 (along with other psalms, as shall be shown further), and some manifestation of the pentateuchal story of exodus and wilderness wandering.

Fourth, this passage shows the variety of ways texts were reappropriated. While some, such as Nahum and the psalm, were quoted as if directly transferable to the new situation, others, such as

Lamentations, were rearranged in content and reversed in meaning. In addition, the texts were at some points quoted at length, but at other points referred to by means of a single phrase. At times they appeared alone; at other times, joined to other texts. Two or more distinct texts, both clearly present, were sometimes overlapped, as were Lam 4:15 and Nah 2:1 in Isa 52:1, and Lam 4:17, Ps 98:8, and Num 14:14 in Isa 52:8.

While the proximity of overlapping brief echoes to much clearer allusions enables modern readers to discern at least some of the fainter echoes in Isaiah 52, they also heighten awareness that such faint echoes may sometimes occur in ways that modern readers cannot easily discern. Only inhabitants of Second Isaiah's own community, cognizant not only of the full range of traditions in the prophetic repertory but also of the social function, connotation, and significance of each of those traditions in exilic Babylon, would be equipped to hear the overtones and undertones of the poet's message. When modern readers reach beyond the obvious to discern subtleties of the message, much will inevitably be missed. Yet as I will show in the rest of this chapter, there is much beneath the surface that can be identified.

Recollections of Language about Jerusalem's Destruction

None of the remaining recollections in this section are as explicit as the passages I have cited above. What they share in common, however, is that they hark back to language already known to be relevant to the times in which Second Isaiah wrote, and with which the poet struggled—language already used in connection with the defeat of Jerusalem. Since the recollections here are less explicit, it is more difficult to argue that Second Isaiah is recalling texts as specifically as was seen above. Some of the recollections here are quite likely allusions to specific texts that are still available, more loosely referred to for a variety of reasons; on the other hand some may be more general recollections of the types of language and concerns that are expressed in the previous literature that resembles them. Whether Second Isaiah is here responding to specific texts identifiable by us, specific texts no longer identifiable by us, or only general tenors of discourse exemplified by texts we know, what is clear is that Second Isaiah continues to speak as response—not creating new media of discourse, but reshaping the discourse with which forebears and contemporaries have already been expressing their concerns. Second Isaiah's keying of new words to the forms and cadences of older speech alerts readers to the rhetorical context in which the new words are to be read. The more the new words resemble old expressions, the more they can take their place beside them—or in some cases, instead of them.

For convenience I have divided this discussion into three parts corresponding to the three panels of the "Awake, Awake" triptych. In the first part, Isa 51:9–16, three distinct kinds of language are discernible: that resembling a certain circle of lament psalms; that resembling Jeremiah; and that resembling Lamentations. In the second section, Isa 51:17–23, the predominant mode of discourse resembles that of Lamentations, especially Lamentations 4. Because more specific quotations abound in the third section, Isa 52:1–2 and 7–12, most of it has already been discussed above, and what is left is to explore is one complex of Lamentations imagery in the opening two verses.

Recollections in Isaiah 51:9–16

In the first four verses of this section, Isa 51:9–12, three recollections of other language about Jerusalem's destruction are laid side by side. The first resembles closely laments now present in Psalms; the second, Jeremiah's book of consolation, and the third, Lamentations. The language of lament psalmody, with its concentration on motivating YHWH to act again as in the past, sets the course followed especially in the opening verse of each section and in the closing of its entirety. Jeremiah's language and language forms are especially noticeable in this first section, while Lamentations concerns are addressed in a variety of ways within all three parts of this section. Below I will draw out the themes each has contributed, and finally will describe their effects in concert with the quotations discussed above.

Psalmic Recollections of YHWH's Might

The passage opens with a call to YHWH to arise on behalf of the people, and a remembrance of God's deeds in bygone days—mythical times, in fact—when God struggled with, and overcame, Rahab, the dragon, the sea and the great deep:[28]

Isa	Awake, awake, put on strength,	עוּרִי עוּרִי לִבְשִׁי־עֹז
51:9	arm of YHWH.	זְרוֹעַ יְהוָה
	Awake as in days of old,	עוּרִי כִּימֵי קֶדֶם
	generations long ago.	דֹּרוֹת עוֹלָמִים
	Are you not she, the crusher of Rahab,	הֲלוֹא אַתְּ־הִיא הַמַּחְצֶבֶת רַהַב
	the piercer of the dragon?	מְחוֹלֶלֶת תַּנִּין
51:10	Are you not she, the one drying the sea,	הֲלוֹא אַתְּ־הִיא הַמַּחֲרֶבֶת יָם
	the waters of the great deep,	מֵי תְּהוֹם רַבָּה
	the one making the depths of the sea a road	הַשָּׂמָה מַעֲמַקֵּי־יָם דֶּרֶךְ
	for the redeemed to pass?	לַעֲבֹר גְּאוּלִים

As the verses progress, the roster of adversaries defeatcd by YHWH's arm moves from powcrful mythological beings, Rahab and the dragon, to Yam/the sea and Tehom/the deep, adversaries once personified in myth who have in Second Isaiah's setting lost much of their potency as cosmic opponents, and now coincide with aspects of the natural world, which YHWH controls.[29] At the same time there is a progression from the recollection of mythical battles with adversaries, with their creation overtones, to a recollection of the crossing of the Red Sea, the moment of redemption for the

[28] Although Gunkel, in *Schöpfung und Chaos in Urzeit und Endzeit* (Göttingen: Vandenhoeck und Rubrecht, 1895), especially pp. 30–33, proposed that Judahite references to this mythological struggle reflected Babylonian influence, Day has argued that a Canaanite influence is more likely (1).

[29] Wakeman (98) observed, "In Isa 51:9 actions appropriate to the sea are distinguished from those appropriate to the monster, and the statements about *yam* appear to be naturalistic reinterpretations of the mythological references."

nation of Israel specifically. The blending of creation and redemption themes will recur in Isa 51:16–17.

Elements of these verses correspond to appeals made to YHWH in several lament psalms, most notably Psalms 44, 74, 77, and 89. There is also some correspondence to the shortest and probably most ancient of the enthronement psalms, Psalm 93. No case can be made for an exclusive or continuous resonance with any one of these texts; however, the presence of several shared elements demonstrates that it is this genre of communal lament that the poet means to invoke:

1) Several elements of these verses correspond closely to the short and probably Canaanite-influenced Ps 93:1–4, which celebrates YHWH's power over the forces of the sea.[30]

Ps 93:1	YHWH is king! In magnificence clothed,	**יְהוָה מָלָךְ** גֵּאוּת **לָבֵשׁ**
	clothed is YHWH, with strength he has girded himself.	**לָבֵשׁ יְהוָה עֹז** הִתְאַזָּר
	Indeed, established is the world, unshakable.	אַף־תִּכּוֹן תֵּבֵל בַּל־תִּמּוֹט
93:2	Established is your throne from of old,	נָכוֹן כִּסְאֲךָ מֵאָז
	from everlasting you are.	**מֵעוֹלָם** אָתָּה
93:3	The rivers lifted up, YHWH,	נָשְׂאוּ נְהָרוֹת יְהוָה
	the rivers lifted up their voice,	נָשְׂאוּ נְהָרוֹת קוֹלָם
	the rivers lift up their crashing.	יִשְׂאוּ נְהָרוֹת דָּכְיָם
93:4	More than the noise of mighty waters,	מִקֹּלוֹת **מַיִם רַבִּים**
	mightier than the breakers of the sea,	אַדִּירִים מִשְׁבְּרֵי־**יָם**
	mighty on the height is YHWH.	אַדִּיר בַּמָּרוֹם **יְהוָה**

The metaphor of God's being clothed with power (לָבֵשׁ עֹז) is found nowhere else in the Hebrew Bible; in fact, the verb לבשׁ is rarely used of YHWH, occurring elsewhere only in the later and possibly dependent Isa 59:17 and in Ps 104:1, in which YHWH is clothed with "honor and majesty." In Psalm 93, as in Isaiah 51, the motifs of YHWH's wearing strength and YHWH's eternity (מֵעוֹלָם)

---

[30] Helen Jefferson, "Psalm 93," showed that 80% of the vocabulary of Psalm 93 is to be found in Second Isaiah. Important parallels in thought occur at many points as well. This indicated to her satisfaction "that Deutero-Isaiah knew and reflected the language and ideas of this psalm" (157–58).

are expressed together, along with YHWH's reign (יְהוָה מָלָךְ, see Isa 52:7, where this motif comes to fruition). Immediately, as in Isaiah, YHWH's strength is challenged by the tumult of the waters. Verses 3–4 depict the rivers' voices rising, and affirm YHWH's power over the mighty waters (מַיִם רַבִּים, see Isa 51:10) and the waves of the sea (יָם, see Isa 51:10). The roaring of the waves in this psalm, which despite their power are no match for YHWH's decrees, bespeaks the same theme as in Isa 51:15 of YHWH's ability to declare boundaries for the natural order. Psalm 93 is the only psalm in which absolutely no creaturely life plays any role. Yet its anthropomorphic description of the waters suggests the roar of human throngs as well, and helps illuminate why a discussion of YHWH as more powerful than the sea might be an argument against fearing human foes.

2) Elements characteristic of the speech of the lament Psalms 44, 74, and 77, and the royal psalm with lament, Psalm 89, are found intensely echoed in Isa 51:9–10. Although each of these psalms shares several elements of language and thought with Isa 51:9–10, none of them contains all of the elements. It is possible, of course, that a psalm of this genre, now lost, inspired Second Isaiah's language to a greater degree than any of those that still exist; such a possibility can neither be denied nor affirmed. What can be affirmed, however, is that this portion of Isaiah is keyed to recall a particular type of lament exemplified by elements shared with Psalms 74, 77, 89, and 44:

a) Psalm 74 is a communal lament considered by most to reflect the destruction of the temple in 587. It begins by questioning YHWH for casting off "the sheep of your pasture" (צֹאן מַרְעִיתֶךָ, see Isa 40:11 and especially 49:9) and asking God to remember the congregation which "you acquired long ago and redeemed" (קָנִיתָ קֶּדֶם גָּאַלְתָּ, verse 2, see Isa 51:9, 10). After a poignant description of the smashing and burning of the sanctuary by the enemies, God is asked why the divine hand is held back (verse 11, see Isa 51:9). This leads to a remembrance in which several motifs found in this section of Isaiah appear:

Ps 74:12	But God is my king from of old,	*וֵאלֹהִים מַלְכִּי מִקֶּדֶם*
	working salvation in the midst of the earth.	פֹּעֵל *יְשׁוּעוֹת* בְּקֶרֶב הָאָרֶץ
74:13	You yourself split by your strength the Sea,	אַתָּה פוֹרַרְתָּ *בְעָזְּךָ יָם*
	you broke the heads of dragons on the waters.	שִׁבַּרְתָּ רָאשֵׁי *תַנִּינִים עַל־הַמָּיִם*
74:14	You yourself crushed the heads of Leviathan;	אַתָּה רִצַּצְתָּ רָאשֵׁי לִוְיָתָן
	You gave him as food for the sharks (?).	תִּתְּנֶנּוּ מַאֲכָל לְעָם לְצִיִּים
74:15	You yourself split open spring and stream,	אַתָּה בָקַעְתָּ מַעְיָן וָנָחַל
	You yourself dried up ever-flowing rivers.	אַתָּה הוֹבַשְׁתָּ נַהֲרוֹת אֵיתָן

Here appear several themes which reappear in a similar complex in Isaiah. The reign of God (וֵאלֹהִים מַלְכִּי, see Isa 52:7), once again described as ancient (מִקֶּדֶם, see Isa 51:9), is evidenced by divine strength over the sea (אַתָּה פוֹרַרְתָּ בְעָזְּךָ יָם, see Isa 51:9–10) and its dragons (תַנִּינִים, see Isa 51:9), by God's ability to provide water or to dry it (see Isa 51:10). Following this description of YHWH's former deeds, the psalmists discuss YHWH's established boundaries of day, night, summer and winter, and plead with YHWH to remember the scoffing of the enemy and the uproar of the adversaries, to "rise up, plead your cause" (קוּמָה אֱלֹהִים רִיבָה רִיבֶךָ, see Isa 51:22, in which YHWH is described as one who pleads for the people, יָרִיב עַמּוֹ).

Although Psalm 74 is, unlike Psalm 93, a lament rather than a celebration, the two psalms share major themes, both of them explicitly relating YHWH's kingship to victory over the sea. As Day pointed out, the correlation of these two themes occurs in Canaanite and Babylonian myths as well. Both Baal's victory over Yam and Nahar, and Marduk's victory over Tiamat, are followed by enthronement.[31] This section of Second Isaiah correlates these two themes as well, beginning with a reminder of YHWH's victory over watery enemies, and ending with a declaration of YHWH's kingship and a celebration of divine reign.

---

[31] Day, 19.

b) Psalm 77 is a lament employing first person singular pronouns and yet expressing communal concerns. This psalm explicitly invokes the crossing of the Red Sea as evidence of YHWH's ancient power. The psalmist remembers times past in terms very similar to those used in Isa 51:9 (עוּרִי כִּימֵי קֶדֶם דֹּרוֹת עוֹלָמִים):

Ps 77:6	I thought about the days of old,	חִשַּׁבְתִּי יָמִים מִקֶּדֶם
	years of long ago.	שְׁנוֹת עוֹלָמִים

After wondering whether YHWH will be angry forever, the psalmist returns to YHWH's deeds of old: "you displayed your strength (עֻזֶּךָ, 77:15, see Isa 51:9); you redeemed (גָּאַלְתָּ, 77:16, see Isa 51:10) your people with your arm (זְרוֹעַ, 77:16, see Isa 51:9)." The Red Sea is described anthropomorphically:

Ps 77:17	The waters saw you, God,	רָאוּךָ מַּיִם אֱלֹהִים
	the waters saw you and writhed;	רָאוּךָ מַּיִם יָחִילוּ
	the depths themselves trembled. . . .	אַף יִרְגְּזוּ תְהֹמוֹת
77:20	In the sea was your road,	בַּיָּם דַּרְכֶּךָ
	and your path in the mighty waters,	וּשְׁבִילְךָ בְּמַיִם רַבִּים
	but your footprints were unknown.	וְעִקְּבוֹתֶיךָ לֹא נֹדָעוּ
77:21	You led like sheep your people,	נָחִיתָ כַצֹּאן עַמֶּךָ
	by the hand of Moses and Aaron.	בְּיַד־מֹשֶׁה וְאַהֲרֹן

This description of YHWH's making a road in the water is very similar to that in Isa 51:10, in which YHWH's arm is identified as the one "making the depths of the sea a road for the redeemed to pass" (הַשָּׂמָה מַעֲמַקֵּי־יָם דֶּרֶךְ לַעֲבֹר גְּאוּלִים). Like the others, Psalm 77 combines motifs also found combined in Isa 51:9–10: the remembrance of times past, the redeeming strength of God's arm, and God's victory over the sea. Here it is not a battle that is suggested (although the sea anthropomorphically reacts as if afraid of battle, revealing a remnant of the mythological story), but the exodus crossing to the wilderness.

c) Psalm 89 is also echoed.[32] This psalm begins as a celebration of YHWH's majesty and of the derived majesty of God's chosen

---

[32] Day (92) argued for Second Isaiah's dependence on Psalm 89 here and in other parts of Second Isaiah. Ginsberg (153) also argued for this connection.

servant David. Only after thirty-eight verses of triumphant language does the psalm describe a new reality of divine rejection of the chosen. The attaching of lament to a previous song of victory enacts what other lament psalms only recall: the gulf between YHWH's victories in the past and YHWH's absence in the present. As before, it is the language of the past that dominates the recollection in Isaiah 51.

Psalm 89 begins with a celebration of YHWH's power, specifically described as the ability to "rule the raging of the sea" and to still its waves. Just as Isa 51:9 does, Psalm 89:11 combines in one verse motifs of YHWH's "strong arm" (זְרוֹעַ עֻזֶּךָ) and the piercing of Rahab (דִכִּאתָ כֶחָלָל רָהַב), following these quickly with proclamations of YHWH's creation of heaven and earth (see Isa 51:13):

Ps 89:11 You yourself crushed Rahab like one pierced; אַתָּה דִכִּאתָ כֶחָלָל רָהַב
with your strong arm you scattered
your enemies. בִּזְרוֹעַ עֻזְּךָ פִּזַּרְתָּ אוֹיְבֶיךָ
89:12 Yours are the heavens; yours also the earth, לְךָ שָׁמַיִם אַף־לְךָ אָרֶץ
the world and all that fills it— תֵּבֵל וּמְלֹאָהּ אַתָּה יְסַדְתָּם
you founded them.

References to the mythic battle with Rahab are quite rare, occurring otherwise only in Job 9:13 and 26:12. A cryptic line in Isa 30:7 (see also Ps 87:4) indicates a relationship between Rahab and the nation of Egypt. The reference is so brief that little of certainty can be learned from it. It should be noted, however, that the defeat of Rahab in Isa 51:9 is followed almost immediately by a reference to the story of the Israelites' exodus from Egypt.[33] Recollections of this psalm, with its very specific covenant language for David, will be noted in other parts of Second Isaiah as well.

---

[33] Day (88–92) and Wakeman (60) made more of this, understanding Rahab as a designation for Egypt that equates the defeat of Rahab with the defeat of Egypt in the crossing of the Red Sea. According to Day, "Rahab is both the monster defeated at creation and Egypt at the time of the Exodus and also, by implication, it may be argued, the thought is extended to Babylon at the time of the prophet himself" (92).

d) Finally, Psalm 44, a communal lament following a serious military defeat, begins with remembrance of YHWH's deeds on behalf of the people of Israel in days of old (בִּימֵי קֶדֶם, verse 2, see Isa 51:9), when YHWH's arm (זְרוֹעֲךָ, verse 4, see Isa 51:9, 52:10) gave victory (הוֹשִׁיעָה, verse 4, see Isa 52:7, 10). As in other lament psalms and as in Isa 52:7, God is declared both king and savior (אַתָּה־הוּא מַלְכִּי אֱלֹהִים צַוֵּה יְשׁוּעוֹת יַעֲקֹב, verse 5). Following these affirmations, the psalmists recount their complaints against YHWH for allowing, or rather orchestrating, their defeat and humiliation. They protest that they have not forgotten YHWH (לֹא שְׁכַחֲנוּךָ, verse 18, see Isa 51:13). The psalm ends with a plea to YHWH to awake (עוּרָה, verse 24, see Isa 51:9, 52:1), arise (קוּמָה, verse 27, see Isa 52:2), and ransom them (וּפְדֵנוּ, verse 27, see Isa 51:11).[34]

Of all the psalms cited here as connected with Isa 51:9–10, Psalm 44 is the only one lacking clear reference to YHWH's battle. In that light Day's suggested translation of 44:20 is interesting.[35] After the people protest innocence they claim, according to the MT, that YHWH "crushed us in the place of jackals" (דִכִּיתָנוּ בִּמְקוֹם תַּנִּים). On the basis of the use of the same verb for the crushing of Rahab in Psalm 89, and of other instances of confusion of תַּנִּים (jackals) with תַּנִּין (dragon), and in agreement with the Peshitta, Day suggested translating the phrase "crushed us instead of the dragon"—which, historicized, is a complaint that YHWH defeated Judah rather than its enemies. The presence of several other motifs normally surrounding the dragon's defeat, that is, YHWH's kingship, days of old, victory, and YHWH's arm, supports that reading.

From the above it is clear that Isa 51:9–10 condenses and combines key discourse of psalms lamenting public distress. This

---

[34] Patrick Miller (94) pointed out that the terminology עוּרָה (awake) and קוּמָה (arise) is common for stirring up battle in Israel's holy wars, used to call both Israel and YHWH to battle. A striking similarity can be seen with the repeated "awake, awake" in the song of Deborah (Judg 5:12).

[35] Day, 112.

language is quite distinct from that of Lamentations. Here YHWH's role as protector king is invoked. YHWH's past victory over watery forces is recalled repeatedly as the speakers seek analogous victories in the present. YHWH's strong arm is emphasized, and YHWH is bid to arise or awake. Verbs such as "redeem" or "ransom" are used to describe God's action on behalf of Israel. The common element submerged in this language is the question of YHWH's reign over the unruly forces of the political universe.

Isaiah 51:9–10 not only shares all these major elements but has compacted them into five extremely dense and referential lines.[36] The genre of appeal to YHWH on the basis of mythological deeds is appropriated to express a prayer which not only sounds familiar to the audience but also guides them toward the poet's formulations of the present. By invoking both the divine conflict myth and the exodus story in which that myth was presented on the political level, Second Isaiah taps into Judah's "imaginative matrix," the "texts-in-the-mind" that provide the community's shared self-understanding, enabling them to view the present moment in terms of typologically similar memories. Framing the language in terms of these longings for YHWH's reign over unruly forces, the poet positions the audience to view the directive to leave Babylon not as one person's impulsive suggestion, but as God's answer to long-spoken prayers. The call to leave Babylon, when it comes in chapter 52, will be seen as an even more glorious exodus than the first: not only an answer to the prayers of a remembering community, but a transposition into a new key of God's recognized dealings with Judah.

Jeremiah's Vision of Restoration

The prophet's recollection of a major verse in Jeremiah's book of consolation, in which God's faithfulness to Israel is envisioned as enduring like the cosmos itself, has already been investigated.

---

[36] Day (22) noted that the references to the myth in Psalms 89 and 74 and in Isaiah 51 clearly indicate that the mythology was already "well established in pre-exilic Israel."

Another prominent reutilization of language from that same chapter occurs in Isaiah 51:11.[37] In Jeremiah 31:11–13, redemption for the scattered people is envisioned:

Jer 31:11	For YHWH has ransomed Jacob,	כִּי־פָדָה יְהוָה אֶת־יַעֲקֹב
	and has redeemed him from a hand	וּגְאָלוֹ מִיַּד
	too strong for him.	חָזָק מִמֶּנּוּ
31:12	And they will come and sing out	וּבָאוּ וְרִנְּנוּ
	on the height of Zion,	בִמְרוֹם־צִיּוֹן
	and be radiant over the goodness of YHWH,	וְנָהֲרוּ אֶל־טוּב יְהוָה
	Over the grain, and over the wine,	עַל־דָּגָן וְעַל־תִּירֹשׁ
	and over the oil,	וְעַל־יִצְהָר
	and over the children of flock and herd.	וְעַל־בְּנֵי־צֹאן וּבָקָר
	Their life will be like a watered garden,	וְהָיְתָה נַפְשָׁם כְּגַן רָוֶה
	and they will not languish any more.	וְלֹא־יוֹסִיפוּ לְדַאֲבָה עוֹד
31:13	Then the young women will rejoice	
	in a dance,	אָז תִּשְׂמַח בְּתוּלָה בְּמָחוֹל
	and the young men and old men together.	וּבַחֻרִים וּזְקֵנִים יַחְדָּו
	I will turn their mourning into joy,	וְהָפַכְתִּי אֶבְלָם לְשָׂשׂוֹן
	and I will comfort them, and I will	וְנִחַמְתִּים
	give them gladness for groaning.	וְשִׂמַּחְתִּים מִיגוֹנָם

Many of the terms in which Jeremiah imagines this redemption are echoed in the prayer in Isa 51:11 and the lines immediately before and after it:

Isa 51:10	Are you not she, the one drying the sea,	הֲלוֹא אַתְּ־הִיא הַמַּחֲרֶבֶת יָם
	the waters of the great deep,	מֵי תְּהוֹם רַבָּה
	the one making the depths of the sea a road	הַשָּׂמָה מַעֲמַקֵּי־יָם דֶּרֶךְ
	for the redeemed to pass?	לַעֲבֹר גְּאוּלִים
51:11	Then let the ransomed of YHWH return	וּפְדוּיֵי יְהוָה יְשׁוּבוּן
	and come to Zion with singing,	וּבָאוּ צִיּוֹן בְּרִנָּה
	and everlasting gladness on their head.	וְשִׂמְחַת עוֹלָם עַל־רֹאשָׁם
	Let joy and gladness overtake them;	שָׂשׂוֹן וְשִׂמְחָה יַשִּׂיגוּן
	let suffering and groaning flee.	נָסוּ יָגוֹן וַאֲנָחָה
51:12	I, I am he, your comforter . . .	אָנֹכִי אָנֹכִי הוּא מְנַחֶמְכֶם

Not only is an abundance of terms from the Jeremiah passage clustered together, but they occur in the same sequence: "ransom"

[37] Paul, 108; Eldridge, 144–45.

and "redeem"; "come to Zion with singing"; "joy," "gladness," and "groaning"; YHWH's "comfort." The close correspondence of expressions by which the hope for return is articulated has led readers for many generations to recognize an unmistakable relationship between these two texts. In fact, it is similarity to Isa 51:11 that has caused many to insist that this section of Jeremiah imitates Second Isaiah.[38] However, as I show in the appendix, Jer 31:11–13 is no less a part of Jeremiah's style of discourse, and no less indebted to the earlier words of Hosea, than the other passages around it are. Linguistic links between the two passages are far more likely to have resulted from Second Isaiah's having appropriated for the opportune historical moment Jeremiah's expectations for the future, than to have been created fresh by Second Isaiah, and subsequently blended with Jeremiah's own themes and terms to create a belated word of consolation about a future already in sight.

Whether the Isaiah passage should be translated in the jussive is difficult to determine on the basis of grammar. Since the previous two verses are presented as human supplication, and there is no indication yet that YHWH has answered, the more natural reading in context is that verse 11 is the prayer to which the previous verses have been leading. The original audience, however, would not have been forced to choose between indicative and jussive—both readings would have been available simultaneously. Joining the lament psalms' appeals to the past with prophetic expectations of the future, the poet both echoes exilic prayer and directs it toward a particular hope already available, courtesy of Jeremiah, to public imagination, formulating the request to suit the response which the poet will subsequently assert that YHWH is making.

YHWH's voice answers immediately in verse 12 and continues for the rest of the section. The direct quotation of Jer 31:35, discussed above, occurs near the end, referring the audience to

---

[38] See for instance Carroll, *Jeremiah*, 569 and 593–94; Holladay, 185; D. R. Jones, *Jeremiah*, NCB (Grand Rapids, MI: Eerdmans, 1992) 389, and many others.

Jeremiah's pledge that YHWH who controls the natural world will protect the nation's future, that is, will enforce once again Zion's security. This reference is surrounded by several phrases recalling language typical of, though not always exclusive to, Jeremiah. YHWH's initial self-identification as comforter in verse 12 is followed by a series of rhetorical questions. The audience is accused of forgetting YHWH (תִּשְׁכַּח יְהוָה, verse 13, a very prevalent theme in Jeremiah; see Jer 2:32, 3:21, 13:25, 18:15, and 23:27). This YHWH they have forgotten is their maker, who stretched out the heavens (עֹשֶׂךָ נוֹטֶה שָׁמַיִם, verse 13, see Jer 10:12: עֹשֵׂה אֶרֶץ בְּכֹחוֹ...וּבִתְבוּנָתוֹ נָטָה שָׁמָיִם). Accusing the audience of fearing the oppressor (הַמֵּצִיק, verse 13) from whom YHWH is about to rescue them, the poet uses a term which is extremely rare in the Bible, but which echoes a phrase repeated three times in Deuteronomy and once in Jeremiah, in which the term appears as both noun and verb: בְּמָצוֹר וּבְמָצוֹק אֲשֶׁר יָצִיק לְךָ אֹיְבֶךָ, "in the siege and in the oppression with which your enemies will oppress you," see Deut 28:53, 55, 57; Jer 19:9.[39] Quick release, rescue from death in the pit, and plenty of bread are assured. As the passage concludes, the quotation of Jer 31:35 is followed by two phrases which combine "I have put my words in your mouth" (וָאָשִׂים דְּבָרַי בְּפִיךָ, see Jer 1:9: נָתַתִּי דְבָרַי בְּפִיךָ, "I have put my words in your mouth") with "in the shadow of my hand I have hidden you" (see Isa 49:2 and its discussion in chapter 4), and then a repetition of the creation language "stretching out the heavens, founding the earth" (לִנְטֹעַ שָׁמַיִם וְלִיסֹד אָרֶץ, see above and Jer 10:12: עֹשֵׂה אֶרֶץ...נָטָה שָׁמָיִם), culminating in YHWH's affirmation to Zion, "my people you are."

Anchored by direct allusions to Jeremiah's consoling words near its beginning and end, this passage displays rich familiarity with a broad range of language known from the prophet. By partaking of such speech, Second Isaiah both declares loyalty to the prophetic

[39] In all four of these instances the authors insist that that the siege will lead people to eat their own children—a subject that will not be far away from the poetry that follows in Isaiah.

tradition and leads it in a new direction. While acknowledging the sin of forgetting, Second Isaiah applies it differently. It is no longer an accusation for which they will be punished, but an obstacle to faith that the prophet attempts to overcome, reminding the audience that God who once rescued their ancestors from Egypt, who created and controls all that is, whose call to a particular people is intimately attached to creation of all the world, has renewed their vocation as God's chosen: "My people you are."

Lamentations 1 and the Comforter

The prophet's propensity to blend references to disparate texts, which was noted already in Isa 52:1 and 8, can be seen in this section as well, in a third layer of language to be distinguished in these verses. Once again a longer section from a precursor text reappears in a more condensed form:

Lam	Bitterly she weeps in the night,	בָּכוֹ תִבְכֶּה בַּלַּיְלָה
1:2	and her tears are on her cheeks.	וְדִמְעָתָהּ עַל לֶחֱיָהּ
	There is no comforter for her	אֵין־לָהּ **מְנַחֵם**
	among all who love her.	מִכָּל־אֹהֲבֶיהָ
	All her friends betrayed her;	כָּל־רֵעֶיהָ בָּגְדוּ בָהּ
	they became her enemies.	הָיוּ לָהּ לְאֹיְבִים
1:3	Judah has gone into exile with affliction	גָּלְתָה יְהוּדָה מֵעֹנִי
	and great labor.	וּמֵרֹב עֲבֹדָה
	She has dwelt among the nations,	הִיא יָשְׁבָה בַגּוֹיִם
	she has found no resting place.	לֹא מָצְאָה מָנוֹחַ
	All her pursuers have overtaken her	כָּל־רֹדְפֶיהָ **הִשִּׂיגוּהָ**
	in narrow straits.	בֵּין הַמְּצָרִים
1:4	Zion's roads are mourning	דַּרְכֵי צִיּוֹן אֲבֵלוֹת
	with lack of festival travelers.	מִבְּלִי בָּאֵי מוֹעֵד
	All her gates are desolate;	כָּל־שְׁעָרֶיהָ שׁוֹמֵמִין
	her priests groan.	כֹּהֲנֶיהָ **נֶאֱנָחִים**
	Her virgins suffer,	בְּתוּלֹתֶיהָ **נוּגוֹת**
	and she—it is bitter for her.	וְהִיא מַר־לָהּ

Drawing contrasts, Isaiah 51 now says:

Isa 51:11	Then let the ransomed of YHWH return	וּפְדוּיֵי יְהוָה יְשׁוּבוּן
	and come to Zion with singing,	וּבָאוּ צִיּוֹן בְּרִנָּה
	and everlasting gladness on their head.	וְשִׂמְחַת עוֹלָם עַל־רֹאשָׁם
	Let joy and gladness overtake them;	שָׂשׂוֹן וְשִׂמְחָה *יַשִּׂיגוּן*
	let suffering and groaning flee.	נָסוּ *יָגוֹן וַאֲנָחָה*
51:12	I, I am he, your comforter.	אָנֹכִי אָנֹכִי הוּא ***מְנַחֶמְכֶם***
	Who are you that you fear the human who will die,	מִי־אַתְּ וַתִּירְאִי מֵאֱנוֹשׁ יָמוּת
	the mortal who will fade like grass. . . .	וּמִבֶּן־אָדָם חָצִיר יִנָּתֵן

The centrality in Lamentations 1 of the theme of Zion's having no comforter (Lam 1:2, 9, 16, 17, 21) has already been discussed above in relation to Isa 52:9. There the many repetitions throughout Second Isaiah of the counter-claim of Zion's comfort were noted. Of all the affirmations of this theme, the emphatic announcement in Isa 51:12, "I, I am he, your comforter," is the most dramatic in terms of its speaker, its placement, and its syntax. Placed in YHWH's mouth, directly after lament-styled pleas for divine answer, its three pronouns where one would have sufficed echoing the question asked twice of YHWH's arm in 51:9–10, "Are you not she?", the language dramatically signals the end of divine silence and the beginning of comfort that has been foreseen already in Isa 40:1, 49:13, and 51:3.

So placed, the statement enacts a divine response not only to the lament questions posed in Isa 51:9–10, but also, and more pointedly, to the complaints of "no comforter" (אֵין מְנַחֵם) that Lamentations had left starkly unanswered. The availability of the lament to Second Isaiah's community is hardly in doubt, and is supported by the use of Lam 4:15 and 17 in Isaiah 52. The masculine singular piel participial form of נחם which is used here is nearly unique to Lamentations 1 and to this verse. As the lament's most repeated, most memorable word, it reverberates in Second Isaiah's recollection, which coheres precisely as counterpoint and answer.

Once this recollection is recognized, it can also be seen that verse 11 calls for the reversal of specific conditions described in the same lament: Whereas Judah had once gone into exile (Lam 1:3), and the roads to Zion mourned (1:4), Second Isaiah prays for the exiles' return, for roads filled with celebration (Isa 51:11).[40] Whereas once pursuers overtook Zion (הִשִּׂיגוּהָ, Lam 1:3), now the poet prays that joy and gladness will overtake those returning (יַשִּׂיגוּן, Isa 51:11). Whereas once YHWH imposed suffering (נוּגוֹת, Lam 1:4) and groaning (נֶאֱנָחִים, Lam 1:4), now, the poet prays, let suffering and groaning flee (נָסוּ יָגוֹן וַאֲנָחָה, Isa 51:11).[41]

Whereas Lamentations 1 drew attention to the sorrow of the city and her inhabitants, and Jeremiah 31 foresaw a reversal of that sorrow, here the poet prays that the terms of the reversal come into effect now. Then, as if moved by the prayer stressing the contrast between what is and what is desired, YHWH's own voice breaks in, changing everything. Zion does indeed have a comforter—none other than YHWH. The assertion "I, I am he, your comforter" (Isa 51:12) could not be more precisely aimed not only at the question formulated in Isa 51:9–10 to anticipate this announcement, but more importantly at Zion's bitter plight articulated in Lamentations 1.

Immediately following this answer to the heart of lament prayer, several verses draw a sharp contrast between YHWH, who made heaven and earth (verse 13, see verse 16), and Jerusalem's human enemy, a distinction that will continue through chapter 52. The idea that YHWH is on Judah's side stands in great tension with other interpretations of Jerusalem's destruction, including those shared by Jeremiah and Lamentations, as well as by Second Isaiah itself. Isaiah 42:24–25 explicitly attributes the nation's destruction to YHWH's anger, and in Isa 43:28 YHWH announces, "I delivered Jacob to utter destruction and Israel to reviling."[42] Furthermore, both of the other sections on Daughter Zion also portray YHWH

---

[40] Newsom, 76.

[41] Turner, 201.

[42] It should be noted that both of these passages, as well as Isa 43:1–2 in which YHWH promises to protect Israel from further harm, echo Lam 2:2–4 closely. Both Lamentations and Second Isaiah portray YHWH's destructive anger as a raging fire burning Israel. While the lament depicts YHWH as the enemy, the prophet blames the people who did not walk in God's ways.

reflecting on this rejection of Jerusalem (see Isa 50:1 and 54:7–8). Nevertheless, here YHWH quite distinctly claims the positive role of comforter, over against the human destroyers. Important reasons for distancing YHWH from past violence will become clear as the section progresses into Second Isaiah's most explicit representation of Jerusalem's losses.

Summary

In the first four verses of this section, Isa 51:9–12, three distinct types of language are represented, all of them in one way or another formulations that attempt to organize, protest against, and find hope in the midst of the disaster that befell Jerusalem. Psalmic language of lament presupposes a God who once acted creatively, and though currently dormant retains the power to act again, if so persuaded. This understanding of YHWH, presented at the beginning and subsequently echoed in the opening verse of each subsection, undergirds the structure of Isa 51:9–52:12 as a whole. By contrast, and not without some tension with the lament psalms, Jeremiah and Lamentations both envision a God who did in fact act—acted not creatively, but destructively, to punish. In their understanding it is not YHWH's inaction but YHWH's action that brought Jerusalem to its present condition. Jeremiah's role as prophet meant casting hopeful visions in the form of assurances rather than prayers, and these assurances are invoked in Second Isaiah's language. These reassurances prepare for the more difficult task facing the poet, the task of joining with, and overthrowing, the most pain-filled language of all, the language of Lamentations. In this language, it was YHWH who acted as enemy, so there could be no comforter, and the only source of hope was the lamenters' ability to call by name, and thus to defy, what had befallen them. It is this language of deepest anguish, introduced in the first portion, with which Second Isaiah reckons in Isa 51:17–23, the second portion of this section.

Recollections in Isaiah 51:17–23: Defusing Lamentations 4

The second panel of the "Awake, awake" triptych shares two major themes with the descriptions of Jerusalem in the book of Lamentations, especially in the fourth chapter: the wrath of YHWH and the children of Zion. Clearly these are two themes very difficult to combine in the same discussion because their juxtaposition raises innumerable questions about the justice of YHWH's wrath. For the lament to articulate the problems is to lay bare a grievance virtually unaddressable: what is there to say "in the presence of the burning children"?[43] For Second Isaiah to attempt a response to this grievance is to tackle a nearly insurmountable theological and, consequently, rhetorical, problem.

I have already noted, through Second Isaiah's direct quotation of Lam 4:15 in Isa 52:11, that Lamentations 4 was known by the poet, and that Second Isaiah displays an interest in recalling and reconfiguring its language. Linkages between that lament and Isa 51:17–23 are not so copious as to remind audiences of the whole of that poetry's brutality, but they are repetitive enough to suggest to hearers that Second Isaiah is aware of, and sympathetic with, its concerns.[44] At the same time, Second Isaiah's message presses to move on from the lament, to blaze a trail by which those who knew the worst of Jerusalem's sorrows could move from alienation and despair to hopeful envisionment. This is a delicate operation: to dwell on the lament too much might raise indignant and even insurmountable objections concerning YHWH's violent excesses.

---

43 According to Irving Greenberg's principle for discourse after the Shoah, "No statement, theological or otherwise, should be made that would not be credible in the presence of the burning children." ("Cloud of Smoke, Pillar of Fire: Judaism, Christianity, and Modernity after the Holocaust," in *Auschwitz: Beginning of a New Era?*, ed. Eva Fleischner, New York: Ktav Publishing House, 1977, 23).

44 Westermann (*Lamentations*, 104) affirmed a close intertextual relationship between this section of Second Isaiah and Lamentations: "The laments which appear in Deutero-Isaiah's announcement of salvation so closely resemble the material in Lamentations that the latter is almost certainly presupposed in the former. This can be seen, for example, in the case of Isa 51:17b–20."

On the other hand, to minimize the destruction and its effects would risk never engaging those most moved by the events of recent history. Accordingly, Second Isaiah both invokes and rings changes on the structure as well as the emphases of Lamentations 4. In order to recognize the effect of Second Isaiah here it is necessary to look more closely at the lament.

Children and YHWH's Wrath in Lamentations 4

The fourth lament opens with the disturbing image of children lying scattered "at the head of every street":

Lam	How the gold is darkened,	אֵיכָה יוּעַם זָהָב
4:1	how the pure gold has changed!	יִשְׁנֶא הַכֶּתֶם הַטּוֹב
	The sacred stones are poured out	תִּשְׁתַּפֵּכְנָה אַבְנֵי־קֹדֶשׁ
	at the head of every street.	**בְּרֹאשׁ כָּל־חוּצוֹת**
4:2	The precious children of Zion,	**בְּנֵי צִיּוֹן** הַיְקָרִים
	who were valued as gold—	הַמְסֻלָּאִים בַּפָּז
	how they are reckoned as clay pots,	אֵיכָה נֶחְשְׁבוּ לְנִבְלֵי־חֶרֶשׂ
	the work of a potter's hands!	מַעֲשֵׂה יְדֵי יוֹצֵר

The phrase בְּרֹאשׁ כָּל־חוּצוֹת, always used of children, and always used to describe the extremity of disaster, is shared with Lam 2:19 and Nah 3:10. From this distance it is difficult to judge whether the phrase was a typical lament formulation, or whether it passed from Nahum to one or both of the laments. Clearly it has a history associated with the worst imaginable depictions of disaster: in Nahum's formulation it is the infants of Thebes who have been "dashed in pieces at the head of every street." By comparison, the lament puts it rather delicately, substituting "sacred stones" at first for the children, and leaving the audience to infer what those who value children as clay pots are doing (neglecting? shattering? pouring out?).

This delicacy only invites audiences further in for further pain. Language about the children's fate grows in horror from verse 1 to verse 10. The children are not being cared for by their parents (verse 3); no one shares bread with them (verse 4); they are searching ash heaps for food (verse 5); beautiful princes, compared with sapphire and coral, are now shriveled and unrecognizable (verses 7–8); they would have fared better dying by the sword (verse 9); in fact, their own mothers are eating them (verse 10). The first half of the lament concludes its litany of particular vignettes of death with a summary of YHWH's role. These perversions happened not by chance nor by divine neglect or incompetence but by design: the slaughter of the innocents resulted from YHWH's burning anger, which devoured Zion's foundations. The last two verses of the litany and the dreadful conclusion state:

Lam	Those pierced by sword were better off	טוֹבִים הָיוּ חַלְלֵי־חֶרֶב
4:9	than those pierced by famine,	מֵחַלְלֵי רָעָב
	whose life drained away,	שֶׁהֵם יָזוּבוּ מְדֻקָּרִים
	far from the produce of the field.	מִתְּנוּבֹת שָׂדָי
4:10	The hands of compassionate women	יְדֵי נָשִׁים רַחֲמָנִיּוֹת
	boiled their own children;	בִּשְּׁלוּ יַלְדֵיהֶן
	they became their food	הָיוּ לְבָרוֹת לָמוֹ
	in the destruction of my poor people.	בְּשֶׁבֶר בַּת־עַמִּי
4:11	YHWH carried his wrath to completion,	כִּלָּה יְהוָה אֶת־חֲמָתוֹ
	poured out the heat of his anger.	שָׁפַךְ חֲרוֹן אַפּוֹ
	And he kindled a fire in Zion,	וַיַּצֶּת־אֵשׁ בְּצִיּוֹן
	and it devoured her foundations.	וַתֹּאכַל יְסוֹדֹתֶיהָ

Now attention shifts to the adult population in and around Zion. The world's rulers did not believe Zion could be breached (verse 12). Blame for the death of the innocents is laid on prophets and priests (verse 13), who are now so defiled that they are treated among the nations as lepers (verses 14–15). Not even priests and elders are honored (verse 16). In verse 17 the voice becomes plural, as if all the victims who have been seen now speak in one voice: "Our eyes wore themselves out—for our help, in vain, from our watchpost we were watching. . . ." The pursuit and capture of "YHWH's anointed" is vividly described (verse 19–20). YHWH is never addressed, not even in the final call for vengeance. Rather, in the penultimate verse, the collective voice addresses Daughter Edom, threatening that Zion's "cup" will transfer to her. In the final two verses, YHWH's actions from verse 11 are reversed as the futures of Daughters Zion and Edom are laid out in close antithetical parallel, punning on the dual meaning of גלה:

Lam 4:21	Rejoice and be glad, Daughter Edom,	שִׂישִׂי וְשִׂמְחִי בַּת־אֱדוֹם
	living in the land of Uz.	יוֹשֶׁבֶת בְּאֶרֶץ עוּץ
	To you also the cup will pass—	גַּם־עָלַיִךְ תַּעֲבָר־**כּוֹס**
	you will become drunk and strip yourself bare.	**תִּשְׁכְּרִי** וְתִתְעָרִי
4:22	Your iniquity, Daughter Zion, is expiated;	תַּם־עֲוֹנֵךְ בַּת־צִיּוֹן
	he will not continue to exile you.	לֹא יוֹסִיף לְהַגְלוֹתֵךְ
	Your iniquity, Daughter Edom, he has punished;	פָּקַד עֲוֹנֵךְ בַּת־אֱדוֹם
	he will lay bare your sins.	גִּלָּה עַל־חַטֹּאתָיִךְ

Children and YHWH's Wrath in Isaiah 51:17–23

The second portion of the "awake awake" section, Isa 51:17–23, also dwells at length on the theme of the fate of Jerusalem's children, connecting it, as the lament did, with the theme of YHWH's wrath. In Second Isaiah these two major themes are arranged in a ring pattern, one enclosed within the other. The outside ring, verses 17 and 21–23, focuses on YHWH's wrath, and the inner ring, verses 18–20 focuses on Zion's children.

YHWH's wrath is described by the image of the cup of wrath (כּוֹס חֲמָתוֹ), the same imagery invoked in (though not original to) Lam 4:21–22, in which enemy Daughter Edom is warned that she too will drink of this cup and become drunk. Here it is Daughter Zion herself who has drained the cup and is drunk with sorrow, but who is promised in the end, as in the end of the lament, that the cup will be taken from her hands and given to her enemies:

Isa 51:17	Wake yourself, wake yourself,	הִתְעוֹרְרִי הִתְעוֹרְרִי
	rise up, Jerusalem,	קוּמִי יְרוּשָׁלַםִ
	who has drunk from YHWH's hand	אֲשֶׁר שָׁתִית מִיַּד *יְהוָה*
	the cup of his wrath.	**אֶת־כּוֹס חֲמָתוֹ**
	The goblet of reeling	אֶת־קֻבַּעַת **כּוֹס** הַתַּרְעֵלָה
	you have drunk, you have drained . . .	שָׁתִית מָצִית
51:21	Therefore hear this, afflicted one,	לָכֵן שִׁמְעִי־נָא זֹאת עֲנִיָּה
	drunk, but not from wine:	**וּשְׁכֻרַת** וְלֹא מִיָּיִן

51:22	Thus says your Lord YHWH,	כֹּה־אָמַר אֲדֹנַיִךְ יְהוָה
	your God, who will contend for his people,	וֵאלֹהַיִךְ יָרִיב עַמּוֹ
	See, I have taken from your hand	הִנֵּה לָקַחְתִּי מִיָּדֵךְ
	the cup of reeling,	אֶת־כּוֹס הַתַּרְעֵלָה
	The goblet of my wrath	אֶת־קֻבַּעַת כּוֹס חֲמָתִי
	you will no longer drink.	לֹא־תוֹסִיפִי לִשְׁתּוֹתָהּ עוֹד
51:23	But I will put it into the hand	וְשַׂמְתִּיהָ בְּיַד־מוֹגַיִךְ
	of your tormentors . . .	

The imagery of drinking wrath and becoming drunk is that used in the lament. But whereas the lament described the consequences of YHWH's wrath in concrete terms, describing the physical states of individual members of the population, these individuals have been subsumed in Second Isaiah under the metaphor of the representative Daughter Zion. Even her suffering is not visualized concretely, but only as the imagined drinking of a cup. So while the imagery is quite vivid, as the metaphorical action of a metaphorical figure it is expressed in a way that removes attention from concrete realities either past or present.

The sorrow from which Daughter Zion suffers is examined in verses 18–20, which presents the other major theme: the suffering of the children. In these three verses, themes from throughout the first half of Lamentations 4 are glimpsed, till at the end the children's fate is directly—though only momentarily—connected with YHWH's fierce activity. These verses begin with an assertion echoing with suspicious imprecision the assertions of "no comforter" in Lamentations 1, catching their cadance, syntax, and sound, but substituting a different verb. Instead of "no comforter," אֵין מְנַחֵם לָהּ (Lam 1:9), this section begins with אֵין־מְנַהֵל לָהּ, "no guide" suggesting that Zion's suffering was exacerbated not by YHWH's absence but by her lack of human leadership. Parent-child roles are reversed as the "mother," rather than her children, is pictured needing care:

Isa	There is no one to guide her	אֵין־מְנַהֵל לָהּ
51:18	among all the children she bore,	מִכָּל־בָּנִים יָלָדָה
	and there is no one to grasp her hand	וְאֵין מַחֲזִיק בְּיָדָהּ
	among all the children she raised.	מִכָּל־בָּנִים גִּדֵּלָה

51:19	These two things have happened to you	שְׁתַּיִם הֵנָּה קֹרְאֹתַיִךְ
	—who will grieve over you?	מִי יָנוּד לָךְ
	—devastation and destruction and famine and sword	הַשֹּׁד **וְהַשֶּׁבֶר וְהָרָעָב וְהַחֶרֶב**
	—how shall I comfort you?	מִי אֲנַחֲמֵךְ
51:20	Your children fainted;	בָּנַיִךְ עֻלְּפוּ
	they lay at the head of every street	שָׁכְבוּ **בְּרֹאשׁ כָּל־חוּצוֹת**
	like an antelope in a net,	כְּתוֹא מִכְמָר
	filled with the wrath of YHWH,	הַמְלֵאִים **חֲמַת־יְהוָה**
	the rebuke of your God.	גַּעֲרַת אֱלֹהָיִךְ

Of all the children Jerusalem bore (בָּנִים יָלָדָה, Isa 51:18, see Lam 4:10), none is left. By famine and sword (הָרָעָב וְהַחֶרֶב, Isa 51:19, see Lam 4:9) they have suffered destruction (שֶׁבֶר, Isa 51:19, see Lam 4:10), and were scattered "at the head of every street" (בְּרֹאשׁ כָּל־חוּצוֹת, Isa 51:20, see Lam 4:1), filled with "the wrath of YHWH" (חֲמַת־יְהוָה, Isa 51:20, see Lam 4:11).

Clear continuities exist between the many specific images in the lament and those in Second Isaiah. As in the lament, the children lie in the street and are no more; destruction, famine, and sword have prevailed. As in the lament, so here, God's consuming wrath is pictured as "YHWH's cup," which makes its drinker drunk with suffering. Both texts claim that YHWH's wrath against Jerusalem is spent, but against her enemies it has just begun.

But distinct discontinuities are distinguishable in Second Isaiah's softening and depersonalizing of the lament's brutal language. Whereas the lament described the death of the children explicitly several times (verses 5, 9, and 10), this death remains only indirectly expressed in Second Isaiah. The lament discussed cannibalism, but Second Isaiah only suggests loss. The lament described YHWH's wrath as having been carried to completion. Second Isaiah' strongest statement about YHWH's wrath is contained by a displacing metaphor, preceded by indications that it is already over:

Isa	Wake yourself, wake yourself,	הִתְעוֹרְרִי הִתְעוֹרְרִי
51:17	rise up, Jerusalem,	קוּמִי יְרוּשָׁלַםִ
	who has drunk from YHWH's hand	אֲשֶׁר שָׁתִית מִיַּד יְהוָה
	the cup of his wrath.	אֶת־כּוֹס חֲמָתוֹ
	The goblet of reeling	אֶת־קֻבַּעַת כּוֹס הַתַּרְעֵלָה
	you have drunk, you have drained.	שָׁתִית מָצִית

Most significantly of all, while the speaker in the lament was appalled at the suffering of the children, in Second Isaiah their own suffering is no longer the focus, but rather the suffering of their "mother," Zion, a representative figure who has taken the place of flesh-and-blood people, both parents and children. It is not these people, but Zion, who has drained the cup, who lacks care and guidance, who needs mourners and comforters, and who is finally promised an end to her suffering. The children of Zion who in the lament have been destroyed do not, in Second Isaiah, stay dead: rather, in chapters 49 and 54, it is the returning exiles who are called Zion's "children." By displacing the locus of suffering from the children to Zion, Second Isaiah sets the stage for envisioning the comfort of comfortless Zion in the form of the return of the exilic community. Recalling concerns articulated in Lamentations 4 just enough in this section to capture and subtly alter its emphases, Second Isaiah prepares now to offer its full answer to exilic lament complaints.

Recollections in Isaiah 52:1–2: The Restoration of Daughter Zion

Besides the "cup of wrath" which was repeated so frequently in the second portion of the section, another prevailing theme of destruction in lament literature is abasement, often expressed in terms of physical disgrace such as being raped, being thrown to the ground, or sitting in the dust. The last verse of the middle portion puts into the mouths of Jerusalem's enemies a brief reminder of this image:

Isa	. . . who said to you,	אֲשֶׁר־אָמְרוּ לְנַפְשֵׁךְ
51:23	"Bow down, and let us pass.	שְׁחִי וְנַעֲבֹרָה
	Make your back like the ground,	וַתָּשִׂימִי כָאָרֶץ גֵּוֵךְ
	and like the street for those passing through."	וְכַחוּץ לַעֹבְרִים

This imagery, which Second Isaiah shares very fully with Lamentations, becomes in the third portion of the "awake awake" triptych the guiding metaphor of Zion's restoration. In order to recognize all that Second Isaiah does with this imagery, it is important to backtrack briefly not only into Lamentations, but also into a previous portion of Second Isaiah, chapter 47, which calls down a similar fate on Daughter Zion's enemy and counterpart, Daughter Babylon.

Imagery of Humiliation in Lamentations

Imagery of disgrace is shared by Lamentations 1, 2, and 3. Lamentations 1:8–10 exemplifies one complex of related metaphors suggested by such downward movement: here Zion's fall is associated with sexual imagery suggestive of rape:

Lam	Jerusalem sinned terribly;	חֵטְא חָטְאָה יְרוּשָׁלִַם
1:8	therefore she has become an impurity.	עַל־כֵּן לְנִידָה הָיָתָה
	All who honored her despise her,	כָּל־מְכַבְּדֶיהָ הִזִּילוּהָ
	for they have seen her nakedness.	כִּי־**רָאוּ עֶרְוָתָהּ**
	She herself groans,	גַּם־הִיא נֶאֶנְחָה
	and turns away.	וַתָּשָׁב אָחוֹר
1:9	Her uncleanness was in her skirts;	**טֻמְאָתָהּ** בְּשׁוּלֶיהָ
	she did not remember her end.	**לֹא זָכְרָה אַחֲרִיתָהּ**
	And she fell extraordinarily—	**וַתֵּרֶד פְּלָאִים**
	she has no comforter.	אֵין מְנַחֵם לָהּ
	"See, YHWH, my suffering,	רְאֵה יְהוָה אֶת־עָנְיִי
	for the enemy is exalted!"	כִּי הִגְדִּיל אוֹיֵב
1:10	The foe spread out his hand	יָדוֹ פָּרַשׂ צָר
	over all her delights;	עַל כָּל־מַחֲמַדֶּיהָ
	for she saw nations—	כִּי־רָאֲתָה גוֹיִם
	they came into her sanctuary—	**בָּאוּ מִקְדָּשָׁהּ**
	those of whom you commanded, "they shall not come	אֲשֶׁר צִוִּיתָה **לֹא־יָבֹאוּ**
	into your assembly."	בַקָּהָל לָךְ

Lamentations 2 begins with the picture of Daughter Zion's having been thrown to the ground by YHWH:

Lam	How the Lord in his anger	אֵיכָה יָעִיב בְּאַפּוֹ
2:1	has humiliated Daughter Zion!	אֲדֹנָי אֶת־**בַּת־צִיּוֹן**
	He threw from heaven to earth	הִשְׁלִיךְ מִשָּׁמַיִם אֶרֶץ
	the splendor of Israel!	**תִּפְאֶרֶת** יִשְׂרָאֵל
	And he did not remember his footstool	וְלֹא־זָכַר הֲדֹם־רַגְלָיו
	in the day of his anger.	בְּיוֹם אַפּוֹ

After several verses of describing YHWH's destructive wrath against Zion, the lament describes the reaction of the city's citizens, who also sit in humiliation:

Lam	They sit on the ground, they are silent,	**יֵשְׁבוּ לָאָרֶץ יִדְּמוּ**
2:10	the elders of daughter Zion,	זִקְנֵי **בַת־צִיּוֹן**
	They have thrown dust on their heads,	הֶעֱלוּ **עָפָר** עַל־רֹאשָׁם
	they have put on sackcloth;	חָגְרוּ שַׂקִּים
	They bow their heads to the ground,	**הוֹרִידוּ לָאָרֶץ** רֹאשָׁן
	the virgins of Jerusalem.	**בְּתוּלֹת יְרוּשָׁלָםִ**

The picture of humiliation in Lamentations 3 uses very similar language—of silence, of sitting, of bowing down toward the dust:

Lam	He will sit alone and be silent	**יֵשֵׁב** בָּדָד **וְיִדֹּם**
3:28	when it is heavy upon him.	כִּי נָטַל עָלָיו
3:29	He will put his mouth to the dust—	יִתֵּן **בֶּעָפָר** פִּיהוּ
	perhaps there is hope.	אוּלַי יֵשׁ תִּקְוָה
3:30	He will give to his attacker the cheek;	יִתֵּן לְמַכֵּהוּ לֶחִי
	he will be filled up with insult.	יִשְׂבַּע בְּחֶרְפָּה

Imagery of Humiliation in Isaiah 47

This imagery of humiliation plays a very important role in Second Isaiah. Around it is structured the exchange of Jerusalem's fortune and Babylon's. Soon I will note the way in which the beginning of the third "awake, awake" poem gathers this imagery into a dramatic reversal of Zion's fortunes. But first it is necessary to glance backward to a section that precedes and foreshadows the glorification of Zion: chapter 47, in which Daughter Babylon's humiliation is imagined point for point as Jerusalem's was portrayed in Lamentations. The chapter begins with a striking repetition of the description of Zion's elders and virgins:

Isa 47:1	Go down and sit in dust, virgin daughter Babylon! Sit on the ground without a throne, daughter Chaldea! For you will no longer be called tender and delicate.	**רְדִי וּשְׁבִי** עַל־**עָפָר** **בְּתוּלַת בַּת**־בָּבֶל **שְׁבִי־לָאָרֶץ** אֵין־כִּסֵּא **בַּת**־כַּשְׂדִּים כִּי לֹא תוֹסִיפִי יִקְרְאוּ־לָךְ רַכָּה וַעֲנֻגָּה

The whole first line of 47:1 is composed of words found in Lam 2:10, except for the change in cities. The next line of verse 1 (שְׁבִי־לָאָרֶץ) and the first line of verse 5 (שְׁבִי דוּמָם) correspond to the first three words of the verse (יֵשְׁבוּ לָאָרֶץ יִדְּמוּ). These are the only two instances in the Bible of the idiom ישׁב לָאָרֶץ. The combination דמם . . . ישׁב is likewise quite unusual.

In verses 2–3 Babylon is told to remove her clothing and uncover her legs, so that, like Zion in Lam 1:8 (רָאוּ עֶרְוָתָהּ), her nakedness is uncovered and her shame is seen (תִּגָּל עֶרְוָתֵךְ גַּם תֵּרָאֶה חֶרְפָּתֵךְ). In verse 5 she is told to sit in silence (שְׁבִי דוּמָם; see Lam 2:10—יֵשְׁבוּ לָאָרֶץ יִדְּמוּ). In verse 7, Babylon's thoughtless arrogance is described in the same terms in which Zion's was in Lam 1:9 (לֹא זָכְרָה אַחֲרִיתָהּ):

Isa 47:7	You said, "I will be mistress forever," you did not lay these to heart, you did not remember its end.	וַתֹּאמְרִי לְעוֹלָם אֶהְיֶה גְבָרֶת עַד לֹא־שַׂמְתְּ אֵלֶּה עַל־לִבֵּךְ **לֹא זָכַרְתְּ אַחֲרִיתָהּ**

This three-word idiom concerning failure to remember one's end occurs nowhere else in the Bible. The only difference between the two instances is in the verb: 3fs in Lamentations ("she did not remember") and 2fs in Isaiah ("you did not remember").[45] The

---

45 Gottwald (*Studies*, 44) recognized the use of Lam 1:9 in Isa 47:7. Where one might expect in Isaiah a corresponding change to a 2fs pronominal suffix in the preposition אַחֲרִית, the Isaiah passage retains the 3fs pronoun exactly as in the Lamentations passage. This pronoun differs from the idiom, which is אַחֲרִית + personal pronoun, as in Num 23:10 ("my end"), Deut 8:16 ("your end") and 32:20 ("their end"), and others, in that it lacks an antecedent for "her."

Scribes both ancient and modern have been troubled by this form. Muilenburg noted that some manuscripts read "your end," and that a Dead Sea Scroll (that is, 1QIsa[a]) reads אחרונה, "what was to follow." The NRSV and the NASB,

change of subject from Zion to Babylon hints that the fate Zion already suffered will yet befall her oppressor. This message answers the hope, expressed in Lam 1:21–22, that YHWH punish Zion's enemies as Zion has been punished. Despite her arrogant claim to the contrary (Isa 47:8–9), Babylon is warned that she will be confronted in a single moment by two misfortunes that had once characterized Zion (see Lam 1:1, 20): widowhood (אַלְמֹן) and bereavement (שְׁכוֹל).

This humiliation of Daughter Babylon, recollected so densely in terms echoing descriptions of Zion and her people in Lamentations, is described in Isa 47:6 as punishment for Babylon's own cruelty to Jerusalem. In depicting YHWH as turning the punishment against the punisher, the poet both addresses Lamentations' frequently voiced prayer for revenge and vindicates YHWH's reputation in the eyes of those Jerusalemites indignant at all they were forced to bear. Babylon's downfall, so vividly pictured in Isaiah 47, does not simply clear the way for the rescue of the exiles. The opportunity to imagine atrocities against the oppressor invites remembrance of, and rage at, all that was suffered by the previous generation. The poet's keying this downfall to the terms by which Judahites remembered their own humiliation suggests

---

without textual support, pluralize the pronoun ("their end" and "the outcome of them," respectively), while the NJB omits it altogether ("the future"). These emendations attempt to correct what might appear to be a grammatical problem.

Although it would seem, especially in comparison with Lam 1:9, that Isa 47:7 is grammatically problematic, there is an alternative idiom attested in biblical Hebrew which uses אַחֲרִיתָהּ without a prior fs referent. Amos 8:10 (וְשַׂמְתִּיהָ כְּאֵבֶל יָחִיד וְאַחֲרִיתָהּ כְּיוֹם מָר—"I will make it like the mourning for an only son, and its end like a bitter day") uses the fs pronoun without a referent anywhere in the verse. Proverbs 14:12 makes this even clearer: יֵשׁ דֶּרֶךְ יָשָׁר לִפְנֵי־אִישׁ וְאַחֲרִיתָהּ דַּרְכֵי־מָוֶת—"There is a straight way (ms) before a man, but its end (fs) are ways (mp) of death" (see also Prov 16:25, 25:8, and Jer 5:31). According to this idiom, the 3fs pronoun in Isa 47:7 would refer not to any noun present in the text, but to an abstraction: the end result of Babylon's course of action. By employing this idiom rather than the other, the poet is able to retain the wording of Lam 1:9 as closely as possible while still addressing Babylon directly.

that the suffering coming to Babylon will equal, or perhaps even surpass, all that befell Jerusalem, and offers a ready reason for exiles to depart from the doomed city.

Imagery of Rising in Isaiah 52

But Daughter Babylon's humiliation is not complete without the reversal of Zion's fortune. Isaiah 51:9–16 began with the prayer that YHWH awaken (עוּרִי) and rescue the people as in former days, and continued with reassurances that YHWH would not allow oppressions to continue. Isaiah 51:17–23 bid Zion to wake up (הִתְעוֹרְרִי), as if from a stupor. When this intoxication is portrayed as a numbness brought on by the magnitude of the motherly sorrow Zion had endured, it may serve to suggest that contemporary indifference to the ravages of the past may not be lack of interest at all, but rather stupor from the cup of YHWH's wrath. Out of all of this, Zion is awakened to confront once again her own pain.

Finally, in Isa 52:1–2, Zion is again bidden to awaken in strength. All the conditions of redemption are set in place, and it is only for her to rise to the occasion. Thc language of lament psalmody bidding YHWH to "awake," addressed in modified form to Zion in 51:17, is reutilized once more. Like YHWH, Zion is told to "put on strength." Such a structuring emphasizes the reciprocal role that Zion plays in her own redemption—the one calling YHWH to arise must also be prepared to act.

As the poet bids Jerusalem to rise up from the dust, many of the terms of her humiliation from the book of Lamentations are blended together:

52:1	Awake, awake,	עוּרִי עוּרִי
	put on your strength, Zion!	לִבְשִׁי עֻזֵּךְ צִיּוֹן
	Put on your splendid garments,	לִבְשִׁי בִּגְדֵי **תִפְאַרְתֵּךְ**
	Jerusalem, the holy city;	יְרוּשָׁלַםִ עִיר **הַקֹּדֶשׁ**
	for he shall no longer come into you,	כִּי **לֹא** יוֹסִיף **יָבֹא**־בָךְ עוֹד
	uncircumcised and unclean.	עָרֵל **וְטָמֵא**

52:2	Shake yourself from the dust, rise up, sit down, Jerusalem; loose the bonds on your neck, captive daughter Zion!	הִתְנַעֲרִי **מֵעָפָר** קוּמִי שְׁבִי יְרוּשָׁלִָם הִתְפַּתְּחִי מוֹסְרֵי **צַוָּארֵךְ** שְׁבִיָּה **בַּת־צִיּוֹן**

According to Lam 1:9, Zion fell splendidly (**תֵּרֶד פְּלָאִים**), skirts unclean (טֻמְאָתָהּ בְּשׁוּלֶיהָ). But in Isa 52:1 she is bidden to arise in splendid garments (בִּגְדֵי תִפְאַרְתֵּךְ),[46] and the invaders are called unclean (טָמֵא). In the lament, Zion's transgressions created a yoke on her neck (**צַוָּארִי**, Lam 1:14), weakening her strength, but Second Isaiah bids her to put on her strength and loose the bonds from her neck (**צַוָּארֵךְ**, Isa 52:2). Rather than putting dust (**עָפָר**, Lam 2:10) on her head, she is told to shake herself free of dust (**עָפָר**, Isa 52:2). In Lam 1:10 nations entered (**בָּאוּ**) her sanctuary (literally, "sacred place," מִקְדָּשָׁהּ), which they had been forbidden to enter (לֹא־יָבֹאוּ), but in Isa 52:1, Jerusalem the sacred city (עִיר הַקֹּדֶשׁ) is assured that these unclean ones will no longer enter her (כִּי לֹא יוֹסִיף יָבֹא־בָךְ).[47] Thus in two verses, Second Isaiah both echoes the twofold image of Zion as defiled woman and defiled place, and reverses her defilement in both modes, completing the reversal of roles with Babylon that was initiated in Isaiah 47. The laments had portrayed Daughter Zion as a bereaved and lonely widow, polluted, violated, weak and naked, comfortless on account of her own sin, her lack of foresight, and the invasion of nations. In response, Second Isaiah announces YHWH's comfort to Jerusalem, who will be purified, strengthened and clothed, forgiven of sin, and protected from invaders, while her persecutor "Daughter Babylon" is left bereaved, widowed, naked and utterly humiliated.

Isaiah 51:9–52:12 in Review

Of all the parts of this highly referential book, Isa 51:9–52:12 is the section most frankly repetitive of other texts. The explicitness with which Second Isaiah quotes several very different texts makes

[46] Newsom, 76.
[47] Newsom, 76.

it clear that direct citation is always available to the poet. Its use here illustrates the mental processes of one living with "texts-in-the-mind." Old imprecations are typologically reapplied to new enemies. Elements of ancient stories attain significance on new planes when language once ordinary is spiritualized or reversed. Psalms imagining the stability of YHWH's reign in a monarchical setting are reaffirmed, even though their validity is no longer self-evident. Even laments expressing humiliation can be turned inside out. Second Isaiah takes full advantage of the plasticity of language, creating out of old materials powerful new assertions. The forms and messages of the old, still visible in this new creation, highlight both the continuity of the language and the alterations in its use.

Though some of Second Isaiah's citations are clear and direct, others are not so distinct, and in some cases they leave open the possibility that Second Isaiah may be recalling unpreserved material or simply a manner of speaking that is exemplified for us by these texts. Yet similarities between these texts, both linguistically and thematically, are great enough to suggest at the most that they are in fact the texts the prophet had in mind, and at the least that they are a suitable backdrop against which to read this section of Second Isaiah.[48]

In this section, the exiles' return to Jerusalem is posited as the appropriate response to a variety of previously known voices: not only the cries of Daughter Zion and the hopes of Jeremiah, but the supplications of lament psalmists and the narrations of Judah's traditional identity. The reuse of these languages, along with some alterations and blending, positions Second Isaiah in relation to various previous formulations of Jerusalem's destruction, suggesting commonalities among the divergent voices and emphasizing their resolution.

---

[48] In addition to the relationships I have described, there are of course many fainter possibilities of echoes. Earliest readers might have understood more fully their importance for the prophet, but for us these echoes are too fleeting to interpret with any certainty. They stand for us as illustrations of the open-ended and seemingly endless nature of textual resonances that may be present but are simply too difficult to discern with clarity.

The section began with an allusion to an allusion: multiple and dense echoes of communal lament discourse, discourse itself founded on allusions to YHWH's mythic ascendancy over the forces of the sea. By recollecting psalms from Judah's past that dwell on these themes, Second Isaiah constructs an expectation through which the rest of the section is read. Common to several of these psalms, but missing in these first verses, are repeated references to YHWH's reign as king. This element—which would have been anticipated by audiences familiar with the motif—is deferred until the dramatic moment in Isa 52:7 when YHWH is seen returning in victory to Jerusalem.

The opening voice goes on (Isa 51:11) to describe a contemporary equivalent of earlier victories: the return of those exiled by Babylon. The poet's prayer for return accords with the expectation already voiced by Jeremiah, the very prophet who had warned of defeat. Immediately and decisively (51:12) YHWH replies, declaring in response to Zion's comfortlessness in Lamentations 1, "I, I am he, your comforter." Continuing to review the problem of Jerusalem's foes, the poet invokes Jeremiah's promise of security as steadfast as nature's boundaries, and connects the creation of heaven and earth with the constitution of the nation. This amalgamation of differing traditions will be mirrored in the blending of disparate texts at the end of this section.

These reassurances cushion the discussion that follows in Isa 51:17–23, in which Zion's suffering is reviewed. This suffering is expressed in terms reminiscent of Lamentations 4, in which Zion's children were consumed by YHWH's wrath. At the same time, what the lament had made painfully concrete, Second Isaiah distills. What is described is not the suffering of the children, nor even of their mothers, but rather that of the metaphoric figure Zion. This minimized and distilled suffering is described as already past. The only future envisioned is the waking of Jerusalem from her stupor and the transfer of her suffering to her enemies.

This exchange of fortune is fully envisioned in Isa 52:1–12. Imagery of humiliation prevalent throughout Lamentations had already been reapplied to Daughter Babylon in Isaiah 47. Here the roles are reversed. Zion is invited to rise up, and key images of her humiliation are quickly overturned. Now Zion herself is told to awaken, put on her strength, and arise, coordinating her actions with YHWH's. The sacred city, once raped by enemies, is promised that the uncircumcised will no longer enter.

The section ends with a chorus of texts telling one story. Nahum's messenger of peace, who once proclaimed Assyria's defeat, now proclaims Babylon's (verse 7). Sentinels who in Lamentations watched in vain for help now see YHWH eye-to-eye as Moses once did (verse 8). As YHWH marches back in victory, the watchers join the chorus of praise that heaven and earth, mountain and forest, have already sung (see Isa 44:23). The ruins of Jerusalem itself are invited to join this chorus, celebrating YHWH's longed-for comfort (verse 9). The ends of the earth now see YHWH's victory (verse 10). Only when salvation has been proclaimed in the language of four distinct traditions encompassing torah, prophets, and liturgical writings are the exiles themselves asked to set out (verse 11). No longer unclean themselves, they depart because the surrounding nations arc unclean. As they had once departed Egypt, carrying spoils for YHWH's tabernacle, now they depart carrying the sacred vessels, Judah's own belongings (verse 12). Rather than fleeing, they process, surrounded before and behind by YHWH their God.

Chapter 4
"Lift up Your Eyes All Around and See": Isaiah 49:1–50:3

The section examined in chapter 3, Isa 51:9–52:12, was the central of three sections in Isaiah 49–54 which concern the figure Daughter Zion. Not only was it a centerpiece to the book rhetorically, but it also contains the most overt intertextual allusions discernible in Second Isaiah. In this chapter I will backtrack to examine Isa 49:1–50:3, the first major section in which Daughter Zion appears, and in which the "servant" first emerges as a speaker. Some preliminary observations about the roles of these two figures within Second Isaiah will help clarify their relationship in this passage and in those that follow. Futher observations on their construction and relationship will follow in chapter 5.

Characterization in Second Isaiah: Zion, the Servant, and the Plural "You"

Since the time of Bernhard Duhm, discussion of these two recurring personified figures, Daughter Zion and the Servant of YHWH, has been obscured by the isolation of four "servant songs" in Isaiah 42, 49, 50, and 53 as qualitatively different from mentions of the servant in the rest of the text.[1] Many recent studies have raised serious doubts, however, about the validity of such a separation, and there has been a growing movement to base interpretation of this figure on all the texts in which he is discussed: that is, to

---

[1] Duhm, *Das Buch Jesaia.* For discussions of the history of this paradigm, see H. H. Rowley, *The Servant of the Lord and Other Essays on the Old Testament* (London: Lutterworth Press, 1952) 1–57; C. R. North, *The Suffering Servant in Deutero-Isaiah* (London: Oxford University Press, 1948) 6–116; and especially H. Haag, *Der Gottesknecht bei Deuterojesaja* (Darmstadt: Wissenschaftliche Buchgesellschaft, 1985) 34–116, whose discussion begins with the first century C.E. and covers both Jewish and Christian interpretive history.

include in the discussion chapters 41–45 and 48.[2] Since the servant is repeatedly identified with "Israel" and "Jacob" in these texts (as well as in Isa 49:3), a consequence of this widening of boundaries has been increasing recognition of the servant's collective nature. While modern scholars (and interpreters throughout the centuries) have posed the question as "Who is the servant of YHWH?" the question the text seems bent on answering rather is "Who is Israel in relation to YHWH?" The oft repeated answer in Isaiah 41–45 is, "Israel is YHWH's servant." (See especially Isa 41:8–10, 43:10, 44:1–2, 21–22, in which Israel is pointedly given this designation.)

With this connection in mind, recent researchers have brought to light interesting correspondences between the two figures Zion and Israel/the servant. For instance, both are described in terms both individual and collective; both have doubled geopolitical names (Zion/Jerusalem; Israel/Jacob); both are introduced complaining about their treatment at YHWH's hands; both are described as suffering and are promised redemption and vindication.[3]

[2] Duhm's ideas were disputed early on by K. Budde, "The So-Called 'Ebed-Yahweh Songs,' and the Meaning of the Term 'Servant of Yahweh' in Isaiah, Chapters 40–55," *American Journal of Theology* 3 (1899) 499–540; and E. König, *Das Buch Jesaja*. Major criticisms of Duhm's theory include: 1) the observation that these four passages do not share enough formal similarities to belong to a common *Gattung* distinct from the rest of Second Isaiah (R. Melugin, *The Formation of the Book of Isaiah*, BZAW 141, New York: Walter de Gruyter, 1976, 64–74, and T. Mettinger, *A Farewell to the Servant Songs: A Critical Examination of an Exegetical Axiom*, Lund, Sweden: CWK Gleerup, 1983, 16–17); 2) the assertion, contrary to Duhm, that the language and content of the texts is continuous with their immediate contexts (see North's detailed vocabulary studies, *The Suffering Servant*, 156–91, and Muilenburg's studies of vocabulary and motif, 407); and 3) the objection that these four passages cannot be distinguished in any decisive way from the other passages in Second Isaiah that deal with YHWH's servant (Eissfeldt, *Old Testament*, 340–41). In the view of some, Duhm's creating a separate category for these passages proceeds from, and bolsters, the impulse to understand YHWH's servant as someone other than the obvious, Israel. Mettinger (*Farewell*, 44–45) saw the theory of the servant songs as "an ingenious but unsuccessful attempt to create a defensive bastion to protect the individual interpretation of the Servant."

[3] For comparisons of these figures see O. H. Steck, *Gottesknecht und Zion*, especially chapter 8, "Zion als Gelände und Gestalt"; J. Sawyer, "Daughter of

As I will show, many individual characteristics of the two figures run parallel as well: their origins, vocations, the language with which they speak and with which they are addressed all revolve around many of the same themes and motifs.

The significance of these two entities must carefully be sought both before and within Second Isaiah. Because her name and role are more focused, it is easier to find textual precedents for Daughter Zion than for Second Isaiah's Israel/servant. The masculine figure that appears parallel to Daughter Zion is, at least initially, rather more elusive. "Israel" is not an easily delineated entity in biblical literature—the name designates variously a person, a people, a united monarchy, a northern kingdom, and an idea. Nor does the designation "servant of YHWH" come with an easily defined set of textual precedents.[4]

Study of the servant has often been frustrated by the perception of inconsistency in the character's description within Second Isaiah as well. Duhm's isolation of four "servant songs" from other servant passages was one attempt to create a coherent figure out of the vividly but paradoxically presented servant. Yet hyperbole and paradox, and the logical tensions that result from them, permeate not only this character, but the entire text of Second Isaiah, and are not easily resolved on a rational level. Those called deaf are told to listen, those called blind to look up and see (42:18). In one verse YHWH is a warrior returning from battle (40:10; 42:13), and in the next a tender shepherd of lambs (40:11) or a laboring woman (42:14). If Second Isaiah's paradoxes are both vividly compelling and impossible to take literally, so are its images: city ruins that sing

---

Zion and Servant of the Lord in Isaiah: A Comparison," *JSOT* 44 (1989) 89–107; L. E. Wilshire, "The Servant-City: A New Interpretation of the 'Servant of the Lord' in the Servant Songs of Deutero-Isaiah," *JBL* 94 (1975) 356–67; and K. Jeppesen, "Mother Zion, Father Servant: A Reading of Isaiah 49–55," in *Of Prophets' Visions and the Wisdom of Sages: Essays in Honour of R. Norman Whybray on his Seventieth Birthday*, ed. H. McKay and D. Clines, JSOTSup 162 (Sheffield: Sheffield Academic Press, 1993) 109–25.

[4] This issue will be discussed further in chapter 5.

and trees that clap their hands signal that this text was meant not to describe the real world but to fire its audience's imagination.

Second Isaiah populates this imaginative world with a variety of figures whose words and deeds ought not in the first instance to be considered actual. This is easy to see with the talking, grieving, mountain-climbing woman Jerusalem, but is often overlooked when YHWH's servant is discussed. Inconsistency and paradox help make the characters interesting and "round" as opposed to predictable and "flat." But even more, as symbolic representations, metaphors for entities that are not necessarily, and not even probably, individuals, Daughter Zion and the servant have the prerogative to shift roles and duties as the rhetorical situation demands.

To complicate the matter of characterization further, Second Isaiah does not always portray its figures in third person and identify them by name. Sometimes they are identified only as "I" or "you." The female addressed in Isaiah 54, for instance, is never called Zion or Jerusalem by name, and in fact some elements in her description stand in tension with other portrayals. However, clear patterns in Second Isaiah's use of pronouns may be traced. These provide clues to the identities and relationships of the poetry's figures and help clarify where the prophet is positioning the audience in relation to them.

Despite their often collective nature, Israel and Jacob are predominantly referred to in scripture as a grammatically singular entity.[5] This masculine singular designation begins with the eponymous patriarch's stories in Genesis and continues in relation to the nation as a whole in Exodus. (See for instance Exod 4:22, "Israel is my first-born son.") By contrast, both before and within Second Isaiah, the designations "children of Israel," "offspring (seed) of Israel," and "house of Israel" are regularly given

---

[5] See, for instance, Number 23–24, Deuteronomy 32–33, many Psalms, Lam 1:17, 2:3–4, and nearly all the prophets: Isa 9:10, 29:22; Jer 10:25, 30:7, Hos 10:11; Amos 6:8; Obad 10; Mic 2:12. John J. Schmitt, in "The Gender of Ancient Israel," *JSOT* 26 (1983) 115–25, has argued that in the Bible nations are consistently given masculine singular pronouns, and cities, feminine singular.

masculine plural markers.[6] Cities, such as Jerusalem, are grammatically feminine, and when they are addressed they are regularly given feminine singular markers, even when it is clearly the people of the city who are being addressed by the city's name.[7] With such sharply delineated grammatical usages, an examination of the use of pronouns within Second Isaiah can help distinguish who is being addressed at various points in the poetry.[8] Certain important observations come to light:

The singular addressees are decisively separated. With slight exceptions, addresses that employ the masculine singular "you" occur only in chapters 40–45 and 48, and addresses to a feminine singular "you" occur only in chapters 40, 47, 49–52, and 54. However, masculine plural addressees are found throughout, in nearly every chapter.

In chapters 41–45, the masculine singular audience is always addressed by YHWH, never by a human speaker. In chapters 41–44, this entity is Israel/Jacob. YHWH never speaks to the servant in singular without calling him Israel. YHWH does speak to Jacob/Israel without calling him servant in 43:1–7—that is, only if the designation from the end of the previous chapter is not meant to carry over.

When Zion enters in Isa 49:14, YHWH ceases speaking to the masculine singular addressee. From then on, when the servant is mentioned, he is either speaking (50:4–9) or being discussed (50:10–11, 52:13–53:12). Although parallel in many ways, the

---

[6] See for instance 2 Kings 17:20; Ps 22:24; Ex 16:31; Num 20:29; Hos 1:6, Amos 5:1; Isa 45:19, 25.

[7] See for instance Jud 1:8; 2 Sam 24:16; 1 Kings 11:32, 20:1; Neh 2:13; Ps 122:2, 3, 6; 137:5, 7–9, Isa 37:10, 22; and especially Isa 3:8, in which Jerusalem and Judah occur in parallel, and Hos 8:5–8, in which Samaria is feminine and Israel is masculine. For an example that sets all three usages in relation to each other see Jer 2:2–4, in which Jerusalem is fs, Israel is ms, and the house of Israel is mpl, all in immediate sequence.

[8] Although I will not be treating Isaiah 53 in detail, I found David Clines' book *I, He, We, and They: A Literary Approach to Isaiah 53*, JSOTSup 1 (Sheffield: Sheffield Academic Press, 1976) quite helpful in pointing out the importance of tracing the various pronouns used by Second Isaiah.

figures Zion and Israel/the servant never appear in the same scene, nor are they discussed in relation to each other. The alternating sections in which they appear often abut one another dramatically, their links unsmoothed by transitional verses. The two figures give the impression of occupying, so to speak, universes of discourse that run parallel but do not converge. However, both Zion and Israel/the servant are found in relation to the masculine plural addressees.

The plural audience's relationship to the two singular entities differs markedly. Alternation between masculine singular and plural addressees in the book's first half is often fluid. Among the masculine plural addressees is an audience that is unidentified at first, but in Isa 43:10 is called by YHWH "my witnesses" (plural) and "my servant" (singular). In several instances (42:22, 43:6–8, 43:21) there is considerable slippage between singular and plural. In chapters 45–48 the plural group is called the "offspring" and "house" of Israel/Jacob.

Usage differs considerably in relation to Zion. Though masculine plural addressees continue in the Zion sections, they are distinct from her, not intermingled as with the servant and Israel. The Zion sections introduce another "they": Zion's children, returning from exile (Isa 49:20–25, 54:1, 13). In 52:11–12 and 55:12 these returnees merge with the masculine plural "you."

From these observations some preliminary conclusions may be reached:

First, the one addressee tying all the sections together is the masculine plural "you" who appears from beginning to end. Among all the audiences portrayed in the book, this one seems to correspond most closely to the prophet's actual audience. This plural audience is identified with "the offspring of Israel," and with "my witnesses, my servant," and thus is doubly aligned with the figure "Israel/Jacob my servant/chosen." In addition, they are identified with the "children" of Zion who are soon to return. The frequent references to their return signal that they are envisioned in exile.

Second, while the servant's location is not given, his frequent intermingling with the masculine plural "you" probably indicates that he too is envisioned as exiled. Despite the pronoun distinctions, the masculine plural audience is fully identified with the masculine singular addressee in a variety of ways. That is to say, the prophet's audience are invited to envision themselves as YHWH's servant(s) Israel.

Third, unlike these two, Jerusalem is envisioned as a distinct entity, still separated from the exiles by the expanse of wilderness in between. Significantly, she is also textually separate from masculine addressees, both singular and plural. What the poet says to Jerusalem is not directly addressed to the audience, but rather is strategically "overheard" by them. Perhaps the frequent alternation between the servant and Zion in chapters 49–55 is on some level an attempt to bridge the barrier of distance between the city and exilic "Israel." Before they have even set out from Babylon, they are allowed to see what they look like to the city as they approach it.

In sum, the three addressees receiving frequent attention in Second Isaiah are discernible by the pronouns by which they are addressed. They are the feminine singular figure representing the city, Zion/Jerusalem; the masculine singular figure representing the nation, Israel/Jacob, who is also called YHWH's servant; and the masculine plural audience who is identified as "my witnesses, my servant," "offspring of Israel/Jacob," "house of Israel/Jacob," and "your (Zion's) children."

Isaiah 49:1–50:3

Chapter 49 marks a crucial transition point in Second Isaiah, the beginning of the alternation of attention between Israel and Zion that will continue through chapter 54. In the first part of this chapter, servant Israel emerges as a speaking character who echoes the words addressed to him by YHWH throughout the early chapters. Once this speaking voice is established, in verse 14, Zion too enters as a speaking character. Some distinct ties with both Lamentations and Jeremiah can be traced in this section.

49:1	Listen, coastlands, to me,	שִׁמְעוּ אִיִּים אֵלַי
	and attend, peoples from afar.	וְהַקְשִׁיבוּ לְאֻמִּים מֵרָחוֹק
	YHWH called me from birth,	יְהוָה מִבֶּטֶן קְרָאָנִי
	from the womb of my mother he called	
	my name.	מִמְּעֵי אִמִּי הִזְכִּיר שְׁמִי
49:2	And he made my mouth like a sharp	וַיָּשֶׂם פִּי כְּחֶרֶב חַדָּה
	sword;	בְּצֵל יָדוֹ הֶחְבִּיאָנִי
	in the shadow of his hand he hid me.	וַיְשִׂימֵנִי לְחֵץ בָּרוּר
	He made me a sharpened arrow;	בְּאַשְׁפָּתוֹ הִסְתִּירָנִי
	in his quiver he kept me hidden.	
49:3	And he said to me, My servant you are,	וַיֹּאמֶר לִי עַבְדִּי־אָתָּה
	Israel, in whom I will be glorified.	יִשְׂרָאֵל אֲשֶׁר־בְּךָ אֶתְפָּאָר
49:4	But I said, in vain I have wearied myself;	וַאֲנִי אָמַרְתִּי לְרִיק יָגַעְתִּי
	for emptiness and vanity	
	I have exhausted my strength.	לְתֹהוּ וְהֶבֶל כֹּחִי כִלֵּיתִי
	Nevertheless, my right is with YHWH,	אָכֵן מִשְׁפָּטִי אֶת־יְהוָה
	and my reward is with my God.	וּפְעֻלָּתִי אֶת־אֱלֹהָי
49:5	And now YHWH has said—	וְעַתָּה אָמַר יְהוָה
	who formed me from the womb as his servant,	יֹצְרִי מִבֶּטֶן לְעֶבֶד לוֹ
	bringing Jacob back to him,[9]	לְשׁוֹבֵב יַעֲקֹב אֵלָיו
	and Israel he will gather to him,	וְיִשְׂרָאֵל לוֹ יֵאָסֵף
	and I am honored in YHWH's eyes,	וְאֶכָּבֵד בְּעֵינֵי יְהוָה
	and my God has become my strength—	וֵאלֹהַי הָיָה עֻזִּי
49:6	he said, It is easy, since you are my servant,	וַיֹּאמֶר נָקֵל מִהְיוֹתְךָ לִי עֶבֶד
	to raise up the tribes of Jacob,	לְהָקִים אֶת־שִׁבְטֵי יַעֲקֹב
	and to bring back the survivors of Israel.	וּנְצוּרֵי יִשְׂרָאֵל לְהָשִׁיב
	I will appoint you as light to the nations,	וּנְתַתִּיךָ לְאוֹר גּוֹיִם
	that my salvation may be	לִהְיוֹת יְשׁוּעָתִי
	to the end of the earth.	עַד־קְצֵה הָאָרֶץ

[9] Here and in verse 6 I follow Mettinger (*Farewell,* 35) and others who argue that the three infinitives in these two verses refer not to the servant but to YHWH.

49:7	Thus has YHWH said,	כֹּה אָמַר־יְהוָה
	the redeemer of Israel and his holy one,	גֹּאֵל יִשְׂרָאֵל קְדוֹשׁוֹ
	to one deeply despised, to one abhorred by nations,	לִבְזֹה־נֶפֶשׁ לִמְתָעֵב גּוֹי
	to a servant of rulers,	לְעֶבֶד מֹשְׁלִים
	"Kings shall see and stand up,	מְלָכִים יִרְאוּ וָקָמוּ
	princes, and they shall bow down,	שָׂרִים וְיִשְׁתַּחֲווּ
	on account of YHWH, who is faithful,	לְמַעַן יְהוָה אֲשֶׁר נֶאֱמָן
	the Holy One of Israel, who has chosen you."	קְדֹשׁ יִשְׂרָאֵל וַיִּבְחָרֶךָּ
49:8	Thus has YHWH said,	כֹּה אָמַר יְהוָה
	at a time of favor I answered you,	בְּעֵת רָצוֹן עֲנִיתִיךָ
	and on a day of salvation I helped you;	וּבְיוֹם יְשׁוּעָה עֲזַרְתִּיךָ
	and I have kept you and given you	וְאֶצָּרְךָ וְאֶתֶּנְךָ
	as a covenant to the people,	לִבְרִית עָם
	establishing the land,	לְהָקִים אֶרֶץ
	bequeathing the desolate inheritances;	לְהַנְחִיל נְחָלוֹת שֹׁמֵמוֹת
49:9	saying to the prisoners, Go out,	לֵאמֹר לַאֲסוּרִים צֵאוּ
	and to those in darkness, Be revealed.	לַאֲשֶׁר בַּחֹשֶׁךְ הִגָּלוּ
	Along the roads they will graze,	עַל־דְּרָכִים יִרְעוּ
	and on every bare height is their pasture.	וּבְכָל־שְׁפָיִים מַרְעִיתָם
49:10	They will not hunger and they will not thirst,	לֹא יִרְעָבוּ וְלֹא יִצְמָאוּ
	and the burning heat and sun will not strike them,	וְלֹא־יַכֵּם שָׁרָב וָשָׁמֶשׁ
	for the one who pities them will lead them,	כִּי־מְרַחֲמָם יְנַהֲגֵם
	and by springs of water will guide them.	וְעַל־מַבּוּעֵי מַיִם יְנַהֲלֵם
49:11	And I will make all my mountains into road,	וְשַׂמְתִּי כָל־הָרַי לַדָּרֶךְ
	and my highways will be raised up.	וּמְסִלֹּתַי יְרֻמוּן
49:12	Behold, these from far away will come,	הִנֵּה־אֵלֶּה מֵרָחוֹק יָבֹאוּ
	and behold, these, from the north and west,	וְהִנֵּה־אֵלֶּה מִצָּפוֹן וּמִיָּם
	and these, from the land of Syene.	וְאֵלֶּה מֵאֶרֶץ סִינִים
49:13	Cry out, heavens, and rejoice, earth,	רָנּוּ שָׁמַיִם וְגִילִי אָרֶץ
	and break forth, mountains, with a cry.	וּפִצְחוּ הָרִים רִנָּה
	For YHWH has comforted his people,	כִּי־נִחַם יְהוָה עַמּוֹ
	and his suffering ones he will pity.	וַעֲנִיָּו יְרַחֵם
49:14	But Zion says, "YHWH abandoned me,	וַתֹּאמֶר צִיּוֹן עֲזָבַנִי יְהוָה
	and the Lord forgot me."	וַאדֹנָי שְׁכֵחָנִי
49:15	Can a woman forget her nursing child,	הֲתִשְׁכַּח אִשָּׁה עוּלָהּ
	not pity the child of her womb?	מֵרַחֵם בֶּן־בִּטְנָהּ
	Even these will forget.	גַּם־אֵלֶּה תִשְׁכַּחְנָה
	But I will not forget you.	וְאָנֹכִי לֹא אֶשְׁכָּחֵךְ

49:16	See, on my palms I inscribed you,	הֵן עַל־כַּפַּיִם חַקֹּתִיךְ
	your walls are before me always.	חוֹמֹתַיִךְ נֶגְדִּי תָּמִיד
49:17	Your children come quickly;	מִהֲרוּ בָּנָיִךְ
	your destroyers and devastators depart from you.	מְהָרְסַיִךְ וּמַחֲרִבַיִךְ מִמֵּךְ יֵצֵאוּ
49:18	Lift up your eyes all around and see,	שְׂאִי־סָבִיב עֵינַיִךְ וּרְאִי
	they are all gathered, they come to you.	כֻּלָּם נִקְבְּצוּ בָאוּ־לָךְ
	As I live, says YHWH,	חַי־אָנִי נְאֻם־יְהוָה
	you shall put them all on like ornaments,	כִּי כֻלָּם כָּעֲדִי תִלְבָּשִׁי
	and bind them on like a bride.	וּתְקַשְּׁרִים כַּכַּלָּה
49:19	As for your ruins and your desolations,	כִּי חָרְבֹתַיִךְ וְשֹׁמְמֹתַיִךְ
	and your destroyed land—	וְאֶרֶץ הֲרִסֻתֵךְ
	Now you will be crowded with settlers,	כִּי עַתָּה תֵּצְרִי מִיּוֹשֵׁב
	and those who swallowed you will be far away.	וְרָחֲקוּ מְבַלְּעָיִךְ
49:20	Still they will say in your ears,	עוֹד יֹאמְרוּ בְאָזְנַיִךְ
	the children of your bereavement,	בְּנֵי שִׁכֻּלָיִךְ
	"The place is too crowded for me;	צַר־לִי הַמָּקוֹם
	make room for me to settle."	גְּשָׁה־לִּי וְאֵשֵׁבָה
49:21	And you will say in your heart,	וְאָמַרְתְּ בִּלְבָבֵךְ
	who bore me these?	מִי יָלַד־לִי אֶת־אֵלֶּה
	I was bereaved and desolate,	וַאֲנִי שְׁכוּלָה וְגַלְמוּדָה
	exiled and sent away,	גֹּלָה וְסוּרָה
	and these, who raised them?	וְאֵלֶּה מִי גִדֵּל
	See, I was left behind, alone,	הֵן אֲנִי נִשְׁאַרְתִּי לְבַדִּי
	these, where were they?	אֵלֶּה אֵיפֹה הֵם
49:22	Thus says the Lord YHWH:	כֹּה־אָמַר אֲדֹנָי יְהוִה
	See, I will lift up to nations my hand,	הִנֵּה אֶשָּׂא אֶל־גּוֹיִם יָדִי
	and to peoples I will raise my signal.	וְאֶל־עַמִּים אָרִים נִסִּי
	And they will bring your sons in their arms,	וְהֵבִיאוּ בָנַיִךְ בְּחֹצֶן
	and your daughters will be carried on their shoulders.	וּבְנֹתַיִךְ עַל־כָּתֵף תִּנָּשֶׂאנָה
49:23	Kings shall be your caretakers,	וְהָיוּ מְלָכִים אֹמְנַיִךְ
	and their queens your nursemaids.	וְשָׂרוֹתֵיהֶם מֵינִיקֹתַיִךְ
	Faces to the ground they shall bow down to you,	אַפַּיִם אֶרֶץ יִשְׁתַּחֲווּ לָךְ
	and the dust of your feet they will lick.	וַעֲפַר רַגְלַיִךְ יְלַחֵכוּ
	And you will know that I am YHWH;	וְיָדַעַתְּ כִּי־אֲנִי יְהוָה
	the one who hopes in me will not be shamed.	אֲשֶׁר לֹא־יֵבֹשׁוּ קֹוָי
49:24	Can prey be taken from the mighty,	הֲיֻקַּח מִגִּבּוֹר מַלְקוֹחַ
	or the captives of a tyrant be rescued?	וְאִם־שְׁבִי צַדִּיק יִמָּלֵט

49:25	But thus says YHWH:	כִּי־כֹה אָמַר יְהוָה
	Even the captives of the mighty will be taken,	גַּם־שְׁבִי גִבּוֹר יֻקָּח
	and the tyrant's prey will escape.	וּמַלְקוֹחַ עָרִיץ יִמָּלֵט
	For I myself will contend with your	
	contenders,	וְאֶת־יְרִיבֵךְ אָנֹכִי אָרִיב
	and I myself will save your children.	וְאֶת־בָּנַיִךְ אָנֹכִי אוֹשִׁיעַ
49:26	I will make your oppressors eat	
	their own flesh,	וְהַאֲכַלְתִּי אֶת־מוֹנַיִךְ אֶת־בְּשָׂרָם
	and, as with wine, with their own blood	
	they will be drunk.	וְכֶעָסִיס דָּמָם יִשְׁכָּרוּן
	And all flesh will know	וְיָדְעוּ כָל־בָּשָׂר
	that I am YHWH your Savior,	כִּי אֲנִי יְהוָה מוֹשִׁיעֵךְ
	and your Redeemer, the Mighty One of Jacob.	וְגֹאֲלֵךְ אֲבִיר יַעֲקֹב
50:1	Thus has YHWH said:	כֹּה אָמַר יְהוָה
	Where is your mother's certificate of	
	divorce,	אֵי זֶה סֵפֶר כְּרִיתוּת אִמְּכֶם
	with which I sent her away?	אֲשֶׁר שִׁלַּחְתִּיהָ
	Or to which of my creditors	אוֹ מִי מִנּוֹשַׁי
	did I sell you?	אֲשֶׁר־מָכַרְתִּי אֶתְכֶם לוֹ
	See, because of your sins you were sold,	הֵן בַּעֲוֺנֹתֵיכֶם נִמְכַּרְתֶּם
	and because of your transgressions	
	your mother was sent away.	וּבְפִשְׁעֵיכֶם שֻׁלְּחָה אִמְּכֶם
50:2	Why did I come and there was no one,	מַדּוּעַ בָּאתִי וְאֵין אִישׁ
	I called, and there was no answerer?	קָרָאתִי וְאֵין עוֹנֶה
	Is my hand too short to ransom?	הֲקָצוֹר קָצְרָה יָדִי מִפְּדוּת
	Is there not in me strength to rescue?	וְאִם־אֵין־בִּי כֹחַ לְהַצִּיל
	See, with my rebuke I will dry the sea,	הֵן בְּגַעֲרָתִי אַחֲרִיב יָם
	and make the rivers wilderness.	אָשִׂים נְהָרוֹת מִדְבָּר
	Its fish will stink from lack of water,	תִּבְאַשׁ דְּגָתָם מֵאֵין מַיִם
	and die of thirst.	וְתָמֹת בַּצָּמָא
50:3	I will clothe the heavens in mourning,	אַלְבִּישׁ שָׁמַיִם קַדְרוּת
	and sackcloth I will make their covering.	וְשַׂק אָשִׂים כְּסוּתָם

Isaiah 49 begins with what has traditionally been called the "Second Servant Song." YHWH's servant announces that he has been designated for particular purposes. Although these purposes are expressed unspecifically, they clearly respond to previous divine discourse about the servant, particularly in chapter 42. The picture that emerges is that the speaker is to be YHWH's servant, YHWH's witness to the nations of the world.

In verses 7–12, the message of redemption continues with a vision of YHWH's release of prisoners, leading them back from all directions. While the metaphor is not spelled out, such words as "graze," "pasture," "lead," and "guide," make it clear that YHWH is imagined as a shepherd (see 40:9–11). A doxological verse (verse 13) follows, calling heavens, earth, and mountains to rejoice because "YHWH has comforted his people."

What immediately follows, verse 14, is pivotal to the structure of both this section and Second Isaiah as a whole. Here Zion speaks for the first and only time, voicing a strenuous complaint: "YHWH abandoned me, and the Lord forgot me." On the heels of YHWH's announced plans to return the captives home, Zion's words appear quite oblivious of all that the audience already knows. Though the complaint is disarmed for the audience even before it is presented, this section continues to reassure Zion that her complaint is no longer valid. YHWH has not forgotten Zion. On the contrary, her children are returning. Their arrival is so immanent that if she will simply look up she will see them. This return will signal fundamental changes in Zion's situation: instead of desolation there will be crowding; instead of humiliation, homage from the kings and queens of surrounding nations. In the final three verses, Isa 50:1–3, YHWH disputes contrary understandings of the catastrophe itself: God never intended to divorce Zion, but rather sent her away in order to redeem her.

Although I have offered a rather straightforward synopsis, Second Isaiah's language is anything but straightforward. It is imagistic and referential, suggesting far more than it spells out, alluding to one motif, then leaping to another. Second Isaiah presents a rhetorical reframing of several motifs already in use to describe the alienation between the people and their God. By echoing words from the past, the poet reconfigures their meaning, suggesting to hearers an appropriate response to the altered political situation.

Negotiating the "Elastic Environment"

Apparently useful to Second Isaiah in this enterprise is a decided difference of perspective between the two earlier texts most heavily recollected in this section, Lamentations and Jeremiah. Their divergent views create, in Bakhtin's words, "an elastic environment of other, alien words," a range of viewpoints on both God and Jerusalem already available to both prophet and audience.[10] Crucial to the imagery of both Jeremiah and Lamentations is the personification of the people as a woman. But the two texts develop this image in decidedly different ways. The female imagery enabled Jeremiah to envision human apostasy as marital infidelity, and the people of YHWH as faithless children. The point of view throughout Jeremiah is sympathetic with divine charges against the woman and the children. Though sometimes their suffering is seen empathetically, there is never a moment when their viewpoint is taken over against YHWH's.

The viewpoint differs in Lamentations, however. Though the first chapter acknowledges Zion's past sins (Lam 1:5, 8, 20) and hints that her disgrace is sexual (1:8–10, 19), and thus moves the closest of all the laments to sympathizing with Jeremiah's evaluation of the disaster, the voices speaking throughout Lamentations are neither divine nor prophetic, but rather emanate consistently from the viewpoint of the victims of God's wrath.[11] As such, Lamentations' envisioning of Daughter Zion and of her children, while recognizable, differs radically from Jeremiah's. Jeremiah had offered occasional glimpses of Zion's suffering, hedged about by reasons why it was so or assurances that it would not continue. Lamentations offers not only persistent images of her suffering, but

---

[10] Bakhtin, 276.

[11] As Provan (23) and Dobbs-Allsopp (54–55) noted, while Lamentations presents the orthodox prophetic view that Jerusalem's destruction is punishment for sin, this viewpoint is presented in a perfunctory way that is seriously undercut by its unspecific nature and by the much greater space given to exploring the people's misery and to questioning the appropriateness of YHWH's punishment.

also verse upon verse of her anguished self-descriptions. Unlike the prophet, Lamentations has no need to justify the ways of YHWH; in fact, God's harshness is relentlessly accented. In Isa 49:1–50:3, intertextual relationships with this female imagery in Jeremiah and Lamentations predominate as Second Isaiah creates a role for Daughter Zion that echoes both of these divergent views, and in doing so forges links between them.

Recollections of Lamentations

Lamentations 1 and Zion's Comforter

Just before Zion's entrance as a speaking character, a doxology occurs that, like the very similar expression already examined in Isa 52:9, combines language of Psalm 98 with Second Isaiah's frequently recurring response keyed to the "no comforter" language in Lamentations 1:

Isa	Cry out, heavens, and rejoice, earth,	רָנּוּ שָׁמַיִם וְגִילִי אָרֶץ
49:13	and break forth, mountains, with a cry.	וּפִצְחוּ הָרִים רִנָּה
	For YHWH has comforted his people,	כִּי־***נִחַם*** יְהוָה עַמּוֹ
	and his suffering ones he will pity.	***וַעֲנִיָּו*** יְרַחֵם

This is the first of four repetitions in Second Isaiah of the claim that YHWH has comforted. Intertextual relations of this concept of comfort with Zion's comfortless in Lamentations have already been discussed at length in chapter 3. Here YHWH's comfort of the people is paired with pity for YHWH's suffering ones (עֲנִיָּו)—a word corresponding precisely to Zion's first self-description in Lamentations. In Lam 1:9, immediately after being called comfortless, Zion voices her first plea: "See, YHWH, my suffering (עָנְיִי)." A description of the enemy's encroachment on Zion's sanctuary follows, one of many descriptions in the lament of the onslaught of the enemies and the removal of Zion's people. Both of these dislocations will be addressed in Isaiah 49. This announcement of YHWH's comfort is followed in the next verse, Isa 49:14, by a second strategic echo of Lamentations.

Lamentations 5 and YHWH's Abandonment

Immediately after the "comfort" language of Isa 49:13, Zion begins to speak:

Isa 49:14	But Zion says, "YHWH abandoned me, and the Lord forgot me."	וַתֹּאמֶר צִיּוֹן **עֲזָבַנִי** יְהוָה וַאדֹנָי **שְׁכֵחָנִי**

Zion's opening words recall a similar complaint: Israel's first words in Isa 40:27: "My way is hidden from YHWH, and by my God is my right disregarded." That complaint had been thoroughly addressed by YHWH in the opening chapters. Zion's entrance with very similar speech signals that her concerns as well will now be addressed.

If Isa 40:27 alludes to any actual lament, it is unavailable to us now. But Daughter Zion's speech resembles very closely a climactic question near the end of the book of Lamentations:[12]

Lam 5:20	Why have you so long forgotten us, abandoned us for all our days?	לָמָּה לָנֶצַח **תִּשְׁכָּחֵנוּ** **תַּעַזְבֵנוּ** לְאֹרֶךְ יָמִים

The pairing of these two verbs might seem at first glance to be a common one. But they actually appear together rarely in biblical texts, and in no other instance in reference to YHWH's abandonment. If Second Isaiah's audience were aware of Lamentations at all, these words, iterated in the context of Jerusalem's suffering, could hardly fail to evoke the lament's anguished final plea.

But both the placement and the revised form counteract the sympathy the question elicited in its original setting. In Lamentations it occurred after eighteen verses, or in the final form, nearly five chapters, of devastating descriptions of YHWH's wrath,

[12] Gottwald (*Studies,* 44 note 1) noted this correspondence. Linafelt (56) suggested more explicitly that Isa 49:14–26 was a direct answer to Lamentations, beginning with a distinct citation of Lam 5:20 in verse 14. He also listed a number of thematic, and sometimes linguistic, correspondences between the remainder of the chapter and the book of Lamentations. Westermann (*Isaiah 40–66,* 219) noted a thematic similarity to Lam 5:22, yet maintained that "What Deutero-Isaiah then quotes in verse 14 is a lament that was actually made. They are words that were used in worship, and well-known to everyone who heard them."

following plea after plea to a silent and unyielding deity. The people's plight was described in poignant particulars: they are orphans; they are disinherited, paying even for water and wood. All—women, princes, elders, boys, old and young—have been violated. Their claim of YHWH's abandonment arises as a searching question at the climax of desperate prayers.

Its recollection in the mouth of Daughter Zion in Isaiah 49, however, follows eight chapters of nearly continuous divine speech promising help, presence, strength, and deliverance. It is preceded by a vivid portrait of YHWH's "day of salvation" (verse 8), the freeing of prisoners, and their return to Zion from all corners of the world. Heaven, earth, and mountains are bid to break forth at the news of YHWH's comfort and compassion. This cosmic celebration heightens the discord of Zion's opening accusation, "YHWH abandoned me and my Lord forgot me." Words once appropriate to sum up valid grievances clash conspicuously with their new setting.

The prayer of Lamentations is not only recontextualized but also recast. It is no longer a question, but a flat statement. It no longer addresses YHWH, but rather accuses YHWH to someone else. It is no longer spoken by a group, but by a single figure contemplating her own welfare. In its present context and form, it exhibits blindness to all that God has been doing to renew and restore, a blindness quite congruent with Second Isaiah's descriptions of Israel in chapter 42. Thus the lines in their new form and context reinterpret the issue: it is not YHWH, but Zion, who is inattentive.

Lamentations 5 had continued after the question, not with a response from YHWH, but with the acknowledgment that the prayer may not be answered. The absence of YHWH's voice and the necessity for the people to envision the possibilities themselves underscore the crisis of their question. But the response in Second Isaiah is quite different. Not only is it preceded by a promise of comfort, but it is followed by an immediate challenge: "Can a woman forget her nursing child, not pity the child of her womb?" At first sight the rhetorically demanded answer would seem to be,

"Of course not!" But Lamentations itself has borne witness to the ravages that war may visit even on maternal care: "Should women eat their own fruit, the little ones they have borne?" (Lam 2:20).[13] YHWH supplies the surprising answer, "Even these will forget. But I will not forget you" (Isa 49:15).

The rest of the chapter reinforces this theme of YHWH's remembering Zion. This section, which envisions the gathering of the exiles from afar, also gathers themes and key words from throughout Lamentations. Many of the reminiscences, viewed singly, would be unimpressive. But their cumulative density is quite significant. Jerusalem's wall (חוֹמַת בַּת־צִיּוֹן, Lam 2:18) was once told to cry to YHWH, to lift its palms (כַּפַּיִךְ, verse 19) to YHWH for the children's lives. Now Zion is inscribed on YHWH's palms, and her walls are continually before God (כַּפַּיִם and חוֹמֹתַיִךְ, Isa 49:16). Once no one came on the roads to Zion (Lam 1:4), but now they all come to her (Isa 49:18).[14] Once it was YHWH who swallowed Zion (בִּלַּע, Lam 2:5; see also verses 2, 8), but now the swallowers (מְבַלְּעָיִךְ, Isa 49:19) are sharply distinguished from YHWH, and are far away. Once Zion begged YHWH to see her narrow straits brought on by death and bereavement (צַר־לִי, Lam 1:20), but now the returning children will complain of narrow straits—of overcrowding (צַר־לִי, Isa 49:20). Zion who was bereaved (שִׁכְּלָה, Lam 1:20), exiled (גָּלְתָה, Lam 1:3), and sent away (סוּרוּ, Lam 4:15) will remember, "I was bereaved and desolate, exiled and sent away" (וַאֲנִי שְׁכוּלָה וְגַלְמוּדָה גֹּלָה וְסוּרָה, Isa 49:21), and will wonder who bore her these offspring.[15] Whereas once the kings of the earth (מַלְכֵי־אֶרֶץ, Lam 4:12) witnessed in horror the city's destruction, now these kings (מְלָכִים, Isa 49:7; 49:23) bear witness

---

[13] Without more linguistic clues, it is not clear that cannibalism is the form of forgetting that is being recalled in this verse, nor that mention in Lamentations of this atrocity is being directly echoed. However, Isa 49:26 illustrates that the idea of eating one's own flesh is not far away.

[14] Newsom (76) noted the reversal of both destroyed walls and languishing roads in Isaiah 49, as well as the return in 49:18 and 51:11 of the scattered populace of Lam 1:3, 5.

[15] Turner (186) also noted some of these correspondences.

to its exaltation, bringing home its exiles and bowing to Zion. Affirming the hope of Lam 3:25, "Good is YHWH to one who hopes in him" (טוֹב יְהוָה לְקֹוָו), YHWH announces, "The one who hopes in me will not be shamed" (לֹא־יֵבֹשׁוּ קֹוָי, Isa 49:23). In accordance with the request of Lam 3:58, "Contend, Lord, with my contenders" (רַבְתָּ אֲדֹנָי רִיבֵי נַפְשִׁי), YHWH promises "I myself will contend with your contenders" (וְאֶת־יְרִיבֵךְ אָנֹכִי אָרִיב, Isa 49:25). In fact, YHWH promises to make Zion's enemies resort to the atrocities to which her people had resorted: "I will make your oppressors eat their own flesh, and as with wine with their own blood they will be drunk" (Isa 49:26; see Lam 2:20; 4:10, 21). Thus Zion's introductory complaint has unleashed a cascade of arguments that YHWH has not forgotten at all.

Summary

Recollections of Lamentations 1 and 5 occur back to back in Isaiah 49:13 and 14, as Zion is introduced. These linguistic recollections, which reverse the earlier complaints, are followed by other reversals that illustrate resolution not only of Jerusalem's predicament in general, but also of many specific expressions of dismay found in Judah's laments. Moreover, in recontextualizing and rephrasing the climactic question of Lamentations 5, Second Isaiah does not simply position itself in relation to previous speech, but also repositions previous speech in relation to its own claims. Rather than presenting the city's plea as a legitimate complaint, long unanswered but finally addressed, Second Isaiah subtly shifts sympathy away from human longing and toward divine response. Zion's complaint is heard not in the context of the divine silence experienced by witnesses to Jerusalem's destruction but in the more panoramic context of divine action understood to have begun long before with the choosing of the patriarchs and the deliverance of their descendants from Egypt. This context will find its fullest development in the subsequent Zion passages.

Recognition of exegetical reuses of the lament in this passage affirms the ancient view of Isaiah as speech that addresses and remedies the pain of Lamentations 1. YHWH's promise to comfort Zion may be viewed as a response not merely to the destroyed state of the city but to a Judahite liturgical complaint that would have been presented to YHWH frequently for several decades. While the lament ends as a prayer unheard, without a word from YHWH, Second Isaiah's antiphonal response not only to its central claim but also to many of its specific terms both affirms and proposes to conclude, or to render no longer applicable, the lament's complaint.

The language of Lamentations in this section, however, is only the finer thread interwoven with much thicker allusions to Jeremiah 1–3 and related passages in Jeremiah. The most important and distinct recollections of Jeremiah occur at the beginning, midpoint, and end of this section, with suggestive echoes scattered throughout the remainder.

Recollections of Jeremiah

Jeremiah 1 and the Servant's Call

Similarities between the portrayal of Jeremiah the prophet and the suffering servant in Second Isaiah have often been noted, even to the point that some have viewed Jeremiah himself as the servant, or at least the servant's model.[16] Linguistic relationships between the depiction of Jeremiah's call at the book's beginning and this servant passage are indeed obvious. After the book's superscription,

---

16 For instance, according to Ibn Ezra, Saadia Gaon understood Isaiah 53 to refer to Jeremiah (S. R. Driver and A. D. Neubauer, *The Fifty-Third Chapter of Isaiah according to the Jewish Interpreters,* New York: Ktav Publishing House, 1969, originally published in 1877, 43–44). In this century, O. Eissfeldt, in *Der Gottesknecht bei Deuterojesaja* (Halle: Max Niemeyer Verlag, 1933) 17; S. Blank, in *Prophetic Faith in Isaiah* (London: Adam and Charles Black, 1958) 100–104, and others have suggested that Jeremiah served as a model for the servant. Eldridge (218–25) discussed particular parallels between Jeremiah and the Servant in Isaiah 53: "lamb led to the slaughter" and "cut off from the land of the living" in Jer 11:19 and 53:7–8; "bear sins" in Jer 10:19 and Isa 53:4. These parallels led him to conclude that "the language of the Servant in Isaiah 53:4–8 is strongly influenced by Jeremiah's laments, especially in the so-called confessional passages."

Jeremiah relates what YHWH said in commissioning him. These verses, as well as the corresponding section in Isaiah 49, bear some well-known resemblances to Egyptian texts concerning God's consecration *in utero* of the royalty:[17]

Jer 1:4	The word of YHWH came to me:	וַיְהִי דְבַר־יְהוָה אֵלַי לֵאמֹר
1:5	Before I formed you in the womb I knew you;	בְּטֶרֶם אֶצָּרְךָ בַבֶּטֶן יְדַעְתִּיךָ
	And before you went out from the womb I consecrated you;	וּבְטֶרֶם תֵּצֵא מֵרֶחֶם הִקְדַּשְׁתִּיךָ
	A prophet to the nations I appointed you.	נָבִיא לַגּוֹיִם נְתַתִּיךָ

These verses are echoed in several ways in Isaiah 49. The word בֶּטֶן ("womb") is used twice, first in the introduction (49:1): "YHWH called me from the womb (יְהוָה מִבֶּטֶן קְרָאָנִי)," and then in a duplication of the phrase from Jer 1:5:[18]

Isa 49:5	And now says YHWH,	וְעַתָּה אָמַר יְהוָה
	who formed me from the womb as his servant . . .	יֹצְרִי מִבֶּטֶן לְעֶבֶד לוֹ

The phrase "form in/from the womb" only occurs in these two texts and in Isa 44:2 and 44:24. Both those passages employ the participial form as Isa 49:5 does, and explicitly refer to Israel.

Not only does servant Israel claim, as Jeremiah did, to have been formed in the womb for God's purposes, but his appointment resembles Jeremiah's semantically. In Jer 1:5, YHWH said to Jeremiah, "A prophet to the nations I appointed you (נָבִיא לַגּוֹיִם נְתַתִּיךָ). Similarly, in Isa 49:6, YHWH says to the servant, "I will appoint you as light to the nations (וּנְתַתִּיךָ לְאוֹר גּוֹיִם)."[19] This

---

[17] See especially W. Beyerlin, *Near Eastern Religious Texts Relating to the Old Testament* (Philadelphia: Westminster Press, 1975) 27–30, who quotes several of these texts, such as this one: "He (Re-Harakhti) formed me to do what he has done, and to bring into being what he has commanded to be done. He named me shepherd of this land . . . he appointed me Lord of the two parts of the land while (I was still) a child. . . . Even as an embryo he set me aside (?) to be in the palace, before I had come from my mother's loins. . . ."

[18] Cassuto, "Formal and Stylistic Relationship," 156; Eldridge, 189–91.

[19] Eldridge, 192–94.

phrasing occurs only in these two passages and in Isa 42:6, where it is paired with another phrase from Isaiah 49, "covenant to the people."

Additional similarities may be seen between Isaiah 49 and Jeremiah 1:

1) Both are composed from the viewpoint of a human speaker, reporting YHWH's words both to and about the speaker. This is rather uncommon in prophetic literature, which devotes the bulk of its attention to YHWH's speech to people other than the prophet.

2) Both speakers tell their story in retrospective terms. Jeremiah recounts an encounter that has already taken place, including both his own objections and God's responses to them. Israel also recounts his previous objections and God's responses. In fact, this account places in Israel's mouth what the audience has already heard from God in preceding chapters: YHWH's repeated announcements that Israel is "my servant," "formed in the womb" (Isa 44:2, see 49:1, 3), in whom YHWH "will be glorified" (יִתְפָּאָר, Isa 44:23, see 49:3); Israel's own initial objections concerning "my right" (מִשְׁפָּטִי, Isa 40:27, see 49:4), and YHWH's reassuring promise that even the weary (יגע, Isa 40:28, 30, 31; see 49:4) will be given strength (כֹּחַ, 40:29, see 49:4).

3) Both passages claim YHWH's appointment of the speaker to a task as messenger. But as I shall show below, the medium of their message may differ.

4) Both mention YHWH's hand and the speaker's mouth, and relate them to one another. After Jeremiah's objection and YHWH's response:

Jer	Then YHWH put out his hand	וַיִּשְׁלַח יְהוָה אֶת־יָדוֹ
1:9	and touched my mouth,	וַיַּגַּע עַל־פִּי
	and YHWH said to me,	וַיֹּאמֶר יְהוָה אֵלַי
	"Now I have put my words in your mouth."	הִנֵּה נָתַתִּי דְבָרַי בְּפִיךָ

In Isaiah, the description of YHWH's actions preparing the servant is more prolix:

Isa 49:2	And he made my mouth like a sharp sword;	וַיָּשֶׂם פִּי כְּחֶרֶב חַדָּה
	in the shadow of his hand he hid me.	בְּצֵל יָדוֹ הֶחְבִּיאָנִי
	He made me a sharpened arrow;	וַיְשִׂימֵנִי לְחֵץ בָּרוּר
	in his quiver he kept me hidden.	בְּאַשְׁפָּתוֹ הִסְתִּירָנִי

That Second Isaiah views this new saying in Isa 49:2 as related to the previous one in Jer 1:9 is demonstrated further on, in Isa 51:16, in which lines from both verses are combined:

Isa 51:16	And I have put my words in your mouth,	וָאָשִׂים דְּבָרַי בְּפִיךָ
	and in the shadow of my hand I hid you.	וּבְצֵל יָדִי כִּסִּיתִיךָ

In short, the servant of YHWH, identified as Israel, is here styled in the manner of YHWH's servant the prophet Jeremiah. Similarities between these two texts are well known and have been much discussed. Although "call narratives" to which both have been compared, especially of Moses in Exodus 3–4 and of Gideon in Judges 6, share with these two passages several motifs such as the dialogue between the divine commissioner and the human appointee and the reluctance of the one called, they do not share either the first-person perspective or the common language that is found in both Jeremiah and Isaiah.[20]

Dependence of Jeremiah 1 on Isaiah 49 has been argued by some who view similarities between Jeremiah and Second Isaiah as indications of secondary editing in Jeremiah. On that basis this opening chapter is, like Jeremiah 30–31, viewed as a postexilic addition to the Jeremiah story. This view might be more convincing if the figure speaking in Isaiah 49 were the prophet himself. But if the speaker is Israel, as he is called in verse 3, then these verses describe the reception of call not by an individual prophet, but by a whole nation, a reception whose literary styling recollects the prophetic call tradition. It is more logical to view the Jeremiah text as a variation on the "call to the individual" motif that is also found

---

[20] Clifford (150) and others have pointed out the similarity between Isaiah 49 and not only Jeremiah 1 but also the call narratives of Moses (Exod 3:1–4:17) and Gideon (Judg 6:11–24). Jeremiah provides by far the closest parallels. The theme of objection and doubt is quite truncated in Isaiah, and may represent simply a bow in the direction of the typical pattern.

in narrative accounts, and the Isaiah text as an intertextual linking of Israel's calling to the call of an individual prophet, than it is to understand Second Isaiah as making the major leap from individual to collective call as well as from narrative to prophecy, and the prophet Jeremiah as afterwards being fashioned in the likeness of collective Israel.

This passage suggests clear parallels between the servant and Jeremiah, parallels that will find further elucidation in Isaiah 53.[21] But even as Israel is posited as a new Jeremiah, some adaptations of the figure also appear. Unlike Jeremiah, who is clearly presented as an individual prophet, the servant in Second Isaiah is given a national name: Israel/Jacob. Unlike Jeremiah, whose primary role in his book is to deliver YHWH's message to the inhabitants of Judah, the servant who is portrayed here is not represented as the one delivering the words in the rest of the book. More often than this servant speaks, he is spoken to (Isaiah 41, 43–44) or about (Isa 42, 53). In fact, when he last appears in Isaiah 53 it is not his speech but his silent presence and the events surrounding him that reveal "YHWH's arm" to the nations. Jeremiah was called "prophet to the nations," but Israel is here called not prophet, but "light to the nations," suggesting a visual, rather than verbal, dimension to the message.

As I will demonstrate in chapter 5, Jeremiah is by no means the only individual model from which the prophet draws the servant's collective character. Further intertextual investigation will show Second Isaiah's envisioned servant Israel to be a composite figure, constructed out of several elements of Judah's tradition. Here it can initially be noted that one of the analogies by which this new Israel is constructed is that of YHWH's prophet Jeremiah.

Jeremiah 2 and the Bridal Ornaments

The second recollection of Jeremiah becomes apparent when both the language and the argumentation in Jeremiah 2 is compared with that of Isaiah 49. A complex of allusions to Jeremiah's

---

[21] See note 16 above.

imagery of the adulterous wife of YHWH appears in this poetry; only now, she has been restored from her shame. The series of references to Zion in Isaiah 49–50 suppress the image of sexual lawlessness that was relentlessly highlighted in Jeremiah, but enough details of that picture remain to indicate that Second Isaiah is imagining an analogous "woman."

Immediately following Zion's complaint that YHWH has forgotten and abandoned her, Second Isaiah presents YHWH's response, in which YHWH is first compared, and then contrasted, with a nursing mother:

Isa	Can a woman forget her nursing child,	*הֲתִשְׁכַּח* אִשָּׁה עוּלָהּ
49:15	not pity the child of her womb?	מֵרַחֵם בֶּן־בִּטְנָהּ
	Even these will forget.	גַּם־אֵלֶּה *תִשְׁכַּחְנָה*
	But I will not forget you.	וְאָנֹכִי לֹא *אֶשְׁכָּחֵךְ*

The theme of forgetting was a crucial one in Jeremiah 2–3 as well. There, however, what was at stake was human forgetfulness rather than divine neglect. Jeremiah 2 began with the metaphor of the people as a bride in the wilderness: "I remember the devotion of your (fs) youth, the love of your (fs) betrothal" (Jer 2:2). This metaphor is not consistently maintained through the chapter; at times metaphorical language is dropped altogether, and at other times it shifts to other images, such as plunder, vine, or a restive camel. Similarly, the pronouns shift several times, not so much according to the images as according to the nouns by which the addressee is identified.

In verse 32 the bridal analogy returns:

Jer	Can a virgin forget her ornaments,	*הֲתִשְׁכַּח* בְּתוּלָה *עֶדְיָהּ*
2:32	a bride her bands?	*כַּלָּה קִשֻּׁרֶיהָ*
	But my people have forgotten me,	וְעַמִּי *שְׁכֵחוּנִי*
	days without number.	יָמִים אֵין מִסְפָּר

Even though the form הֲתִשְׁכַּח is found nowhere else in the Bible than these two verses, the relationship between Jer 2:32 and Isa 49:15 may not be at first glance readily apparent. After all, Jeremiah imagines a virgin; Second Isaiah a mother. The first text concerns frivolous ornaments, the second, precious children. The first implies that the bride will not forget these objects, while the second states, shockingly, that a mother may in fact forget her child. The first turns out to be about human forgetting, the second about God's. The next two verses in Isaiah 49 elaborate on YHWH's remembering, claiming that Zion is inscribed in YHWH's hand, and that Zion's children are approaching. Isaiah 49:18 returns to the Jeremiah passage in a startling way:[22]

Isa 49:18	Lift up your eyes all around and see, they are all gathered, they come to you. As I live, says YHWH, you shall put them all on like ornaments, and bind them on like a bride.	שְׂאִי־סָבִיב עֵינַיִךְ וּרְאִי כֻּלָּם נִקְבְּצוּ בָאוּ־לָךְ חַי־אָנִי נְאֻם־יְהוָה כִּי כֻלָּם כַּעֲדִי תִלְבָּשִׁי **וּתְקַשְּׁרִים כַּכַּלָּה**

Zion, who had thought she was forgotten, is invited to lift up her eyes and see that this is not true at all. This verse employs not only the unusual word עֲדִי (ornaments) that had appeared in Jer 2:32, but uses it in connection with two other words in the verse: כַּלָּה (bride) and a verbal form of קִשֻּׁרִים (bands), which only appears otherwise in the Bible in a list of women's ornaments in Isa 3:20. Here the words appear in a simile in which those returning from distant lands to Jerusalem become the decorative wear of YHWH's bride, the signs of her husband's love, adorning the city with their presence.

The shifts in imagery are dizzying in both passages, and in the Isaiah passage especially have led to curious interpretations.[23] In Jer

---

[22] Cassuto ("Formal and Stylistic Relationship," 157) noted the similarity of both of these verses to Jer 2:32. Paul (114) and Eldridge (197–99) discussed it as well.

[23] T. Ridderbos, *Isaiah* (Grand Rapids, MI: Zondervan, 1985, originally published in Dutch in 1950–51) 444, called this image of Zion donning her inhabitants in the way a bride dons an ornamental waistband a "curious picture." Muilenburg (575) mistook YHWH for the bride: "The returning exiles are YHWH's jewels. YHWH will adorn himself with them as a bride adorns herself." Westermann (*Isaiah 40–66*, 220) attempted to explain away the imagery: "Here the term 'ornament' is not really an aesthetic one. Adornment is 'what renders someone beautiful in the sight of others,' splendour or dignity. It is not here conceived in terms of its objective value or beauty. It means making beautiful and dignified in the eyes of others. The

2:32 it is the masculine plural "my people" who are compared with a feminine singular bride, and only after this verse does the address shift back to feminine singular. In Isa 49:15 it is YHWH who is compared with the feminine singular mother, and Zion becomes her child, but by verse 18 it is Zion who has become the bride, and her own children who are the ornaments. The mixing of metaphors in both texts create difficulties in sorting out one-to-one correspondences. Yet Jeremiah's words supply a context missing from Second Isaiah's surface, so that links between the bride's ornaments and the mother's children can be discerned. The poet's recollections of Jeremiah point toward a logic such as this: YHWH has been accused of having forgotten Zion. Yet this forgetting, Second Isaiah reminds the audience, was not unilateral. Echoing the syntax of an old accusation against the people as forgetting YHWH like a foolish bride might forget decorations, YHWH asks whether a woman could forget her own child. The implied answer is "no." Yet YHWH then points out (as Jeremiah had) that humans do forget. It is YHWH who does not forget. God will restore Zion to her own bridal state and rejoin her with her "ornaments," the children that YHWH claims to have remembered even more faithfully than had their mother. Even if a bride could forget her decorations, even though Jerusalem did in fact forget YHWH, even though the bitter conditions may have led some women even to forget their own young, nevertheless, despite all human forgetting, YHWH bridges the chasm of disaster by continuing to remember Jerusalem. As a sign of the undoing of estrangement, the returning children become the mother's ornaments, now donned in celebration. Second Isaiah has changed the ingredients of an accusation into those of a promise.

Jeremiah 3 and the Certificate of Divorce

The third close connection between this part of Second Isaiah and the initial chapters of Jeremiah occurs near the end of the

---

reason why Israel regains her honour and standing in the world's eye is the vast number of those who return."

section, in Isa 50:1, which reverses Jeremiah's warning of irreconcilable estrangement. Jeremiah had introduced the imagery, as I have shown, in the beginning of his address in Jer 2:2, calling the addressee (who is, according to the first part of the verse, Jerusalem) YHWH's bride. Before returning to this analogy, Jeremiah cycles through several others, in which the addressees are compared with fruit (2:3), prey (2:14), diggers of cisterns (2:13, 18), a slave (2:20), a vine (2:21), a camel (2:23), a thief (2:26). Finally, invoking a statute of divorce between humans, Jer 3:1 asks:

Jer		לֵאמֹר
3:1	If a man sends his wife away,	הֵן ***יְשַׁלַּח*** אִישׁ אֶת־אִשְׁתּוֹ
	and she leaves him,	וְהָלְכָה מֵאִתּוֹ
	And marries another man,	וְהָיְתָה לְאִישׁ־אַחֵר
	can he return to her again?	הֲיָשׁוּב אֵלֶיהָ עוֹד
	Would not that land be greatly defiled?	הֲלוֹא חָנוֹף תֶּחֱנַף הָאָרֶץ הַהִיא
	You have solicited many lovers,	וְאַתְּ זָנִית רֵעִים רַבִּים
	and would you return to me?	וְשׁוֹב אֵלַי נְאֻם־יְהוָה
	says YHWH.	

In very similar language, Deuteronomy 24:1–4 had outlawed a man's taking again (לָשׁוּב לְקַחְתָּהּ) his estranged wife once he has written her a certificate of divorce (סֵפֶר כְּרִיתֻת) and sent her away (וְשִׁלְּחָהּ), allowing her to leave and marry another man (וְהָלְכָה וְהָיְתָה לְאִישׁ־אַחֵר). Such an action would bring guilt on the land (הָאָרֶץ). Scholars have debated whether Jeremiah was referring to this particular formulation of the law of divorce.[24] The relationship seems clear both thematically and linguistically, but how moderns understand Jeremiah is actually less important than how the tradition itself understood the passage. Jeremiah 3:6–11 is a prose elaboration that may stand at some years distant.[25] It displays cognizance of the exegetical relationship between Jer 3:1

---

[24] In addition to the commentaries, see for example J. D. Martin, "Forensic Background to Jeremiah 3:1," *VT* 19 (1969) 82–92, T. R. Hobbs, "Jeremiah 3:1–5 and Deuteronomy 24:1–4," *ZAW* 86 (1974) 23–29, and Burke Long, "The Stylistic Components of Jeremiah 3:1–5," *ZAW* 88 (1976) 386–90.

[25] So argue McKane (*Jeremiah*, vol. 1, 64–69) and Carroll (*Jeremiah*, 145).

and the Deuteronomic law by repeating a specific clause of the law that is missing in Jer 3:1: שִׁלַּחְתִּיהָ וָאֶתֵּן אֶת־סֵפֶר כְּרִיתֻתֶיהָ אֵלֶיהָ ("I sent her away and gave her certificate of divorce to her"). This clause is used in reference to YHWH's rejection of Israel, and stands as a warning to Judah lest the same happen to her. For our purposes it confirms that the question in Jer 3:1 was understood by its readers not simply by general reference to divorce laws but specifically in references to the expression in Deut 24:1–4.

Like Jeremiah, Second Isaiah does not employ the metaphor of marriage as a sole, or even primary, description of the divine-human relationship. According to Second Isaiah, Zion is YHWH's herald (Isa 40:9), city (Isa 44:26–28; 49:16–17; 52:1), child (Isa 49:15), and widow (54:4), and YHWH is Zion's mother (49:15), rescuer (49:26), gardener (51:3), torturer (51:17), king (52:7), and protector (54:14–16). Among these diverse analogies is that of YHWH as Zion's estranged—but not divorced—husband. This metaphor will recur in chapter 54, in which YHWH confesses to having once deserted Zion, but promises not to do so again. In Isaiah 49, YHWH denied having forgotten Zion and claimed to remember her faithfully; here in Isa 50:1, YHWH denies having either divorced Zion or sold her children:[26]

Isa 50:1	Thus has YHWH said:	כֹּה אָמַר יְהוָה
	Where is your mother's certificate of divorce,	אֵי זֶה סֵפֶר כְּרִיתוּת אִמְּכֶם
	with which I sent her away?	אֲשֶׁר *שִׁלַּחְתִּיהָ*
	Or to which of my creditors	אוֹ מִי מִנּוֹשַׁי
	did I sell you?	אֲשֶׁר־מָכַרְתִּי אֶתְכֶם לוֹ
	See, because of your sins you were sold,	הֵן *בַּעֲוֺנֹתֵיכֶם* נִמְכַּרְתֶּם
	and because of your transgressions your mother was sent away.	*וּבְפִשְׁעֵיכֶם שֻׁלְּחָה* אִמְּכֶם

Jeremiah had used the law to demonstrate that a woman who has been with another man is not only loathsome but actually forbidden to her first husband. Because the people's sins against YHWH were tantamount to a wife's unfaithfulness, Jeremiah asked

---

[26] Eldridge, 199–203.

how they could expect to then return to YHWH. Second Isaiah employs the vocabulary of the divorce law for a contrary purpose, saying, in effect, if Jerusalem is thus rejected, where is the certificate of divorce? Where is the legal paper necessitating the permanence of the separation? In other words, who says the analogy actually applies? Like Jer 3:13 ("only know your guilt—עֲוֹנֵךְ—that against YHWH your God you transgressed"—פָּשָׁעַתְּ), this verse goes on to identify the problem as sins (עֲוֹנֹתֵיכֶם) and transgressions (פִּשְׁעֵיכֶם). Though Jeremiah attributes these to the wife, Second Isaiah blames the children.

These three echoes of the first chapters of Jeremiah, located as they are at the beginning, middle, and end of this passage, signal that Zion's first section is profitably to be read not only in terms of Lamentations, but also against the background of Jeremiah, the prophet of Jerusalem's destruction. Whereas Jeremiah had been depicted as a solitary figure crying to deaf ears, his successor Israel is the one whose own ears have finally become unstopped, and who is now himself responsive to God's call. Whereas Jeremiah, using female imagery, had accused the hearers of estrangement from YHWH, Second Isaiah uses variations of the same imagery to announce reconciliation.

Echoes of Jeremiah's words in chapter 13, which is closely related to chapter 3, may also be heard in this section in language such as "lift up your eyes and see" (Isa 49:18, see Jer 13:20), the imagery of the scattered/returning flock (Isa 49:9–10, see Jer 13:20), "you will say in your heart" (Isa 49:21, see Jer 13:22), labor pains and birth (Isa 49:21, see Jer 13:21), exile (Isa 49:21, see Jer 13:19), and the humbling of kings and queens (Isa 49:23, see Jer 13:18). In all these cases, imagery that was used to communicate devastation is here reversed to sum up restoration: what Zion sees is not her coming enemies but her coming children, no longer her flock being driven away but her flock being led back; what she says in her heart expresses no longer dismay but surprised delight; what she experiences is no longer labor without birth but birth without labor. She is no longer exiled but restored; and it is no longer her royalty, but that of other nations, who are humbled. They come bowing down before Zion.

Jeremiah 31 and Descriptions of the Return

The language of consolation and return in Jeremiah 30–31 reverses threat language found in the prophetic oracles of the earlier part of Jeremiah. In my previous chapter, I examined close exegetical relationships between parts of Jeremiah 31 and Isaiah 51, relationships testifying that the well-known similarities between Jeremiah's book of consolation and Second Isaiah are quite purposefully executed. Images and phrases occurring in that section of Jeremiah are scattered throughout Second Isaiah, from its first chapter to its last, often so briefly as to provide modern ears, unfamiliar with the rich context, only fleeting echoes. One such complex of echoes is to be found in Isaiah 49:9–13. Without other support for recognizing Second Isaiah's knowledge of Jeremiah 31, these echoes, though certainly tantalizing, could easily be counted as coincidentally similar reversals of the same prophecies of threat. If viewed against the background of Jeremiah's earlier hopes of return, however, this new poetry displays free play with, and enlargement upon, the constructions of Jeremiah's visions.

1) In Isa 49:9, the returning exiles are pictured as the flock of sheep that YHWH had once driven away. This description resembles the portrayal of return in Jer 31:10: "The one who scattered Israel will gather him (יְקַבְּצֶנּוּ), and will keep him as a shepherd his flock (כְּרֹעֶה עֶדְרוֹ)." In fact, the first image of return in Second Isaiah's introduction (Isa 40:11) had echoed this Jeremian passage even more closely. There YHWH was pictured shepherding the flock like a shepherd (כְּרֹעֶה עֶדְרוֹ יִרְעֶה), gathering (יְקַבֵּץ) the lambs and leading the ewes.

2) This description of pasturage is extended in Isa 49:10 with an assurance that they will be led by springs of water. It corresponds to the description of return in Jer 31:9, in which YHWH promises to lead the returnees by brooks of water.[27]

[27] Cassuto, "Formal and Stylistic Relationship," 151; Eldridge, 141.

3) In Isa 49:11 it is not just the pasture land and water that become inviting. Road (דֶּרֶךְ) and highways appear in the mountains to smooth the way home. Similarly, directly after the description of brooks of water, Jer 31:9 describes a road (דֶּרֶךְ) on which the returnees will not stumble.

4) The direction from which the returnees come is given in Jer 31:8 as "the land of the north" (מֵאֶרֶץ צָפוֹן, the same direction from which the invaders came in Jer 13:20, etc.) and "the farthest parts of the earth." In Isa 49:12 the returnees come from far away, from the north (מִצָּפוֹן) and west.[28]

5) The description of the returnees concludes in Isa 49:13 with a hymnic passage in which the elements are told to cry out (רָנּוּ) because "YHWH has comforted his people" (נִחַם יְהוָה עַמּוֹ). The Jeremiah passage begins with a similar cry. There it is a prayer to YHWH, in which the people cry out (רָנּוּ), "save, YHWH, your people (הוֹשַׁע יְהוָה אֶת־עַמְּךָ)."[29]

6) In addition to all this, the entire chapter in Isaiah begins with an address to the coastlands that is very similar to that in Jer 31:10, which begins:

Jer	Hear the word of YHWH, nations,	***שִׁמְעוּ*** דְבַר־יְהוָה גּוֹיִם
31:10	and declare in the coastlands far away.	וְהַגִּידוּ ***בָאִיִּים מִמֶּרְחָק***

The Isaiah chapter likewise begins:[30]

Isa	Listen, coastlands, to me,	***שִׁמְעוּ אִיִּים*** אֵלַי
49:1	attend, peoples from afar.	וְהַקְשִׁיבוּ לְאֻמִּים ***מֵרָחוֹק***

In no other place are the "coastlands" addressed as here.

Whether Second Isaiah intends the audience to relate this poetry to Jeremiah's specific words is not clear. Given the missed opportunities to repeat verbatim formulations that are here only paraphrased, it is doubtful that the poet seeks more than to tap into known images of return. What is clear is that the visions of

---

28 Cassuto, 150; Eldridge, 140.

29 Cassuto, 150; Eldridge, 139.

30 Cassuto, 151; Eldridge, 142.

return expressed here are not Second Isaiah's own creation, but are pictures of hope already formed in the community's mental landscape. What the prophet does that is new is to apply to a particular historical moment what was once a hope about an indefinite time in the future, and to claim that the things formerly declared have now come to pass. Renewing the notion of a "servant of YHWH" called in the tradition of Jeremiah, the poet invites the understanding that what is being said now is what Jeremiah himself would have said, had he lived so long. Setting up the beginning of this section as a renewal of Jeremiah's call, now made to the nation as a whole, the poet then begins radically to reverse the estranged divine-human relationship that Jeremiah had announced. Thus Second Isaiah is portrayed not as standing over against the preexilic prophet, but as carrying his message to its logical conclusion. Whereas Jeremiah employed the metaphor of the people as the unfaithful wife of YHWH in an effort to convey to his hearers the magnitude of their apostasy toward their God, Second Isaiah uses elements of Jeremiah's language to recall that metaphor and to place the new speech in its context, and yet to proclaim an end to the punishment threatened by Jeremiah.

In this passage Second Isaiah enlists the voice of a messenger who, like Jeremiah, is authorized by his pre-birth election by YHWH. Jeremiah had claimed that Jerusalem's memory was more frivolous than that of a shallow young girl; Second Isaiah claims that YHWH's memory is more enduring than that of the most doting mother. Jeremiah had suggested an impending divorce; Second Isaiah proclaims reconciliation. Nothing Jeremiah had claimed is denied outright, although in keeping with rapprochement, its terms are softened and cushioned—nowhere does Second Isaiah use the violent sexual language that Jeremiah often employs. Second Isaiah's proclamation of salvation, however, is keyed to the terms of Jeremiah's threats as if to say that the prophecies, having been fulfilled, are now being disassembled—the time of alienation and grief is over, and the time of redemption is at hand.

Isaiah 49:1–50:3 in Review

The beginning of Isaiah 49 marks a turning point in Second Isaiah. Immediately following a major section addressed primarily to Israel/Jacob, which concluded in chapter 48 with the rousing call to "go out from Babylon, flee from Chaldea," this chapter turns to address Daughter Zion, who has not been addressed since the introduction. Elements of Jeremiah's words of censure and threat recur abundantly here. Motifs, phrases, and arguments from Jeremiah 1–3 and 13 reemerge. Here they bring not condemnation but consolation.

The entrance of Daughter Zion as a central figure in the second half of Second Isaiah is accompanied by allusions not only to Jeremiah, but also to two other Zion traditions, both of them liturgical: the enthronement hymn celebrating YHWH's reign as king protecting Jerusalem, and its logical transposition, the book of Lamentations, which mourned the destruction of Jerusalem and its abandonment by YHWH.[31] The enthronement language had begun to appear in Second Isaiah with a dramatic repetition of the first line of Psalm 98 in Isa 42:10, directly after the first announcement of YHWH's purpose for God's chosen servant. In this chapter the psalmic language begins to be combined with the specific announcement that "YHWH has comforted his people," an announcement that addresses the complaint that was left unanswered in Lamentations 1, "Zion has no comforter." As I showed in chapter 3, the language will dramatically resurface in Isa 52:9–10, in response to the announcement in Isa 52:7 of YHWH's return to reign in Zion.

The announcement of YHWH's comfort is elucidated not just by the reversal of Jeremiah's threats, but also by repeated allusions to specific complaints from Lamentations. The question that had summed up Jerusalem's predicament is recollected in Zion's opening words, although given a very different setting and tone in

---

[31] The ironic citation of Psalm 48 in Lam 2:15 accentuates the overturned royal Zion theology fundamental to Lamentations.

Second Isaiah. Enemies who in Lamentations tormented Jerusalem are imagined departing, and the city's own people, who in the lament were exiled and killed, are imagined returning on the shoulders of foreign rulers, in such numbers that the desolate city will be crowded. These themes so predominant in Lamentations—the sufferings of Zion, the loss of her people and the torment by her enemies—resurface each time Zion is addressed, in Isa 51:9–52:12 and again in Isaiah 54. Each time, the issues are subtly redefined by Second Isaiah, who forges out of Lamentations' complaints a question for which Cyrus's ascendancy and the exiles' return becomes the appropriate answer.

Immediately following Isa 50:3 is a second (and the only other) section in which the servant speaks. This section, along with the final "servant" section in Isaiah 53, will be dealt with next. Then I will examine Daughter Zion's last section, Isaiah 54, showing how Second Isaiah brings the two figures, Israel and Zion, into relationship with each other.

Chapter 5
"My Back I Gave to Attackers": Isaiah 50:4–11 and 52:13–53:12

In both Isa 49:1–50:3 and 51:9–52:12, previous Judahite language is recalled which connects the devastated city of Jerusalem and the exiled people of Israel with their textual past, and negotiates a rhetoric by which they might envision anew their theological identity. The female figure, who is recollected from both Jeremiah and Lamentations as a woman rejected by God, is offered renewal and reconciliation. The city's people, whom both Jeremiah and Lamentations described suffering destruction and exile, are imagined returning in triumph from afar, reenacting the nation's originating story of exodus.

In this chapter and the next I will examine the sections most closely related to those already explored: two sections on the servant of YHWH standing between the Zion sections, Isa 50:4–11 and Isa 52:13–53:12, and the final section on Daughter Zion, Isaiah 54. This will complete the exploration of the two predominant figures in Second Isaiah's "Zion section," Daughter Zion and the Servant of YHWH.

As was discussed in chapter 3, intertextual precedents for Daughter Zion are easy to find and remain relatively stable. Second Isaiah never spells out who Daughter Zion is, but rather seems to assume that the figure is self-evident.[1] By contrast, as was pointed out in chapter 4, the prophet repeatedly identifies the servant of YHWH with Israel and Jacob, and never identifies the servant by

---

[1] In his discussion of the debate about the servant (*Farewell,* 39), Mettinger pointed out the discrepancy in the scholarly treatment of the two figures with this remark: "In Isa 54:1–8 we have a portrait of Zion which is so rich in detail that scholars would be writing penetrating monographs about this unknown female figure, if we did not already know that the prophet is here speaking about Jerusalem."

any other name, thus repeatedly answering not the question "who is YHWH's servant?" but "who is Israel in relation to God?" Over and over Second Isaiah asserts that Israel is YHWH's servant.

Though both the concept of "YHWH's servant" and the personification of the nation of Israel as a masculine singular figure are well known from previous Judahite texts, they are not generally combined. As was noted in chapter 4, previous references to Israel as a masculine singular entity are quite plentiful. Likewise, previous portions of the Bible note many servants of YHWH, including Moses, David, the prophets in general, and even Nebuchadrezzar of Babylon (Jer 25:9). Occasionally the term designates Abraham, Isaac, and Israel (Ex 32:13, Dt 9:27) or Jacob alone (Ezek 37:25). Leviticus 25:55 refers to the children of Israel (בְּנֵי־יִשְׂרָאֵל) as YHWH's servants, plural (see also verse 42).

In all the previous literature, only Jeremiah addresses the masculine singular nation as "my servant": in Jer 30:10 (see also 46:27–28) YHWH announces, "But now do not fear, my servant Jacob, says YHWH, and do not be dismayed, Israel, for I am saving you from afar, and your offspring from the land of their captivity." Similarities between that verse and parts of Second Isaiah (see especially Isa 41:8–10 and 43:5) have often been noted. It is possible that Second Isaiah's identification of Israel with the servant was inspired by Jeremiah's remark. Nevertheless, it was Second Isaiah who articulated in detail the implications of this new association.

Westermann has noted that the imagery by which the servant is described connects with several elements of Judah's traditions.[2] I have already shown an analogy drawn between this servant and Jeremiah, whose call is recollected in Isa 49:1–13. Relationships have also been suggested to the patriarchs, particularly in the "do not fear" passages early in the book,[3] and to David, on account of the descriptions of Israel as both "servant" and "chosen," a combination that occurs otherwise only of David and his

---

[2] Westermann, *Isaiah 40–66*, 20–21.

[3] See especially Gen 26:24 and Isa 41:8–10; Gen 28:13–15 and Isa 43:5–6.

descendants.[4] This relationship to David will be explored in chapter 6.

But a striking clue to the servant figure in Second Isaiah which has never, to my knowledge, been explored involves recollections of Lamentations 3 in the final two major servant passages, primarily Isa 50:4–11 and, secondarily, Isa 52:13–53:12.

Isaiah 50:4–11

50:4	The Lord YHWH gave me	אֲדֹנָי יְהוִה נָתַן לִי
	the language of those taught,	לְשׁוֹן לִמּוּדִים
	to know how to sustain (?)[5] the weary	לָדַעַת לָעוּת אֶת־יָעֵף
	with a word.	דָּבָר יָעִיר
	He wakens in the morning, in the morning he wakens my ear,[6]	בַּבֹּקֶר בַּבֹּקֶר יָעִיר לִי אֹזֶן
	to hear as those taught.	לִשְׁמֹעַ כַּלִּמּוּדִים
50:5	The Lord YHWH opened my ear,	אֲדֹנָי יְהוִה פָּתַח־לִי אֹזֶן
	and I did not rebel;	וְאָנֹכִי לֹא מָרִיתִי
	I did not turn away.	אָחוֹר לֹא נְסוּגֹתִי
50:6	My back I gave to attackers	גֵּוִי נָתַתִּי לְמַכִּים
	and my cheeks to beard-pluckers.	וּלְחָיַי לְמֹרְטִים
	My face I did not hide	פָּנַי לֹא הִסְתַּרְתִּי
	from insults and spittle.	מִכְּלִמּוֹת וָרֹק

[4] See especially Ps 89:4, 20–21; 78:70 and Isa 41:8, 9; 42:1; 43:10; 44:1, 2; and 45:4. For discussions of these see Eissfeldt ("Promises of Grace," 204–5) and Mettinger (*Farewell*, 44).

[5] לָעוּת is a hapax legomenon and according to BDB very dubious. BHS lists several alternatives. RSV and NRSV translate as "sustain"; Westermann, following LXX, has "answer" (*Isaiah 40–66*, 225). JPS and Clifford both emend the word to לָעֵת, "in the time" (Clifford, 157) or "timely" (JPS). BDB and BHS both list several other suggestions, but there is no clear solution.

[6] The first יָעִיר, though it occurs in the previous verse, is marked by a *munach* connecting it with what follows. BHS editors suggest the word's deletion. Westermann likewise considers it redundant and deletes it (*Isaiah 40–66*, 225). JPS and NRSV both repeat "rouses" or "wakens," though not in the order in which the words occur in Hebrew. Clifford (157), supplying a personal pronoun, translates the phrase as "He roused me each morning, he roused my ear . . ." The text is unavoidably problematic. I have chosen, following the *munach*, to associate the first יָעִיר with the line that follows, and to translate as literally as possible.

50:7	And the Lord YHWH will help me,	וַאדֹנָי יֱהוִה יַעֲזָר־לִי
	therefore I have not been disgraced.	עַל־כֵּן לֹא נִכְלָמְתִּי
	Therefore I set my face like flint,	עַל־כֵּן שַׂמְתִּי פָנַי כַּחַלָּמִישׁ
	and I knew that I would not be ashamed.	וָאֵדַע כִּי־לֹא אֵבוֹשׁ
50:8	My vindicator is near; who will plead against me?	קָרוֹב מַצְדִּיקִי מִי־יָרִיב אִתִּי
	Let us stand up together.	נַעַמְדָה יָּחַד
	Who is the adversary of my right?[7]	מִי־בַעַל מִשְׁפָּטִי
	Let him approach me.	יִגַּשׁ אֵלָי
50:9	See, the Lord YHWH will help me;	הֵן אֲדֹנָי יֱהוִה יַעֲזָר־לִי
	who will condemn me?	מִי־הוּא יַרְשִׁיעֵנִי
	See, they all like a garment will wear out;	הֵן כֻּלָּם כַּבֶּגֶד יִבְלוּ
	a moth will eat them.	עָשׁ יֹאכְלֵם
50:10	Who among you fears YHWH,	מִי בָכֶם יְרֵא יְהוָה
	listening to the voice of his servant,	שֹׁמֵעַ בְּקוֹל עַבְדּוֹ
	who walked in darkness,	אֲשֶׁר הָלַךְ חֲשֵׁכִים
	and had no light?	וְאֵין נֹגַהּ לוֹ
	He will trust in the name of YHWH,	יִבְטַח בְּשֵׁם יְהוָה
	and rely upon his God.	וְיִשָּׁעֵן בֵּאלֹהָיו
50:11	See, all of you are lighting fire,	הֵן כֻּלְּכֶם קֹדְחֵי אֵשׁ
	kindling sparks.	מְאַזְּרֵי זִיקוֹת
	Walk in the light of your fire,	לְכוּ בְּאוּר אֶשְׁכֶם
	and in the sparks you have ignited.	וּבְזִיקוֹת בִּעַרְתֶּם
	By my hand this has happened to you:	מִיָּדִי הָיְתָה־זֹּאת לָכֶם
	in a bed of travail you lie.[8]	לְמַעֲצֵבָה תִּשְׁכָּבוּן

[7] Other uses of the word בַעַל as a construct are translated in terms of "one given to" something or "one who has" something. See, for instance, Gen 37:19, 2 Kings 1:8, Nah 1:2, Pr 22:24, 23:2, Ec 7:12, and Isa 41:15. On that basis it seems that the more natural translation of this phrase would not be "adversary," but "advocate." On the other hand, the parallel questions in 8a and 9a seem also to carry a negative connotation. With NRSV, JPS, Westermann (*Isaiah 40–66,* 226), Clifford (157), and the overwhelming majority, I have translated according to context. In view of the wider context that will be discussed, I still have misgivings about this translation.

[8] Although most translators interpret this verse negatively, the rather sarcastic comment that this generates in the second line ill fits the context. Clifford (158) has attempted a tentative positive translation which he says has the merit of connecting more easily with what follows. Both the preceding and the following verses address the audience positively. Furthermore, the problem presented in verse 10 is the darkness in which the servant is made to walk, so encouragement to walk in whatever light is available dovetails with the

This section follows abruptly upon the concluding verses of the first section on Daughter Zion, Isa 49:14–50:3, without obvious transitional markers. As in chapter 49, the servant himself speaks. But whereas there the concern was YHWH's call and commissioning, here most of the passage concerns the figure's adversaries. Four factors complicate interpretation of this passage: 1) several syntactic and linguistic difficulties render the translation itself obscure (see translation notes); 2) the language is condensed and referential, even elliptical, giving the impression that even where the verses themselves are understandable, context is missing; 3) determining the speaker is problematic in the final two verses, rendering it difficult to assess the relationship between these verses and the previous speech; and 4) although the main speaker is identified as the servant in verse 10, the vocabulary and concerns of this section are rather different from those of the speaking servant in the previous chapter.

Not all of these problems can be resolved. However, some intertextual features of this passage do assist our understanding. As does chapter 49, this passage echoes several of the motifs found in YHWH's own words earlier in the book. The servant describes YHWH as having "opened my ear" (פָּתַח־לִי אֹזֶן, 50:5; see 42:20 and 48:8). Though he receives insults (כְּלִמּוֹת) he is confident he will not be disgraced (לֹא נִכְלָמְתִּי) or ashamed (לֹא אֵבוֹשׁ, 50:6–7; for all three of these see 45:16–17). He is confident that YHWH will help him (יַעֲזָר, 50:7, 9; see 41:10–14, etc.). As has been voiced several times before in connection with servant Israel, there is concern for "my justice" or "my right" (מִשְׁפָּטִי, 50:8; see especially 40:27, 42:1–4, 49:4). In fact, several terms connected with judicial conflict are reutilized (קָרוֹב, יָרִיב, יַחַד, מִשְׁפָּט, יִגַּשׁ, 50:8; see 41:1, 21–22). The question "who among you . . . will listen" is repeated (מִי בָכֶם . . . שֹׁמֵעַ, 50:10; see 42:23), and walking in darkness is

preceding verse. The word מַעֲצֵבָה is a hapax and could be related to either meaning of the verb עצב, that is, either "hurt, pain, grieve," or "shape, fashion." Although I have translated it in accordance with most others, the transformational overtones that may be present here should not be overlooked.

mentioned once again (הָלַךְ חֲשֵׁכִים וְאֵין נֹגַהּ לוֹ, 50:10; see 42:16). The primary difference is that it is no longer YHWH speaking to or about the servant. Rather, the servant himself has adopted these words. He alludes to these many reassurances elliptically, referring quickly to what YHWH already explored at length, as if to communicate thoroughly but concisely that conceptions which earlier in the text were YHWH's about the servant are here the servant's about himself. Thus he stands in the intermediate position between YHWH and the audience, as one who has heard (verse 4), and therefore has a word that others should hear (verse 10), an example that others should follow.

Besides reframing earlier parts of Second Isaiah, this section closely echoes another voice from earlier Judahite literature, the male figure in Lamentations 3.[9]

Recollections of Lamentations 3

While the other four poems of Lamentations all concern themselves explicitly with Jerusalem as a place and often as a woman, the middle poem does not mention Jerusalem and its fall. Nor does it use the same voice as the other poems. In Lamentations 1, 2, and 4

---

[9] Other intertextual connections with Isaiah 50 have been suggested, but in my opinion they are not as strong as what I will propose. Westermann found parallels between this passage and the book and figure of Jeremiah, specifically in chapters 11–20. His list is more concerned with thematic parallels than with verbal repetitions (*Isaiah 40–66*, 227–28). Although Clifford did momentarily draw a comparison between the figure in Isaiah 50 and the one in Lamentations 3, he perceived verbal repetitions of Isaiah 30:8–14 in the words "hear," "rebel," "trust," and "rely" (162). Williamson (106–15), noting that the word לִמּוּדִים occurs in Isa 8:16, theorized that Second Isaiah considered himself the one to open Isaiah's long-sealed book of judgment. In support of this idea he cited congruences such as YHWH's "hiding his face" from the house of Jacob in 8:17 and the servant's not hiding his face from shame in 50:6—a frequent cliché hardly unique to these two texts.

Although Gottwald (*Studies*, 45) did not compare these chapters in detail, he did make the form-critical observation that Lam 3:1–18, 1:13–15, Isa 50:4–9, and Isa 52:13–53:12 are all "songs bewailing national suffering under the figure of a person enduring great pain and ostracism." He further stated (116), "the personalizing of national grief and suffering in Lamentations was one of the definite forerunners of the Suffering Servant conception."

an ungendered observer describes Jerusalem's condition, interacting in chapters 1 and 2 with Daughter Zion, and giving way in chapter 4 to a collective "we." In chapter 3 the speaker is a male figure who contemplates his own sufferings in many of the terms in which Daughter Zion had described herself.[10] Thus he becomes her counterpart, a figure who, like Zion, embodies the suffering of many. Unlike Zion, who expresses her theology by calling YHWH to account, the *geber* expresses his by attempting, midway through the lament, to reason his way to hope.

Giving to the Attacker One's Cheek

On the linguistic level, the relationship between Isaiah 50 and Lamentations 3 is easiest to see in the middle third of the poem. I will begin the exploration in the center, with the ט and י stanzas:

Lam 3:25	Good is YHWH to one who hopes in him,	טוֹב יְהוָה לְקֹוָו
	to the soul that seeks him.	לְנֶפֶשׁ תִּדְרְשֶׁנּוּ
3:26	Good it is that one should wait in silence	טוֹב וְיָחִיל וְדוּמָם
	for the salvation of YHWH.	לִתְשׁוּעַת יְהוָה
3:27	Good it is for a man that he carry	טוֹב לַגֶּבֶר כִּי־יִשָּׂא
	the yoke in his youth.	עֹל בִּנְעוּרָיו
3:28	He will sit alone and be silent	יֵשֵׁב בָּדָד וְיִדֹּם
	when it is heavy upon him.	כִּי נָטַל עָלָיו
3:29	He will put his mouth to the dust—	יִתֵּן בֶּעָפָר פִּיהוּ
	perhaps there is hope.	אוּלַי יֵשׁ תִּקְוָה
3:30	He will give to his attacker the cheek;	יִתֵּן לְמַכֵּהוּ לֶחִי
	he will be filled up with insult.	יִשְׂבַּע בְּחֶרְפָּה

Every key image and most of the key words from these verses recur in Second Isaiah in one way or another.[11] The relationship

[10] Provan (80) pointed out on the basis of the reference to "his wrath" in the first verse (referring back to 2:22 without supplying the nominal antecedent for the ms possessive pronoun) that Lamentations 3 was composed with the second lament in mind. He further noted that the speaker used expressions reminiscent of those in chapters 1 and 2.

[11] The parallel suggestions to hope (קוה), wait (יחל), and seek (דרשׁ) recur in Isa 40:31 (see also 49:23), 55:6, and 51:5 (see also 42:4). While יחל

between this passage and Second Isaiah's servant is, however, most distinctly signaled by Lam 3:30, where it describes the stance of humility that the *geber* recommends: יִתֵּן לְמַכֵּהוּ לֶחִי יִשְׂבַּע בְּחֶרְפָּה, "He will give to his attacker the cheek, he will be filled up with insult." Second Isaiah's figure represents himself doing this very thing:

Isa 50:6	My back I gave to attackers	גֵּוִי נָתַתִּי לְמַכִּים
	and my cheeks to beard-pluckers.	וּלְחָיַי לְמֹרְטִים
	My face I did not hide	פָּנַי לֹא הִסְתַּרְתִּי
	from insults and spittle.	מִכְּלִמּוֹת וָרֹק

Here the phrase יִתֵּן לְמַכֵּהוּ לֶחִי, which occurs nowhere else in the Hebrew Bible, has been adapted and expanded.[12] The order of the words has remained the same though their syntax has shifted; nouns parallel to "cheek" (i.e. "back") and "attackers" (i.e. "beard-pluckers") have been added to the beginning and end of the phrase to expand the one phrase into two parallel ones. The peaceful submission to abuse that was prescribed by the *geber* has thus been carried out, and carried further, by the first-person figure in Isaiah 50, who is identified in verse 10 as YHWH's servant.

Several other verbal connections are made between Lamentations' *geber* and Second Isaiah's servant. The collection into this short poem of terms and ideas from throughout the lament suggests that, as in other chapters, the poet is here creating not a

---

and דרשׁ are common verbs voicing expectancy toward God, especially in the psalms, קוה is relatively rare.

The vocabulary of sitting in silence (יֵשֵׁב בָּדָד וְיִדֹּם) with mouth to the dust (יִתֵּן בֶּעָפָר פִּיהוּ), bearing the yoke (עֹל) are, like corresponding language in Lamentations 2, evoked in Isaiah 47's imperatives to Daughter Babylon; see Isa 47:1, 5, and 6. In fact, דּוּמָם only appears adverbially in Lam 3:26 and Isa 47:5. These images are again evoked in the address to Daughter Zion in Isa 52:1–2.

[12] The word לֶחִי is used in combination with various forms of נכה in I Kings 22:24; 2 Chr 18:23; Job 16:10; Ps 3:8; and Mic 4:14. But the participle "attackers" only appears in Lam 3:30 and Isa 50:6, and the combination with נתן is likewise unique. Gottwald (*Studies*, 44) noted this correspondence between Lam 3:30 and Isa 50:6, as well as מִשְׁפָּטִי in Lam 3:59 and Isa 40:27, 49:3, but not 50:8.

scribal exegesis from a manuscript, but an evocation of words and images remembered in association with the *geber* figure.

1) In Isa 50:4, 5, and 10, as in Lamentations 3, there is a great concern for the ears and for hearing. But whereas the *geber* had pleaded with YHWH to be the one hearing and not hiding his ear (קוֹלִי שָׁמָעְתָּ; אַל־תַּעְלֵם אָזְנְךָ, Lam 3:56), the speaker in Isa 50:4–5 claims that YHWH has wakened and opened his own ear to hear (יָעִיר לִי אֹזֶן לִשְׁמֹעַ; אֲדֹנָי יְהוִה פָּתַח־לִי אֹזֶן), and the audience is subsequently challenged by an observer to hear the voice of this servant (שֹׁמֵעַ בְּקוֹל עַבְדּוֹ, Isa 50:10).

2) Similarly, both passages treat the subject of rebellion. The *geber* prays, "We—emphatic—transgressed and rebelled," (וּמָרִינוּ, Lam 3:42), but follows this confession with a parallel phrase pointing out YHWH's response, "You—emphatic—did not forgive." The speaker in Isa 50:5 repeats this emphatic form in first person singular, only to negate it: "I—emphatic—did not rebel" (מָרִיתִי). The first person form of מרה is not found anywhere else in the Bible than in these two passages and in Lam 1:18 and 20, in which Zion confessions her rebellion. Paradoxically, the *geber's* own confession signals a turn from rebellion—and it is this attitude, not the former one, that the servant chooses to describe.

3) The *geber* describes YHWH's steadfast love and mercy as constant, "new every morning" (חֲדָשִׁים לַבְּקָרִים, Lam 3:23). Similarly, the servant is awakened to hear YHWH "morning by morning" (בַּבֹּקֶר בַּבֹּקֶר, Isa 50:4). The understanding common to both is that awareness of divine presence and care is renewed daily.

4) In Isa 50:8, an entire complex of requests verbalized by the *geber* is echoed. The *geber* had pleaded with YHWH to come near (קָרַבְתָּ, Lam 3:57), to plead his cause (רַבְתָּ אֲדֹנָי רִיבֵי נַפְשִׁי, verse 58), to judge his right (שָׁפְטָה מִשְׁפָּטִי, verse 59). Likewise, in the same sequence, the speaker in Isa 50:8 affirms that his vindicator is near (קָרוֹב), and asks who will plead against him (מִי־יָרִיב), and who is the adversary of his right (מִי־בַעַל מִשְׁפָּטִי).[13] While

[13] Or "advocate of my right"; see note 7 above. In view of Lam 3:57–59, "advocate" may make more sense.

attention in that section of Lamentations finally rests on the foes plotting against the speaker, attention in Isaiah 50 comes to rest on YHWH's assistance and the consequent ineffectiveness of the speaker's adversaries.

5) When in Isa 50:10 another voice concludes the speaker's words, the servant is once again identified with a key phrase: he goes into darkness (הָלַךְ חֲשֵׁכִים) without light, just as the *geber* had described himself as the one whom YHWH made go into darkness (וַיֹּלַךְ חֹשֶׁךְ) without light (Lam 3:2). In Isaiah 50 the observer surpasses the *geber's* self-description: "yet trusts in the name of YHWH and relies upon his God."

Similarities between the two texts run deeper than the words. Just as this is the only portion of Lamentations in which a male figure speaks, so this section of Second Isaiah is one of two passages in Second Isaiah in which a human male speaks, the other being in Isaiah 49.[14] Like Lamentations 3, Isaiah 50 depicts the speaker discussing suffering and trust, and reflecting on the struggle to maintain faith through darkness and adversity. In both books, he interrupts the interplay between other voices, adding a voice and a section that is more monologic, and is congruent with surrounding themes without indicating a common setting. That is, in both Lamentations 3 and Isaiah 50, the speakers suffer in undefined places, in circumstances less particularized than those in surrounding chapters. In neither text is Jerusalem mentioned, although the city surrounds both texts. Rather, the concentration is on the spiritual struggle of the speaker, his coming to grips with suffering in a constructive way, and his attempts to convey a model of persevering trust to listeners who are encouraged to follow his example. In short, just as Second Isaiah seems to have reemployed Daughter Zion from Lamentations 1–2, likewise the poet seems to have recollected the figure of Lamentations 3, casting him in the role of YHWH's servant.

---

[14] The pronoun in 40:6 is "I" (ungendered) in LXX but "he" in MT. A likewise ungendered, and according to many commentators, interpolated, "me" appears briefly in 48:16.

While the Isaiah passage shares many of the same themes and words as the lament, the emphasis has been reshaped in important ways. First, by taking most of its material from the middle portion of the lament, Isaiah places more emphasis on the speaker's hopeful words than on his laments and complaints, which were originally far more numerous. Second, the speaker in Second Isaiah describes himself as displaying the qualities that the Lamentations figure does not claim, but merely envisions and prescribes. Third, all complaint language is removed from the sufferer's mouth and attributed to another speaker, who in verse 10 emphasizes the darkness in which the speaker has had to walk. In fact, God's role is subtly reshaped: while the *geber* not only hopes in God but also complains that it is God who is afflicting him (see Lam 3:1–18, 43–45), the servant does not himself discuss this problem. God's role as afflicter enters in only in relation to those addressed in verse 11. In these ways the figure of Lamentations 3 is preserved, affirmed, and even extended. He exemplifies those who contend with confusion and opposition, yet maintain hope for the future. While Lamentations 3 had displayed human grappling with God's faithfulness, the emphasis in Isaiah 50 has been subtly transformed into a study, by means of a single paradigmatic figure, of human faithfulness.

Connections with Isaiah 52:13–53:12

While the allusions to Lamentations 3 occur more densely in Isaiah 50 than anywhere else, several words and themes of Lamentations 3 recur as well in Isaiah 53. As before, a man is described as YHWH's servant, who suffers and hopes in silence. Here, however, the concentration is on the servant's suffering more than his hope. As the *geber* in Lamentations 3 had prescribed (Lam 3:28), he does not speak. Rather, others speak for him. He is rejected by others (Isa 53:3; see Lam 3:46, 53, 60–63); stricken (נכה, Isa 53:4; see Lam 3:30); afflicted and crushed (ענה, דכא, Isa 53:4–5; see Lam 3:33–34—this combination is very rare); he suffers the perversion of justice (מִשְׁפָּט, Isa 53:8, see Lam 3:35); he is cut off (נגזר, Isa 53:8, see Lam 3:54 and also Jer 11:19) and buried (Isa

53:9, see Lam 3:53, 55. The *geber* had imagined being thrown alive into a well, but in Second Isaiah it is a grave.). He places himself in solidarity with sinners even while interceding for them (Lam 3:8, 40–42; Isa 53:11–12). The outcome that the *geber* only hoped for is enacted in Second Isaiah. The *geber* had suggested that there may yet be hope, that God would not allow injustice to continue unchecked (Lam 3:29, 34–39), but the speakers in Second Isaiah describe the servant's coming vindication in posterity, length of life, satisfaction, and prosperity (Isa 53:10–12). If YHWH was sufficient as the *geber's* portion (חֵלֶק as a noun, Lam 3:24), now he is given a portion (חלק as a verb, Isa 53:12) of the spoil.

Summary

Similarities of Isaiah 53 to Lamentations 3 augment the stronger relationship between Isaiah 50 and the lament. The collection of so many different elements of Lamentations 3 into the space of seven verses in Isaiah 50 is impressive, and the repetition of many of the lament's themes in Isaiah 53 supplements the suspicion that the *geber* acted as one of the models for the suffering servant figure. Thematic coherence is very clear; the servant acts the role that the *geber* prescribes, in circumstances quite similar to those described. When, in addition, the larger literary factors are noted, that is, the male figure's interruption of Jerusalem-oriented passages in order to develop a similar theme in a different sphere, the lack of clues to geographical location in both texts, and the monologic speech embedded in a text that is on the whole far more prone to interactive voices, compelling similarities emerge between the lament and Isaiah 50.

While a direct relationship between the *geber* and the servant of YHWH has not often been posited, interpreters throughout time have connected both of these characters to Jeremiah, the servant of YHWH who suffers and laments on Jerusalem's behalf.[15] A

---

[15] For the connections that have been drawn between Jeremiah and the servant, beginning with Saadia Gaon in the tenth century, see chapter 4, note 16.

As for the connections made between Jeremiah and the lament, ancient

relationship between the lament and the Isaiah texts may offer solutions to some of the interpretive problems in the latter: on its own terms, Isaiah 50 seems to jump abruptly from theme to theme, and its flow is not obvious. But if it is seen as a series of condensed, exegetical comments on a text already known, its brevity and abruptness make more sense.

The Servant of YHWH and Daughter Zion: Comparisons and Contrasts

Daughter Zion and the Geber: Parallels in Lamentations

While recognition of this allusion to the *geber* solves some interpretive problems, it nevertheless raises hermeneutical ones. The *geber's* closest counterpart in the book of Lamentations is Daughter Zion herself. His self-description parallels her own in numerous ways. The two figures speak in unison over against God, as parallel representatives of the people's suffering and prayers. Both describe their suffering as resulting from God's wrath. Both are described as desolate (שֹׁמֵם, 3:11; שֹׁמֵמָה, 1:13) and bitter (בַמְּרוֹרִים, 3:15; מַר־לָהּ, 1:4). Both confess their rebellion (מָרִינוּ, 3:42; מָרִיתִי, 1:18, 20) and lift their hands/hearts to God (נִשָּׂא לְבָבֵנוּ אֶל־כַּפָּיִם, 3:41; שְׂאִי אֵלָיו כַּפַּיִךְ, שִׁפְכִי כַמַּיִם לִבֵּךְ, 2:19). Both perceive God as "killing without mercy" (הָרַגְתָּ לֹא חָמָלְתָּ, 3:43; הָרַגְתָּ . . . לֹא חָמָלְתָּ, 2:21) and protest the harshness of God's deeds. Both are tormented by "enemies" who "open against us/her their

---

tradition (including the LXX, Vulgate, Syriac, Aramaic Targum, and the Talmud) nearly unanimously ascribed Lamentations to Jeremiah, and many critical scholars of the twentieth century (including Löhr, Rudolph, Haller, Meek, and Brandscheidt) have suggested in various ways that Lamentations 3 was written to be read as if by Jeremiah. For these claims, see Max Löhr, "Threni III und die jeremianische Autorschaft des Buches der Klagelieder," *ZAW* 24 (1904) 1–16; W. Rudolph, "Der Text der Klagelieder," *ZAW* 56 (1938) 101–22; M. Haller, *Die Klagelieder*, in M. Haller and K. Galling, *Die fünf Megilloth*, HAT 1/18 (Tübingen: Mohr [Paul Siebeck], 1940) 91–113; T. J. Meek, "The Book of Lamentations," in *IB*, vol. 6, ed. G. A. Buttrick et al. (New York: Abingdon Press, 1956); R. Brandscheidt, *Das Buch der Klagelieder*, GSAT 10, (Düsseldorf: Patmos, 1988). For discussions of this history, see Provan (8–11) and Westermann (*Lamentations*, 24–34).

mouths" (פָּצוּ עָלֵינוּ פִּיהֶם כָּל־אֹיְבֵינוּ, 3:46; פָּצוּ עָלַיִךְ פִּיהֶם כָּל־אוֹיְבַיִךְ, 2:16), and both call down God's punishment on their enemies (3:64–66; 1:21).

Daughter Zion and the Servant: Parallels in Second Isaiah

Like Lamentations, Second Isaiah posits parallels between Daughter Zion and Israel/Jacob as the servant.[16] Israel was formed by YHWH in the womb (44:2), and Zion is the child of YHWH's own womb (49:15). Both are introduced protesting vigorously against YHWH's neglect (40:27; 49:14). Both have been abused by enemies (50:6; 51:23). Both are cajoled by YHWH with exhortations not to fear (41:10; 54:4) and promises that they will not be forgotten (44:21; 49:15) or rejected (41:9; 54:7–8). Neither need be ashamed or dismayed (45:17; 54:4), because all their enemies will be routed (41:12; 54:15–17) and will even bow down to them (49:7, 23). Both are described with threefold adjectives of affliction (49:7; 54:11); both are promised a joyful return of offspring from faraway lands (43:5; 54:3). Both are depicted individually as well as collectively, and while their geopolitical identities (as nation; as city) are not forgotten, their highest moments of pathos are also their most personal. Through both, YHWH's arm is revealed before all the nations (52:10; 52:15, 53:1). Both will prosper as a result (53:12; 54:11, 12). In each, the story line moves from abuse, shame, despair, and recrimination to promise, vindication, fulfillment, and exaltation.

Moreover, both figures are depicted paradoxically. Both are portrayed not only as recipients of messages, but as messengers as well (40:9; 50:4). For both figures, the issue of guilt or innocence is ambiguous: Zion has both suffered overmuch for her own sins (40:2) and suffered vicariously for her children's sins (50:1); Israel has suffered the consequences of his own sins (43:24) and will bear the iniquities of others (53:11). In fact, Second Isaiah's indictments

---

[16] For cues to some of these observations I am indebted to Steck (*Gottesknecht*), Sawyer, Wilshire, and Jeppesen.

against Israel/Jacob and their offspring are far harsher than those against Zion, before whom YHWH is portrayed as conciliatory.

Daughter Zion and the Servant: Contrasts in Second Isaiah

The above parallels notwithstanding, Second Isaiah does not maintain Lamentations' strong parallelism of function. This is especially seen in the positioning of the masculine plural audience in relation to the two figures. This audience is at times identified with Israel the servant, such as in Isa 43:10 when God tells them: "You are my witnesses (plural) and my servant (singular)." But they are held distinct from Zion until the very last verse addressed to her, in which they become servants of YHWH *in* Zion (54:17). They are not her; they are not yet even with her, but rather are told to go to her. Zion is portrayed as alone, empty and barren until the addressees return to her. Invoked in Lamentations to represent those remaining in the land, she is in Second Isaiah no longer a community but a place, a destination. She is no longer a subject to act, but an object awaiting the actions of others. Whereas Israel is seen working out his salvation by assuming his calling as servant, and the masculine plural audience is envisioned working out their salvation by returning to Zion, her salvation is in the end not something that she enacts but something that happens to her, when God and God's people return.

This subtle differentiation in role is furthered by a differentiation in speaking voice. Israel's first words in the book are a complaint against God. In succeeding chapters he is addressed by God, cajoled, exhorted, redefined. Israel himself begins speaking in chapter 49 and continues in chapter 50, describing himself in many of the same terms in which he was described by God. When Zion appears in chapter 49 she occupies approximately the same relation to God that Israel first did in chapter 40: as a complainer in need of divine correction. Like Israel, she is in chapter 49 and in succeeding chapters addressed by God, cajoled, exhorted, redefined. Like Israel, she is told what God says to her, what she has said, what she will say, what she should say, what she should do. But unlike Israel, Zion never regains her speaking voice.

It is striking that the male figure who once commended silence before God (Lam 3:28) and is described as silent (Isa 42:2; 53:7) actually speaks quite a bit (49:1–6, 50:4–9), while the one who was outspoken in Lamentations, and in Second Isaiah is told to raise a shout (54:1), to raise her voice with strength, to announce from a mountaintop YHWH's presence (40:9), instead becomes mute, never speaking for herself again. Though told to rise up and put on her strength, she no longer displays the strength she showed in Lamentations. She fares well by comparison with the female figure in Jeremiah—at least Second Isaiah does not excoriate her with obscene speech. But compared with Daughter Zion in Lamentations, she loses her voice even as she is being told to speak. Although much is announced to her as good news, we never actually hear what Zion herself thinks of the news that the exiles are returning.[17]

---

[17] Prophetic interpretation of the two figures may in fact have contributed to the skewing of modern interpretation and even translation of Lamentations, obscuring the parallels between them by interpreting the *geber* positively, and Zion negatively, in textually unwarranted ways. For instance, of Daughter Zion it is said in Lam 1:2, אֵין־לָהּ מְנַחֵם מִכָּל־אֹהֲבֶיהָ. This has traditionally been translated as an implicit accusation of wrongdoing, as in the NRSV ("among all her *lovers* she has no one to comfort her"). But as Provan (*Lamentations,* 36) has pointed out, there is no warrant for this translation of the participial form of "to love." In fact, in none of the other sixty-five uses in the Bible of the participle אֹהֵב would a translation like "lover" or "paramour" make sense: it would make Abraham God's lover (Isa 41:8), Isaac his son Esau's paramour (Gen 25:28), and the Lord God the sexual partner of strangers and righteous alike (Deut 10:18; Ps 146:8).

While translation practices work against Zion's image, they work in favor of her colleague in chapter 3. At several points he expresses much more ambivalence toward God than translators allow. For instance, verses 34–36 read most literally:

Lam	Crushing under his foot	לְדַכֵּא תַּחַת רַגְלָיו
3:34	all the prisoners of the earth,	כֹּל אֲסִירֵי אָרֶץ
3:35	turning aside a man's justice	לְהַטּוֹת מִשְׁפַּט־גָּבֶר
	before the face of the Most High,	נֶגֶד פְּנֵי עֶלְיוֹן

This reconfiguration of roles is apparently due to the interests Second Isaiah set out to support. Although previous Judahite literature reflected a wide range of attitudes toward both Israel and Zion, and had often used them interchangeably, Daughter Zion's role as the city itself, and her identity in Lamentations as the figure of the Jerusalemite remnant, suggested for her a Judahite, not exilic, location.[18] But Israel/Jacob, the wandering nation, was free to be imagined in exile. Indeed, in Lamentations itself Israel and Jacob are hardly mentioned, much less personified, and disappear from the text in the aftermath of the battle. In suggesting to the exiled community that the solution to their own crisis lay in repatriation, Second Isaiah cast them as Zion's children by whose return the city itself would be redeemed. In that schema, change is set in motion by an altered perspective within the exilic community, in which they reinterpret their sufferings as purposeful and their own calling as redemptive. Because the behavioral result of this change of heart is repatriation, there is little room in Second Isaiah's scheme for Zion to enjoy a change of perspective independent of the exiles' return.

3:36	subverting a man in his lawsuit,	לְעַוֵּת אָדָם בְּרִיבוֹ
	the Lord did not see.	אֲדֹנָי לֹא רָאָה

The subject of the first three verbs is lacking, so it is not at all clear for the first two and a half verses whose actions are being discussed. In fact, the *geber* has already accused God of terrific violence. When in verse 36b God's position in the sentence is given, it is ambiguous, perhaps even intentionally ambivalent. It may suggest that God does not see doing these things, or that God does not see when they are done, or even that God does them without seeing. Standard translations regularly resolve the ambiguity in one direction, however, either converting the statement, which has no interrogative marker, to a question, "Does the Lord not see?" (NJB, NRSV), or converting the simple verb רעה to something else: "The Lord does not choose, or approve" (Gordis, 143; Gottwald, *Studies*, 14; JPS; NEB). Provan (97–98) noted, "However we translate *'adonai lo ra'ah* in v. 36, then, we have the paradoxical picture of God standing apart from events for which he is described as responsible elsewhere in the stanza."

[18] Nevertheless, her location was more fluid in previous literature. In Lam 1:3 and 7, for instance, she is envisioned going into exile or wandering. See Newsom, 76.

Since there actually was a community in Jerusalem grappling with the destruction's meaning, a prophet like Second Isaiah could well have developed their mother Zion, like their ancestor Israel, as an ideal theological role model, rehabilitated and extended quite independently from the prospect of the exilic community's return.[19] But, as Newsom pointed out, and as I have shown, there is no marker in the text for the inhabitants of Judah who were not exiled.[20] It does not seem to be part of the prophet's program to reeducate them. Like that of Zion into whom they are subsumed, their redemption is imagined only in their fellow citizens' return. The malleable nature of the personifications, and their resulting changes of fortune and role, should serve to remind readers of their constructed, imaginative character.

Isaiah 50:4–11 and 52:13–53:12 in Review

Although both Israel as a masculine singular figure and the designation "YHWH's servant" are widely found in previous Judahite literature, these two are identified with each other only a single time in Jer 30:10 before Second Isaiah repeatedly and insistently connects them together. Descriptions of the servant in Second Isaiah echo several distinct traditions, gradually developing a template for the exilic addressees' own self-understanding. This chapter explored in depth the textual connections between the *geber* in Lamentations 3 and the servant as depicted in Isa 50:4–11 and 52:13–53:12.

---

[19] In fact, later on in tradition Zion does regain her role as a speaking, theologizing mother. Although she maintains a silent, still personified presence in Third Isaiah (see especially Isaiah 60, 62, and 66:8–12), she reemerges several centuries later as a major speaking figure in Baruch 4:5–29, encouraging her "children" to take courage, cry to God, and await divine deliverance. For an examination of her role in Baruch and its relations to previous literature, see P. Willey, "Baruch," in *The Women's Bible Commentary*, rev. ed., ed. C. Newsom and S. Ringe (Louisville, KY: Westminster/John Knox, 1998).

[20] Newsom, 77.

Postures and understandings that the *geber* of Lamentations 3 commends to his audience, Second Isaiah incorporates into character traits for YHWH's chosen servant. Like the *geber,* this servant seeks a stance of faithful trust in the face of war, exile, confusion, and even divine injustice. Linguistic parallels between these two figures include not only the recollection in Isa 50:6 of "he will give to the attacker his cheek" (Lam 3:30), but also concerns with ears and hearing, rebellion, renewal in the morning, YHWH's role as defending attorney and judge, and the figure's trust while walking in darkness without light. Isaiah 53 likewise echoes themes of suffering such as silence, rejection, affliction, perversion of justice, burial, intercession, and vindication. In both books the figures' passages interrupt more interactive passages to display the inner struggles of suffering and trust. Yet while Lamentations 3 remains a human meditation on divine faithfulness, subtle shifts in Second Isaiah transform the discussion into a meditation on human faithfulness. All the *geber's* fondest hopes are fulfilled in YHWH's final words concerning the servant: on account of his righteousness in the face of overwhelming oppression, he is in the end vindicated by YHWH, given a portion with the great, spoil with the strong.

Parallels and contrasts drawn between the masculine and feminine personifications in the two texts betray Second Isaiah's disposition to objectify the female and invite identification with the male. In Lamentations, Daughter Zion and the *geber* were described, and described themselves, in linguistically parallel terms, displayed similar attitudes toward God, and occupied similar roles in envisioning lament and restoration. In Second Isaiah many parallels between Zion and the Servant still exist, and the similarities of language used to describe them confer upon them strikingly similar story lines that move from despair and abandonment to restoration, vindication, and hope. Yet contrasts appear in the positioning of the two figures in relation to the pervasive masculine plural audience. While the audience is invited to identify themselves with Servant Israel and will eventually emerge as

YHWH's servants, they are not identified with Zion but are instead invited to regard her as their mother, who will be comforted by their return. Objectification of the female figure is also evident in her silence, which is particularly striking in view of the facts that she is told several times to speak up, and that it is the Servant who is called silent even though he speaks several times. Since all traces of the Judahite population have been subsumed into the collective figure Zion, her speechlessness is in effect their own.

The various imagined audiences, having developed gradually throughout Second Isaiah, will finally converge in the final two chapters, in which the children of Zion, envisioned as the servants of YHWH regaining their heritage in Jerusalem, receive as their own the Davidic promise of divine protection.

Chapter 6
"Open Wide the Site of your Tent": Isaiah 54:1–17

Last to be studied is Isaiah 54, the third and final section of Second Isaiah in which the female figure is addressed. This section is not only rich in its referents to other Israelite literature, but also intertextually rich in terms of Second Isaiah itself, collecting themes from throughout the previous chapters which will finally bring Daughter Zion and Israel into relationship with each other.

Isaiah 54:1–17

54:1	Cry out, barren one who did not bear;	רָנִּי עֲקָרָה לֹא יָלָדָה
	break forth into cries and shout,	פִּצְחִי רִנָּה וְצַהֲלִי
	you who did not travail.	לֹא־חָלָה
	For more will be the children of the desolate one	כִּי־רַבִּים בְּנֵי־שׁוֹמֵמָה
	than the children of the married one,	מִבְּנֵי בְעוּלָה
	says YHWH.	אָמַר יְהוָה
54:2	Enlarge the site of your tent,	הַרְחִיבִי מְקוֹם אָהֳלֵךְ
	and the curtains of your dwellings spread out;	וִירִיעוֹת מִשְׁכְּנוֹתַיִךְ יַטּוּ
	do not hold back;	אַל־תַּחְשֹׂכִי
	lengthen your tent-cords	הַאֲרִיכִי מֵיתָרַיִךְ
	and your stakes strengthen.	וִיתֵדֹתַיִךְ חַזֵּקִי
54:3	For to the right and to the left you will burst out,	כִּי־יָמִין וּשְׂמֹאול תִּפְרֹצִי
	and your offspring will possess the nations,	וְזַרְעֵךְ גּוֹיִם יִירָשׁ
	and the desolate cities they will settle.	וְעָרִים נְשַׁמּוֹת יוֹשִׁיבוּ
54:4	Do not fear, because you will not be ashamed,	אַל־תִּירְאִי כִּי־לֹא תֵבוֹשִׁי
	and do not be dismayed,	וְאַל־תִּכָּלְמִי
	because you will not be disgraced,	כִּי לֹא תַחְפִּירִי
	For the shame of your youth you will forget,	כִּי בֹשֶׁת עֲלוּמַיִךְ תִּשְׁכָּחִי
	and the disgrace of your widowhood	וְחֶרְפַּת אַלְמְנוּתַיִךְ
	you will remember no more.	לֹא תִזְכְּרִי־עוֹד

54:5	For the one marrying you is the one who made you	כִּי בֹעֲלַיִךְ עֹשַׂיִךְ
	—YHWH Sabaoth is his name.	יְהוָה צְבָאוֹת שְׁמוֹ
	And the one redeeming you is the Holy One	
	of Israel	וְגֹאֲלֵךְ קְדוֹשׁ יִשְׂרָאֵל
	—the God of all the earth he is called.	אֱלֹהֵי כָל־הָאָרֶץ יִקָּרֵא
54:6	For as a woman abandoned	כִּי־כְאִשָּׁה עֲזוּבָה
	and hurt in spirit, YHWH has called you,	וַעֲצוּבַת רוּחַ קְרָאָךְ יְהוָה
	and as a wife of youth when she is rejected,	וְאֵשֶׁת נְעוּרִים כִּי תִמָּאֵס
	says your God.	אָמַר אֱלֹהָיִךְ
54:7	In a brief moment I abandoned you,	בְּרֶגַע קָטֹן עֲזַבְתִּיךְ
	but in great pity I will gather you.	וּבְרַחֲמִים גְּדֹלִים אֲקַבְּצֵךְ
54:8	In a flood of anger I hid	בְּשֶׁצֶף קֶצֶף הִסְתַּרְתִּי
	my face for a moment from you,	פָנַי רֶגַע מִמֵּךְ
	but in eternal love I have pitied you,	וּבְחֶסֶד עוֹלָם רִחַמְתִּיךְ
	says your redeemer YHWH.	אָמַר גֹּאֲלֵךְ יְהוָה
54:9	Like the waters of Noah this is to me,[1]	כִּי־מֵי נֹחַ זֹאת לִי
	which I swore	אֲשֶׁר נִשְׁבַּעְתִּי
	would not again pass over the earth,	מֵעֲבֹר [מֵי־נֹחַ] עוֹד עַל־הָאָרֶץ
	likewise I have sworn	כֵּן נִשְׁבַּעְתִּי
	not to be angry with you or rebuke you.	מִקְּצֹף עָלַיִךְ וּמִגְּעָר־בָּךְ
54:10	For the mountains will depart,	כִּי הֶהָרִים יָמוּשׁוּ
	and the hills will totter,	וְהַגְּבָעוֹת תְּמוּטֶנָה
	but my steadfast love will not depart from you,	וְחַסְדִּי מֵאִתֵּךְ לֹא־יָמוּשׁ
	and my covenant of peace will not totter,	וּבְרִית שְׁלוֹמִי לֹא תָמוּט
	says the one who pities you, YHWH.	אָמַר מְרַחֲמֵךְ יְהוָה
54:11	Suffering one, storm-tossed, not comforted,	עֲנִיָּה סֹעֲרָה לֹא נֻחָמָה
	see, I am laying your stones in	
	antimony,	הִנֵּה אָנֹכִי מַרְבִּיץ בַּפּוּךְ אֲבָנַיִךְ
	and your foundations in sapphires,	וִיסַדְתִּיךְ בַּסַּפִּירִים
54:12	and I have made rubies your pinnacles,	וְשַׂמְתִּי כַּדְכֹד שִׁמְשֹׁתַיִךְ
	and your gates sparkling stones,	וּשְׁעָרַיִךְ לְאַבְנֵי אֶקְדָּח
	and all your walls precious stones,	וְכָל־גְּבוּלֵךְ לְאַבְנֵי־חֵפֶץ
54:13	and all your children disciples of YHWH—	וְכָל־בָּנַיִךְ לִמּוּדֵי יְהוָה
	and abundant is the peace of your children.	וְרַב שְׁלוֹם בָּנָיִךְ

---

[1] Here I follow the BHS textual apparatus which, following Greek manuscripts, suggests deleting the yod from the verse's first word (כִּי becomes כְּ) and מֵי־נֹחַ from the third colon.

54:14	In righteousness you will be established.	בִּצְדָקָה תִּכּוֹנָנִי
	You will stay far from oppression,	רַחֲקִי מֵעֹשֶׁק
	for you will not fear,	כִּי־לֹא תִירָאִי
	and from ruin, for it will not come near you.	וּמִמְּחִתָּה כִּי לֹא־תִקְרַב אֵלָיִךְ
54:15	If someone stirs up strife it is not from me.	הֵן גּוֹר יָגוּר אֶפֶס מֵאוֹתִי
	Who will strive with you?	מִי־גָר אִתָּךְ
	On your account he will fall.	עָלַיִךְ יִפּוֹל
54:16	Behold, I myself created the smith	הִנֵּה אָנֹכִי בָּרָאתִי חָרָשׁ
	who blows the coal fire	נֹפֵחַ בְּאֵשׁ פֶּחָם
	and who brings out the tools for his work;	וּמוֹצִיא כְלִי לְמַעֲשֵׂהוּ
	and I myself created the spoiler to destroy.	וְאָנֹכִי בָּרָאתִי מַשְׁחִית לְחַבֵּל
54:17	No tool fashioned against you will succeed,	כָּל־כְּלִי יוּצַר עָלַיִךְ לֹא יִצְלָח
	and every tongue arising against you	וְכָל־לָשׁוֹן תָּקוּם־אִתָּךְ
	for judgment, you will condemn.	לַמִּשְׁפָּט תַּרְשִׁיעִי
	This is the heritage of YHWH's servants,	זֹאת נַחֲלַת עַבְדֵי יְהוָה
	and their righteousness from me, says YHWH.	וְצִדְקָתָם מֵאִתִּי נְאֻם־יְהוָה

Isaiah 54 is the third major section in which Zion is personified and addressed as a woman. It begins without transition as soon as the last servant passage ends. This abrupt shift in focus juxtaposes the two figures, suggesting continuities that are not explicated. As soon as it is announced that the servant has borne the sin of many and interceded for transgressors, the female figure is told to cry out. Her delight, it is quickly discovered, is not over her renewed spiritual state but over her body's fertility.

Unlike the two previous Zion sections, chapter 54 never addresses Zion by name. Moreover, some shifts occur here in the metaphor that is used of her. Although the addressee in this passage is still viewed as both woman and city, as one who suffered estrangement from YHWH and now needs comfort and restoration—a series of themes connecting her with Zion as characterized in the two previous passages—the addressee in this passage is no longer portrayed as bereft, but as barren, not having either travailed or borne children. As in Isaiah 49, she is told that she will be crowded with offspring. Unlike Isaiah 49, this chapter never details the origin of these inhabitants.

The chapter's central focus is the broken relationship between Zion and YHWH, here portrayed, as in Isa 50:1, as her estranged husband. Here YHWH at last admits to having abandoned Zion (see Isa 49:14), but promises at length never to do so again. As the metaphor shifts from Zion as wife to Zion as city, she is promised jeweled foundations, pinnacles, gates, and walls, safety and prosperity for her children.

This chapter, nearly at the end of Second Isaiah, returns to themes and motifs from throughout the book, including many that previously occurred primarily in the first half. It begins by repeating the same words from Psalm 98 that have recurred frequently in refrains throughout the book: רָנִּי ("cry out"), and פִּצְחִי רִנָּה ("break forth into cries"). In two previous refrains, the heavens had been told to cry out and the mountains to break forth (Isa 44:23; 49:13). In Isa 52:8–9 the locus of rejoicing moved closer: Jerusalem's sentinels were pictured crying out and Jerusalem's ruins were told to break forth. In Isa 54:1 the locus of rejoicing is Zion herself.

Furthermore, like YHWH's servant Israel in numerous passages, and echoing the initial injunction to her in Isa 40:9, Zion is told "do not fear" (אַל־תִּירְאִי, 54:4; see 41:10–13; 43:1, 5; 44:2). Like YHWH's servant, she need not be ashamed or dismayed (לֹא תֵבוֹשִׁי; אַל־תִּכָּלְמִי; 54:4; see 45:17; 50:7). Whereas previously her descendants were always called "your children" (בָּנָיִךְ), and the word זֶרַע (offspring/seed) was used only in connection with servant Israel, here Zion is graced with offspring (זַרְעֵךְ, 54:3; see 43:5; 44:3; 45:19, 25; 48:19; 53:10). YHWH who was called the maker (עֹשֶׂךָ, 44:2) of servant Jacob is now called Zion's maker (עֹשַׂיִךְ, 54:5). With all these recurrences of motifs that had previously surrounded addresses to servant Israel, it is not so surprising that in the very last verse, Isa 54:17, עַבְדֵי יְהוָה, "servants of YHWH," appear for the first and only time in connection with Zion. The last line addressed to Zion in the book is also the final mention of YHWH's servant. The two parallel motifs are brought together, and the term "servant" is found in plural form for the first and only time, rendering the connection between Zion's children and YHWH's servant finally explicit: YHWH's servants *are* Zion's children, finally returned to their mother city.

Alongside the servant motifs in this chapter, Zion motifs also display both continuity and change. Zion's children, who were discussed along with Zion in both her previous sections, are once again prominent, although configured differently. Whereas in Isaiah 51 they were filled with YHWH's wrath, unable to aid their mother, perhaps even dead, and in Isaiah 49 they were returning on the shoulders of foreign rulers, here they are already settlers spreading out to inhabit the desolate cities (54:3). Their mother Zion, who was introduced complaining bitterly of YHWH's abandonment (Isa 49:14), is now promised that she will never be abandoned again (54:7, 10). Zion is called the afflicted one, not comforted (Isa 54:11; see 51:19, 21) and promised relief from enemies and restoration (Isa 54:14; see 49:26, 51:23, 52:1). Previously envisioned as YHWH's wife, sent away on account of her children's transgressions (Isa 50:1), Zion is now envisioned as once again reconciled to her husband YHWH, who promises everlasting love (54:8). This undoing of Zion's complaints asserts strenuously that the city's condition as "not comforted" is now past.

Like the previous two Zion sections, this chapter draws exegetically upon both Jeremiah and Lamentations. Even more prominently, however, this chapter draws upon pentateuchal tradition and royal Zion psalms. In fact, the distressed language of Lamentations and Jeremiah which was so crucial to earlier parts of the book is in many ways laid aside here as the reconnections with the more positive previous traditions are strengthened.

Recollections of Lamentations

Lamentations 5 and YHWH's Abandonment

The statement with which Zion first appeared in Isa 49:14, a statement that echoed Lam 5:20, accused YHWH of both forgetting and abandoning her. The question of forgetting had been answered immediately in 49:15, but the second accusation was left unaddressed. In chapter 54 it is finally answered. Several terms from the last four verses of Lamentations 5 recur here: not only "forget" and "abandon" (שׁכח and עזב) from verse 20, but also "despise" and "be angry" (מאס and קצף) from the conclusion, verse 22:

Lam	You, YHWH, are forever;	אַתָּה יְהוָה לְעוֹלָם
5:19	your throne will endure	תֵּשֵׁב כִּסְאֲךָ
	from generation to generation.	לְדֹר וָדוֹר
5:20	Why have you so long forgotten us,	לָמָּה לָנֶצַח **תִּשְׁכָּחֵנוּ**
	abandoned us for all our days?	**תַּעַזְבֵנוּ** לְאֹרֶךְ יָמִים
5:21	Return us, YHWH, to yourself, and let us return;	הֲשִׁיבֵנוּ יְהוָה אֵלֶיךָ וְנָשׁוּבָה
	renew our days as of old,	חַדֵּשׁ יָמֵינוּ כְּקֶדֶם
5:22	unless you have utterly rejected us,	כִּי אִם־**מָאֹס מְאַסְתָּנוּ**
	have become exceedingly wrathful against us.	**קָצַפְתָּ** עָלֵינוּ עַד־מְאֹד

The terms מאס and קצף appear together nowhere else in the Bible, except in Isa 54:6–8, where they appear along with עזב. In verse 4 Zion is told, "The shame of your youth you will forget (תִּשְׁכָּחִי)." Verse 5 identifies YHWH as Zion's husband, and verses 6–8 draw out the analogy:

Isa	For as a woman abandoned	כִּי־כְאִשָּׁה **עֲזוּבָה**
54:6	and hurt in spirit, YHWH has called you,	וַעֲצוּבַת רוּחַ קְרָאָךְ יְהוָה
	and a wife of youth when she is rejected,	וְאֵשֶׁת נְעוּרִים כִּי **תִמָּאֵס**
	says your God.	אָמַר אֱלֹהָיִךְ
54:7	In a brief moment I abandoned you,	בְּרֶגַע קָטֹן **עֲזַבְתִּיךְ**
	but in great pity I will gather you.	וּבְרַחֲמִים גְּדֹלִים אֲקַבְּצֵךְ
54:8	In a flood of anger I hid	בְּשֶׁצֶף **קֶצֶף** הִסְתַּרְתִּי
	my face for a moment from you,	פָנַי רֶגַע מִמֵּךְ
	but in everlasting love I have pitied you,	וּבְחֶסֶד עוֹלָם רִחַמְתִּיךְ
	says your redeemer YHWH.	אָמַר גֹּאֲלֵךְ יְהוָה

In chapter 49 YHWH's forgetting was vigorously denied. But here it is admitted that YHWH did in fact abandon Zion, though only for a moment, and in order to return compassionately to her. The syntactic structure of the verses moves repeatedly from admission of the validity of the terms of Lamentations to reversal of these terms. In all three verses, and with increasing forcefulness, a certain rhetorical rhythm emerges: first the admission of rejection (e.g., v. 7a: "In a brief moment I abandoned you"), and then, in syntactically parallel terms, its reversal (v. 7b: "but in great pity I will gather you"). The parallelism of terms is intricate: "brief (literally, 'small') moment"; "great (literally, 'large') pity"; "I abandoned you"/"I will gather you"; בְּחֶסֶד עוֹלָם/בְּשֶׁצֶף קֶצֶף (a parallelism difficult to render in English, but something like: "in an angry flood"/"in an everlasting love"); "I hid my face from you"/"I pitied you." Even alliteration encourages the perception that all events took place within an ordered, symmetrical environment of divine logic.

This repeated admission, laced with reversal, both validates the laments' final questions—and the perception of divine abandonment that had inspired them—and declares an alternate timetable to that asserted in the lament: YHWH's abandonment, though actual, was by no means either enduring or excessive. The laments had lodged their protest during the brief moment in which all was not yet seen. Zion's abandonment was only a small interlude, more than matched by both the durability and the depth of God's renewed commitment of compassionate love. Addressing decisively the two alternative scenarios left hanging at the end of Lamentations ("return, renew"/"utterly rejected"), YHWH promises that not anger but steadfast love is the final word. As in chapter 49, this promise is significantly addressed not to the plural community of Lamentations 5, but to Zion as the female figure representing the city.

As Albrektson has pointed out, Lamentations frequently reflects upon the overturned tradition of Jerusalem's inviolability.[2] The last several verses, Lam 5:19–22, he noted, belong to a specific group of traditions linked to Zion as God's abode. As I will show below, in the midst of replying to these laments over the violation of Zion's divinely assured security, Second Isaiah reasserts this very tradition,

---

[2] Albrektson, 219–30.

recollecting psalmic discourse that celebrated God's promises both to Jerusalem and to the Davidic monarchy.

Several terms from the beginning of Lamentations 5 are also recalled in this chapter and in the beginning of chapter 55. The first two verses of the lament had invoked YHWH, saying:

Lam 5:1	Remember, YHWH, what has befallen us; look and see our disgrace:	זְכֹר יְהוָה מֶה־הָיָה לָנוּ הַבִּיטָה וּרְאֵה אֶת־חֶרְפָּתֵנוּ
5:2	our heritage has been turned over to aliens, our houses to foreigners.	נַחֲלָתֵנוּ נֶהֶפְכָה לְזָרִים בָּתֵּינוּ לְנָכְרִים

This disgrace is undone in Isa 54:3–4, where Zion is told that her offspring will possess not only their own land, but the nations, that their dwellings will spread out in all directions, and that she will no longer remember (לֹא תִזְכְּרִי) her disgrace (חֶרְפַּת). At the end of the chapter (verse 17), the inhabitants' lost heritage (נַחֲלָתֵנוּ) is recalled as the heritage (נַחֲלַת) of YHWH's servants. Here as well, the response to collective, Jerusalemite discourse is addressed to the figurative mother Zion, into whom the city's remaining inhabitants are apparently subsumed. The repopulation of Zion will mark the end of its disgrace.

The lament's next complaint was likewise made in reference to humans:

Lam 5:3	Orphans we have become, without a father, our mothers widows.	יְתוֹמִים הָיִינוּ אֵין אָב אִמֹּתֵינוּ כְּאַלְמָנוֹת

Once again, ever reluctant to mention the city's actual population, Second Isaiah responds metaphorically, attributing widowhood not to those who lost husbands but to the city itself (חֶרְפַּת אַלְמְנוּתַיִךְ, "disgrace of your widowhood," Isa 54:4)—another slippage of metaphors if it is recalled that in Isa 50:1 Zion was not widowed but separated from her husband. Attribution of widowhood to Zion, if even only briefly, allows Second Isaiah both to acknowledge the widowhood suffered by actual women, and to subsume it in language of reconciled love. Since YHWH was the husband of whom Zion was bereaved, her reconciliation to God offers a symbolic restitution for the bereavements of war and destruction.

This series of reversals of the beginning of Lamentations 5 continues past chapter 54 into the beginning of Isaiah 55 with an image that, while rich in itself, makes more sense when read against the lament background. In Lam 5:4 the people complained about the cost of goods that should have been free:

Lam	Our water with money we drink,	מֵימֵינוּ בְּכֶסֶף שָׁתִינוּ
5:4	and our wood comes with a price.	עֵצֵינוּ בִּמְחִיר יָבֹאוּ

Several of the terms of this verse reappear immediately after the end of the last Zion passage, with its announcement concerning the heritage of YHWH's servants:

Isa	Ho, all who thirst, go to the water,[3]	הוֹי כָּל־צָמֵא לְכוּ לַמַּיִם
55:1	and everyone without money, go,	וַאֲשֶׁר אֵין־לוֹ כָּסֶף לְכוּ
	buy and eat,	שִׁבְרוּ וֶאֱכֹלוּ
	go and buy without money,	וּלְכוּ שִׁבְרוּ בְּלוֹא־כֶסֶף
	and without price, wine and milk.	וּבְלוֹא מְחִיר יַיִן וְחָלָב

Buying water (מַיִם) with money (כֶּסֶף) is only discussed otherwise in Deut 2:6, 28 in the directive to Israel to buy from Edom when journeying there, the point clearly being that these commodities were not the Israelites' for the taking in the lands that were given by God to their neighbors. The convergence of the three terms מַיִם, כֶּסֶף, and מְחִיר is unique to this lament and to Second Isaiah, and the context is quite similar. According to the lament, those who lost their heritage to encroaching foreigners were forced to pay money even for natural resources freely found by those owning property. The complaint expresses displacement and dispossession. Second Isaiah, however, announces free access first to water and then, more extravagantly, to wine and milk. In the first line, the complaint is reversed and normal living conditions are returned.

---

[3] Although the NRSV translates the four instances of הלך in this verse and in verse 3 as "come," the message of Second Isaiah, in relation to the masculine plural audience, is not "come," but "go": see Isa 48:20, 55:12, and especially Isa 52:12.

The next line, however, depicts the returnees becoming as rich in Jerusalem as the lamenters were once poor. Not only are they exempt from buying basic necessities, but even luxuries are envisioned in free abundance.[4]

Lamentations 5, which was already recollected at the very beginning of Zion's first section in chapter 49, has provided the final Zion section rich images of destitution inviting reversal. The heritage of land and resources will be restored and even enhanced; the disgrace of oppression and want will be forgotten. The problem of widowhood is subsumed into the category of divine abandonment, and reversed: whereas the lamenters feared that YHWH was abandoning, rejecting, and continuing forever in unmitigated rage, the poet asserts that God's abandonment, while severe, was only momentary, that reconciliation was always the end in view.

Second Isaiah's disposition to imagine Jerusalem not as a group of human citizens, but as the personified figure Zion, which was already noted in the treatment in Isaiah 49 and 51–52 of other

---

[4] An apparent reversal of the very next verse of Lamentations occurs at the beginning of Second Isaiah. In Lam 5:5 the people complain יָגַעְנוּ וְלֹא הוּנַח־לָנוּ, "we are weary, and we are not allowed to rest." Further on, they describe the labor of young men and boys:

Lam	Young men carry the grinding mill,	בַּחוּרִים טְחוֹן נָשָׂאוּ
5:13	and boys stagger with wood.	וּנְעָרִים בָּעֵץ כָּשָׁלוּ

In Isaiah 40, the speaker describes YHWH as the creator who never grows weary (לֹא יִיגָע, 40:28), who gives strength to those who wait for God:

Isa	Boys will grow tired and be weary,	וְיִעֲפוּ נְעָרִים וְיִגָעוּ
40:30	and young men will utterly stumble,	וּבַחוּרִים כָּשׁוֹל יִכָּשֵׁלוּ
40:31	but those waiting for YHWH will renew their strength;	וְקוֵֹי יְהוָה יַחֲלִיפוּ כֹחַ
	they will rise up on the wing like eagles.	יַעֲלוּ אֵבֶר כַּנְּשָׁרִים
	They will run and not be weary;	יָרוּצוּ וְלֹא יִיגָעוּ
	they will walk and not grow tired.	יֵלְכוּ וְלֹא יִיעָפוּ

Though the verb כשל is used often in prophetic texts to describe the stumbling of Israel on account of sin, these passages in Lamentations and Second Isaiah are the only two places that describe the literal stumbling of young men and boys. This is striking also in that Second Isaiah does not otherwise tend to discuss individuals: the words בַּחוּרִים and נְעָרִים never reappear in the poetry.

Lamentations themes, is especially conspicuous here, since the entire poem being recollected was articulated in a plural voice, and the plights of various members of the society were pointedly highlighted. By distilling away these human entities and addressing the city itself, the poet is able both to deal with the theological problem of abandonment and to envision a solution for that problem, on the literal level, as the repopulation and physical restoration of an abandoned city structure. Images from Lamentations 4 become particularly helpful as the discussion in Isaiah 54 turns from Zion as wife to Zion as city.

Lamentations 4 and the Sacred Stones

Echoes of the fourth lament can be detected in Isaiah 54:11–13. This was the lament that had described the sufferings of Jerusalem's children so brutally, and had been recollected already in Isaiah 51–52. Here its opening imagery is reversed. The lament, which positioned the children and princes, foundations and gates, prophets and priests alike as belonging personally to Zion, began with an analogy between Jerusalem's "sacred stones" which were scattered "at the head of every street" and "the precious children of Zion," who were treated like clay pots:

Lam	How the gold is darkened,	אֵיכָה יוּעַם זָהָב
4:1	how the pure gold has changed!	יִשְׁנֶא הַכֶּתֶם הַטּוֹב
	The sacred stones are poured out	תִּשְׁתַּפֵּכְנָה **אַבְנֵי**־קֹדֶשׁ
	at the head of every street.	בְּרֹאשׁ כָּל־חוּצוֹת
4:2	The precious children of Zion,	**בְּנֵי** צִיּוֹן הַיְקָרִים
	who were valued as gold—	הַמְסֻלָּאִים בַּפָּז
	how they are reckoned as clay pots,	אֵיכָה נֶחְשְׁבוּ לְנִבְלֵי־חֶרֶשׂ
	the work of a potter's hands!	מַעֲשֵׂה יְדֵי יוֹצֵר

But in Isaiah 54:11–13, specifics of Zion's prosperity are listed:

54:11	Suffering one, storm-tossed, not comforted,	עֲנִיָּה סֹעֲרָה לֹא נֻחָמָה
	see, I am laying your stones in antimony,	הִנֵּה אָנֹכִי מַרְבִּיץ בַּפּוּךְ **אֲבָנַיִךְ**
	and your foundations in sapphires,	וִיסַדְתִּיךְ ***בַּסַּפִּירִים***

54:12	and I have made rubies your pinnacles,	וְשַׂמְתִּי כַּדְכֹד שִׁמְשֹׁתַיִךְ
	and your gates sparkling stones,	וּשְׁעָרַיִךְ לְאַבְנֵי אֶקְדָּח
	and all your walls precious stones,	וְכָל־גְּבוּלֵךְ לְאַבְנֵי־חֵפֶץ
54:13	and all your children disciples of YHWH—	וְכָל־בָּנַיִךְ לִמּוּדֵי יְהוָה
	and abundant is the peace of your children.	וְרַב שְׁלוֹם בָּנָיִךְ

Zion's sacred stones, אַבְנֵי־קֹדֶשׁ (Lam 4:1), have now become sparkling stones (אַבְנֵי אֶקְדָּח, Isa 54:12), precious stones (אַבְנֵי־חֵפֶץ, Isa 54:12), stones set in antimony (מַרְבִּיץ בַּפּוּךְ אֲבָנַיִךְ, Isa 54:11); her foundations, once devoured by YHWH's fire (תֹּאכַל יְסוֹדֹתֶיהָ, Lam 4:11), are now foundations set in the sapphires (סַדְתִּיךְ בַּסַּפִּירִים, Isa 54:11) to which princes were once compared (סַפִּיר, Lam 4:7) before hunger disfigured their appearance. The gates of Jerusalem (שַׁעֲרֵי יְרוּשָׁלָ͏ִם, Lam 4:12), once violated by her enemies, now sparkle with precious stones (שְׁעָרַיִךְ לְאַבְנֵי אֶקְדָּח, Isa 54:12), and, in the same breath, the precious children of Zion (בְּנֵי צִיּוֹן הַיְקָרִים, Lam 4:2), who had been counted as clay pots, will now be disciples of YHWH (וְכָל־בָּנַיִךְ לִמּוּדֵי יְהוָה, Isa 54:13), and will enjoy abundant peace (וְרַב שְׁלוֹם בָּנָיִךְ, Isa 54:13).

This close connection between physical wealth and children has already appeared in Second Isaiah both in the images of nations coming to pay homage to Jerusalem (in Isa 45:14 they come bringing wealth and merchandise; in 49:22–23 they bring sons and daughters); and in the striking image of Zion, discussed in chapter 4, wearing her children as ornaments (Isa 49:18). While Lamentations 4 uses the analogy of precious stones to highlight the value of the city's children and the costliness of their loss, Second Isaiah connects the children and the stones, but emphasizes the physical structures of the city: not only will what was ruined be rebuilt, but it is—hyperbolically, at least—imagined as more magnificent than any city in existence, a place in which Zion's children, in abundant security, can become disciples of God.

Recollections of both Lamentations 4 and 5 in Isaiah 54 display patterns of reinterpretation similar to what has been discovered in the other Zion sections: reification of the addressees from human citizenry to the personified city figure, reduction of the human presence in the text from a variety of kinds of people to the simpler category of "children" (here of ambiguous origin but bearing similarities to the exilic addressees), and an increased attention to physical prosperity, articulated through descriptions of luxurious commodities and jeweled structures. Attention to the city's walls, gates, and foundations in Lamentations 4 facilitates a shift in focus in the midst of Isaiah 54 from Zion as abandoned woman to Zion as city soon to be repaired. In that shift she moves from person to place awaiting residents, who in the following chapter will be urged once again to make the journey home to her.

Recollections of Jeremiah

Jeremiah 4, 10 and Jerusalem's Tent

These reversals of misfortune described in the laments are further reinforced by recollections of Jeremiah's language of threat. First the poet recollects a lament that Jeremiah twice attributed to the city of Jerusalem. In Jer 4:14–18 the prophet announces that besiegers have closed in around Jerusalem. The city's response to this disaster is then imagined by the prophet: first she shouts her anguish in terms evoking the pangs of childbirth ("My anguish! My anguish! I writhe in pain!" 4:19). Then she describes her destruction:

<table>
<tr><td>Jer
4:20b</td><td>Suddenly my tents are devastated,
my curtains in a moment.</td><td>פִּתְאֹם שֻׁדְּדוּ אֹהָלַי
רֶגַע יְרִיעֹתָי</td></tr>
</table>

The same metaphor is repeated in Jeremiah 10. Once again these words are imagined being spoken in response to the threat of siege:

<table>
<tr><td>Jer
10:20</td><td>My tent is devastated,
and all my tent-cords are snapped;
my children have gone out from me,
and they are no more.
There is no longer anyone stretching out my tent,
or setting up my curtains.</td><td>אָהֳלִי שֻׁדָּד
וְכָל־מֵיתָרַי נִתָּקוּ
בָּנַי יְצָאֻנִי
וְאֵינָם
אֵין־נֹטֶה עוֹד אָהֳלִי
וּמֵקִים יְרִיעוֹתָי</td></tr>
</table>

The verses that follow describe Jerusalem's people as scattered, and portray the approaching enemy bent on making the cities of Judah "a lair of jackals."

In a response that reverses Jeremiah's imagery, Isa 54:1–2 employs the metaphor of the tent once again, this time speaking to rather than for the city. Zion is told:

Isa 54:1	Cry out, barren one who did not bear,	רָנִּי עֲקָרָה **לֹא** יָלָדָה
	break forth into cries and shout,	פִּצְחִי רִנָּה וְצַהֲלִי
	you who did not travail.	לֹא־חָלָה
	For more will be the children of the desolate one	כִּי־רַבִּים **בְּנֵי**־שׁוֹמֵמָה
	than the children of the married one,	**מִבְּנֵי** בְעוּלָה
	says YHWH.	אָמַר יְהוָה
54:2	Enlarge the site of your tent,	הַרְחִיבִי מְקוֹם **אָהֳלֵךְ**
	and the curtains of your dwellings stretch out;	**וִירִיעוֹת** מִשְׁכְּנוֹתַיִךְ **יַטּוּ**
	do not hold back;	אַל־תַּחְשֹׂכִי
	lengthen your tent-cords	הַאֲרִיכִי **מֵיתָרַיִךְ**
	and your stakes strengthen.	וִיתֵדֹתַיִךְ חַזֵּקִי

She must expand her tent in order to make room for all her children, who in Jeremiah had left her and disappeared, and in Second Isaiah have become numerous once again. Here the very specialized combination of terms used in the Jeremiah passages, אֹהָלַי/אָהֳלִי ("my tents/tent," Jer 4:20, 10:20), יְרִיעֹתָי ("my curtains," Jer 4:20, 10:20), מֵיתָרַי ("my tent-cords," Jer 10:20) and נֹטֶה ("stretch out," Jer 10:20) all reappear in condensed form in Isa 54:2, in which Zion herself is instructed to set up and enlarge her tent. In addition, while Jer 10:20 spells out the meaning of this image in terms of the loss of Zion's children, Isa 54:1–2 makes the sudden increase of her children the occasion for reestablishing and enlarging Zion's tents.

In the Hebrew scriptures, the common noun "tent" is occasionally used in this metaphorical sense to describe personal death, as in Isa 38:12, in which Hezekiah describes his mortal illness as the removal of his tent and the rolling up of his cloth from a weaver's loom, and in Ps 52:5, in which death is described as being torn from one's tent. But the dense parallels in language in reference to Zion's own tents are found nowhere else than in these two passages. A metaphor for individual death, appropriated by Jeremiah for particular use in describing the death of a city, is here reemployed to describe the city's rejuvenation.[5] Likewise the term רֶגַע, "moment," used in Jer 4:20 to describe the suddenness of the destruction, is reinterpreted in Isa 54:7. Now it is used to describe the destruction's duration: רֶגַע קָטֹן, "a brief moment."

Jeremiah 2, 3, 31 and Zion's Shame

In chapter 3 I discussed instances of textual overdetermination, in which a single verse or phrase blends recollections from two and even three distinct sources. Without independent evidence that these source texts are being echoed, such overdeterminations are difficult to assess. On the basis of surrounding quotations of Lamentations 4, Psalm 98, and Numbers 14, a blending of elements of these texts was detected, for instance, in Isa 52:8.

A similar instance seems to occur in verses 4–8 of this passage, most particularly verse 4. It has already been noted that responses to Lamentations 5 which began in Isaiah 49 are resumed here as the subject of YHWH's abandonment is discussed. Presently I will note echoes of Psalm 89 within these same verses. Since Lamentations 5 echoes the royal Zion tradition exemplified by the psalm, it is not surprising that common themes are found in both those prior texts. In terms of both linguistic and thematic similarity, however, when in verse 4 Zion's disgrace is discussed, it is neither the psalm nor the lament that provides the primary vocabulary of disgrace. Rather it is the disgrace described by Jeremiah, which

---

[5] B. Kaiser (169) noted this parallel between Isaiah 54 and Jeremiah 4 and 10, and used it as evidence that the speaker in the Jeremiah passages was the city—or, more precisely, the prophet imputing the words to Zion. G. Glassner, *Vision eines auf Verheissung gegründeten Jerusalem: Textanalytische Studien zu Jesaja 54*, Österreichische Biblische Studien 11 (Klosterneuburg: Österreichisches Katholisches Bibelwerk, 1991) 229–42, suggested several parallels between Isaiah 54 and Jeremiah 4, including this one. The others he mentioned included the use of מַשְׁחִית in Jer 4:7 and Isa 54:16; the mountains and hills as quaking or being removed in Isa 54:10 and Jer 4:24; the storm language in Jer 4:11–13, see Isa 54:11; and the ironic contrast of Jerusalem as devastated yet decked in gold ornaments in Jer 4:29–31, see Isa 54:11–17. Thematic connections seem to exist here, but they do not seem continuous enough, exclusive enough, or linguistically clear enough to be considered here.

resulted not from divine abandonment of the city but from human abandonment of YHWH.

Immediately after the reversal of the tent metaphor, Second Isaiah recollects the image by which Jeremiah had first introduced his discussion of Jerusalem, her youthful betrothal to YHWH:

Jer 2:1	YHWH's word came to me, saying:	וַיְהִי דְבַר־יְהוָה אֵלַי לֵאמֹר
2:2	Go and call in the ears of	
	Jerusalem,	הָלֹךְ וְקָרָאתָ בְאָזְנֵי יְרוּשָׁלַםִ לֵאמֹר
	"Thus says YHWH:	כֹּה אָמַר יְהוָה
	I remember the steadfast love of your youth,	***זָכַרְתִּי*** לָךְ ***חֶסֶד נְעוּרַיִךְ***
	the love of your betrothal.	אַהֲבַת כְּלוּלֹתָיִךְ
	You followed me in the desert,	לֶכְתֵּךְ אַחֲרַי בַּמִּדְבָּר
	in a land not sown."	בְּאֶרֶץ לֹא זְרוּעָה

This early bliss did not, according to Jeremiah, last long. Both Jer 3:24–25 and 31:19 portray the people confessing the shame and disgrace of their sins since their youth (נְעוּרִים). In the first passage the people acknowledge:

Jer	The shame devoured	וְ***הַבֹּשֶׁת*** אָכְלָה
3:24	our ancestors' labor from our youth;	אֶת־יְגִיעַ אֲבוֹתֵינוּ ***מִנְּעוּרֵינוּ***
	their flocks and their herds,	אֶת־צֹאנָם וְאֶת־בְּקָרָם
	their sons and their daughters.	אֶת־בְּנֵיהֶם וְאֶת־בְּנוֹתֵיהֶם
3:25	Let us lie down in our shame	נִשְׁכְּבָה ***בְּבָשְׁתֵּנוּ***
	and let our dismay cover us,	וּתְכַסֵּנוּ ***כְּלִמָּתֵנוּ***
	for against YHWH our God we sinned,	כִּי לַיהוָה אֱלֹהֵינוּ חָטָאנוּ
	we and our ancestors, from our youth	אֲנַחְנוּ וַאֲבוֹתֵינוּ ***מִנְּעוּרֵינוּ***
	and up to this day,	וְעַד־הַיּוֹם הַזֶּה
	and we did not listen to the voice	וְלֹא שָׁמַעְנוּ בְּקוֹל
	of YHWH our God.	יְהוָה אֱלֹהֵינוּ

Similarly, the collective figure Ephraim later on reflects:

Jer	For after I turned, I repented,	כִּי־אַחֲרֵי שׁוּבִי נִחַמְתִּי
31:19	and after I was discovered,	וְאַחֲרֵי הִוָּדְעִי
	I struck my thigh.	סָפַקְתִּי עַל־יָרֵךְ
	I was ashamed, and indeed dismayed,	***בֹּשְׁתִּי*** וְגַם ***נִכְלַמְתִּי***
	for I bore the disgrace of my youth.	כִּי נָשָׂאתִי ***חֶרְפַּת נְעוּרָי***

As in many other instances, what Jeremiah portrays in a variety of ways, sometimes in terms of Jerusalem, sometimes in relation to the people, Second Isaiah collapses into the figure Zion, who is reassured in Isa 54:4:

Isa 54:4	Do not fear, because you will not be ashamed,	אַל־תִּירְאִי כִּי־לֹא **תֵבוֹשִׁי**
	and do not be dismayed,	וְאַל־**תִּכָּלְמִי**
	because you will not be disgraced,	כִּי לֹא תַחְפִּירִי
	For the shame of your youth you will forget,	כִּי **בֹשֶׁת** עֲלוּמַיִךְ תִּשְׁכָּחִי
	and the disgrace of your widowhood	וְ**חֶרְפַּת** אַלְמְנוּתַיִךְ
	you will remember no more.	**לֹא תִזְכְּרִי**־עוֹד

Here, the two synonyms of shame used in Jer 3:25 (כְּלִמָּה, בֹּשֶׁת) and the three used in Jer 31:19 (בֹּשֶׁת, כלם, and חֶרְפָּה) are recollected together—a density unique to these passages. As in the Jeremiah passages, this shame has been hers since her youth. A different word is used at this point—a word connecting with Psalm 89 (see below). But two verses later, in Isa 54:6, Jeremiah's word נְעוּרִים reappears in a description of Zion as אֵשֶׁת נְעוּרִים, "wife of youth."

YHWH's response in Jer 3:26 is an exhortation to return (שׁוּב), which is repeated in Jer 31:21. But discussion of return is significantly missing in Isaiah 54. It is not Jerusalem who is imagined needing to return in Second Isaiah, but rather YHWH (52:8) and the exiles (44:22; 49:5–6; 51:11) who return to Jerusalem. Before the exhortation to return, Jer 31:20 added a note of grace, in which YHWH emphatically claims to remember and pity Ephraim (רַחֵם אֲרַחֲמֶנּוּ . . . זָכֹר אֶזְכְּרֶנּוּ). In Isa 54:4, it is Jerusalem who will not remember (לֹא תִזְכְּרִי) her shame, and in both Isa 54:8 and 10, YHWH repeats promises to pity (מְרַחֲמֵךְ/רִחַמְתִּיךְ) and show steadfast love (חֶסֶד), thus restoring Jerusalem to the original marital devotion that Jeremiah had envisioned. And whereas Jeremiah repeatedly accused her of having abandoned YHWH (Jer 2:13, 17, and 19), now YHWH repeatedly promises not to abandon her (Isa 54:6, 7).

In the previous literature, the accusations of abandonment had flown both ways, in Jeremiah by YHWH of Jerusalem, and in

Lamentations by Jerusalem of YHWH. By using constructions found in both, and thus reinterpreting them, Second Isaiah reassures the city that YHWH's abandonment, rejection, and wrath, have ended. At the same time the poet informs Jerusalem that she will forget the shame Jeremiah had said resulted, not from YHWH's abandonment of the city, but from their abandonment of YHWH. As when Second Isaiah reminded the audience of former things by telling them not to remember them, the exhortation to forget in this chapter is a not-so-subtle nudge to remember. The virtual absence of such vocabulary of shame from Lamentations suggests that it was a category not uppermost in the minds of lamenters. Even when the word חֶרְפָּה was used (Lam 3:30, 61; 5:1) it was not connected with the population's sins but with their sufferings. Second Isaiah's references to disgrace, using the vocabulary of Jeremiah, put the audience on notice that even though YHWH is offering reconciliation, YHWH was not really the one in the wrong. Reconciliation flows from God's abundant, though arguably undeserved, pity.

Pentateuchal Recollections

Barren Women

As in chapters 51–52, here as well pentateuchal themes reappear. In Isa 54:1 the female figure is addressed as עֲקָרָה לֹא יָלָדָה, "barren woman who did not bear." Stories of barren women of old, beginning with Sarah, are recalled by the term עֲקָרָה (Gen 11:30, etc., see particularly Jud 13:2 and 3, where the whole phrase עֲקָרָה לֹא יָלָדָה describes Samson's mother). In fact, Sarah's pregnancy was specifically mentioned in Isa 51:2 as a precedent for hope against hope. However, the term in the second line, שׁוֹמֵמָה, "ruined," which is contrasted with בְּעוּלָה, "married," may signal a somewhat different, though complementary, metaphor. In the feminine singular form it is found otherwise only in Lam 1:13, in which Zion describes the condition YHWH inflicted upon her, and 2 Sam 13:20, where it describes Tamar's condition after she was raped by Amnon and ruined for marriage—and thus for childbearing.[6]

The analogies drawn to traditions of female childlessness by means of these adjectives help extend the metaphor of Zion into a direction never used in Lamentations, and not previously used in Second Isaiah. Sorrow over dying Judahite children present throughout Lamentations, and recalled in Isaiah 51, dissolves in this new image: unlike the Zion of Isaiah 49 and 51 who had been bereaved of children, the Zion of chapter 54 may never have had them to begin with. Unlike the Zion of chapter 51, whose children were lost, and the Zion of Isaiah 49, who wondered what surrogate bore her the children unexpectedly brought to her from the nations, the Zion of chapter 54 is found to have children whose origin is neither stated nor speculated upon. Emphasizing marital reconciliation, the chapter implies that children are born of the reunion of YHWH with the now fertile wife, but this implication is not drawn out explicitly. In this way enough ambiguity is maintained to blur the lines between the various families of Zion: Zion's children are here explicitly identified neither with descendents still living in Jerusalem nor with descendents of the Babylonian exiles, though both groups, understanding themselves as children of the city, are free to read themselves into the text. If, according to the traditional stories, miraculous fertility inevitably follows barrenness, if Sarah who was one could become many, then literary logic dictates a similar outcome for the underpopulated, languishing city.

Noah's Flood

A further analogy to the Genesis story is made explicit immediately following the discussion of marital reconciliation.

---

[6] The connection with both Sarah and Tamar was suggested by Mary Callaway, *Sing, O Barren One: A Study in Comparative Midrash*, SBLDS 91 (Atlanta: Scholars Press, 1986) 67–68. Since David's court narrative is not otherwise recollected in Second Isaiah, it may not be Tamar herself who is being remembered, but rather the condition that her story exemplifies.

Verse 8 describes YHWH's earlier rage as "a flood of anger" (שֶׁצֶף קֶצֶף). The very next verse recalls the quintessential tradition of "a flood of anger" in Genesis 6–9, and YHWH's subsequent promise to Noah never again to destroy the earth with a flood:

54:9	Like the waters of Noah this is to me,	כִּי־מֵי נֹחַ זֹאת לִי
	which I swore	אֲשֶׁר נִשְׁבַּעְתִּי
	would not again pass over the earth,	מֵעֲבֹר עוֹד עַל־הָאָרֶץ
	likewise I have sworn	כֵּן נִשְׁבַּעְתִּי
	not to be angry with you or rebuke you.	מִקְּצֹף עָלַיִךְ וּמִגְּעָר־בָּךְ

The explicit reference to Noah in 54:9 recalls a tradition with clear typological links with Jerusalem's destruction, since both of these disasters are distinctly understood as having been caused by divine anger over human evil. Second Isaiah draws the analogy to its logical conclusion in the promise of God to Zion, analogous to that to Noah: "likewise I have sworn not to be angry with you or rebuke you." Both Noah and Zion are in the end instructed to repopulate and refill the empty lands.

Since the verbal echoes are faint here, consisting only of the name "Noah" and the common words "covenant," "waters," "earth," and "again," it is impossible to tell whether Second Isaiah was reading Genesis text in its present form or in one of its earlier manifestations.[7] Clearly, however, the version known by Second Isaiah, like the story's final form, involved divine promises enforcing an unprecedented level of commitment to future protection, and this is the point upon which the poet capitalizes in reasserting next, in 54:10, the security of Jerusalem. The analogies to Noah are clear and apt: as in that story, although well-deserved destruction occurred once before, the decision not to carry out such a destruction again is founded not on human moral improvement but on divine grace.[8] After the flood, according to Second Isaiah, the sea was not allowed again to transgress (עבר, Isa

7 Tantalizingly, however, Gen 8:21 connects the promise never to destroy the earth again with the recognition that the inclination of the human heart is evil from youth (נְעֻרָיו, see 54:4, 6).

8 On this point see B. Anderson, "Exodus and Covenant," 347–49.

54:9) its boundaries. The analogy between divine control of the watery chaos and divine protection against transgressing enemies was already imagined at length in Isaiah 51. This metaphor emerges once again as YHWH assures "storm-tossed" Zion (54:11) that no enemy weapons will again prevail against her (54:14–17).

Significantly, the recurrent term by which the analogy to Noah is established (נִשְׁבַּעְתִּי, "I promised") does not occur at all in the Genesis narrative. Rather, this term is closely associated with the covenant between God and the Davidic king, a covenant expressed most directly in Psalm 89, which also lends language to this chapter and becomes an explicit precedent in chapter 55.

Psalmic Recollections

Although the importance of Lamentations, Jeremiah, and pentateuchal traditions for Isaiah 54 has already been outlined, some of the richest intertextual work in this chapter involves three psalms which reflect the tradition of YHWH's covenant with the Davidic king and protection of the royal city, Psalms 89, 72, and 46. Psalm 89 was already discussed above in chapter 3 in connection with the combat imagery in Isa 51:9–10. That imagery opened a section which, in the tradition of several collective lament psalms, invoked God's renewed power by recalling the primal combat myth. The language of such psalms went on to shape the outline of the entire section, which ended with a dramatic portrayal of YHWH's return, announced by means of Psalm 98's proclamation of YHWH's reign. Although Psalm 89 specifically outlines the divine covenant with Davidic royalty and highlights its overthrow, the issue of human royalty and its defeat does not explicitly emerge in Isaiah 51–52. Isaiah 54 and 55 will bear more directly on this question.

Psalm 72, a second royal hymn, portrays the conferral of divine dominion, and with it the responsibility for maintaining peace and justice, on the subject king. He is described as exercising power over the other nations and protection over his own. Psalm 46, the language of which is deeply linked to that of the royal psalms, describes YHWH's protection of the city in which the deity dwells.

Psalm 89

Throughout the early chapters of Second Isaiah, Israel was repeatedly identified by YHWH as "my servant" (עַבְדִּי, Isa 42:1, 19; 44:21; 45:4; 48:20; 49:3, 6; see also 49:5; 50:10; 52:13; 53:11) and "my chosen" (בְּחִירִי, Isa 42:1; 45:4; see also 43:20; 49:7), and even as "my servant whom I have chosen" (עַבְדִּי אֲשֶׁר בָּחָרְתִּי, Isa 43:10; see also 41:8, 9; 44:1, 2). Aside from Servant Israel in Second Isaiah, David is the only servant of YHWH described in this way, as both "my servant" (עַבְדִּי) and "my chosen" (בְּחִירִי), most predominantly in Psalm 89:4 (see also verses 20, 21, 40, and 51):

Ps 89:4	I have made a covenant with my chosen,	כָּרַתִּי בְרִית לִבְחִירִי
	I have sworn to David my servant.	נִשְׁבַּעְתִּי לְדָוִד עַבְדִּי

It seems evident, as was mentioned in chapter 5, that an analogy is being drawn between the former status of the royal house and the new role of Israel as Second Isaiah imagines it. Speculation on this point is not necessary, however, since Second Isaiah's final chapter renders this relationship explicit, in Isa 55:3:[9]

Isa 55:3	Incline your ears and come to me;	הַטּוּ אָזְנְכֶם וּלְכוּ אֵלַי
	listen, and you will live:	שִׁמְעוּ וּתְחִי נַפְשְׁכֶם
	I will make with you an everlasting covenant,	**וְאֶכְרְתָה לָכֶם בְּרִית עוֹלָם**
	my faithful steadfast love for David.	**חַסְדֵי דָוִד הַנֶּאֱמָנִים**
55:4	See, a witness to the peoples I made him,	הֵן עֵד לְאוּמִּים נְתַתִּיו
	a leader and commander for the peoples.	נָגִיד וּמְצַוֵּה לְאֻמִּים

---

[9] Anderson ("Exodus and Covenant," 348) noted this transferring of promises of grace originally given to the Davidic dynasty to the people themselves, particularly marked by the masculine plural pronoun in Isa 55:3. Eissfeldt ("Promises of Grace") also noted the strong relationship between Psalm 89 and Isa 55:1–5, and supplemented this observation with a long list of other passages throughout Second Isaiah that correspond to Psalm 89, including many that were noted in my chapter 3 in relation to Isaiah 51:9–16. As I observed in my first chapter, however, Eissfeldt viewed the relationship between the two works as "formal and superficial" (206) only, since Second Isaiah envisioned the promises as applying now to Israel rather than to the monarch.

These verses explicitly allude to the language of divine covenant with David that is found in its fullest form in Psalm 89, not only naming David himself as the covenant's recipient, but recollecting the phrase "I have made a covenant with my chosen" (כָּרַתִּי בְרִית לִבְחִירִי) and applying it directly to the masculine plural audience (לָכֶם) who have already been established as YHWH's chosen (see especially Isa 43:2, 10), and in fact, like David, as YHWH's witnesses as well (עֵדַי, Isa 43:10, 12; 44:8). In this reference to David, the poet makes explicit what has been implicit throughout the text, that the covenant once conferred upon David is now, along with all the concommitant titles, being conferred upon the masculine plural audience.

This direct allusion to monarchic discourse is further bolstered by the repetition of other language from Psalm 89. In the last several verses of the celebrative section of the psalm, just before the lament mourning YHWH's rejection of the royal servant, YHWH's affirmation of David is cited in soaring language:

Ps 89:34	My steadfast love will not depart from him, and I will not betray my faithfulness.	וְחַסְדִּי לֹא־אָפִיר מֵעִמּוֹ וְלֹא־אֲשַׁקֵּר **בֶּאֱמוּנָתִי**
89:35	I will not profane my covenant, and what went out from my lips I will not change.	לֹא־אֲחַלֵּל **בְּרִיתִי** וּמוֹצָא שְׂפָתַי לֹא אֲשַׁנֶּה
89:36	Once I have sworn in my holiness; to David I will not lie:	אַחַת נִשְׁבַּעְתִּי בְקָדְשִׁי אִם־לְדָוִד אֲכַזֵּב
89:37	his offspring will continue forever, and his throne, like the sun before me,	זַרְעוֹ **לְעוֹלָם** יִהְיֶה וְכִסְאוֹ כַשֶּׁמֶשׁ נֶגְדִּי
89:38	like the moon, established forever, a faithful witness in the sky.	כְּיָרֵחַ יִכּוֹן **עוֹלָם** **וְעֵד** בַּשַּׁחַק **נֶאֱמָן**

The language of promise and covenant is echoed in the lament portion of the psalm, and becomes especially poignant when a question directly challenging the sworn covenant is asked:

Ps 89:50	Where is your steadfast love from the first, Lord, which your swore to David in your faithfulness?	אַיֵּה **חֲסָדֶיךָ** הָרִאשֹׁנִים אֲדֹנָי נִשְׁבַּעְתָּ **לְדָוִד** **בֶּאֱמוּנָתֶךָ**

Vocabulary used richly in these sections, and indeed throughout the psalm, characterizes the reference to David in Isa 55:3–4: not only David's name (Ps 89:50 and Isa 55:3) but also "my steadfast love" (חַסְדִּי, Ps 89:34, 50 and Isa 55:3; see also Ps 89:2, 3, 15, 25, 29, 34; Isa 54:8, 10); "faithfulness"/"faithful" (נֶאֱמָן/אֱמוּנָה, Ps 89:34, 38, 50 and Isa 55:3; see also Ps 89:2, 3, 6, 9, 25); "covenant" (בְּרִית, Ps 89:35 and Isa 55:3; see also Ps 89:4, 29, 35, 40; Isa 54:10); "forever" (עוֹלָם, Ps 89:37, 38 and Isa 55:3; see also Ps 89:2, 3, 5, 29, 53; Isa 54:8); "witness" (עֵד, Ps 89:38 and Isa 55:4). The only missing element in Isaiah 55 is the verb נִשְׁבַּעְתִּי, "I swore," so prominent in Psalm 89. It will be discussed below in connection with Isaiah 54.

The rich utilization of this vocabulary makes it clear that Isa 55:3–4 is referring not simply to the David tradition in the abstract, but to the tradition as it is rendered in such a royal psalm. Reflecting language employed in Psalm 89 to articulate both YHWH's promise to David and the violation of that promise, Second Isaiah establishes a strong reconnection with that promise, conferring it now on all who are YHWH's chosen servants.

The direct reference to David in Isa 55:3, in the midst of a vocabulary particularly reminiscent of the royal covenant, draws explicit attention to a language complex growing throughout Isaiah 54 that is best recognized by reference to Psalms 89, 46, and 72. Each of these psalms emphasizes an aspect of the complex of preexilic ideology which had connected YHWH's choice of David's family with YHWH's protection of Jerusalem, the chosen city. Whereas this Jerusalem ideology had been invoked in Lamentations in order to express dismay and shock over its failure, Second Isaiah invokes the ideology to announce its—and with it, Jerusalem's—reinstatement.

Recollections of Psalm 89 within the Zion passage itself are complex, involving both the language of promise from the psalm's hymnic section and the language of disgrace from its lament section. Perhaps the easiest way to begin approach this question is to reexamine the same verses noted above:

Ps	I have made a covenant with my chosen,	כָּרַתִּי **בְרִית** לִבְחִירִי
89:4	I have sworn to David my servant.	**נִשְׁבַּעְתִּי** לְדָוִד **עַבְדִּי**
89:34	My steadfast love will not depart from him,	**וְחַסְדִּי** לֹא־אָפִיר מֵעִמּוֹ
	and I will not betray my faithfulness.	וְלֹא־אֲשַׁקֵּר בֶּאֱמוּנָתִי
89:35	I will not profane my covenant,	לֹא־אֲחַלֵּל **בְּרִיתִי**
	and what went out from my lips I will not change.	וּמוֹצָא שְׂפָתַי לֹא אֲשַׁנֶּה
89:36	Once I have sworn in my holiness;	אַחַת **נִשְׁבַּעְתִּי בְקָדְשִׁי**
	to David I will not lie:	אִם־לְדָוִד אֲכַזֵּב
89:37	his offspring will continue forever,	**זַרְעוֹ לְעוֹלָם** יִהְיֶה
	and his throne, like the sun before me,	וְכִסְאוֹ כַשֶּׁמֶשׁ נֶגְדִּי
89:38	like the moon, established forever,	כְּיָרֵחַ **יִכּוֹן עוֹלָם**
	a faithful witness in the sky.	וְעֵד בַּשַּׁחַק נֶאֱמָן
89:50	Where is your steadfast love from the first, Lord,	אַיֵּה **חֲסָדֶיךָ** הָרִאשֹׁנִים אֲדֹנָי
	which your swore to David in your faithfulness?	**נִשְׁבַּעְתָּ** לְדָוִד בֶּאֱמוּנָתֶךָ

The dense recurrence in Isa 54:8–10 of the terms "steadfast love" (חַסְדִּי/חֶסֶד, 54:8, 10), "forever" (עוֹלָם, 54:8), and "covenant" (בְּרִית, 54:10) have already been noted. These are fairly unremarkable words in themselves and it is only the reference to David and the addition of more acute language such as "faithfulness" and "witness" that clarifies the relationship between Isaiah 55 and the psalm. But in addition, Isa 54:9 reutilizes a word, missing from chapter 55, which had recurred three times in the psalm and is crucial to its arguments: נִשְׁבַּעְתִּי, "I swore" (Ps 89:4, 36, 50):

Isa	In a flood of anger I hid	בְּשֶׁצֶף קֶצֶף **הִסְתַּרְתִּי**
54:8	my face for a moment from you,	פָנַי רֶגַע מִמֵּךְ
	but in eternal love I have pitied you,	**וּבְחֶסֶד עוֹלָם** רִחַמְתִּיךְ
	says your redeemer YHWH.	אָמַר גֹּאֲלֵךְ יְהוָה
54:9	Like the waters of Noah this is to me,	כִּי־מֵי נֹחַ זֹאת לִי
	which I swore	אֲשֶׁר **נִשְׁבַּעְתִּי**
	would not again pass over the earth,	מֵעֲבֹר עוֹד עַל־**הָאָרֶץ**
	likewise I have sworn	כֵּן **נִשְׁבַּעְתִּי**
	not to be angry with you or rebuke you.	מִקְּצֹף עָלַיִךְ וּמִגְּעָר־בָּךְ

54:10	For the mountains will depart,	כִּי הֶהָרִים יָמוּשׁוּ
	and the hills will totter,	וְהַגְּבָעוֹת תְּמוּטֶנָה
	but my steadfast love will not depart from you,	וְחַסְדִּי מֵאִתֵּךְ לֹא־יָמוּשׁ
	and my covenant of peace will not totter,	וּבְרִית שְׁלוֹמִי לֹא תָמוּט
	says the one who pities you, YHWH.	אָמַר מְרַחֲמֵךְ יְהוָה

Like the language in the surrounding verses, the key word נִשְׁבַּעְתִּי, "I swore," which is completely absent from the Noah story in Genesis, reflects the tradition of YHWH's covenant with David. By analogy to Noah, by using language of oath to David, Second Isaiah does something new: this covenant is now offered directly to Jerusalem without the royalty's mediation. As we will see below, references to the safety of Zion herself as articulated in Psalm 46 smooth the way for this transfer of the divine oath to the city itself.

Once this connection is seen, other linguistic similarities between the psalm's lament section and Isaiah 54 can be noted, such as בּוּשָׁה ("shame," Ps 89:46; see Isa 54:4), חֶרְפָּה ("disgrace," Ps 89:42, 51; see Isa 54:4), and in connection with these, the peculiar word עֲלוּמִים ("youth," Ps 89:46, found otherwise only in Job), which appears in Isa 54:4 as עֲלוּמַיִךְ, where it replaces the synonym נְעוּרִים used in the Jeremiah passages, apparently in order to provide a more direct parallel for its near homonym אַלְמְנוּתַיִךְ ("widowhood"). Whereas the psalmist perceives YHWH hiding (תִּסָּתֵר, Ps 89:47) from him forever, YHWH in Isa 54:8 reflects upon having hid (הִסְתַּרְתִּי) from Zion for only a moment. Whereas Ps 89:41 claims that YHWH has burst (פָּרַצְתָּ) the walls of David's city, has made (שַׂמְתָּ) his strongholds a ruin (מְחִתָּה), Isaiah 54 envisions a massive rebuilding project which includes not only Zion's bursting out (תִּפְרֹצִי, Isa 54:3) in growth, but also YHWH's making (שַׂמְתִּי, Isa 54:12) her pinnacles of rubies and keeping ruin (מְחִתָּה, Isa 54:14) far away from her. Laments once raised on the king's behalf are answered as if Zion herself had spoken them.

Earlier chapters (see especially Isaiah 44–45) had argued strenuously for viewing the Persian Cyrus as YHWH's "shepherd" who would rebuild Jerusalem and its temple (44:28), and even as YHWH's "anointed" (45:1)—all roles once reserved for David, Solomon, and their descendents. The poet had even anticipated objections to this proposal by means of analogies to a potter's sovereignty over the vessels he makes (45:9–13). In view of Judah's continued vassalage and the opportunities Cyrus represented, it is clear that this prophet did not view the reinstitution of the Judahite monarchy, whether desirable or not, as expedient. True to the mood of Second Isaiah, which transforms even liabilities and setbacks into reflections of the divine purpose, arguments against Davidic kingship are not made directly, but rather by filling in all the semantic spaces once occupied by the kingship, rendering it rhetorically superfluous. The divine promise once mediated through the king is now mediated through the city itself.

Psalm 46

In addition to Davidic language, language once associated even more directly with the safety of the royal city is invoked in Isaiah 54. Psalm 46 celebrated the eternal security of Zion. Even should the physical world fall into tumult, there would be no need for the residents to fear:

Ps 46:2	God is our refuge and strength, a help in distress, ever sufficient.	אֱלֹהִים לָנוּ מַחֲסֶה וָעֹז עֶזְרָה בְצָרוֹת נִמְצָא מְאֹד
46:3	Therefore we will not fear when the earth changes, when the mountains totter in the heart of the seas.	עַל־כֵּן לֹא־נִירָא בְּהָמִיר אָרֶץ וּבְמוֹט הָרִים בְּלֵב יַמִּים

Further on, in verse 7, similar instability is attributed to the political world: the nations roar, kingdoms totter (מָטוּ), the earth melts. Yet since God is the city's refuge it will not totter (בַּל־תִּמּוֹט).

Likewise in Isa 54:10 Zion, who has been told not to fear (אַל־תִּירְאִי, Isa 54:4), is assured of her security:[10]

---

10 Anderson ("Exodus and Covenant," 348) noted this correspondence between Isaiah 54 and Psalm 46.

Isa 54:10	For the mountains will depart,	כִּי **הֶהָרִים** יָמוּשׁוּ
	and the hills will totter,	וְהַגְּבָעוֹת **תְּמוּטֶנָה**
	but my steadfast love will not depart from you,	וְחַסְדִּי מֵאִתֵּךְ לֹא־יָמוּשׁ
	and my covenant of peace will not totter,	וּבְרִית שְׁלוֹמִי **לֹא תָמוּט**
	says the one who pities you, YHWH.	אָמַר מְרַחֲמֵךְ יְהוָה

Here as elsewhere Second Isaiah expands the previous poetry by adding synonyms and homonyms creating new parallelisms, rendering even more explicit what was implied in the psalm. Not merely the mountains, but the hills as well are in an uproar; they not only totter (מוט) but they depart altogether (מוש). But the attributes of God's loyalty to Jerusalem, "steadfast love" and "covenant of peace," showing themselves more stable even than the physical world around, will neither totter nor depart. Even more explicitly, the final verses of the chapter explain that because of God's protection no weapon or enemy will be able to prevail against the city.

This is a crucial reassurance in view of the importance of Zion's inviolability in earlier imagination, and in view of the confidence which Jerusalem's destruction by Babylon had broken. Assurances that the city is once again a secure place serve not only to renew trust in YHWH's protection and good will, but also to address the practical question of physical safety in what undoubtedly seemed to the residents of Babylon to be the wild west. In the previous Zion passage, YHWH was seen returning to Zion (Isa 52:8); here Zion is reinstated as YHWH's dwelling-place, the geographical anchor of Judah's religious self-understanding.

Psalm 72

Psalm 72 illuminates the background from which the language of Zion's peace and righteousness emanates, particularly as it is articulated in Isa 54:13–14. That psalm connects the themes of monarchy and civic protection, emphasizing YHWH's support of Judah's monarch, who in turn guarantees the righteousness, peace, and security of the city. It is the king's wise rule that crushes the oppressor and brings days of righteousness and abundance of peace to the people:

Ps 72:3	May the mountains yield peace to the people,	יִשְׂאוּ הָרִים **שָׁלוֹם** לָעָם
	and the hills, in righteousness.	וּגְבָעוֹת **בִּצְדָקָה**
72:4	May he judge the poor of the people,	יִשְׁפֹּט עֲנִיֵּי־עָם
	and deliver the needy children,	יוֹשִׁיעַ **לִבְנֵי** אֶבְיוֹן
	and crush the oppressor. . . .	וִידַכֵּא **עוֹשֵׁק**
72:7	May righteousness bloom in his days,	יִפְרַח־בְּיָמָיו **צַדִּיק**
	and abundance of peace,	**וְרֹב שָׁלוֹם**
	till the moon is no more.	עַד־בְּלִי יָרֵחַ

Similarly, in Isa 54:13–14, Zion is promised abundance of peace, establishment in righteousness, and distance from oppression:[11]

Isa	. . . and all your children disciples of YHWH—	וְכָל־**בָּנַיִךְ** לִמּוּדֵי יְהוָה
54:13	and abundant is the peace of your children.	**וְרַב שְׁלוֹם בָּנָיִךְ**
54:14	In righteousness you will be established;	**בִּצְדָקָה** תִּכּוֹנָנִי
	you will stay far from oppression,	רַחֲקִי **מֵעֹשֶׁק**
	for you will not fear,	כִּי־לֹא תִירָאִי
	and from ruin, for it will not come near you.	וּמִמְּחִתָּה כִּי לֹא־תִקְרַב אֵלָיִךְ

This combination of phrases is unique to Psalm 72 and Isaiah 54.[12] Promises once mediated to the city through the righteous reign of the king are now reiterated, though no king is in sight.

---

[11] Porteous (240) recognized in the terms שָׁלוֹם and צְדָקָה in both Psalm 72 and Isaiah 54 words historically connected with the city of Jerusalem, perhaps even in its pre-Israelite mythology.

[12] Once this relationship is seen, an echo of Psalm 72 in Isaiah 49 becomes more obvious. According to the psalm, not only are oppressors crushed but they are immediately envisioned bowing down to Judah's king:

Ps	May his foes bend the knee before him,	לְפָנָיו יִכְרְעוּ צִיִּים
72:9	And may his enemies lick the dust.	וְאֹיְבָיו **עָפָר יְלַחֵכוּ**
72:10	May the kings of Tarshish and the coastlands	**מַלְכֵי** תַרְשִׁישׁ וְאִיִּים
	bring gifts,	מִנְחָה יָשִׁיבוּ
	The kings of Sheba and Seba	מַלְכֵי שְׁבָא וּסְבָא
	bring tribute.	אֶשְׁכָּר יַקְרִיבוּ
72:11	May all kings bow down to him,	**וְיִשְׁתַּחֲווּ־לוֹ כָל־מְלָכִים**
	and all nations serve him.	כָּל־גּוֹיִם יַעַבְדוּהוּ

This vision of the subservience of the nations and their kings is echoed in Isa 49:23, in which kings and queens similarly bow down and lick the dust before Zion:

While the theology of preexilic Zion involved an intricate relationship between YHWH, YHWH's chosen servant the king, and YHWH's protection of the city through the king's righteous reign, Second Isaiah has altered the terms. Zion's security, peace and protection are reinstated, but the covenant through which these are upheld is no longer with a king, but with Zion herself and with her children, the returning plural audience who in Isaiah 55 inherit the monarchic promise. Second Isaiah never discusses directly the issue of David's dynasty. Rather, the poet fills the semantic spaces once filled by the king: YHWH is Jerusalem's king (Isa 52:7), Israel is YHWH's chosen and servant (45:4, etc.), Cyrus is YHWH's shepherd, temple-builder, and anointed (44:28, 45:1), and Zion herself is the one established in righteousness (54:14) and told to sit on her throne (52:2, see 47:1).[13]

Isa 49:23	Kings shall be your caretakers, and their queens your nursemaids.	וְהָיוּ **מְלָכִים** אֹמְנַיִךְ וְשָׂרוֹתֵיהֶם מֵינִיקֹתַיִךְ
	Faces to the ground they shall bow down to you, and the dust of your feet they will lick.	אַפַּיִם אֶרֶץ **יִשְׁתַּחֲווּ לָךְ** **וַעֲפַר** רַגְלַיִךְ **יְלַחֵכוּ**
	And you will know that I am YHWH; The one who waits upon me will not be shamed.	וְיָדַעַתְּ כִּי־אֲנִי יְהוָה אֲשֶׁר לֹא־יֵבֹשׁוּ קֹוָי

In the psalm, it is tribute that is brought to the king by other nations; in Isaiah 49 this tribute becomes the returning children themselves. But see Isa 45:14, in which other nations are envisioned bowing down to Jerusalem and bringing their wealth. There, as in Ps 72:10, Sabeans are mentioned specifically. In Isa 60:14, which is textually dependent on Isaiah 49, the tribute that is brought to Zion is once again material wealth.

[13] According to Gottwald ("Social Class," 54), Isaiah 40–55 "parcels out the functions of the former Davidic dynasty, some to Cyrus and some to the exiled community, thereby dissolving any need for a Judahite prince." This usage in Second Isaiah, Gottwald points out, differs from other programmatic visions of the restored community such as Ezekiel's and the Deuteronomistic History, which both indicate hope in the return of Davidic rule. Eissfeldt ("Promises of Grace," 203–6) similarly noted that Second Isaiah differs from not only Jeremiah and Ezekiel concerning the status of the monarchy, but also with Haggai and Zechariah, and that Second Isaiah applies language once used of the monarchy to Cyrus the anointed, YHWH the king, and Israel itself as the elect servant.

The least that could be said about this series of echoes is that Second Isaiah imagines Zion being given a renewal of assurance quite continuous with earlier psalmic constructions. Strong evidence has been cited for viewing Psalms 89, 46, and 72 as sources for Second Isaiah's adapted language. As preexilic psalms clearly connected with the royal city, they were available to Second Isaiah and their use in discussions of Jerusalem's renewal is historically plausible. The language of Isaiah 54 itself is very similar to passages from the psalms, in some cases uniquely so. The psalms are used in Isaiah 54 to continue development of a line of reasoning that coheres thematically with their use in monarchic times, reinvesting the psalmic claims with new validity in spite of alterations in Judah's political status. Understandings of God's unique relationship to Zion that had been called radically into question by the city's destruction are given new voice and configuration in this adaptation of monarchic formulations.

The degree of explicitness with which the circle of discourse surrounding preexilic Zion theology is echoed here is confirmed by the recollections in Isaiah 51–52 of other psalms reflecting this same circle of discourse: the enthronement psalms, 93 and 98, and the communal laments over the nation's downfall, 44, 74, and 77 as well as 89. In fact, the explicit transfer of Davidic promises to the returning Israelites in chapter 55 culminates a reutilization of royal Zion psalmody that has been gaining force throughout Second Isaiah. Suggestions of divine kingship begin early in chapter 40 with images of royal procession (verses 3–5, 9; see Ps 98:9), the might of YHWH's arm (verse 10; see Ps 98:1), and YHWH's role as shepherd (verse 11; see Ps 95:7), followed by a psalmic section focusing on YHWH's incomparability (verses 18, 25; see Ps 89:6) and political power (verses 15–17, 23–24; see Ps 72:8–11). Beginning in Isa 41:21 (see also 43:15 and 44:6), YHWH is called Jacob's King. Quotations of Psalm 98 begin in Isa 42:10 with "Sing to YHWH a new song," and continues by repeated references throughout the rest of text (see for instance 44:23; 49:13; 54:1; 55:12). Roles of "servant and chosen" and of "shepherd and anointed" are reassigned. YHWH's rival gods are humiliated (46:1–2), their city is dethroned (Isa 47:1), and foreign rulers come bowing to Zion (49:22–23). Leaning most heavily on the tradition, Isaiah 51–52 invokes psalmic discourse of divine victory and kingship, recalling communal laments and praises which themselves recalled the motifs of cosmic battle, enthronement, and reign, culminating in the herald's announcement: "Your God reigns!" (52:7) and the sentinels' sighting of YHWH's procession toward Zion, marching to the tune of Ps 98:1–3. In the final two chapters, as Zion and her husband YHWH are reunited, language of the city's divine protection once mediated through the king is iterated to Zion herself, and the covenant once made with David is renewed with the plural audience. In the final verses, they are the ones processing like royalty to Zion. The mountains, hills, and trees all celebrate their coming as they had once celebrated the coming of YHWH, with bursts of song and clapping of hands (Isa 55:12; see Ps 98:8; 96:12).

Isaiah 54:1–17 in Review

In Isaiah 54, language from a variety of sources merges upon Zion. The city's future is described in the uniting of terms previously used of Israel as well as of Zion. Themes articulating Zion's destitution in previous chapters are subtly altered, particularly in regard to her imagined marital and maternal state: before seen as abandoned and bereft, now she is envisioned as widowed and barren, yet on the verge of restoration and fecundity. Language once used to describe destruction, destitution, and shame in Lamentations and Jeremiah is restructured to announce healing and restoration: YHWH admits to having abandoned her but promises restoration now; disgrace and widowhood are acknowledged and set aside; restoration of both precious children and priceless city structures is envisioned; Zion's tents, once devastated, are not only restored but expanded, and the disgrace of her youth, so prominent in Jeremiah, is remembered in order to be forgotten.

Precedent for Jerusalem's renewal is drawn from both pentateuchal tradition and psalmic hymnody. Like Sarah, Zion will have children, so many children that the tents she once lamented as destroyed will have to be enlarged. Like Noah and David she is pledged divine favor which will not this time be revoked. Specific pledges of prosperity are voiced in terms familiar from psalms announcing YHWH's protection of Zion through the Davidic regency, particularly Psalms 89, 46, and 72, which inspire the repeated use in Isaiah 54 of terms such as "I swore," "covenant of peace," "abundant peace," and "righteousness." Zion's complaint that YHWH both forgot and abandoned having been refuted, the pain so excruciating in the midst of the previous Zion section disappears, as the dead children are indeed forgotten, and a new family is begun in a city now safe and prosperous.

As for the servant, last seen in Isa 53:12 vindicated and glorified on account of his faithfulness, he remains invisible in chapter 54 until the very last verse where, for the first and only time, he appears as "servants." There all the major addressees, the "she," "he," and "they," are finally brought together: the repatriated children of Zion, her "offspring," are revealed as YHWH's servant, now plural. Both Zion and the servant, the two personified figures who have served throughout Second Isaiah to connect the exiles with their textual heritage, disappear in the next and final chapter, and the masculine singular audience is addressed with appeals to return to YHWH and visions of their procession homeward.

Chapter 7
"From This Time Forward I Make You Hear New Things": Using Memory to Construct a Future

The dense and persistent use in Isaiah 49–54 of recollections from previous texts forms a rich fabric of thought, linking old and new in complex patterns both familiar and surprising. Sometimes texts are recalled in approximately their original form; other times they are recast and even reversed. Throughout the discourse reigns an appeal to Israel's originating story and formative theological myths. This appeal connects the late sixth century with cultural memories, and attempts to establish a bridge over broken or damaged traditions. These memories of the past are marshaled to assert the message that returning to redevelop Jerusalem and YHWH's cult is the logical next chapter in Israel's sacred story.

In its appeal not simply to Judahite themes or traditions, but to actual words and even liturgies of celebration, threat, and lament that had previously shaped Israelite self-understanding, Second Isaiah displays sensitivity both to continuities from the past and to disruptions in the present. In the destruction of Jerusalem, the expectation of YHWH's unfailing defense of Judah and of its royalty had been irreparably ruptured. Repetition of old forms and phrases were no longer adequate to account for new uncertainties. Yet neither was a completely new word likely to take root in hearts still inhabited by unresolved textual conflicts. Any new word purported to be YHWH's had to take this paradox into account, and was therefore obliged to be both continuous and discontinuous with earlier words, to hark back to the "former things" (Isa 46:9) "declared long ago" (48:5) while at the same time setting aside these former words to declare a "new thing" (43:19) "created now, not long ago" (48:7). This rhetorical feat Second Isaiah not only announces, but carries out. By giving old words new contexts, by twisting them on their axis, by blending together disparate and disjunctive traditions, Second Isaiah both appeals to the past and refashions it to argue that current events and programs fulfill what was intended by YHWH all along.

Close attention not only to themes and forms in Second Isaiah but to its use of phrases and word complexes found in other literature has helped pinpoint some of Second Isaiah's details, showing that the poet is not simply responding to ideas but to expressions, habitual formulations, and verbal constructions of the relationship between YHWH and the people. Attention to the language used has made it possible at times to recognize the actual speech to which Second Isaiah replies and to set the poet's words in their rhetorical context. At other times it has enabled identification at least of nearest available language with which to compare Second Isaiah's speech.

This study has only scratched the surface of the subject of Second Isaiah's intertextual recollections. Although Isaiah 49–54 is the most densely and continuously allusive part of the book, the texts that I have observed comprising the rhetorical background for these sections continue to reappear in a variety of ways throughout Second Isaiah. Their appearance becomes more evident once the exegetical nature of Second Isaiah's interest in the previous text has been clarified. The search for intertextual clues does reach a point of diminishing returns, simply because of modern lack of access to all the textual contexts of Second Isaiah. But that point has not been approached for the chapters that I have left relatively untouched. For instance, I have not discussed the echoes of Jer 10:1–16 in Second Isaiah's discussions about idols, nor the several brief allusions to Zephaniah to be found scattered through the text, nor have I dealt in depth with the creation and exodus material in Isaiah 40–48. Even the sections I have discussed contain more possibilities than I have touched upon. I have simply outlined here the most obvious intertextual echoes in order to suggest a methodology, highlight prominent texts, and set some precedents for the type and strength of recollection for which one could reasonably argue.

Echoes of Lamentations in Second Isaiah are quite numerous. The linguistic links are continuous enough, and striking enough, to indicate direct knowledge of at least some, but more probably, of all five of the laments. Some portions of Second Isaiah, notably chapters 50 and 51–52, seem to display dense continuity with particular laments. Other portions seem to recall several together. The terms of Lamentations are expressly referred to frequently enough to suggest to hearers of Second Isaiah that its proclamations are best understood in relation not only to the exile, not only to laments about the exile, but to laments making the particular claims, envisioning the world in the particular ways, that are found in Lamentations.

Second Isaiah takes on the terms of Lamentations not to continue their prayers but to answer them, to dispute, reverse, and reinvent them. In its most argumentative moments it restates the discourse of lament and the lamenters' viewpoints and strenuously disputes their claims, as when they call YHWH their destroyer or ask why YHWH has forgotten them. More often, Second Isaiah acknowledges the validity of the lament's claims and argues that what has been will no longer be: the fallen will rise from the dust, while the oppressors will sink to the ground; the weak will become strong and the hungry will be fed; the abandoned will be redeemed, and most of all, comfortless Zion will be comforted by YHWH.

Reigning throughout all these disputations and reversals is a rhetorical technique that is sometimes quite overt, and at other times quite subtle: the reimagining of the world of Jerusalem in terms that have shifted from those in Lamentations. This shift, which is not expressly pointed out by the poet, is particularly noticeable in two ways. First, identities of figures and persons have shifted. Judahites as people, among whom are both the authors of the laments and those whom they vividly portrayed mourning, have virtually disappeared in the new text. They are represented, if at all, by Daughter Zion, the personification of the city itself. By subtle twists of the text she is represented as unclean and violated, but now called to arise to greet her coming king and to make room for returning children. The male *geber* of Lamentations 3 has been revived and distilled into a model of righteous suffering and perseverance on behalf of others. The disgrace of Judah's leaders is subsumed under the glory of their return. These recast identities rehabilitate the public image of the exiles, who in Lamentations were the leaders who led the city into sin, and in Second Isaiah become the sanctified carriers of YHWH's vessels. The violence and loss of human life, especially that of children, commemorated so bitterly in Lamentations, is offered comfort in the form of Zion's "children," born in exile, returning to their mother.[1]

Second, the locus of theological thinking has shifted. Whereas Lamentations searched for answers that made sense in light of their experience, that is, the disaster of Jerusalem, Second Isaiah begins with the assumption of a gracious God, who punished only to restore. Second Isaiah concentrates on the actions and attitudes desired in the people, often ending complex arguments not with a theological but a practical conclusion—not a description of YHWH, but a call to act: to return to Zion. Most prominent in Second Isaiah, though missing from Lamentations, is the divine voice. Whereas Lamentations recorded human voices pleading with God without answer, Second Isaiah presents God's voice saying both that what happened to Jerusalem was well deserved, and that God's intention for the future is rescue and redemption. Thus unanswered questions of Lamentations are offered response, though some of the lament's terms are suppressed as Second Isaiah shifts the poetry into new directions.

Second Isaiah's recollections of Jeremiah are markedly more harmonious than those of Lamentations. Second Isaiah's primary

---

[1] Gottwald ("Social Class," 52) noted the differences between Lamentations' description of the Judahite and exilic communities and Second Isaiah's, chalking up the lack of interest in the Judahite people either to naiveté or "'hardball' politics" on the part of Second Isaiah. Newsom (75–76) differs on this point, understanding Second Isaiah as working out an "imaginative framework within which these social and ideological problems can be finessed," although the language Second Isaiah offers is "clearly populated with the intentions and interests of the exilic community."

distinction from Jeremiah's message is one of temporal perspective. Jeremiah's warnings of the nation's downfall had already been authenticated by history, but the book's hopes for return had not yet been fulfilled, giving it an open-ended quality with which Second Isaiah was able to connect. The prophet's assessment of the people's wrongdoing is nowhere disputed in Second Isaiah, nor is the cause of the exile given any other interpretation: it was not the power of another nation or deity, but the wrath of YHWH against disobedient subjects that overturned the city. Jeremiah had predicted that Jerusalem would suffer; Second Isaiah declares that Jerusalem has completed her suffering. Prophetic envisionment of the nation's reconstitution, already hoped for during the exile, is assigned to Second Isaiah's own time. Reversals of misfortune already structured into the text of Jeremiah are reutilized by Second Isaiah, who mines the poetry of warning for even more reversals.

Prominent in the reutilizations of Jeremiah is the female figure, who here is stabilized as Zion. What Jeremiah said would happen to her is reversed in Second Isaiah: once humiliated, now she is glorified; once threatened with divorce, now she is assured of YHWH's faithfulness; once mourning the destruction of her "tents," now she is told to make more space for them. Along with these reversals comes a considerable softening of prophetic attitudes toward the figure. Once addressed in humiliating and even obscene language, now she is beckoned with conciliatory words.

Simplifications in the relationships among various entities have occurred. Whereas in Jeremiah feminine singular figures are called by a variety of names, including not only Daughter Zion and Jerusalem but also virgin Israel, Rachel, and Judah, the naming is simplified in Second Isaiah to one city and two nouns, Zion and Jerusalem. Whereas in Jeremiah the female figure, the masculine singular nation of Israel, and the masculine plural people are addressed interchangeably, adapting the pronoun to fit the name but fluidly moving from one to another, Second Isaiah imposes a marked separation between the feminine singular "you" that addresses Zion and the two masculines, the singular Israel/Jacob and the plural offspring or house of Israel. Whereas Jeremiah, like Lamentations, fluidly envisioned the woman herself as exiled (Jer 31:21) and as left behind (10:20), in Second Isaiah she is only envisioned waiting in Judah for her children's return.

Perhaps the most important transformation of the Jeremiah material studied here has been the recollection of the prophetic figure himself. The account of Jeremiah's call and message is recollected in Second Isaiah, but rather than being applied to a new, named prophet such as the implied speaker of the oracles, the prophetic call is issued to the nation of Israel itself. Earlier in the poetry (see Isa 40:27) the prophetic speaker and Israel were clearly differentiated. But at the point at which Jeremiah's call is recollected in chapter 49, the line between the voice of Israel and the voice of the prophet becomes very thin, so thin that it is impossible to tell just when the "I" that initiates chapter 49 ceases to speak. Jeremiah's dual role as both an inhabitant and a critic of Jerusalem was displayed on a narrative level. The figure Israel shares Jeremiah's dual role, both representing and speaking to the people. But the construction of those tensive roles is complicated by the figure's existence only as a metaphor.

Second Isaiah's cohesiveness with and updating of Jeremiah's message, along with the absence of a new clearly marked prophetic figure, may suggest that this new prophetic message is offered as a continuation of the previous one. Authority ascribed to the prophet by dint of the fulfillment of his warnings is appropriated by Second Isaiah, who declares continuity with former words. At the same time, the new model for the community is not the prophetic figure but the personified nation itself, adopting traits and roles once represented by Jeremiah.

Second Isaiah's reutilization of Nahum, Psalms, and pentateuchal material displays considerably more continuity and less alteration than the recollections of either Jeremiah or Lamentations. In these cases, words used in previous times are now applied to a new time, and are given renewed vitality in their contemporized setting. Nahum's celebration of the defeat of Assyria becomes Second Isaiah's celebration of Babylon's defeat. Psalms associated with the Jerusalem and monarchic tradition are remembered, though in altered political circumstances. The celebration of YHWH's reign in the enthronement psalms is validated by the liberation of the exiles. Communal lament psalms that once implored YHWH's help on the basis of the nation's constitutive stories are reiterated and imagined being answered by YHWH. Psalms celebrating the political stability of Jerusalem on the basis of the divine sponsorship of the Davidic dynasty are invoked but with radical changes. Jerusalem is promised protection, but no earthly king. Instead, the absent monarch's roles are distributed among YHWH (who now is the king who shares glory with nobody), Israel (YHWH's new chosen servant), Cyrus (YHWH's anointed), and Zion (the recipient of YHWH's covenant). Jerusalem's tradition of peace and righteousness is renewed with YHWH as its guarantor.

Traditions of origin in the Pentateuch are recollected many times and are used typologically for comparison and contrast. Present circumstances call for a journey like that of the ancestors from Egypt—only now the salvific miracle is not dry land in the water, but water in the dry land. In fact, the new exodus is marked by heightened majesty: the people are envisioned processing rather than fleeing; they are not simply following YHWH but being guarded rear and front. The psalmists' laments of the absence of YHWH's once-powerful arm are answered by a display of divine strength that does not simply mimic the glorious past but rather sets new standards: the first exodus threatens to become merely a foretaste of this new act of nation-building.

Events preceding the exodus are also recalled, from the creation motif to the election of Abraham's family. YHWH's creation of the natural world is linked to YHWH's creation of the nation of Israel. Myths of victory over powerful watery enemies are invoked to reason that YHWH can subdue any human oppressor who arises. The barrenness of matriarchal wombs is recalled to argue that the empty land will be repopulated. The oath to Noah after the flood is recollected to assert the permanence of YHWH's unconditional promise of peace to Jerusalem.

By recoiling from Lamentations, intersecting with the lament psalms, aligning with Jeremiah, and merging with pentateuchal stories, Second Isaiah locates itself in relation to its discursive context. Rejecting many of the formulations of lament literature, the text offers a coherent conclusion to recent events, one attempting to minimize the theological crisis raised by the city's destruction and to create continuity with more hopeful images from the nation's past. The suffering of the dead and the survivors, not personally remembered by most of the poet's contemporaries but memorialized in Lamentations' searing poetry, is modulated and offered two alternative rationalizations. On the one hand, the nation's suffering resulted from sin and required drastic but temporally limited punishment. On the other hand a large space is created, on the basis of the *geber's* protestations, for the vindication of innocent suffering much stressed in Lamentations, for its recasting as a redemptive act of service. Once abhorred by the nations, Israel will now become the object of amazement to foreign rulers and peoples. "You will call nations you do not know, and nations that do not know you will run to you" (Isa 55:5), to fulfill a divine purpose beyond human comprehension.

Second Isaiah's appropriation of other texts is quite selective. Substantive signs of influence by the eighth-century prophets Isaiah, Micah, Amos and Hosea are not easily found. Nor are the prophecies of Ezekiel recollected here, even though both prophets evidently communicated their messages in Babylon, and even though both prophets were deeply indebted to Jeremiah.[2] Most strikingly, there is no explicit recollection of Moses, the Sinai tradition, or the Deuteronomic formulation of YHWH's conditional covenant with Israel. This is particularly noticeable since the exodus and other covenants are recalled, and since both Lamentations and Jeremiah connect Jerusalem's destruction with

---

[2] See especially Walther Zimmerli, "Der 'neue Exodus'" in which he explores the differences between Ezekiel's and Second Isaiah's uses of Exodus traditions.

the people's breach of the Mosaic covenant.[3] Yet though Second Isaiah neglects the conditionality of the wilderness covenant, and opts instead for expressions of unilateral grace such as the story of the deliverance from Egypt itself and the covenants with Noah and David, the text still holds the people accountable for their sin and still projects a model Israel which studies and obeys the Torah.[4]

Second Isaiah's rhetorical positioning relative to previous texts, then, involves not only stances in relation to acknowledged texts, but also a series of omissions of texts that others might have considered relevant. Though for modern interpreters the significance of such omissions is difficult to assess, they may be just as strategically chosen as are the rearrangements of elements within the texts that are used. Since every new interpretation necessarily appropriates only part of the surplus of tradition, the particularities the poet introduces are not the only possible outcomes prefigured by previous texts. But the poet configures language in such a way as to suggest that there is no other direction that events could have taken, and that YHWH's people are being beckoned simply to cooperate with their destiny.

---

[3] Anderson ("Exodus and Covenant," 350–54) noted that both Hosea and Jeremiah stood primarily in the Mosaic covenant tradition, and yet both also pressed these to their limits. While reconciliation was impossible for those who had broken the covenant, both prophets expressed hope for reconciliation based on the everlasting love of God. Albrektson (231–37) provided an extensive list of specific correspondences between the threats of Deuteronomy 28 and the conditions described in Lamentations.

[4] Anderson ("Exodus and Covenant") found the omission of Sinai themes and theology curious, especially in light of the many references in Second Isaiah to the exodus and wilderness traditions. He viewed Second Isaiah as reflecting a fusion in the Jerusalem cult of the exodus story with mythological battle/kingship motifs derived from Canaanite influence. Although Psalms 89 and 132 reflect some conditional language, they maintain that YHWH's pledge to David will stand despite human unfaithfulness. This, as Anderson noted, contrasts directly with the conditional Sinai covenant. He concluded that Second Isaiah "adopts the Exodus pattern of symbolization, though separating it from the conditional Mosaic covenant with which it had been bound from the very first; and he adopts the unconditional covenant with David, though separating it from the unhappy history of the Davidic dynasty and transferring its promises of grace to the people" (357).

Second Isaiah stakes its claim in tensive relationships to previous religious language that was both revered and problematic. Its rhetorical power derives neither from its continuity with all that was authoritative in previous tradition, nor from its incontestability as divine revelation. Though staking a claim to revelatory status, the poetry depended upon its audience to validate its authority. Since the return and revitalization of Jerusalem never reached the majestic scope envisioned by the prophet, we may surmise that Second Isaiah was never validated on the basis of its accuracy about the future. Rather, the poetry gained its audience by means of its power to join itself with—and to rekindle—the imaginations of its hearers, to reenvision YHWH's story with Jerusalem, to articulate hope despite the ambiguities of the present, and to invite hearers to participate in its joyful expectancy. The frequent recollections of Second Isaiah itself in later texts of both Judaism and Christianity testify to this poetry's power to inhabit the minds of later audiences still hoping to witness its full actualization.

Appendix

Evidence for the Exilic Dating of Jeremiah 30–31

For most of this century the idea has persisted that parts of Jeremiah 30–31 come from post-exilic times and are dependent upon Second Isaiah. This notion particularly applies to Jer 30:10–11; 31:7–14; and 31:35. In the preceding chapters I have shown Second Isaiah's close relationships not just to these passages but to parts of Jeremiah that are generally considered quite early and original to the prophet, and thus that textual relationships between to two books can hardly be written off as scribal additions to Jeremiah based on Second Isaiah.

In this appendix, I will examine the book of consolation, especially the verses in question, in relation to both Jeremiah's early chapters and the book of Hosea, to show that the claims that these sections have closer ties with Second Isaiah than with these two earlier traditions are not warranted. Of necessity this will be a cursory examination; however, I hope it will contribute to the ongoing conversation concerning Jeremiah's redactional history.

Relationships to Jeremiah's Prophecies of Doom

A deep continuity exists between Jeremiah 30–31 and Jeremiah's threats in the early part of the book. This continuity extends to the passages, such as Jer 30:10–11, 31:7–14, and 31:35 which are most frequently considered dependent upon Second Isaiah. A comprehensive list of the thematic and linguistic linkages observable between Jeremiah 30–31 and Jeremiah's "A" material is not necessary here; rather, I will briefly present the continuity of the most disputed verses of Jeremiah 30–31, and passages immediately surrounding them, with Jeremiah's message.[1]

[1] For a more general survey of these relationships, see for instance Taro Odashima, *Heilsworte im Jeremiabuch: Untersuchungen zu ihrer vordeuteronomistischen Bearbeitung* (Stuttgart: W. Kohlhammer, 1989), who studied the close

1) Jeremiah 30:10–11 shares with Jer 1:8 the common "do not fear" and "I am with you" formulas, both of which are phrases that proliferate in early parts of Second Isaiah. With Jer 10:24–25 this passage shares the phrase יסר בְּמִשְׁפָּט/לַמִּשְׁפָּט "discipline justly," a phrase that appears otherwise only in Isa 28:26. In addition, according to the people's request, YHWH promises not to make an end to Israel, but rather to destroy the other nations. This particularly close relationship to chapter 10 is intensified by several other neighboring linguistic relationships between the two chapters.

2) Both Jer 2:2 and 31:2 begin their addresses with honeymoon recollections of the nation's wilderness period. Whereas in chapter 2 this early relationship between God and the nation is recalled in order to contrast it with the more recent estrangement, in chapter 31 the wilderness is recalled in order to assert that the relationship will once again be renewed. Both passages characterize the relationship of YHWH to Israel with the words חֶסֶד (kindness) and אַהֲבָה (love). This second word is rarely used of the relationship between YHWH and Israel, and its combination with recollections of the wilderness in both these passages is striking.

3) In Jer 4:15–16, a voice declares disaster from Mt. Ephraim (מֵהַר אֶפְרָיִם): watchers (נֹצְרִים) are arising against Jerusalem from a distant land. Jeremiah 6:4–5 similarly uses language of attack against Jerusalem, representing the attackers as saying to one another twice, "Rise, let us go up" (קוּמוּ וְנַעֲלֶה). In Jer 31:6, voices once again speak from Mt. Ephraim (בְּהַר אֶפְרָיִם), but this time they are the watchers (נֹצְרִים) proclaiming a pilgrimage, saying "Rise, let us go up" (קוּמוּ וְנַעֲלֶה) to Zion. Jeremiah 4:15, 31:6, and 50:12 are the only places in the prophets where the term הַר אֶפְרָיִם occurs, and Jer 6:5 and 31:6 are the only two places at all where the "rise, let us go up" phrase occurs in this form.

---

linguistic relationships between Jeremiah 30–31 and the earlier prophecies in order to discern what he perceived as an early exilic, pre-Deuteronomistic redaction Jeremiah adding oracles of hope corresponding to the earlier oracles of doom.

4) Jeremiah 6:9 and 31:7, both immediately following the passages mentioned above, discuss the "remnant of Israel" (שְׁאֵרִית יִשְׂרָאֵל). As above, in chapter 6 the phrase has to do with the remnant's doom; in chapter 31 with its promising future.

5) Jeremiah 31:8 refers to bringing the exiles from the land of the north—a direction from which, it is repeatedly warned in Jeremiah's prophecies, enemies will come. See especially Jer 4:6 and 6:22, which are linguistically very close to Jer 31:8.

6) In Jer 6:21, YHWH threatens to lay before the people stumbling blocks on which they will stumble. In Jer 31:9, YHWH promises a level road on which they shall not stumble.

7) Jeremiah 31:10 opens with a phrase (שִׁמְעוּ דְבַר־יְהוָה, "hear the word of YHWH") that is unknown in Second Isaiah, but is found ten times in Jeremiah, more frequently than in any other book, beginning with Jer 2:4. The same verse goes on to employ other words found frequently in Jeremiah's early poetry: וְהַגִּידוּ ("declare," see Jer 4:5, 5:20, etc.), אִיִּים ("coastlands," see Jer 2:10, etc.), מִמֶּרְחָק ("far away," see Jer 4:16, 5:15, 6:20). The message declared in this verse employs a metaphor (the people of the nation as a flock of sheep scattered) that has been employed several times in the early poetry. See especially Jer 10:21, Jer 13:17 and 20.

8) Jeremiah 6:11 envisions YHWH's wrath being poured out on a variety of people in the city, including young men together (בַּחוּרִים יַחְדָּו) and old men (זָקֵן). Jeremiah 31:13 envisions these groups of people, including the young men and old men together (בַּחֻרִים וּזְקֵנִים יַחְדָּו) rejoicing at their salvation and prosperity.

9) In the last section of Jeremiah 3, YHWH expresses having hoped that Israel would behave like a son to YHWH, and would call YHWH "father." In 3:21f, Israel's children weep over their sins, are bid by YHWH to return, and are imagined returning. Jeremiah 31:15 and 18 pick up these themes in very similar words and phrases.

Both passages go on in subsequent verses to depict Israel speaking of its own shame. Jeremiah 3:24–25 describes the shame and dismay that had been with Israel since their youth. In Jer

31:19b these same terms reappear. The following three verses continue the wordplay on שׁוּב as chapter 3 did.

10) The next twelve verses of Jeremiah 31 (verses 23–34) are mostly prose and are generally considered late. Before the chapter ends, however, there is a three-verse poetic reassurance that is usually considered late because part of it is duplicated in Isa 51:15. It too is quite relevant to the early poetry of Jeremiah. In Jer 5:22, YHWH contrasts the disobedience of Israel to the inability of the natural world to transgress boundaries set by YHWH:

Jer 5:22	Do you not fear me? says YHWH.	הַאוֹתִי לֹא־תִירָאוּ נְאֻם־*יְהוָה*
	Do you not tremble before me,	אִם מִפָּנַי לֹא תָחִילוּ
	Who placed the sand as a boundary for the sea,	אֲשֶׁר־שַׂמְתִּי חוֹל גְּבוּל ***לַיָּם***
	an eternal rule, that it cannot transgress.	חָק־עוֹלָם וְלֹא יַעַבְרֶנְהוּ
	They toss and do not prevail,	וַיִּתְגָּעֲשׁוּ וְלֹא יוּכָלוּ
	its waves roar and do not transgress it.	***וְהָמוּ גַלָּיו*** וְלֹא יַעַבְרֻנְהוּ

Jeremiah 31:35–36 similarly invokes the rules of the natural order. Here, however, it is not to complain of Israel's unfaithfulness but to affirm YHWH's faithfulness to Israel:

Jer 31:35	Thus says YHWH,	כֹּה אָמַר *יְהוָה*
	who gives the sun for light by day,	נֹתֵן שֶׁמֶשׁ לְאוֹר יוֹמָם
	the laws of the moon and stars	***חֻקֹּת*** יָרֵחַ וְכוֹכָבִים
	for light by night,	לְאוֹר לָיְלָה
	who stills the sea, though its waves roar—	רֹגַע ***הַיָּם וַיֶּהֱמוּ גַלָּיו***
	YHWH Sabaoth is his name.	*יְהוָה* צְבָאוֹת שְׁמוֹ
31:36	If these rules ever fail	אִם־יָמֻשׁוּ ***הַחֻקִּים*** הָאֵלֶּה
	before me, says YHWH,	מִלְּפָנַי נְאֻם־יְהוָה
	Then the seed of Israel also will cease	גַּם זֶרַע יִשְׂרָאֵל יִשְׁבְּתוּ
	from being a nation before me for all time.	מִהְיוֹת גּוֹי לְפָנַי כָּל־הַיָּמִים

Here the rules of the boundaries of day and night, as well as the boundaries of the sea, are invoked. The metaphor of the bounded sea operates on a further plane in Jer 31:35–36. A common description of enemy forces overrunning a city is that of the uncontainable sea. Jeremiah 6:23, for instance, describes the nation that will invade from the north, saying קוֹלָם כַּיָּם יֶהֱמֶה, "their sound is like the roaring sea." In Jeremiah 31 the sea's boundaries are invoked in the midst of a promise to keep the enemies from overwhelming Israel.

The above comparisons show that the language and ideas of Jeremiah 30–31 continue and extend themes already found in Jeremiah's prophecy of doom, even in sections that have previously been considered unrelated to Jeremiah and dependent upon Second Isaiah.

Relationships to the Book of Hosea

There is also a close relationship between parts of Jeremiah 30–31 and the prophecies of the earlier Hosea. This relationship cuts right through the midst of the verses many consider dependent on Second Isaiah. As is well known, in both these verses and in Jeremiah 3 the twin metaphors of Israel as both the beloved, faithless wife and the adored, ungrateful child are found, both metaphors already poignantly explored in Hosea. Furthermore, this section of Jeremiah employs geographical terminology appropriate to the northern kingdom and never used of Judah. The term "Ephraim" is unattested in Second Isaiah, but is especially prominent in Hosea. Below a few specific further examples of relationships between Hosea and sections of Jeremiah 31 are noted:

1) Hosea 4:5, 5:5, 14:2, and 14:10 all speak of Israel as stumbling (כשל) in its sin. Hosea 14:10 especially elaborates this metaphor:

Hos	Who is wise and understands these?	מִי חָכָם וְיָבֵן אֵלֶּה
14:10	discerning and knows them?	נָבוֹן וְיֵדָעֵם
	For level are the roads of YHWH,	כִּי־יְשָׁרִים דַּרְכֵי יְהוָה
	and the righteous walk in them,	וְצַדִּקִים יֵלְכוּ בָם
	But transgressors stumble in them.	וּפֹשְׁעִים יִכָּשְׁלוּ בָם

It has already been noted that this metaphor is shared by Jer 6:15–21 and Jer 31:9. Like the Hosea passage, Jeremiah 6 emphasizes a moral journey in which people who do not obey YHWH will stumble. Jeremiah 31:9 uses many of the same terms to lend a moral dimension to the return of exiles:

Jer 31:9	With weeping they will come,	בִּבְכִי יָבֹאוּ
	and with consolations I will lead them;	וּבְתַחֲנוּנִים אוֹבִילֵם
	I will let them walk by brooks of water,	**אוֹלִיכֵם** אֶל־נַחֲלֵי מַיִם
	on a level road	בְּדֶרֶךְ יָשָׁר
	on which they will not stumble;	**לֹא יִכָּשְׁלוּ בָּהּ**
	For I have become a father to Israel,	כִּי־הָיִיתִי לְיִשְׂרָאֵל לְאָב
	and Ephraim is my first born.	וְאֶפְרַיִם בְּכֹרִי הוּא

The last part of this verse previews a theme that will be fully developed eleven verses later, in 31:20, Ephraim as YHWH's tenderly loved child. This idea recollects the poignant imagery in Hosea 11:3–4, in which YHWH recalls teaching Ephraim to walk, holding them in parental arms, leading them with bands of love, bending down and feeding them.

2) The beginning of Jer 31:10 (שִׁמְעוּ דְבַר־יְהוָה, "hear the word of YHWH"), which is frequently used in Jeremiah, is also found in Hosea 4:1: שִׁמְעוּ דְבַר־יְהוָה בְּנֵי יִשְׂרָאֵל, "hear the word of YHWH, children of Israel."

3) It is sometimes claimed that Jer 31:11 rings notes of Second Isaiah in its use of the terms גאל (redeem) and פדה (ransom). Carroll, for instance, claims that both of these terms recur frequently in Isaiah 40–55.[2] But this is only half true: גאל appears frequently, but פדה only once, that is, half as often as it does in Jeremiah. The combination is found already in Hos 13:14:

Hos 13:14	From the hand of Sheol I will ransom them,	**מִיַּד** שְׁאוֹל **אֶפְדֵּם**
	from death I will redeem them.	מִמָּוֶת **אֶגְאָלֵם**
	Where are your plagues, death?	אֱהִי דְבָרֶיךָ מָוֶת
	where is your sting, Sheol?	אֱהִי קָטָבְךָ שְׁאוֹל
	Comforting is hid from my eyes.	**נֹחַם** יִסָּתֵר מֵעֵינָי

Jeremiah 31:11 reassures Israel that this ransoming and redeeming has indeed occurred. Verse 13 assures Israel of YHWH's comfort, using a form of נחם as above.

4) In the midst of a verse that is regularly cited as dependent upon Second Isaiah, Jer 31:12 uses a list that is not found anywhere else in Jeremiah and is never used in Second Isaiah. However, this

[2] Carroll, *Jeremiah*, 593.

list is found frequently in Hosea and even more fully in Deuteronomy: "the grain, the wine, and the oil, the flock and herd"—see Hos 2:10, 24; 5:6; Deut 7:13, 11:14, 12:17, etc. As in those two books it is here used to specify economic abundance.

5) Holladay suggested that verse 14 must be from a later time on the basis of the paralleling of people (עַמִּי) and priests (הַכֹּהֲנִים), a construction he deemed foreign to Jeremiah.[3] He discounted as irrelevant a very interesting parallel in Hosea 4:

Hos	And it will be like people, like priest,	וְהָיָה ***כָעָם כַּכֹּהֵן***
4:9	I will punish him for his ways,	וּפָקַדְתִּי עָלָיו דְּרָכָיו
	and his deeds I will return to him.	וּמַעֲלָלָיו אָשִׁיב לוֹ
4:10	They will eat and not be satisfied,	וְאָכְלוּ וְלֹא ***יִשְׂבָּעוּ***
	they will practice prostitution and not increase . . .	הִזְנוּ וְלֹא יִפְרֹצוּ

In contrast, Jer 31:14 promises fullness and satisfaction for both people and priests:

Jer	I will give the priests their fill of fatness,	וְרִוֵּיתִי נֶפֶשׁ ***הַכֹּהֲנִים*** דָּשֶׁן
31:14	and my people will be satisfied with good,	***וְעַמִּי*** אֶת־טוּבִי ***יִשְׂבָּעוּ***
	says YHWH.	נְאֻם־יְהוָה

From all the above it can be seen that, like other portions of Jeremiah, this section is rife with Hosean imagery and language. When all these instances are considered together, and when it is noted that the density of their similarity to Hosean language is quite a bit greater than to that of Second Isaiah, the argument that Second Isaiah is the originator of this language becomes quite unconvincing. Rather that positing an unnecessarily complex history in which Hosea influences the early parts of Jeremiah, these influence Second Isaiah, and early Jeremiah, Hosea, and Second Isaiah together influence Jeremiah 30–31, it is far more reasonable to recognize the role of Hosea's poetry in the development of the poetry of Jeremiah, both that of judgment and of promise, and the role of that poetry, both judgment and promise, in the development of Second Isaiah.

---

[3] Holladay, 162.

BIBLIOGRAPHY

Abrahams, Israel and C. Roth 1971 — "Cassuto, Umberto." *EncJud* 5, cols. 234–36. Jerusalem: Keter Publishing House.

Ackroyd, Peter 1968 — *Exile and Restoration: A Study of Hebrew Thought of the Sixth Century B.C.* Philadelphia: Westminster Press.

Ackroyd, Peter 1987 — "Isaiah 1–12: Presentation of a Prophet." In his *Studies in the Religious Tradition of the Old Testament.* London: SCM Press, 79–104. Original publication, 1978.

Albertz, R. 1990 — "Das Deuterojesaja-Buch als Fortschreibung der Jesaja-Prophetie." In *Die Hebraische Bibel und ihre zweifache Nachgeschichte: FS Rolf Rendtorff,* ed. E. Blum et al., 241–56. Neukirchen: Neukirchener Verlag.

Albrektson, B. 1963 — *Studies in the Text and Theology of the Book of Lamentations.* Lund, Sweden: CWK Gleerup.

Alexander, Joseph A. 1953 — *Commentary on the Prophecies of Isaiah.* 2 vols. Grand Rapids, MI: Zondervan. Original publication as *The Later Prophecies of Isaiah,* 1847.

Anderson, A. A. 1989 — *The Book of Psalms.* 2 vols. NCB. Grand Rapids, MI: Eerdmans. Original publication, 1972.

Anderson, B. W. 1962 — "Exodus Typology in Second Isaiah." In *Israel's Prophetic Heritage: Essays in Honor of James Muilenburg,* ed. B. W. Anderson and W. Harrelson, 177–95. New York: Harper and Brothers.

Anderson, B. W. 1976 — "Exodus and Covenant in Second Isaiah and Prophetic Tradition." In *Magnalia Dei: The Mighty Acts of God,* ed. F. M. Cross et al., 339–60. New York: Doubleday.

1651 — *Annotations upon All the Books of the Old and New Testament.* Additional annotations, London: J. Legatt and J. Raworth, 1658.

Bakhtin, M. M. 1981 — *The Dialogic Imagination.* Edited by Michael Holquist. Austin, TX: The University of Texas Press. Original publication in Russian, 1975.

Baltzer, Dieter
1971 *Ezechiel und Deuterojesaja: Berührungen in der Heiserwartung der beiden grossen Exilspropheten.* BZAW 121. Berlin: Walter de Gruyter.

Baltzer, Klaus
1989 "Schriftauslegung bei Deuterojesaja? Jes 43,22–28 als Beispiel." In *Die Väter Israels: Beiträge zur Theologie der Patriarchenüberlieferungen im AT,* ed. Manfred Görg, 11–16. Stuttgart: Katholisches Bibelwerk.

Barthes, Roland
1971 "De l'oeuvre au texte." In *Revue d'esthetique* 3: 225–32.

Barton, John
1990 "History and Rhetoric in the Prophets." In *The Bible as Rhetoric: Studies in Biblical Persuasion and Credibility,* ed. Martin Warner, 51–64. London: Routledge.

Beal, Timothy
1992 "Glossary." In *Reading Between Texts,* ed. Danna Nolan Fewell, 21–24. Louisville: Westminster/John Knox Press.

Begrich, Joachim
1963 *Studien zu Deuterojesaja.* Munich: Chr. Kaiser Verlag. Original publication, 1938.

Beyerlin, W., ed.
1975 *Near Eastern Religious Texts Relating to the Old Testament.* Philadelphia: Westminster Press.

Biddle, Mark
1991 "The Figure of Lady Jerusalem: Identification, Deification and Personification of Cities in the Ancient Near East." In *The Biblical Canon in Comparative Perspective,* ed. K. L. Younger, et al., 173–94. Lewiston, NY: Edwin Mellen.

Blank, Sheldon
1958 *Prophetic Faith in Isaiah.* London: Adam and Charles Black.

Blenkinsopp, Joseph
1992 *The Pentateuch: An Introduction to the First Five Books of the Bible.* New York: Doubleday.

Bloom, Harold
1973 *The Anxiety of Influence: A Theory of Poetry.* London: Oxford University Press.

Bonnard, P.-E.
1972 *Le Second Isaïe: Son disciple et leurs éditeurs, Isaïe 40–66.* Paris: J. Gabalda.

Brandscheidt, R.
1988 *Das Buch der Klagelieder.* GSAT 10. Düsseldorf: Patmos.

Bright, John
1965 *Jeremiah.* AB 21. Garden City, NY: Doubleday and Co.

Budde, K.
1899 "The So-Called 'Ebed-Yahweh Songs,' and the Meaning of the Term 'Servant of Yahweh' in Isaiah, Chapters 40–55." *American Journal of Theology* 3: 499–540.

Buttenweiser, Moses 1938 — *The Psalms.* Chicago: University of Chicago Press.

Callaway, Mary 1986 — *Sing, O Barren One: A Study in Comparative Midrash.* SBLDS 91. Atlanta: Scholars Press.

Calvin, John 1948 — *Commentary on the Book of the Prophet Isaiah.* 5 vols. Grand Rapids, MI: Eerdmans. Original publication in Latin, 1551.

Carroll, Robert P. 1986 — *Jeremiah.* OTL. Philadelphia: Westminster Press.

Carroll, Robert P. 1992 — "The Myth of the Empty Land. *Semeia* 59: 79–93.

Cassuto, U. 1961 — *The Documentary Hypothesis and the Composition of the Pentateuch.* Jerusalem: Magnes Press. Original publication in Hebrew, 1941.

Cassuto, U. 1973 — "On the Formal and Stylistic Relationship between Deutero-Isaiah and other Biblical Writers." *Biblical and Oriental Studies,* vol. 1, 141–77. Jerusalem: Magnes Press. Original publication, *Rivista Israelitica* VIII (1911): 191–214; IX (1912): 81–90; X, (1913): 1–13.

Chavasse, Claude 1964 — "The Suffering Servant and Moses." *CQR* 165: 152–63.

Cheyne, T. K. 1881 — *The Prophecies of Isaiah,* vol. 2. London: C. Kegan Paul & Co.

Childs, Brevard 1979 — *Introduction to the Old Testament as Scripture.* Philadelphia: Fortress Press.

Christensen, Duane 1988 — "Nahum." In *Harper's Bible Commentary,* ed. J. L. Mays et al., 736–38. San Francisco: Harper and Row.

Clayton, Jay, and Eric Rothstein, eds. 1991 — *Influence and Intertextuality in Literary History.* Madison: University of Wisconsin Press.

Clements, Ronald E. 1982 — "The Unity of the Book of Isaiah." *Int* 36: 117–29.

Clements, Ronald E. 1985 — "Beyond Tradition-History: Deutero-Isaianic Development of First Isaiah's Themes." *JSOT* 31: 95–113.

Clifford, Richard J. 1984 — *Fair Spoken and Persuading: An Interpretation of Second Isaiah.* New York: Paulist Press.

Clines, David 1976 — *I, He, We, and They: A Literary Approach to Isaiah 53.* JSOTSup 1. Sheffield: Sheffield Academic Press.

Clines, David
1988 "Introduction to the Biblical Story: Genesis-Esther." In *Harper's Bible Commentary*, ed. J. L. Mays et al., 74–84. San Francisco: Harper and Row.

Coggins, Richard
1982 "An Alternative Prophetic Tradition?" In *Israel's Prophetic Tradition: Essays in Honour of Peter Ackroyd*, ed. R. Coggins et al., 77–94. Cambridge: Cambridge University Press.

Connerton, Paul
1989 *How Societies Remember.* Cambridge: Cambridge University Press.

Conrad, Edgar
1974 *Patriarchal Traditions in Second Isaiah.* Th.D. diss., Princeton Theological Seminary.

Cornill, Carl H.
1891 *Einleitung in das Alte Testament.* Freiburg: J. C. B. Mohr.

Cornill, Carl H.
1905 *Einleitung in die kanonischen Bücher des Alten Testaments.* Tübingen: J. C. B. Mohr.

Craigie, Peter C.
1983 *Psalms 1–50.* Word Biblical Commentary 19. Waco, TX: Word Books.

Cross, Frank M.
1973 *Canaanite Myth and Hebrew Epic: Essays in the History of the Religion of Israel.* Cambridge: Harvard University Press.

Culler, Jonathan
1981 *The Pursuit of Signs: Semiotics, Literature, Deconstruction.* Ithaca, NY: Cornell University Press.

Dahood, Mitchell
1965 *Psalms I: 1–50.* AB 16. Garden City, NY: Doubleday & Co.

Dahood, Mitchell
1968 *Psalms II: 51–100.* AB 17. Garden City, NY: Doubleday & Co.

Davies, G. I.
1989 "The Destiny of the Nations in the Book of Isaiah." In *The Book of Isaiah—Le Livre D'Isaïe*, ed. J. Vermeylen, 93–120. Leuven: University Press.

Day, John
1985 *God's Conflict with the Dragon and the Sea: Echoes of a Canaanite Myth in the Old Testament*, Cambridge: Cambridge University Press.

Day, John
1988 "Prophecy." In *It Is Written: Scripture Citing Scripture*, ed. D. A. Carson and H. G. M. Williamson, 39–55. Cambridge: Cambridge University Press.

Day, John
1990 *Psalms.* Old Testament Guides. Sheffield: Sheffield Academic Press.

Delitzsch, Franz
1889 *The Prophecies of Isaiah,* 4th ed. 2 vols., transl. S. R. Driver. Edinburgh: T & T Clark.

Deming, Linda
1978
Hymnic Language in Deutero-Isaiah: The Calls to Praise and their Function in the Book, Ph.D. diss., Emory University.

Dentan, R. C.
1962
"Numbers, Book of." *IDB* 3, 567–71. Nashville: Abingdon Press.

Dobbs-Allsopp, F. W.
1993
Weep, O Daughter of Zion: A Study of the City-Lament Genre in the Hebrew Bible. Rome: Pontifical Biblical Institute Press.

Döderlein, J. C.
1775 & 1789
Esaias. Ex resensione textus Hebraei . . ., Altdorf.

Donne, John
1967
Selected Prose. Edited by Helen Gardner and Timothy Healy. Oxford: Clarendon Press. Original publication, 1624.

Driver, S. R., and A. D. Neubauer, eds.
1969
The Fifty-Third Chapter of Isaiah according to the Jewish Interpreters. New York: Ktav Publishing House. Original publication, 1877.

Duhm, Bernhard
1892
Das Buch Jesaia. Göttingen: Vandenhoeck & Ruprecht.

Duhm, Bernhard
1907
Das Buch Jeremia. Tübingen: J. C. B. Mohr. Original publication, 1901.

Eakins, Joel K.
1970
Ezekiel's Influence on the Exilic Isaiah. Ph.D. diss., Southern Baptist Theological Seminary.

Eaton, John
1959
"The Origin of the Book of Isaiah." *VT* 9: 138–57.

Eichhorn, J. G.
1783
Einleitung ins AT, vol. 3. Leipzig: Weidmann.

Eissfeldt, Otto
1933
Der Gottesknecht bei Deuterojesaja. Halle: Max Niemeyer Verlag.

Eissfeldt, Otto
1962
"The Promises of Grace to David in Isa 55:1–5." In *Israel's Prophetic Heritage: Essays in Honor of James Muilenburg,* ed. B. W. Anderson and W. Harrelson, 196–207. New York: Harper and Brothers.

Eissfeldt, Otto
1965
The Old Testament: An Introduction. New York: Harper and Row. Original publication in German, 1934.

Eldridge, Victor
1978
The Influence of Jeremiah on Isaiah 40–55. Ph.D. diss., Southern Baptist Theological Seminary.

Eliot, T. S.
1973
"Tradition and the Individual Talent." In *American Literature: The Makers and the Making,* vol 2, ed. Cleanth Brooks et al., 2828–39. New York: St. Martin's Press. Original publication, 1917.

Emerson, Ralph W. 1875 — *The Complete Works of Ralph Waldo Emerson.* Boston: Houghton Mifflin Co.

Ewald, Heinrich 1867–8 — *Die Propheten des Alten Bundes erklärt,* 2nd ed. 3 vols. Göttingen: Vandenhoeck & Ruprecht. Original publication, 1840–41.

Ewald, Heinrich 1968 — *Die Propheten des Alten Bundes.* 3 vols. Göttingen: Vandenhoeck & Ruprecht. Original publication, 1840–41.

Ferris, P. W., Jr. 1992 — *The Genre of Communal Lament in the Bible and the Ancient Near East.* SBLDS 127. Atlanta: Scholars Press.

Fischer, J. 1939 — *Das Buch Isaias übersetzt und erklärt.* II Teil: Kap. 40–66. Bonn: P. Hanstein.

Fishbane, Michael 1979 — *Text and Texture: Close Readings of Selected Biblical Texts.* New York: Schocken Books.

Fishbane, Michael 1980 — "Revelation and Tradition: Aspects of Inner-Biblical Exegesis." *JBL* 99: 343–61.

Fishbane, Michael 1985 — *Biblical Interpretation in Ancient Israel.* Oxford: Clarendon Press.

Fishbane, Michael 1989 — *The Garments of Torah: Essays in Biblical Hermeneutics.* Bloomington: Indiana University Press.

Fitzgerald, Aloysius 1972 — "The Mythological Background for the Presentation of Jerusalem as a Queen and False Worship as Adultery in the OT." *CBQ* 34: 403–16.

Fohrer, G. 1964 — *Das Buch Jesaja,* vol. 3. Stuttgart: Zwingli Verlag.

Friedman, Richard 1992 — "Torah (Pentateuch)." In *The Anchor Bible Dictionary,* vol. 6, ed. David N. Freedman et al., 605–22. New York: Doubleday.

Friedman, Theodore 1971 — "Isaiah." *EncJud* 9, cols. 44–71. Jerusalem: Keter Publishing House.

Gesenius, Wilhelm 1821 — *Philologisch-kritischer und historischer Kommentar über den Jesaia.* 3 vols. Leipzig: F. C. W. Vogel.

Giesebrecht, F. 1907 — *Das Buch Jeremia: Handkommentar zum Alten Testament,* 2nd ed. Göttingen: Vandenhoeck & Ruprecht.

Gillis, John R., ed. 1994 — *Commemorations: The Politics of National Identity.* Princeton, NJ: Princeton University Press.

Ginsberg, H. L. 1958 — "The Arm of YHWH in Isaiah 51–63 and the Text of Isa 53:10–11." *JBL* 77: 152–56.

Gitay, Yehoshua 1981 — *Prophecy and Persuasion: A Study of Isaiah 40–48.* Bonn: Lingusitica Biblica.

Glassner, Gottfried
1991
Vision eines auf Verheissung gegründeten Jerusalem: Textanalytische Studien zu Jesaja 54. Österreichische Biblische Studien 11. Klosteneuburg: Österreichisches Katholisches Bibelwerk.

Gordis, Robert
1974
The Song of Songs and Lamentations: A Study, Modern Translation and Commentary. New York: Ktav Publishing House.

Goshen-Gottstein, M. H.
1975
"Christianity, Judaism and Modern Bible Study." In *VTSupp* 28, 69–88, Leiden: E. J. Brill.

Gottwald, Norman
1954
Studies in the Book of Lamentations. Studies in Biblical Theology, no. 14. London: SCM Press.

Gottwald, Norman
1992
"Social Class and Ideology in Isaiah 40–55: An Eagletonian Reading." *Semeia* 59: 43–57.

Graf, Karl H.
1862
Der Prophet Jeremia, Leipzig: T. W. Weigel.

Gray, George B.
1903
A Critical and Exegetical Commentary on Numbers. ICC. Edinburgh: T. & T. Clark.

Gray, John
1979
The Biblical Doctrine of the Reign of God. Edinburgh: T. & T. Clark.

Greenberg, Irving
1977
"Cloud of Smoke, Pillar of Fire: Judaism, Christianity, and Modernity after the Holocaust," in *Auschwitz: Beginning of a New Era?,* ed. Eva Fleischner, 7–55. New York: Ktav Publishing House.

Gressmann, Hugo
1914
"Die literarische Analyse Deuterojesajas." *ZAW* 34: 254–97.

Gunkel, Hermann
1895
Schöpfung und Chaos in Urzeit und Endzeit. Göttingen: Vandenhoeck & Ruprecht.

Gunkel, Hermann
1967
The Psalms: A Form-Critical Introduction. Philadelphia: Fortress Press. Original publication in German, 1930.

Gunn, David
1975
"Deutero-Isaiah and the Flood." *JBL* 94: 493–508.

Gwaltney, W. C., Jr.
1983
"The Biblical Book of Lamentations in the Context of Near Eastern Lament Literature." In *Scripture in Context II: More Essays on the Comparative Method,* ed. W. W. Hallo et al., 191–211. Winona Lake, IN: Eisenbrauns.

Haag, Herbert
1985
Der Gottesknecht bei Deuterojesaja. Darmstadt: Wissenschaftliche Buchgesellschaft.

Haller, M.
1940
Die Klagelieder, in M. Haller and K. Galling, *Die fünf Megilloth*, HAT 1/18, 91–113. Tübingen: Mohr (Paul Siebeck).

Haran, Menahem
1981
"Behind the Scenes of History: Determining the Date of the Priestly Source." *JBL* 100: 321–33.

Hayes, J. H., and S. A. Irvine
1987
Isaiah: The Eighth-Century Prophet. Nashville: Abingdon Press.

Hays, Richard
1989
Echoes of Scripture in the Letters of Paul. New Haven: Yale University Press.

Herrmann, Siegfried
1990
Jeremia: Der Prophet und das Buch. Darmstadt: Wissenschaftliche Buchgesellschaft.

Hillers, Delbert R.
1972
Lamentations. AB 7A. Garden City, New York: Doubleday and Co.

Hobbs, T. R.
1974
"Jeremiah 3:1–5 and Deuteronomy 24:1–4." *ZAW* 86: 23–29.

Hobsbawm, Eric, and Terence Ranger, eds.
1983
The Invention of Tradition. Cambridge: Cambridge University Press.

Holladay, William L.
1989
Jeremiah 2. Hermeneia. Minneapolis: Fortress Press.

Hollander, John
1981
The Figure of Echo: A Mode of Allusion in Milton and After. Berkeley: University of California Press.

Howard, David M.
1986
The Structure of Psalms 93–100, Ph.D. diss., University of Michigan.

Hummel, H. D.
1971
"Bible." *EncJud* 4, cols. 899–915. Jerusalem: Keter Publishing House.

Hurvitz, Avi
1982
A Linguistic Study of the Relationship Between the Priestly Source and the Book of Ezekiel. Paris: Gabalda.

Hyatt, J. P.
1956
"Jeremiah." *IB* 5, ed. G. A. Buttrick et al., 777–1142. New York: Abingdon Press.

Ibn Ezra, Abraham
1948
The Commentary of Ibn Ezra on Isaiah, New York: P. Feldheim. Reprinted from edition edited by M. Griedlander, London, 1873.

Janzen, J. Gerald
1989
"An Echo of the Shema in Isaiah 51:1–3." *JSOT* 43: 69–82.

Jefferson, Helen
1952
"Psalm 93." *JBL* 71: 155–60.

Jenny, Laurent 1982 — "The Strategy of Form." In *French Literary Theory Today: A Reader*, ed. T. Todorov, 34–63. Cambridge University Press. Original publication in French, 1976.

Jeppesen, K. 1993 — "Mother Zion, Father Servant: A Reading of Isaiah 49–55." In *Of Prophets' Visions and the Wisdom of Sages: Essays in Honour of R. Norman Whybray on his Seventieth Birthday*, ed. H. McKay and D. Clines. JSOTSup 162, 109–25. Sheffield: Sheffield Academic Press.

Jones, Douglas R. 1955 — "The Traditio of the Oracles of Isaiah of Jerusalem." *ZAW* 67: 226–46.

Jones, Douglas R. 1992 — *Jeremiah*. NCB. Grand Rapids, MI: Eerdmans.

Jones, Gwilym H. 1972 — "Abraham and Cyrus: Type and Anti-Type?" *VT* 22: 304–19.

Kaiser, Barbara Bakke 1987 — "Poet as 'Female Impersonator': The Image of Daughter Zion as Speaker in Biblical Poems of Suffering." *JR* 67: 164–82.

Kaiser, Otto 1975 — *Introduction to the Old Testament: A Presentation of its Results and Problems*. Minneapolis, MN: Augsburg. Translated from the 2nd edition, published in German,1970.

Kaiser, Otto 1981 — "Klagelieder." In *Sprüche, Prediger, Das Hohe Lied, Klagelieder, Das Buch Esther*, ed. H. Ringgren et al., ATD 16, 291–386. Göttingen: Vandenhoeck & Ruprecht.

Kaiser, Otto 1983 — *Isaiah 1–12: A Commentary*, 2nd ed. OTL. Philadelphia: Westminster Press. Original publication in German, 1981.

Kapelrud, A. S. 1964 — "The Date of the Priestly Code (P)." *ASTI* 3: 58–64.

Kissane, E. J. 1943 — *The Book of Isaiah: Translated from a Critically Revised Hebrew Text with Commentary*, vol. 2. Dublin: Browne and Nolan.

Knight, Douglas A. 1985 — "The Pentateuch." In *The Hebrew Bible and its Modern Interpreters*, ed. D. Knight and G. Tucker, 263–96. Chico, CA: Scholar's Press.

Köhler, Ludwig 1923 — *Deuterojesaja stilkritisch untersucht*. BZAW 37. Giessen: Töpelmann.

König, E. 1926 — *Das Buch Jesaja*. Güterslohn: C. Bertelsmann.

Koppe, J. B.
1780
D. Robert Lowth's Jesaias übersetzt mit einer Einleitung und kritischen philologischen und erläuternden Anmerkungen, Leipzig.

Kratz, R. G.
1991
Kyros im Deuterojesaia-Buch: Redaktionsgeschichtliche Untersuchungen zu Entstehung. FAT 1. Tübingen: Mohr (Paul Siebeck).

Kraus, H.-J.
1960
Klagelieder. Neukirchen: Neukirchener Verlag.

Kraus, H.-J.
1989
Psalms 60–150: A Commentary. Minneapolis: Augsburg.

Kristeva, Julia
1980
Desire in Language: A Semiotic Approach to Literature and Art. Edited by Leon S. Roudiez. New York: Columbia University Press. Original publication in French, 1969.

Lanahan, William F.
1974
"The Speaking Voice in the Book of Lamentations." *JBL* 93: 41–49.

Lansberg, Max
1901
"Ab, Ninth Day of." *The Jewish Encyclopedia*, vol. 1, 23–25. New York: Funk and Wagnalls.

Levenson, Jon
1988
Creation and the Persistence of Evil: The Jewish Drama of Divine Omnipotence. Princeton, NJ: Princeton University Press.

Linafelt, Tod
1995
"Surviving Lamentations." *Horizons in Biblical Theology* 17: 45–61.

Lohfink, N.
1980
"Der junge Jeremia als Propagandist und Poet: Zum Grundstock von Jer 30–31." In *Le Livre de Jérémie: Le Prophète et son Milieu, Les Oracles et Leur Transmission*, ed. P. M. Bogaert, 351–68. Leuven: Leuven University Press.

Löhr, Max
1894
"Der Sprachgebrauch des Buches der Klagelieder." *ZAW* 14: 31–50.

Löhr, Max
1904
"Threni III und die jeremianische Autorschaft des Buches der Klagelieder." *ZAW* 24: 1–16.

Long, Burke O.
1976
"The Stylistic Components of Jeremiah 3:1–5." *ZAW* 88: 386–90.

Lowth, Robert
1778
Isaiah: A New Translation with a Preliminary Dissertation and Notes. London: Nichols.

Maier, Walter
1959
The Book of Nahum: A Commentary. St. Louis: Concordia Publishing House.

Margalioth, Rachel
1964
The Indivisible Isaiah: Evidence for the Single Authorship of the Prophetic Book. New York: Sura Institute for Research, Jerusalem Yeshiva University.

Martin, James D. 1969 — "Forensic Background to Jeremiah 3:1." *VT* 19: 82–92.

Matheus, Frank 1990 — *Singt dem Herrn ein neues Lied: Die Hymnen Deuterojesajas*, Stuttgart: Katholisches Bibelwerk.

Mays, James L. 1994 — *Psalms*. Interpretation. Louisville: John Knox Press.

McKane, William 1986 — *A Critical and Exegetical Commentary on Jeremiah*, vol. 1. ICC. Edinburgh: T. & T. Clark.

McKane, William 1996 — *A Critical and Exegetical Commentary on Jeremiah*, vol. 2. ICC. Edinburgh: T. & T. Clark.

McKenzie, John L. 1968 — *Second Isaiah*. AB 20. Garden City, New York: Doubleday & Co.

Meek, T. J. 1956 — "The Book of Lamentations." *IB* 6, ed. G. A. Buttrick et al., 3–38. New York: Abingdon Press.

Melugin, Roy 1976 — *The Formation of the Book of Isaiah*. BZAW 141. New York: Walter de Gruyter.

Merwe, B. J. van der 1956 — *Pentateuchtradisies in die Prediking van Deuterjesaja*. Groningen: J. B. Wolters.

Merwe, B. J. van der 1964/65 — "Echoes from Teaching of Hosea in Isaiah 40–55." *OTWSA*: 90–99.

Mettinger, T. N. D. 1983 — *A Farewell to the Servant Songs: A Critical Examination of an Exegetical Axiom*, Lund, Sweden: C. W. K. Gleerup.

Mettinger, T. N. D. 1986 — "In Search of the Hidden Structure: YHWH as King in Isaiah 40–55." *Svensk Exegetisk Årsbok 51–52*. Lund, Sweden: C. W. K. Gleerup.

Milgrom, Jacob 1991 — *Leviticus 1–16*. AB 3. Garden City, NY: Doubleday and Co.

Millbank, John 1992 — "'I Will Gasp and Pant': Deutero-Isaiah and the Birth of the Suffering Subject." *Semeia* 59: 59–71.

Miller, Patrick 1973 — *The Divine Warrior in Early Israel*. Cambridge: Harvard University Press.

Mintz, Alan 1984 — *Hurban: Responses to Catastrophe in Hebrew Literature*. New York: Columbia University Press.

Miscall, Peter D. 1992 — "Isaiah: New Heavens, New Earth, New Book." In *Reading Between Texts*, ed. Danna Nolan Fewell, 41–56. Louisville: Westminster/John Knox Press.

Morgan, Prys 1983 — "From a Death to a View: The Hunt for the Welsh Past in the Romantic Period." In *The Invention of Tradition*, ed. Eric Hobsbawm and Terence Ranger, 43–100. Cambridge: Cambridge University Press.

Morgan, Thaïs 1989 — "The Space of Intertextuality." In *Intertextuality and Contemporary American Fiction*, ed. P. O'Donnell and R. C. Davis, 239–79. Baltimore: Johns Hopkins University Press.

Movers, F. C. 1837 — *De utriusque recensionis vaticiniorum Ieremiae, Graece Alexandrinae et Hebraicae masorethicae, indole et origine commentatio critica.* Hamburg.

Mowinckel, Sigmund 1914 — *Zur Komposition des Buches Jeremia.* Oslo: J. Dybwad.

Mowinckel, Sigmund 1931 — "Die Komposition des deuterojesanischen Buches." *ZAW* 49: 87–112.

Mowinckel, Sigmund 1946 — *Prophecy and Tradition*, Oslo: J. Dybwad.

Mowinckel, Sigmund 1954 — *He that Cometh.* New York: Abingdon Press. Original publication in Norwegian, 1951.

Mowinckel, Sigmund 1961 — *Psalmenstudien.* 6 vols. Amsterdam: Verlag P. Schippers, 1961. Original publication, 1921–24.

Muilenburg, James 1956 — "Isaiah 40–66." *IB* 5, ed. G. A. Buttrick et al., 381–773. New York: Abingdon Press.

Mulzer, M. 1993 — "Döderlein und Deuterojesaja," *Biblische Notizen* 66: 15–22.

Nägelsbach, C. W. E. 1884 — *The Prophet Isaiah Theologically and Homiletically Expounded.* New York: Charles Scribner's Sons. Original publication in German, 1877.

Neusner, Jacob, ed. 1989 — *Lamentations Rabbah: An Analytical Translation.* Atlanta: Scholars Press.

Newsom, Carol 1992 — "Response to Norman Gottwald, 'Social Class and Ideology in Isaiah 40–55: An Eagletonian Reading.'" *Semeia* 59: 73–78.

North, C. R. 1948 — *The Suffering Servant in Deutero-Isaiah.* London: Oxford University Press.

North, C. R. 1964 — *The Second Isaiah.* Oxford: Clarendon.

Noth, Martin 1962 — *Exodus: A Commentary.* OTL. Philadelphia: Westminster Press. Original publication in German, 1959.

Noth, Martin 1968 — *Numbers: A Commentary.* OTL. Philadelphia: Westminster Press. Original publication in German, 1966.

Odashima, Taro 1989 — *Heilsworte im Jeremiabuch: Untersuchungen zu ihrer vordeuteronomistischen Bearbeitung.* Suttgart: W. Kohlhammer.

O'Day, Gail R.
1990
"Jeremiah 9:22–23 and 1 Corinthians 1:26–31: A Study in Intertextuality." *JBL* 109: 259–67.

Ogden, Graham
1978
"Moses and Cyrus." *VT* 28: 195–203.

Patrick, Dale
1984
"Epiphanic Imagery in Second Isaiah's Portrayal of a New Exodus." *Hebrew Annual Review* 8: 125–41.

Paul, Shalom
1969
"Literary and Ideological Echoes of Jeremiah in Deutero-Isaiah." In *Proceedings of the Fifth World Congress of Jewish Studies*, ed. Pinchas Peli, 102–20. Jerusalem: R. H. Hacohen Press.

Pfeiffer, Robert
1941
Introduction to the Old Testament. New York: Harper and Brothers.

Pope, Marvin
1973
Job. AB 15. Garden City, NY: Doubleday and Co.

Porteous, N.
1961
"Jerusalem-Zion: The Growth of a Symbol." In *Verbannung und Heimkehr*, ed. Arnulf Kuschke, 235–52. Tübingen: J. C. B. Mohr.

Provan, Iain
1991
Lamentations. NCB. Grand Rapids, MI: Eerdmans.

Rabinowitz, Peter
1980
"'What's Hecuba To Us?': The Audience's Experience of Literary Borrowing." In *The Reader in the Text: Essays on Audience and Interpretation*, ed. S. Suleiman and I. Crossman, 241–63. Princeton: Princeton University Press.

Rad, Gerhard von
1965
Old Testament Theology. Vol. 2: *The Theology of Israel's Prophetic Traditions*. New York: Harper & Row. Original publication in German, 1960.

Radday, Yehuda T.
1973
The Unity of Isaiah in the Light of Statistical Linguistics. Hildesheim: H. A. Gerstenberg.

Raitt, Thomas
1977
A Theology of Exile: Judgment/Deliverance in Jeremiah and Ezekiel. Philadelphia: Fortress Press.

Rendtorff, Rolf
1986
The Old Testament: An Introduction. Philadelphia: Fortress Press. Original publication in German, 1983.

Rendtorff, Rolf
1990
The Problem of the Process of Transmission in the Pentateuch. JSOTSupp 89. Sheffield: Sheffield Academic Press. Original publication in German, 1977.

Rendtorff, Rolf
1991
"The Book of Isaiah: A Complex Unity. Synchronic and Diachronic Reading." In *SBL Seminar Papers*, 8–20. Atlanta: Scholars Press.

Rendtorff, Rolf 1993 — *Canon and Theology: Overtures to an Old Testament Theology*. Edited by Margaret Kohl. Minneapolis: Fortress Press. Original publication in German, 1991.

Ridderbos, T. 1985 — *Isaiah*. Grand Rapids, MI: Zondervan. Original publication in Dutch, 1950–51.

Roberts, J. J. M. 1991 — *Nahum, Habakkuk, and Zephaniah: A Commentary*. OTL. Louisville: Westminster/John Knox Press.

Rogerson, John 1985 — *Old Testament Criticism in the Nineteenth Century*. Philadelphia: Fortress Press. Original publication, 1984.

Roudiez, Leon S. 1980 — "Introduction." In *Desire in Language: A Semiotic Approach to Literature and Art* by Julia Kristeva, 1–22. New York: Columbia University Press.

Rowley, H. H. 1952 — *The Servant of the Lord and Other Essays on the Old Testament*. London: Lutterworth Press.

Rudolph, Wilhelm 1938 — "Der Text der Klagelieder." *ZAW* 56: 101–22.

Rudolph, Wilhelm 1947 — *Jeremia*. Tübingen: Mohr (Paul Siebeck).

Sawyer, John 1989 — "Daughter of Zion and Servant of the Lord in Isaiah: A Comparison." *JSOT* 44: 89–107.

Schmid, Hans Heinrich 1976 — *Der Sogenannte Jahwist: Beobachtungen und Fragen zur Pentateuchforschung*. Zurich: Theologischer Verlag.

Schmitt, John J. 1983 — "The Gender of Ancient Israel." *JSOT* 26: 115–25.

Seidel, Moshe 1935 — "Parallels between the Book of Isaiah and the Book of Psalms." In *Minhah leDavid*, 23–47. Jerusalem: Reuben Mas [Hebrew].

Seidel, Moshe 1956 — "Parallels between the Book of Isaiah and the Book of Psalms" *Sinai* 38: 149–72 [Hebrew].

Seitz, Christopher 1990 — "The Divine Council: Temporal Transition and New Prophecy in the Book of Isaiah." *JBL* 109: 229–47.

Seitz, Christopher 1991 — *Zion's Final Destiny: The Development of the Book of Isaiah. A Reassessment of Isaiah 36–39*. Minneapolis: Fortress Press.

Shakespeare, W. 1969 — *William Shakespeare: The Complete Works*, edited by Alfred Harbage. Baltimore: Penguin Books.

Shenkel, J. D. 1965 — "An Interpretation of Ps. 93:5." *Biblica* 46: 401–2.

Silberman, Lou 1982 — "Wellhausen and Judaism." *Semeia* 25: 75–82.

Smend, R. 1991 — "Lowth im Deutschland." In *Epochen der Bibelkritik*, BET 109, 43–62. Munich: Chr. Kaiser.

Soggin, J. Alberto 1976 — *Introduction to the Old Testament.* OTL. Philadelphia: Westminster Press. Translated from the 2nd ed., published in Italian, 1974.

Sommer, Benjamin 1996 — "Allusions and Illusions: The Unity of the Book of Isaiah in Light of Deutero-Isaiah's Use of Prophetic Tradition." In *New Visions of Isaiah*, ed. Roy Melugin and Marvin Sweeney, JSOTSup 214, 156–86. Sheffield: Sheffield Academic Press.

Sommer, Benjamin 1994 — *Leshon Limmudim*: The Poetics of Allusion in Isaiah 40–66. Ph.D. diss., University of Chicago.

Spykerboer, H. C. 1976 — *The Structure and Composition of Deutero-Isaiah with Special Reference to the Polemics against Idolatry.* Meppel: Krips Repro.

Steck, Odil H. 1985 — *Bereitete Heimkehr: Jesaja 35 als redaktionelle Brücke zwischen dem Ersten und dem Zweiten Jesaja.* Stuttgart: Verlag Katholisches Bibelwerk.

Steck, Odil H. 1992 — *Gottesknecht und Zion: Gesammelte Aufsätze zu Deuterojesaja.* Tübingen: Mohr (Paul Siebeck).

Sweeney, Marvin 1996 — "Jeremiah 30–31 and King Josiah's Program of National Restoration and Religious Reform." *ZAW* 108: 569–83.

Tannert, Werner 1956 — *Jeremia und Deuterojesaja: Eine Untersuchung zur Frage ihren literarischen und theologischen Zusammenhanges.* Ph.D. diss., Karl Marx University in Leipzig.

Tate, Marvin 1990 — *Psalms 51–100.* Word Biblical Commentary 20. Dallas: Word Books.

Torrey, C. C. 1928 — *The Second Isaiah: A New Interpretation.* Edinburgh: T. & T. Clark.

Tucker, Gene M. 1985 — "Prophecy and Prophetic Literature." In *The Hebrew Bible and its Modern Interpreters*, ed. D. Knight and G. Tucker, 325–68. Chico, CA: Scholar's Press.

Turner, Mary D. 1992 — *Daughter Zion: Lament and Restoration.* Ph.D. diss., Emory University.

Van Seters, John 1975 — *Abraham in History and Tradition.* New Haven: Yale University Press.

Van Seters, John
1983
In Search of History: Historiography in the Ancient World and the Origins of Biblical History. New Haven: Yale University Press.

Van Seters, John
1992
Prologue to History: The Yahwist as Historian in Genesis. Louisville, KY: Westminster/John Knox Press.

Volz, Paul
1922
Der Prophet Jeremia. Leipzig: A. Deichert.

Volz, Paul
1932
Jesaja II. Leipzig: Verner Scholl.

Wakeman, Mary K.
1973
God's Battle with the Monster: A Study in Biblical Imagery. Leiden: E. J. Brill.

Weinfeld, Moshe
1968
"God the Creator in Genesis 1 and in the Prophecy of Second Isaiah." *Tarbiz* 37/2: 105–132 [Hebrew].

Wellhausen, Julius
1957
Prolegomena to the History of Ancient Israel. Cleveland, OH: World Publishing Co. Original publication in German, 1878, as *Geschichte Israels*, vol. 1.

Westermann, Claus
1965
The Praise of God in the Psalms. Richmond: John Knox Press. Original publication in German, 1961.

Westermann, Claus
1967
Handbook to the Old Testament. Minneapolis: Augsburg. Original publication in German, 1962.

Westermann, Claus
1969
Isaiah 40–66. OTL. Philadelphia: Westminster Press. Original publication in German, 1966.

Westermann, Claus
1981
Sprache und Struktur der Prophetie Deuterojesajas. Stuttgart: Calwer Verlag.

Westermann, Claus
1994
Lamentations: Issues and Interpretation. Minneapolis: Augsburg Fortress. Original publication in German, 1990.

Whybray, R. Norman
1975
Isaiah 40–66. NCB. Grand Rapids, MI: Eerdmans.

Whybray, R. Norman
1987
The Making of the Pentateuch: A Methodological Study. JSOTSupp 53. Sheffield: Sheffield Academic Press.

Whybray, R. Norman
1995
Introduction to the Pentateuch. Grand Rapids, MI: William B. Eerdmans.

Willey, Patricia Tull
1998
"Baruch." In *The Women's Bible Commentary*, rev. ed., ed. C. Newsom and S. Ringe. Louisville, KY: Westminster/John Knox Press.

Williamson, H. G. M.
1994
The Book Called Isaiah: Deutero-Isaiah's Role in Composition and Redaction. Oxford: Clarendon Press.

Wilshire, L. E.
1975
"The Servant-City: A New Interpretation of the 'Servant of the Lord' in the Servant Songs of Deutero-Isaiah." *JBL* 94: 356–67.

Winnett, Frederick 1965 — "Re-examining the Foundations." *JBL* 84: 1–19.

Wright, G. Ernest 1962 — "Exodus, Book of." *IDB* 2, 188–97. Nashville: Abingdon Press.

Ydit, Meir 1971 — "Av, the Ninth of." *EncJud* 3, cols. 936–40. Jerusalem: Keter Publishing House.

Young, E. J. 1954 — *Studies in Isaiah.* London: Tyndale Press.

Young, E. J. 1958 — *Who Wrote Isaiah?* Grand Rapids, MI: Eerdmans.

Young, E. J. 1965–72 — *The Book of Isaiah.* 3 vols. Grand Rapids, MI: Eerdmans.

Zenger, Erich 1987 — "The God of Exodus in the Message of the Prophets as Seen in Isaiah." In *Exodus: A Lasting Paradigm,* ed. Bas Van Iersel and Anton Weiler, 22–33. Edinburgh: T. & T. Clark.

Zerubavel, Yael 1994 — "The Historic, the Legendary, and the Incredible: Invented Tradition and Collective Memory in Israel." In *Commemorations: The Politics of National Identity,* ed. John R. Gillis, 105–23. Princeton, NJ: Princeton University Press.

Zimmerli, Walther 1963 — "Der 'neue Exodus' in der Verkündigung der beiden grossen Exilspropheten." In his *Gottes Offenbarung: Gesammelte Aufsätze zum Alten Testament,* 192–204. München: Chr. Kaiser Verlag.